Philosophy for A Level

Philosophy for A Level is an accessible textbook for the new 2017 AQA Philosophy syllabus. Structured closely around the AQA specification this textbook covers the two units, Metaphysics of God and Metaphysics of Mind, in an engaging and student-friendly way. With chapters on 'How to do philosophy', exam preparation providing students with the philosophical skills they need to succeed, and an extensive glossary to support understanding, this book is ideal for students studying philosophy.

Each chapter includes:

- argument maps that help to develop students' analytical and critical skills
- comprehension questions to test understanding
- discussion questions to generate evaluative argument
- explanation of and commentary on the AQA set texts
- 'Thinking harder' sections
- cross-references to help students make connections
- bullet-point summaries of each topic.

The companion website hosts a wealth of further resources, including PowerPoint slides, flashcards, further reading, weblinks and handouts, all structured to accompany the textbook. It can be found at www.routledge.com/cw/alevelphilosophy.

Michael Lacewing is a teacher of philosophy and theology at Christ's Hospital school, and a former Reader in Philosophy and Vice-Principal Academic at Heythrop College, University of London. He is founder of the company A Level Philosophy (www.alevelphilosophy.co.uk), and advises the British Philosophical Association on matters related to philosophy in schools.

Philosophy for A Level

Metaphysics of God and Metaphysics of Mind

Michael Lacewing

Routledge
Taylor & Francis Group

LONDON AND NEW YORK

First published 2017
by Routledge
2 Park Square, Milton Park, Abingdon, Oxon OX14 4RN

and by Routledge

711 Third Avenue, New York, NY 10017

Routledge is an imprint of the Taylor & Francis Group, an informa business

British Library Cataloguing-in-Publication Data
A catalogue record for this book is available from the British Library

Library of Congress Cataloging-in-Publication Data
Names: Lacewing, Michael, 1971- author.
Title: Philosophy for A level : metaphysics of God and metaphysics of mind /
Michael Lacewing.
Other titles: Metaphysics of God and metaphysics of mind
Description: New York : Routledge, 2017. | Includes index.
Identifiers: LCCN 2017001770 | ISBN 9781138690400 (pbk. : alk. paper)
Subjects: LCSH: Philosophy--Textbooks. | Reasoning--Textbooks.
Classification: LCC BD31 .L26 2017 | DDC 107.6--dc23
LC record available at https://lccn.loc.gov/2017001770

ISBN: 978-1-138-69040-0 (pbk)
ISBN: 9781315164588 (ebk)

Typeset in Frutiger
by Saxon Graphics Ltd, Derby

Visit the companion website: www.routledge.com/cw/alevelphilosophy

MIX
Paper from
responsible sources
FSC® C013056
www.fsc.org

Printed and bound in Great Britain by
TJ International Ltd, Padstow, Cornwall

Contents

Illustrations

Figures

Argument maps

Acknowledgements

Thanks to Rebecca Shillabeer at Routledge and Dave Wright at Saxon Graphics for their work on this textbook, to Jim Thomas for his excellent copy-editing, and to my colleagues at Heythrop College for supporting my work with A Level philosophy. Thanks also to the AQA subject team for answering a number of queries on the interpretation of the syllabus. And a special thanks goes to Joanne Lovesey for her stellar work on compiling the glossary.

CHRIST'S HOSPITAL

A SCHOOL LIKE NO OTHER

Christ's Hospital is an independent co-educational boarding and day school for boys and girls aged 11–18 with 870 pupils. It is unique for a UK independent boarding school in that it educates a proportion of its pupils for free, and many at a reduced rate. This stems from its founding charter as a charitable school. It was established in 1552 by King Edward VI to care for poor and homeless children of the City of London, and the generosity of donors has built up an endowment that enables Christ's Hospital to maintain its charitable tradition. School fees are paid on a means-tested basis, with substantial subsidies paid by the school, so that pupils from a wide range of social and cultural backgrounds are able to have a high quality, independent boarding school education.

The school, set in 1,200 acres of rolling Sussex countryside, has an impressive history of high academic achievement with an average of 12% of pupils each year taking up places at Oxford or Cambridge, and 98% of leavers going on to top Universities in the UK and abroad. Offering a choice of A levels, Pre-U, and International Baccalaureate (IB) courses, it provides a healthy, stimulating and comfortable environment in which pupils learn to be independent, making the most of their abilities, whether in academia, sports, music or fine arts. The pupils grow up with a strong sense of responsibility towards each other, the school and the world around them.

Introduction

The AQA A Level Philosophy course aims to introduce you, as a student, to some key concepts and methods in philosophy, studied as an academic discipline. It focuses on four big philosophical questions: 'What, and how, do we know?', 'What is morally right and good?', 'Does God exist?', and 'What is the mind?' It introduces you to philosophy by considering some of the very best attempts to answer these questions, the arguments of some of the very best philosophers in history as well as recent discussions. In this textbook, we look at the last two issues concerning God and the mind. In an accompanying textbook, we look at the issues of knowledge and morality.

For those readers who are already familiar with the accompanying textbook, *Philosophy for AS and A Level*, many of the points in this introduction are the same. But I include them here both as a reminder and for any readers who do not know the other textbook.

One aim of this textbook is, of course, to cover the ideas and arguments that are on the syllabus. But it aims at more than that. First, it aims to show you *how* to do philosophy – not just to tell you, but to show you, what philosophical thinking and philosophical writing is like. This is important because the A level aims to introduce the methods of philosophy, as well as the ideas. Second, it aims to get you *engaging* in the argument. The discussion is provocative and leaves many lines of thought hanging. So, for instance, you might come up with new objections or replies that haven't yet been discussed, or argue that a particular point is convincing or implausible. That's the idea. This textbook doesn't try to tell you what *should* be said, only (some of) what *could* be said. (That leads to one important difference between this book and your essays. The book tries to be even-handed, and doesn't often draw firm conclusions. In your evaluative essays, you'll be expected to defend a particular point of view.)

How to use this book

How to do philosophy

I expect that most readers have already covered at least some of the material in the other textbook on epistemology or moral philosophy. If so, you'll have learned that philosophy involves reading and thinking in very particular ways, ones that can be quite different from how you normally read and think. (If not, you may need to learn some epistemology as you go through this book.) In Chapter 1, I talk about what is involved in doing philosophy – how to reason, read, and write philosophically. It is repeated from *Philosophy for AS and A Level*, and included here so you don't need to keep turning to the other book. It is intended as a resource to which you can return again and again, as and when you need to. But as you embark on a new philosophical topic, you may want to skim the section on PHILOSOPHICAL ARGUMENT (p. 5) and the best ways of ENGAGING WITH THE TEXT (p. 16) before going on to study Chapter 2 or Chapter 3.

Each paragraph of Chapters 2 and 3 is intended to be taken as a thought to be considered, reread, and reflected on. *Philosophy needs to be read slowly, and more than once, to be understood.* You will probably find, in addition, that you are not able to completely understand a particular theory until you also understand rival theories that oppose it. And so, at the end of each major section (e.g. 'Physicalist theories'), you may feel that you need to return to earlier discussions, to think about them again in the light of what you learned later.

Following the syllabus

Metaphysics of God is covered in Chapter 2 and Metaphysics of Mind in Chapter 3. Each chapter opens with a brief synopsis of what the chapter covers and what you should be able to do by the end of it. This is followed by the AQA syllabus, which I have structured by topic and subtopic. The bullet points from the syllabus are used to structure the discussion, with each section further divided by the main ideas, arguments and objections. However, in some cases, I have not followed the bullet points strictly or in the order they appear in the syllabus. I was able to explain the ideas, theories, objections and debates more clearly by rearranging them. The table of contents, with its many headings and subheadings, shows how each part relates to the others. There is also an INDEX BY SYLLABUS CONTENT on p. 369, which provides the page numbers on which each bullet point of the syllabus is discussed.

Additional features

Alongside the text, there are a number of features in the margin. Most commonly, there are questions that test your understanding and cross-references to other relevant discussions and ideas. To get the most out of the book, stop and answer the questions – in your own words – as you go along. The questions are the kinds that you'll find on the exam, so it is good practice for that. It is also worth following up cross-references, especially when you have read, but forgotten, the sections referred to. (Cross-references marked by a book icon 📖 refer to the companion textbook, *Philosophy for AS and A Level: Epistemology and Moral Philosophy*.) Understanding philosophy is often about being able to make connections. Also in the margin are occasional illustrations, definitions of technical terms, and references to philosophical texts where the argument being discussed can be found.

You'll frequently come across sections called 'Thinking harder'. These discuss more difficult ideas or take the arguments deeper – so you'll need to think harder. They will extend and develop your knowledge, helping you to understand more about the issue being discussed.

Throughout the book, you'll find figures that provide illustrations and examples to support your understanding and connect the issues to real life situations. You'll also find 'argument maps', visual representations of arguments and their logical structure. I explain these further in UNDERSTANDING ARGUMENTS AND ARGUMENT MAPS (p. 9).

At the end of each main section covering a theory or debate, there is a list of 'Key points', summarising clearly the main issues the section has covered. And at the end of each topic, there is a 'Summary' in the form of a list of questions, to show what issues have been addressed. Both the Key points and the Summary should help with exam revision and testing your knowledge.

Set texts

The syllabus includes a list of 'set texts'. Many of the arguments identified in the syllabus content come from these texts. You aren't expected to read all the texts (though it would be good to try to read some of them), but you are expected to understand and be able to evaluate the arguments they discuss. To help with this, you'll find these texts and the arguments they present discussed in gray-shaded boxes. All the texts listed in the syllabus are discussed at some point, and they are included in the INDEX BY SYLLABUS CONTENT (p. 369), so you can look up the discussion of any text in order of author.

Glossary

The glossary provides brief definitions for an extensive list of terms. I have included terms that have a technical philosophical use, that identify an important philosophical concept, or that name a theory, argument or objection. While such terms are explained in the text, if you can't understand or remember the explanation, use the glossary to help you. It should also prove a useful resource for revision.

Companion website and further resources

You can find further resources supporting the study of AQA Philosophy on the Routledge companion website, www.routledge.com/cw/alevelphilosophy. The resources include

1. handouts based on this text, including material on philosophical skills, revision and exam technique
2. PowerPoint presentations
3. extension material, covering a number of philosophical ideas or arguments that are not on the syllabus but are directly relevant to it
4. further reading lists
5. helpful weblinks
6. flashcards, for revising and testing your knowledge of philosophical terms and the names of theories and objections
7. the AQA list of texts with links where available, and
8. a commentary on Descartes' *Meditations*.

How to do philosophy

Philosophy is thinking in slow motion.

John Campbell

This chapter repeats Chapter 1 of my *Philosophy for AS and A Level: Epistemology and Moral Philosophy*. It is included here for convenience, so you don't need to refer to the other book for information and reminders on how to do philosophy well.

The chapter introduces you to a way of thinking about philosophy – as argument – which is also a way of thinking philosophically. It also covers three skills that you need to do philosophy well: reasoning (or argument), reading and writing.

Assuming that you are studying the topics in this book after you have studied Epistemology and/or Moral Philosophy, you will be familiar with how philosophy works. But you can read the chapter through now, as a reminder of the skills that are central, or come back to it when you need to.

Philosophical argument

At the heart of philosophy is philosophical argument. Arguments are different from assertions. Assertions are simply stated; arguments always involve giving reasons. An argument is a reasoned inference from one set of claims – the premises – to another claim, the conclusion. The premises provide reasons to believe that the conclusion is true. If the premises are true, the conclusion is more likely to be true. Arguments seek to 'preserve truth' – true premises will lead to a true conclusion. Philosophers distinguish between two types of argument – deductive and inductive.

Deductive argument

Successful deductive arguments are *valid* – if the premises are true, then the conclusion *must* be true. In this case, we say that the conclusion is *entailed* by the premises. Here is a famous example:

Premise 1: Socrates is a man.
Premise 2: All men are mortal.
Conclusion: Socrates is mortal.

A valid deductive argument with true premises, like this example, is called *sound*.

But a valid deductive argument doesn't have to have true premises. Here is an example (abbreviating 'Premise' to 'P' and 'Conclusion' to 'C'):

P1. There are gnomes in my house.
P2. My house is in Oxford.
C. Therefore, there are gnomes in Oxford.

In this example, if the premises are true, then the conclusion must be true, so the argument is valid. But the first premise is false, because there aren't any gnomes in my house (not even garden gnomes).

It is important to recognise that truth and validity are *different* properties. We've just seen that a valid argument can have false premises. Here's an example of an invalid argument with true premises (and even a true conclusion):

P1. This book was written on a computer.
P2. Computers were invented by people.
C. Therefore, eagles are birds.

Give an example of a) an invalid argument; b) a valid argument with false premises; and c) a sound argument.

As these examples show, there are two ways that a deductive argument can fail. First, it could be *invalid*: even if the premises are true, it is possible that the conclusion might be false (the truth of the premises doesn't mean that the conclusion must be true). Second, it could have false premises, even if the conclusion is entailed by the premises. (As a variant of this, it may be that we don't or cannot *know* whether the premises are true or not.) If a deductive argument is either invalid or it has at least one false premise, it is *unsound*.

Inductive argument

A successful inductive argument is an argument whose conclusion is supported by its premises. If the premises are true, the conclusion is *more likely* to be true; the truth of the premises increases the probability that the conclusion is true. But it is still possible that the conclusion is false. So inductive arguments are not described as 'valid' or 'sound'. Instead, an inductive argument with true premises that provide strong support for the conclusion is sometimes called 'cogent'.

> Explain and illustrate the difference between inductive and deductive arguments.

But inductive arguments can also go wrong in just two ways. First, the premises might not make the conclusion more probable (or, at least, not by much). Second, one or more of the premises may be false. In either case, the premises don't offer good reasons for believing the conclusion is true.

One type of induction is induction through enumeration, as in this famous example:

P1. This swan is white.
P2. This other swan is white.
P3. That third swan is white.
…
P500. That swan is white as well.
C. All swans are white.

The example shows that an inductive argument can be a good argument, but the conclusion can still be false!

There are other types of inductive argument apart from enumerative induction. We shall look at hypothetical reasoning next.

> A hypothesis is a proposal that needs to be confirmed or rejected by reasoning or experience.

HYPOTHETICAL REASONING

In hypothetical reasoning, we try to work out the best hypothesis that would explain or account for some experience or fact.

Medical diagnosis provides an example – what would explain exactly *this* set of symptoms? This isn't a matter of comparing this case with other cases which all have exactly the same symptoms. There may only be some overlap or the case might involve some complication, such as more than one disease being involved. We use hypothetical reasoning – if such-and-such were true (e.g. the patient has disease *x*), would that explain the evidence we have? The evidence supplies the premises of the argument, and the conclusion is that some hypothesis is true because it accounts for the evidence.

When we are using hypothetical reasoning, it is not usually enough to find some hypothesis that *can* explain the evidence. We want to find the *best* hypothesis. To do this, we first need to know what makes for a *good* hypothesis. Philosophers have argued for several criteria.

1. Simplicity: the best-known is probably Ockham's razor, which says 'Don't multiply entities beyond necessity.' Don't put forward a hypothesis that says many different things exist when a simpler explanation will do as well. A simpler explanation is a better explanation, as long as it is just as successful. For example, the explanation that plants flower in the spring in response to an increase in light and temperature is a better explanation than saying that they flower in the spring because that's when the fairies wake them up. The second explanation is committed to the existence of fairies – and we shouldn't think that fairies exist unless there is something we cannot explain without thinking they exist.
2. Accuracy: a good hypothesis fits the evidence that we are trying to explain.
3. Plausibility: a good hypothesis fits with what else we already know.
4. Scope: a good hypothesis explains a wide range of evidence.
5. Coherence: a good hypothesis draws and explains connections between different parts of the evidence.

> **?**
> What makes for a good hypothesis?

The best hypothesis will be the hypothesis that demonstrates all these virtues to a higher degree than alternative hypotheses. A lot of philosophy involves arguing about which theory provides the best hypothesis to account for our experience.

Understanding arguments and argument maps

Understanding arguments is central to doing philosophy well. That is why throughout this book, you will be asked to outline and explain arguments. You'll be asked to do so in the exam as well.

Understanding an argument involves identifying the conclusion, identifying the premises, and understanding how the premises are supposed to provide reasons for believing the conclusion. Use linguistic clues, like 'since', 'because', 'if … then …' and many others, to help you do this. It is also important to distinguish between what someone supposes for the purposes of argument, and what they actually want to assert as reasons for believing the conclusion.

Many arguments involve quite a complex structure, with some premises establishing an initial conclusion, which is then used as a premise to establish a second conclusion. In coming to understand an argument, it can be very helpful to create an *argument map*. This is a visual diagram of how the argument works – its 'logical structure'. Psychologists have shown that using argument maps greatly improves one's ability to think critically.

Here is a simplified example of a map from Moral Philosophy:

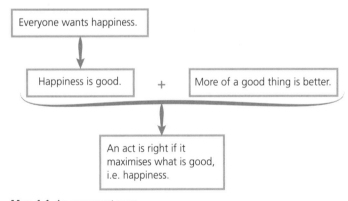

Map 1.1 An argument map

There are argument maps throughout this book, and you will also be asked to construct your own argument maps. To understand the maps and make your own, there are several things you need to know about argument mapping.

You can find out more about argument maps online at https://en. wikipedia.org/wiki/ Argument_map.

1. A simple argument is made up of one conclusion and one reason. The reason may be given in a single premise, but you may need to combine two or more 'co-premises' to make up the reason. Thus

    is a simple argument with a single premise, while

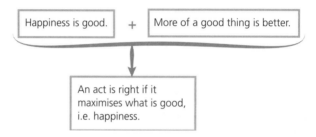

    is a simple argument with two co-premises that must be combined to support the conclusion. This is shown by the '+' between the boxes and the line that runs below both of them.

2. A complex argument is an argument that links several simple arguments. MAP 1.1 is an example.

3. Each box in an argument map should have just one claim inside it, written as a full sentence. And it should contain no reasoning. Thus, 'Happiness is good because everyone wants happiness' should not be entered in a box, but must be broken down as shown.

4. A line ending in an arrow indicates a relation of support. The line leads from the reason and points to the claim supported.

5. A line ending in '-|' indicates an objection. Here is our argument again, but with an objection added. (In this example, the objection is marked against the conclusion, and notes a way that even if the premises are true, the conclusion may be false.)

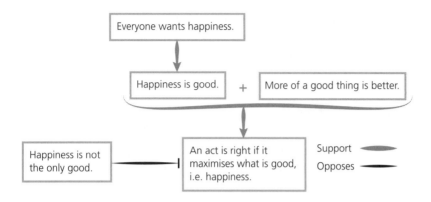

6. Our examples show that you can create argument maps for simple arguments, complex arguments and even debates with arguments for and against the conclusion, objections, responses and so on.

7. Argument maps can be more or less complete. According to some guides, argument maps must all be deductive, with every premise stated. On this approach, our first simple argument should be:

However, there are two difficulties with insisting on deductive completeness. First, if you are trying to map how people actually argue, then it is a mistake to turn every argument into a deduction. For example, hypothetical reasoning is misrepresented if you try to turn it into a deduction. To argue that happiness is good, someone may not want to claim that it is *always* true that what people want is good; they may simply be assuming that if everyone wants something, that is *good evidence* that it is good.

Second, while it can be worthwhile trying to construct a complete argument map, complete maps can become very complicated. A partial one can be sufficient to help one understand the main moves and logical structure of an argument.

In this book, many of the argument maps are *neither complete nor deductive*, but I trust they will be useful in helping you to understand the arguments being discussed.

Evaluating arguments

When you evaluate an argument, you are yourself *making* an argument. You are arguing that the argument evaluated is either a good or bad argument. In other words, the conclusion of your evaluation is that the argument evaluated is a good/bad argument, and you have to provide reasons to support this claim. There are three types of reason you can give, three different ways of evaluating arguments:

1. As already stated above, you can argue that one or more of the premises is false (or unknown). If you are right, then the argument does not give you a reason to believe the conclusion, because it rests on a false (or unknown) premise.

2. As also already stated above, you can argue that the conclusion does not follow from the premises. If you are evaluating a deductive argument, you are claiming that the argument is not valid. If you are evaluating an inductive argument, you are claiming that the argument is not cogent, i.e. the premises do not provide a (good or strong) reason to believe the conclusion. For example, with inferring the best hypothesis, you could argue that the conclusion is not the best explanation for the premises, e.g. that it isn't plausible or simple, or at least that the argument doesn't show that it is, e.g. there may be other explanations that haven't been considered.

3. You can also evaluate the formal features of an argument. Without worrying about whether it is true, you can ask whether it is clear, whether the premises are relevant to the conclusion, whether the support offered by the premises has been demonstrated, and so on. You may want to offer an improvement on the argument, e.g. rephrasing it to be clearer, supplying missing premises, identifying assumptions, and so on.

Evaluating claims

In addition to evaluating arguments, you can evaluate claims on their own. In evaluating a claim, you provide an argument for thinking that it is true or false.

For any claim C (e.g. 'God exists'), we need to distinguish arguments for and against the claim from arguments about these arguments, as shown in this diagram:

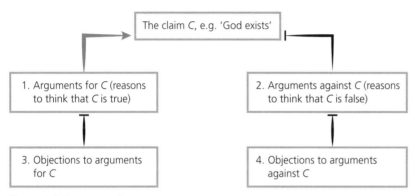

Figure 1.1 Four types of argument

An argument for or against a claim is an argument that the claim is true or false. An argument for or against an argument is an argument that the argument is successful or fails. This means that objections to an argument are not the same as arguments for the opposite claim.

Suppose I provide an argument with the conclusion that God exists (Box 1). You respond by making an objection to my argument, e.g. that one of the premises is false (Box 3). In doing this, you argue that I haven't shown that God exists; you haven't argued that God doesn't exist. At the end of my argument and your objection, we should conclude that we don't yet know whether God exists or not, but we don't have reason to conclude that God doesn't exist. (For that conclusion, we need an argument in Box 2.)

When you are arguing for or against a claim, don't overstate your case. Your claim is only as strong as the reasons that you can provide for it.

In 25-mark essay questions on the exam, you are typically asked to evaluate a claim. You need to break this down into a series of arguments and their evaluation (discussed below in WRITING PHILOSOPHY, p. 18). After you've explained the claim, for each section of the answer, you should consider an argument for or against the claim, objections to that argument, and possible responses. If you use inductive arguments, e.g. hypothetical reasoning, you'll also need to indicate how *strong* or cogent you think the argument is. If you have one argument for a conclusion and another argument against the conclusion, you'll need to consider which argument is stronger, e.g. by using the criteria for a good argument set out in HYPOTHETICAL REASONING (p. 8). You will also need to think about which arguments, and which objections, are the *most important and critical* ones to discuss, given the conclusion you want to reach.

An aside: why reason?

Why, you may wonder, should we place so much importance on reasoning in this way? Is it worth it? Here are four quick reasons in favour of reasoning:

1. To discover the truth
2. To uncover poor reasoning, e.g. fallacies (see below) and sophistry
3. To recognise when, where, and how a dialogue ceases to be reasonable or instructive
4. To probe both sides of a controversial issue in a sensitive and intelligent way.

Can I justify these claims? If I present an argument in favour of reasoning, then I'm using reasoning to justify reasoning, which is circular. Then again, if you object to reasoning for this reason, you are using reasoning to make your objection! An alternative justification of reason is to check the results of reasoning by a different method. Science does this all the time by hypothesis and observation. In many cases, we can confirm, by observation, that the conclusion of a piece of reasoning is correct. Some people are sceptical about reasoning or claim, for example, that all beliefs are equally 'reasonable'. For an excellent discussion dismantling this view, see Stephen Law's *Believing Bullshit*, Ch. 4.

To criticise an argument or claim is not necessarily to reject it. You can be concerned to reject bad reasons because you want to find stronger ones! To show respect to someone does not require that you agree with them. Taking someone else's thought seriously – so seriously that you test it rigorously in your mind – is to pay them a compliment.

It is important to remember that the *point* of philosophical argument is not personal victory.

Fallacies

A fallacy, as philosophers use the word, is not a mistake of fact or truth. A fallacy is an error in reasoning. More exactly, it is an argument in which the premises do not offer rational support to the conclusion. If the argument is deductive, then it is fallacious if it is not valid. If the argument is inductive, it is fallacious if the argument is not cogent, i.e. the premises do not make it (much) more likely that the conclusion is true.

See 'Fallacies', at www.nizkor.org/ features/fallacies/; 'Fallacies: alphabetic list (unique)', at http:// changingminds.org/ disciplines/ argument/fallacies/ fallacies_unique. htm; and 'List of fallacies', at http:// en.wikipedia.org/ wiki/List_of_fallacies

There are many types of fallacy; the *Nizkor Project* lists 42, *Changing Minds* 53, and *Wikipedia* over 100. It's good to become familiar with some of the main types. If you do, it is really important to understand *why* the fallacy is a fallacy.

Spotting fallacies has two purposes: 1) evaluating the strength of an argument and 2) improving it. When learning how to spot fallacies, try to develop the skill of how you would reformulate the argument to avoid committing a fallacy. It is not always clear-cut whether a fallacy is being committed or not, and the answer depends on just how the premises are being deployed or further assumptions being made. The question is always ultimately about the strength of support the premises offer.

To learn how to avoid fallacies in your own work, it can be helpful to learn first how to spot them! Fallacies are always easier to spot in someone else's work, so start with people you don't know, then look at the work of other students, then try to spot them in your own work.

Reading philosophy

The syllabus includes a list of books and articles to read and think about. If you read these texts, you may find it challenging, especially if you haven't read any philosophy before. You may not know much about the background of the text – when was it written and why? The form of the text is difficult – there can be long and complicated arguments, unfamiliar words, an unusual style of language, and abstract ideas. It is unclear just how the text should be interpreted, and commentaries on the texts often disagree. This section provides some guidance that may help. But the first thing to remember is that it is *normal* to feel confused and challenged.

Approaching the text

For these first three points, you'll need to use a commentary on the text, or an introduction:

1. Contextualise: it can help to set the scene, but this shouldn't be restricted to a historical understanding. An awareness of central ideas is useful.
2. Identify what philosophical *problems* the text addresses.
3. Get an overview: look at the title, introductory and concluding paragraphs, and the chapter and section headings. Knowing the conclusion does not ruin the text (it isn't a detective story). Understanding the structure can help fit different arguments and claims together.

These next three points are about how to interact with the text:

4. For long texts, don't feel the need to start at the beginning. Start with what will best get you into the thinking of the author, e.g. connections to previous topics, points of interest, etc.
5. Don't get bogged down in details: reading the text more than once is helpful and often necessary. Read it quickly first, noting the main points, skimming what is most unclear; then read it again more closely.
6. Distinguish the text from secondary interpretation: for example, knowing what other people said Descartes said is not knowing what Descartes said.

Engaging with the text

The following points relate to reading any philosophy, including this textbook:

1. Read slowly and actively: philosophy should not be read like fiction or even most non-fiction. *Philosophy needs to be read slowly, and often more than once, to be understood.* Take notes and constantly question not only whether you've understood what the author is trying to say, but also whether what s/he says is true, and whether the arguments support the conclusions.

2.   Look for signposts: sentences that indicate what the text is about, what has been, is being, or will be argued.
3.   Ask what the passage of text offers: a new concept, a framework for understanding an issue, an argument for a conclusion?
4.   Argument mapping: find the arguments. Identify premises, inferences and conclusions. Break arguments down into steps (there can be many interim conclusions).
5.   Don't be afraid to challenge: try to find inconsistencies in the text, but also try to find ways to interpret the text to remove the inconsistencies.
6.   Ask what interpretation best fits the purpose of the author. Does an interpretation presuppose ideas that were not available to the author?
7.   Know the point of any example used: examples can seize the imagination and memory, but knowing its purpose and what it is supposed to show is central to understanding the text.
8.   Look up key words in a dictionary of philosophy: don't be lazy, and don't use a normal dictionary (for philosophical words) as they won't capture or explain the relevant sense.

Beyond the text

1.   Visualise: if you put the text, or the arguments within it, into some other visual form, that can help generate understanding.
2.   Use secondary sources carefully: always question the authority of secondary sources, and always go back to the text.
3.   Find different ways to think about and interact with the text. These will help you understand more than if you simply read it. For example, you might want to
     a.   practise précis (either rewrite a passage more briefly in your own words or, if you have the text electronically, try deleting words while retaining the argument);
     b.   rewrite a passage of the text in a different genre (e.g. a detective story);
     c.   select quotations that make important points (good for revision);
     d.   mark up the text for premises, conclusions, linguistic clues, etc.;
     e.   do some argument mapping.

Writing philosophy

What you need to know

Different types of knowledge are needed to do well in philosophy. Each is tested by different types of question on the exam. You can be asked to define a term (3-mark questions), explain a claim or an argument (5-mark questions), compare two positions in a debate or explain a position and present an objection (12-mark questions), or, finally, to evaluate a claim (25-mark questions). Here are five types of knowledge that are relevant to doing all this well:

See UNDERSTANDING THE QUESTION, p. 337.

1. *Understanding what the question is asking*: For each type of question, you need to understand what the question is asking you to *do*. So you need to know the difference between a definition, an explanation, and what is needed for an evaluative essay.
2. *Knowledge of the issue*: You need to understand the relevant concept, argument or claim. Evaluating claims is most complex. You'll need to know what the options are, the key arguments defending and attacking the claim, the theories that philosophers have defended that pull different arguments and claims together into a coherent whole.
3. *Structure of arguments*: Knowing how an argument works (or doesn't) is more than knowing the conclusion and the premises used; it is understanding *how* the premises are supposed to connect together to support the conclusion. With your own arguments, you equally need to understand how they work, and you should present them with a clear structure.
4. *Relevance*: A good part of philosophical skill is a matter of selecting ideas, concepts, examples and arguments that you encountered in the material you studied that are relevant to the question. Knowing what is relevant is a special kind of knowledge, which involves thinking carefully about what you know about arguments and theories in relation to the question asked.
5. *Critical discussion*: When you evaluate a claim, it is important to know that *presenting* ideas is distinct from *critically discussing* those ideas. You need to understand whether an argument succeeds or fails and why, and be able to present and compare arguments, objections and

counter-arguments to argue towards the most plausible position. You will usually need to draw on more than one source or author, and above all *think*.

Planning an essay

When you are answering a short-answer question, what you need to do is straightforward. You don't need to make any choices about *what* concepts or arguments to talk about, since that is specified by the question. You should still organise your thoughts before writing. But essays – both coursework essays and in the exam – need to be planned in more detail.

1. Take time to understand the question in detail. Most weak essays are weak because they fail to answer the actual question.
2. Keep the question in mind throughout writing, to ensure that your thought and planning stay relevant. Someone should be able to tell from the essay itself what question it is answering.
3. If it is appropriate, think about challenging the question. Does it make assumptions that can be questioned?
4. Brainstorm to generate ideas of what you might discuss. (In an exam, recall the relevant revision plan.) One way is through 'successive elaboration' – take a single-sentence statement of a position, and then make it more detailed, e.g. by providing some premises, then think what would be necessary to establish the premises, etc. Another is 'conceptual note-taking', simply writing what comes to mind: even starting from 'I don't know anything about *x*' suggests and leads to others, such as 'I don't know what *x* means' and 'So and so defines *x* as …'. Half-formed thoughts are better developed when out on the page.
5. If you are researching the essay, start by making the relevant ideas familiar, but make decisions on what to concentrate on, and narrow your research to achieve depth in a few central areas.
6. An essay needs shape, it is always directed towards a conclusion, so you'll need to decide what to include and what to leave out.
7. Don't aim to cover too much; three main arguments is usually enough. Even fewer can be fine if you go into real depth.
8. Plan an essay that argues for a particular position. You will often want to argue for or against a specific claim (as in a debate). But you don't

have to. For example, you can argue that we can't know either way. Whatever your conclusion (the claim you want to make), you'll need to defend it, even the claim that we can't know something. Have it in mind throughout the plan and writing. The essay should read like one long argument (taking in various smaller arguments, objections and replies) for your conclusion.

9. The evaluative discussion is the most important part of the essay, so only introduce and explain material that you will use in discussion. You can think of this as two halves: the arguments in favour of your conclusion; and the objections to your arguments, or separate arguments against your conclusion, and replies to them. Make sure you consider the objections and counter-arguments. Even if you are defending your point of view strongly (which is fine), you need to consider fairly what can be said against it.

10. In light of all of the above points, write a plan which includes key points (definitions, arguments, objections, etc.) and the paragraph structure.

11. Each paragraph presents an idea. Paragraphs should not be divided on *length*, but as 'units of thought'. If you made a one-sentence summary of each paragraph, would the resulting account of the essay read logically?

Writing an essay

Once again, I'll just provide some advice on the most difficult writing task, the essay:

1. Plan the essay. It is very rare that good philosophical essays are written 'off the cuff', taking each thought as it occurs to you in turn. An essay is not (just) a test of memory, but of intelligence, which includes organisation and clarity.

2. However, new ideas will probably occur as you write. It is fine to deviate from the plan, but think through new ideas before incorporating them to make sure they are good and to structure them.

3. The usual starting point for constructing an argument is explaining other people's ideas. The idea here is to be *accurate* and *sympathetic*. An argument works best when the ideas are presented *as strongly as*

possible – otherwise the opponent can simply rephrase the idea, and your counter-argument falls apart.

4. In general, aim to be concise. Present the kernel of the idea clearly and relevantly. Stick to what you need to present in order to properly discuss the question. This can involve surrounding detail, since you need to show an awareness of the situation of the topic in the subject. But be selective and relevant.

5. Never just *report* or *allude to* the arguments you have read – *make* the argument. To use a metaphor from war, you are not a reporter at the front line, but a combatant engaged for one side or the other.

6. Use the three-part structure: make a point, back it up, show its relevance.

7. In critical discussion, reflect on what a particular argument actually demonstrates, and whether there are counter-arguments that are better. You should be able to argue both for and against a particular view. Relate these arguments to each other, evaluating which is stronger and why. You need to work at shaping the material and 'generating a discussion'.

8. Alternatively, you may want to relate a particular argument to a broader context, e.g. a philosopher's overall theory, other philosophers' ideas on the same issue, etc. – in general, work to understand the relation between the parts and the whole.

9. Understand and be careful about the strength of your assertions. It is important to know whether your arguments indicate that 'all … (e.g. lies are wrong)', 'some …', 'most …', or 'typically …'. It is also important to distinguish between whether this *is* so, or *must* be so, or simply *may be* so.

10. Never introduce new material in the concluding paragraph of the essay. The essay's conclusion should reflect the argument of the essay. Don't feel you have to personally agree with your conclusion! Essays are not confessions of belief.

11. In an exam setting, you also need to keep note of the time, and leave time to review and correct what you've written.

A standard essay structure

1. Introduction: how you understand the question, what you'll argue for (and perhaps some indication of how you will discuss the question)

Alternatively, you may consider objections to each argument (in (3)) in turn as you consider the argument.

There may not be time or space for (5) and (6) in every case, and you can still write a very good essay without them.

2. An explanation of the claim to be evaluated, perhaps including some of the relevant background theory, and either including or followed by …
3. The arguments in favour of the claim (give the arguments, and if you think they work, argue that the reasoning is valid and the premises are true)
4. Objections to these arguments and replies to the objections
5. Arguments against the claim
6. Objections to these arguments
7. Conclusion: a clear statement showing how the claim is supported/ defeated by the arguments discussed. This will require you to make some points, either as you go along or in the conclusion, about which arguments or objections are strongest and why.

General advice

When doing coursework essays:

1. Do not wait until you have finished your research to start writing the essay. If you find, as your research continues, that someone else has written what you've written, then reference it; if you find an objection, then explain it and explain why it is wrong, or, if the objection persuades you, rewrite what you've written as 'one might think …' and use the objection to show why it is wrong.
2. Rewrite the essay – almost no one does themselves justice in one draft.
3. Quotations do not substitute for understanding. Use them when you want to illustrate the precise wording of an idea or back up an interpretation.
4. Don't plagiarise.

In both coursework and exam essays:

5. Be precise, especially with words that have a philosophical meaning, like 'valid', 'assume', 'infer'.
6. Be clear. Being vague gives the reader the sense that you don't really know what you are talking about. Don't hide behind long words – it rarely impresses people who understand them. Use technical terms in

context, and make sure that the philosophical meaning of ordinary words is clear – if not, provide a quick definition.

7. Don't use long and involved sentences. Use active, not passive, constructions, e.g. 'Plato argued ...' not 'It was argued by Plato ...'.

8. Include signposts. Generally speaking, the first sentence of a paragraph should give some indication to a reader as to where you are in the argument (e.g. 'A second criticism of the argument that ...).

9. While it is acceptable to use the first person ('I'), this should not be to say 'I feel ...' or 'I think ...' or 'In my opinion ...' as though such an assertion adds any weight to the plausibility of the conclusion. The whole essay is what you think, however it is phrased.

Chapter 2

Metaphysics of God

Please see the INTRODUCTION (p. 1) for an explanation of the different kinds of marginal boxes and what they mean. Please see CHAPTER 1 HOW TO DO PHILOSOPHY (p. 5) for explanations of philosophical argument and how to understand argument maps.

In his most famous book, *The Critique of Pure Reason*, Immanuel Kant claimed that we are, as rational creatures, interested in the answers to three questions: 'What can I know?', 'What must I do?', and 'What may I hope?' The discussions of epistemology and moral philosophy tackle the first two questions, which leaves the issue of 'What may I hope?' Is this physical life all that there is, or will I continue in some form after my body dies? Is there some divine being or ultimate reality that brings about justice, if not in this life, then the next? In other words, does religious belief make sense?

In this chapter, we will look at just one of these issues – the existence of God. If you have already studied some philosophy, you'll know that while it can be interesting surveying the many views that people hold on philosophical matters, we can often do philosophy with greater understanding and depth by looking more closely at a few debates in detail. But you'll also know that without reminding ourselves of the broader context, we can get lost in the details of theories and arguments. So it is worthwhile repeatedly returning to the fundamental question and its importance to us as human beings. If God exists, that has significant implications for how we understand what we are, the nature of the world and our place in it, and what the future may hold for us.

In this chapter, we will approach the question of whether God exists as a question in metaphysics. To think about this question meaningfully, we first need to have some idea of what we mean by 'God'. The idea of God is very varied in human history and culture. We will look at just one concept of God, deriving from the traditional monotheistic religions of Judaism,

Christianity and Islam. So our first question will be what this concept is and whether it makes sense.

Having understood what God is (according to this tradition), we can then ask whether such a God exists. We will discuss three arguments for the existence of God and one against. The ontological argument claims to prove that God exists just by unpacking our understanding of the concept of God. The argument from design uses the apparent order and purpose of nature to infer the existence of God. The cosmological argument claims that without God, the universe cannot exist or be explained. The problem of evil uses the existence of evil to infer that God, at least as traditionally conceived, does not exist.

We will end by reflecting on whether 'the metaphysics of God' makes sense. When people talk about God – when we use religious language – what are we really doing? Is 'God' the name or concept of a being that exists (or doesn't)? If not, then whether God exists isn't really a metaphysical question after all. So does religious language state facts or is it a way of expressing our values? Is it even meaningful to talk of God?

By the end of the chapter, you should be able to analyse, explain, and evaluate a number of arguments for and against the coherence of the concept of God, the existence of God, and theories of religious language.

A note on referring to God: I have adopted the traditional personal pronoun 'he' in referring to God. English unfortunately has only two personal pronouns, 'he' and 'she', both gendered. If God exists, I don't believe that God is gendered in either way. My use of 'he' is purely to avoid the awkwardness of alternating 'he' and 'she' and of using 's/he'.

> Metaphysics asks questions about the fundamental nature of reality. *Meta-* means above, beyond or after; physics enquires into the physical structure of reality – which may or may not be the fundamental nature of all reality.

Syllabus checklist ✓

The AQA A level syllabus for this topic is:

I. The concept and nature of 'God'

God's attributes:

✓ God as omniscient, omnipotent, supremely good (omnibenevolent), and the meaning(s) of these divine attributes

✓ Competing views on such a being's relationship to time, including God being timeless (eternal) and God being within time (everlasting)
✓ Arguments for the incoherence of the concept of God including:
  ● The paradox of the stone
  ● The *Euthyphro* dilemma
  ● The compatibility, or otherwise, of the existence of an omniscient God and free human beings

II. Arguments relating to the existence of God

For the arguments below, students should pay particular attention to nuances in the logical form of the arguments (deductive, inductive, etc.), the strengths of the conclusions (God does exist, God must exist, etc.), and the nature of God assumed or defended by the argument.

A. Ontological arguments

✓ St Anselm's ontological argument
✓ Descartes' ontological argument
✓ Norman Malcolm's ontological argument

Issues that may arise for the arguments above, including:
✓ Gaunilo's 'perfect island' objection
✓ Empiricist objections to a priori arguments for existence
✓ Kant's objection based on existence not being a predicate

B. Teleological/design arguments

✓ The design argument from analogy (as presented by Hume)
✓ William Paley's design argument: argument from spatial order/ purpose
✓ Richard Swinburne's design argument: argument from temporal order/regularity

Issues that may arise for the arguments above, including:
✓ Hume's objections to the design argument from analogy
✓ The problem of spatial disorder (as posed by Hume and Paley)

✓ The design argument fails as it is an argument from a unique case (Hume)
✓ Whether God is the best or only explanation

C. Cosmological arguments

✓ The Kalām argument (an argument from temporal causation)
✓ Aquinas' First Way (argument from motion), Second Way (argument from atemporal causation) and Third Way (an argument from contingency)
✓ Descartes' argument based on his continuing existence (an argument from causation)
✓ Leibniz's argument from the principle of sufficient reason (an argument from contingency)

Issues that may arise for the arguments above, including:
✓ The possibility of an infinite series
✓ Hume's objection to the 'causal principle'
✓ The argument commits the fallacy of composition (Russell)
✓ The impossibility of a necessary being (Hume and Russell)

D. The problem of evil

✓ Whether God's attributes can be reconciled with the existence of evil
  ● The nature of moral evil and natural evil
  ● The logical and evidential forms of the problem of evil

Responses to these issues and issues arising from those responses, including:
✓ The free will defence (including Alvin Plantinga)
✓ Soul-making (including John Hick)

III. Religious language

✓ The distinction between cognitivism and non-cognitivism about religious language

✓   The empiricist/logical positivist challenges to the status of metaphysical (here, religious) language: the verification principle and verification/falsification (Ayer)
- Hick's response to Ayer (eschatological verification) and issues arising from that response

✓   Further responses: the '*University* debate'
- Anthony Flew on falsification (Wisdom's 'gardener')
- Basil Mitchell's response to Flew (the 'partisan')
- Hare's response to Flew (bliks and the lunatic)

and issues arising from those responses.

I. The concept and nature of 'God'

There are many concepts of God around the world, and different religions have different views on the nature of God. However, almost all agree that God is 'maximally great' – that nothing could be greater than God. This is the conception of God we will start with. But we develop it more narrowly, and the properties of God we will discuss are those which Judaism, Christianity and Islam – the three great monotheistic traditions – have thought central. Even more narrowly, we will look only at how the debate over God's attributes has been understood and developed in the Western Christian tradition. In this section, we will ask how the concept of God has been understood, whether it is coherent, and whether it is consistent with certain views of morality and human freedom.

A. God's attributes

On Christian Doctrine,
Bk 1, Ch. 7

We start with the thought that nothing could be greater than God. Another way this thought has been expressed is that God is perfect. Augustine says that to think of God is to 'attempt to conceive something than which nothing more excellent or sublime exists'. But just thinking of what does exist, and thinking of God as the most excellent of these things, may be too limited. Some philosophers claim that God is the most perfect being that *could* exist.

If God exists, then not only does nothing that is greater than God exist, but it is impossible for anything greater than God to exist.

The idea of perfection has often been linked to the idea of reality in two ways. First, what is perfect has been thought to be more real than what is not. Imperfections involve something failing to exist in a better way. Second, perfection has also been thought to involve complete self-sufficiency – i.e. not to be dependent on anything, and not to lack anything. Again, this connects with being the ultimate reality: that which is not the ultimate reality will depend on that which is, and so not be perfect. So God, as the most perfect being, is traditionally thought of as the ultimate reality – the ground or basis for everything that exists.

> Why would one think God is the 'greatest' being? Could anything be greater than God?

Omniscience

Perfect knowledge is usually taken to mean 'omniscience'. The most obvious definition of omniscience is 'knowing everything' (Latin *omni-*, 'all'; *scient*, 'knowing'). But we need to remember that God is the most perfect *possible* being, and perhaps it is *impossible* to know everything. For example, if human beings have free will, then perhaps it is not possible to know what they will do in the future. So let us say for now that omniscience means 'knowing everything that it is possible to know'.

> We discuss the idea of God as a 'person' in extension material, available on the companion website.

Omniscience is not just a matter of *what* God knows, but also of *how* God knows. Aquinas argues that God knows everything that he knows 'directly', rather than through inference or through understanding a system of representation (such as language or thinking in terms of propositions). To perfectly know something, Aquinas thought, the form of knowledge must match the nature of the object, e.g. we know visible things best through sight. Furthermore, to know each thing as the particular thing it is, rather than just to have general knowledge, is better. Knowing each tree as the tree it is, is more perfect than knowing general facts about trees. So direct knowledge of particulars is superior to knowledge that is mediated by concepts. This is a bit like our knowing objects through sense experience, or better, knowing what you are doing when you are doing it, since everything that exists, thinks Aquinas, exists as a result of God's activity.

> We return to this issue in OMNISCIENCE AND FREE HUMAN BEINGS, p. 48.

> Aquinas, *Summa Theologica*, Pt 1, Q. 14, Arts 5, 6

Other philosophers disagree about whether God's knowledge must always take the form Aquinas claimed. They argue that if God doesn't know all true propositions, then there is something that God doesn't know; so God has conceptual and propositional knowledge as well as direct knowledge.

> What is 'omniscience'?

Omnipotence

Power is the ability to do things. As perfect, God will have perfect power, or the most power possible. The most obvious definition of omnipotence is 'the power to do anything' (Latin *omni-*, 'all'; *potent*, 'powerful'). But once again, we should consider that God is the most perfect possible being, and therefore God's power may be the power to do anything possible and no more. Should we think that the power to do anything includes, for instance, the logically impossible; or is this not a possible power? Could God make $2 + 2 = 5$? Could God create a married bachelor? Some pious philosophers have wanted to say yes – logic is no limit on God's power. However, there is simply no way we can meaningfully say this.

AQUINAS ON OMNIPOTENCE

AQUINAS, *SUMMA THEOLOGICA*, PT 1, Q. 25, ART. 3

Aquinas argues that the correct understanding of God's omnipotence is that God can do anything possible. What is impossible is a contradiction in terms – the words that you use to describe the impossible literally contradict each other. So any description of a logically impossible state of affairs or power is not a meaningful description, because it contains a contradiction. What is logically impossible is not anything at all.

Thus, the *limits* of the logically possible are not *limitations* on God's power. Even if God can't do the logically impossible, there is still nothing that God can't do.

1) Is logic a limitation on God's power? 2) What is 'omnipotence'?

Supreme goodness (omnibenevolence)

There are two ways of understanding perfect, or supreme, goodness. If goodness just is perfection, then saying God is perfectly good is just to say that God is perfectly perfect – or the most perfect possible being. There is more than one way to be perfect (including, as we've seen, perfect power and perfect knowledge), and God is perfect in all ways. This is a metaphysical sense of 'goodness'.

The other sense of 'goodness', which is the sense in which I will understand it in our discussion, is the moral sense. In this sense, 'God is perfectly good' means that God's will is always in accordance with moral values.

Plato and Augustine connect the two understandings of perfect goodness. What is perfect includes what is morally good; evil is a type of 'lack', a 'falling short' or absence of goodness. Evil doesn't have a positive aspect – it isn't a genuine 'force' or an aspect of reality that stands against goodness. What is evil simply fails to be what is good. If evil is a 'lack' or 'failure', what is morally good is more real than what is not. And so what is morally perfect and what is metaphysically perfect are the same thing.

Explain the difference between 'metaphysical' and 'moral' perfection.

We discuss evil further in THINKING HARDER: MIDGLEY ON HUMAN EVIL (p. 128) and in relation to omnipotence in extension material.

God and time

Being perfect, God is self-sufficient, dependent on nothing else for existence. If something brought God into existence, God would be dependent on that thing to exist. If there were something that could end God's existence, then God is equally dependent on that thing (not exercising its power) to continue to exist. If God depends on nothing else, then nothing can bring God into existence or end God's existence. And so (if God exists) God's existence has no beginning or end.

There are two ways in which this can be expressed. If God exists in time, then having no beginning or end, God exists throughout all time. God is a temporal being that is *everlasting*. If God exists outside time, then God is an atemporal being, timeless. In this case, God's existence is *eternal*. God has no beginning or end because the ideas of beginning and end only make sense in time – something can only start or stop existing in time. God is not in time, so God cannot start or stop existing.

Explain the difference between the terms 'everlasting' and 'eternal'.

This idea of God's 'eternal' existence says very little – just that God is atemporal – and even this is negative (God does *not* exist in time). Furthermore, while we can say this, it is very hard to understand what we could mean. What is it for a being, such as God, to exist 'outside time'?

Thinking harder: Stump and Kretzmann on eternity

Consolations of Philosophy

STUMP AND KRETZMANN, 'ETERNITY'

Boethius on eternal being

Stump and Kretzmann begin their analysis of eternity with a famous definition by Boethius. An eternal being such as God, Boethius says, is one that has 'the complete possession all at once of illimitable life'. This life is possessed in its 'whole fullness', 'such that nothing future is absent from it and nothing past has flowed away'. Instead, it is 'always present to itself'.

In another work, *On the Trinity*, Boethius argues that this means that we need to understand the idea of 'now' differently for an eternal being. 'Now' for us, as beings that exist in time, marks the present moment in time and the passage of time. 'Now' is always becoming the past; it is only ever 'now' for an instant. But for an eternal being, 'now' remains and doesn't move – it marks out the whole eternal life of the being.

These are very difficult ideas, and it will take a long time to understand them. But as a start, we can say that an eternal being

1. has 'life';
2. cannot have a beginning or an end, since it is 'illimitable' – not only limitless, but can't be limited;
3. is atemporal in possessing its whole life all at once, giving a distinct meaning to 'now'; and
4. involves a special kind of duration, as no part of its life is ever absent.

We need to understand each of these claims. (1) is fairly straightforward (at least in theory!). The 'life' of eternal being can't be physical or biological. What is physical or biological is temporal. It exists in time and undergoes change. So the life of eternal being must be a 'psychological life'.

(2) is similarly straightforward. This psychological life of an eternal being is not limited. If something has a beginning or an end, then it is limited – it does not exist before its beginning or after its end. So this is a life that has no beginning or end.

These first two conditions are compatible with God being everlasting – existing throughout time but with no beginning or end in time. (3) rejects this interpretation of God's relationship to time and is much harder to understand. The events that constitute the life of an eternal being do not, from its perspective, follow one another in time. Its whole life is experienced as 'now', i.e. as 'present'. That 'present' isn't flanked by past or future, it is not a moment in which future becomes past. It is a non-temporal present.

How can we understand this claim and the relation of an atemporal being, such as God, to temporal beings, such as ourselves? We will need to unpack the idea of 'now'. But first, it may help to have a picture in mind. We are used to thinking of time in timelines, with beings that exist at the same time – simultaneously – as overlapping one another on the line, e.g.

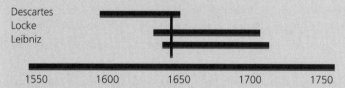

Figure 2.1 A standard timeline

We can figure out whether two beings exist at the same time by drawing straight lines at right angles to the timeline. A line at right angles to the timeline picks out a particular 'moment in time' – a moment that was, at that time, 'present'. Whatever occurs in the same moment is simultaneous – it occurs at the same time. So we can see that, for part of their lives, Descartes, Locke and Leibniz were all alive at the same time (1646–50).

But we cannot show where an eternal being fits using this picture, because it isn't in time at all. The timeline is a picture of how future time becomes present and then past. Whether an event is

> Identify two differences between the temporal sense of 'now' and the eternal sense of 'now'.

future, present or past depends on where on the timeline one is. But an eternal being doesn't have future or past, only present. It needs to be in a different dimension from the timeline.

Boethius suggests this picture instead, with the whole of time as the circumference of the circle and God as the centre point of the circle:

Figure 2.2 A circular timeline

Explain Boethius' circle as an account of God's eternity.

From the centre of the circle, we can draw a line at right angles to *any point on the circumference* (the timeline). God is simultaneous with every point in time. In this diagram, we can map every different moment in time onto just the one moment of God's entire existence.

These are only pictures, and they can be misleading (e.g. Boethius is not suggesting that time goes in a circle!). But they may help us understand the complexity of 'now' or 'simultaneity' when talking about an eternal being. We said there was a time when Descartes, Locke and Leibniz all lived simultaneously. An eternal being is simultaneous with every point in time. We cannot mean 'simultaneous' in the same sense in both sentences. We cannot say that an eternal being exists *at the same time* as an event in time, since it doesn't exist in time. So what can we mean?

Types of simultaneity

Stump and Kretzmann propose two new concepts of simultaneity to explain the relationship of God to time. The familiar concept of simultaneity is that two things are simultaneous if they exist or occur *at one and the same time*. But this is, obviously, a definition that presupposes that the two things are in time. Call our familiar concept 'T-simultaneity' (for temporal simultaneity). Part of the life of Descartes was T-simultaneous with parts of the lives of Locke and Leibniz.

For an eternal being, its whole life is present. This is a new idea of simultaneity, call it 'E-simultaneity' (for eternal simultaneity). Two events or beings are E-simultaneous if they exist or occur in one and the sameeternal present. Any two events in God's life will be simultaneous, since all events in God's life are present, in the eternal 'now'. This is an atemporal concept of simultaneity.

We can use these two concepts of simultaneity to create a third concept which will explain the relationship of an eternal being to time, to say that God is simultaneous with any (and every) event in time, 'ET-simultaneity' (for simultaneity between something eternal and something temporal). The concept is more complicated because we can't say that the two simultaneous things exist at the same time (since one is atemporal) nor that they exist in the eternal present (since one is temporal).

Let's take the event in time as your reading this paragraph. From *God's* perspective, your reading this paragraph is present and so is the whole of God's eternal life. Your reading this paragraph is present in the temporal sense – it is 'now', in between past and future; and the whole of God's life is 'now' in the eternal present. From *your* perspective, your reading this paragraph is now in time, and God is eternally present.

More generally, from our temporal perspective, because God is ET-simultaneous with every moment in time, then God is present at every moment in time. God is never past or future, and no part of God is past or present (so talk of how God 'used to be' or how God 'will be' makes no sense). From God's perspective, every event in time is observed as occurring in the present, ET-simultaneous with all of God's life. As Stump and Kretzmann put it, 'From a temporal

Stump and Kretzmann discuss the relativity of simultaneity, given Einstein's theory of space-time. We discuss this and some implications of their analysis in extension material.

standpoint, the present is ET-simultaneous with the whole infinite extent of an eternal entity's life. From the standpoint of eternity, every time is present, co-occurrent with the whole of infinite atemporal duration.' So God experiences every moment in time as present together, and the whole of God's existence is simultaneous with each moment in time.

The formal definition of ET-simultaneity is this:

Where x is some temporal event and y is some eternal event, x and y are ET-simultaneous if

a. for an eternal being, A, x and y are both present, x observed as temporally present and y as eternally present; and

b. for a temporal being, B, x and y are both present, x observed as temporally present and y as eternally present.

Explain what, according to Stump and Kretzmann, it means to say that you and God exist ET-simultaneously.

Because you are temporal, existing over a period of time, and God is eternal, we should not say that you and God exist at the same time. In other words, you and God do not exist T-simultaneously. Likewise, you do not exist eternally. So you and God do not exist E-simultaneously. But (if God exists and is eternal) you and God exist ET-simultaneously – at each moment when you exist, God also exists eternally.

A last point. Descartes existed (for a time) T-simultaneously with Locke, and Locke existed (at that same time) T-simultaneously with Leibniz. From knowing this, we can infer that Descartes existed (for a time) T-simultaneously with Leibniz. T-simultaneity is a 'transitive' relation. (A transitive relation is just one in which if it holds between x and y, and between y and z, then it holds between x and z. For example, if x is bigger than y, and y is bigger than z, then x is bigger than z.) If x happens at the same time as y, and y happens at the same time as z, then x and z also happen at the same time.

It is important to notice that ET-simultaneity is *not* transitive. If your reading of this paragraph is ET-simultaneous with God, and another temporal event, say your tenth birthday is also ET-simultaneous with God, this doesn't mean that your reading this paragraph is ET-simultaneous, or even T-simultaneous, with your tenth birthday. (If it is your tenth birthday, I'm very impressed, and happy birthday!) We will see *why* this is so important when we discuss OMNISCIENCE AND FREE HUMAN BEINGS (p. 48).

Atemporal duration

The final idea we need to look at is (4), God's existence as a special kind of duration. We said that our present is a moment in time, an instant at which future becomes past. The eternal present, God's present, is not like that, because there is no future or past. What it is like is hard, perhaps impossible, to imagine. It is a type of limitless, pastless, futureless duration. Perhaps the best way to try to understand this is to think about our concept of 'duration'.

Something that 'endures' lasts through time. It persists through time, it continues to exist. It isn't ephemeral or fleeting. These concepts have a resonance for us – endurance, persistence, substance, permanence. But what does the existence of any temporal thing, you for instance, reallyamount to? You exist through time, in the past, the present and the future. When your life is finished, you no longer exist. But right now, you exist. But how? The past does not exist and the future is yet to exist. You existed in the past, but you don't any more – that part of your life is gone. The past of your life does not exist. You will exist in the future, but you don't yet – that part is yet to exist. The future of your life does not exist. So it seems that your existence is only in the present. But what is that? Just a fleeting moment at which the future becomes the past! To exist in time is barely to exist at all, it seems!

We said that something that endures, that has duration, is not fleeting or ephemeral. Yet the existence of anything in time seems to consist in no more than existence in a fleeting moment. Most of its 'existence' is either past or future, so not in existence at all! If

God existed in time, even if God is everlasting, this would be just as true of God as of you. God's past would not exist, nor would God's future. Only that part of God that is present would exist.

But now think of a form of existence in which no part of one's existence has disappeared into the past or has yet to come into existence in the future, an existence the whole of which is present. This is existence in which none of the existence of the thing has already gone and none of it is yet to come. That is what atemporal duration is, and according to Boethius, Stump and Kretzmann, it is the form of existence that God has. Everything that God ever 'was' or 'will be' always 'is'.

What is it for God to exist eternally?

Key points: God's attributes

- Traditional monotheistic conceptions of God stem from the idea that God is the most perfect possible being.
- Omniscience: God knows everything it is possible to know. At least much of what God knows, says Aquinas, he knows directly, without inference or linguistic representation.
- Omnipotence: God has the power to do anything that it is possible to do.
- Supreme goodness (omnibenevolence): God is the most perfect possible being, and because moral goodness is a perfection, God's will is in accordance with moral values.
- Everlasting: God exists through all time, with no beginning or end.
- Eternal: God's existence is atemporal, with no beginning or end. According to Stump and Kretzmann, following Boethius, God's existence is illimitable and wholly present to God, a form of atemporal duration.
- The temporal present ('now') is a moment between past and future. The eternal present ('now') is atemporal.
- Two events are T-simultaneous if they occur at the same time. Two events are E-simultaneous if they both occur as part of the same eternal present. Two events, one temporal and one eternal, are ET-simultaneous

if the temporal event is temporally present and the eternal event is eternally present. The whole life of God is ET-simultaneous with every moment in time.

B. Arguments for the incoherence of the concept of God

If God is the most perfect possible being, then each of the perfections attributed to God must be possible, and the combination of the perfections must also be possible. Both of these requirements lead to difficulties. For example, we have seen that it is unclear what it means to say that 'God knows everything it is possible to know.' If we cannot make the idea of omniscience coherent, then we cannot make the concept of God coherent. Another puzzle is whether God can will evil. Omnipotence suggests 'yes', perfect goodness suggests 'no'. So is the concept of God coherent? If not, then nothing could be God, i.e. God does not and cannot exist. We will look at three arguments that challenge the coherence of the concept of God.

The paradox of the stone

Can God create a stone that he can't lift? If the answer is 'no', then God cannot create the stone. If the answer is 'yes', then God cannot lift the stone. So either way, it seems, there is something God cannot do. If there is something God can't do, then God isn't omnipotent. Indeed, no being can be omnipotent. The concept of an omnipotent being is incoherent, because no being could have the powers to create a stone it can't lift and to lift that stone.

Outline and explain the paradox of the stone.

One reply argues that the paradox fails because it presupposes the possibility of something logically impossible. The claim that someone, *x*, can make something that is too heavy for *x* to lift is not normally self-contradictory. However, it becomes self-contradictory – logically impossible – when *x* is an omnipotent being. 'A stone an omnipotent being can't lift' is not a possible thing; as a self-contradiction, it describes nothing. So, it might be replied, 'the power to create a stone an omnipotent being can't lift' is not a possible power. If God lacks it, God still doesn't lack any possible power.

Explain the claim that 'the power to create a stone an omnipotent being can't lift' is logically impossible.

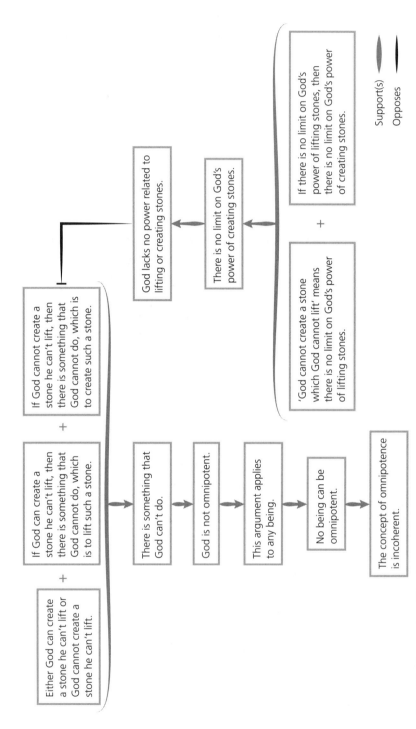

Map 2.1 The paradox of the stone

Either God can create a stone he can't lift or God cannot create a stone he can't lift.

+

If God can create a stone he can't lift, then there is something that God cannot do, which is to lift such a stone.

+

If God cannot create a stone he can't lift, then there is something that God cannot do, which is to create such a stone.

There is something that God can't do.

God is not omnipotent.

This argument applies to any being.

No being can be omnipotent.

The concept of omnipotence is incoherent.

God lacks no power related to lifting or creating stones.

There is no limit on God's power of creating stones.

'God cannot create a stone which God cannot lift' means there is no limit on God's power of lifting stones.

+

If there is no limit on God's power of lifting stones, then there is no limit on God's power of creating stones.

Support(s)

Opposes

But this reply begs the question. It *assumes* that we can coherently talk of an omnipotent being. It assumes that in the phrase 'a stone that an omnipotent being can't lift', there is no problem with the term 'omnipotent being'. But if the concept of an omnipotent being is self-contradictory, then this isn't true. Until we know that the concept of an omnipotent being is a coherent concept, we can't legitimately use the concept, for example in arguing that 'a stone that an omnipotent being can't lift' is a logically impossible state of affairs. Now, the reply is supposed to be trying to *show* that the concept is not self-contradictory, but in order to do this, it has to assume that the concept is not self-contradictory. This is the fallacy of begging the question – an argument that assumes the truth of its conclusion in order to show the truth of its conclusion. So this reply fails.

A better response to the paradox is this. Suppose we allow that God can lift any stone, but cannot create a stone that he can't lift. 'God cannot create a stone which God cannot lift' only means that 'if God can create a stone, then God can lift it'. God can create a stone of any size and can then lift that stone. So is there a stone that God can't create? No. There is no limit on God's power of lifting stones, and so there is no limit on God's power of creating stones. That God cannot create a stone that he can't lift is no limit on the stones that God can create. So God lacks no power related to lifting or creating stones.

> Explain one response to the paradox of the stone.

The Euthyphro *dilemma*

What is the relationship between God and morality? Is morality something independent of God or is morality whatever God wills it to be? Can God make right be wrong, or good bad, or not? The answer, it seems, must be one of the following two options:

1. Morality is independent of what God wills. To be good, God's will must conform to something independent of God. God wills what is morally right because it is right.
2. Morality is whatever God wills. What is morally right is right because God wills it.

There are reasons to think that *neither* answer is satisfactory, creating a dilemma. If (1) is correct, then we place a constraint on God. God would no

Explain the difference between claiming that God wills what is morally right because it is right and claiming that what is morally right is right because God wills it.

longer be omnipotent, because God cannot turn wrong into right. But if (2) is correct, then God can change wrong into right by an act of will. For example, if murdering babies were commanded by God, then it would be morally right of us to murder babies. This violates our sense of morality.

If neither answer is satisfactory, but logically, the relationship between God and morality must be either (1) or (2), then we may question whether our concept of God is coherent (assuming our concept of morality is coherent). How can we best make sense of our concept of God in relation to morality?

PLATO'S DILEMMA

The debate derives from a discussion of a closely related issue in Plato's dialogue *Euthyphro*. In his dialogue, Plato considered the question 'what is piety?' Is piety doing whatever the gods want or do the gods want what is pious? Our version is different in two respects. First, it substitutes 'morality' for 'piety' and the classical monotheistic concept of God for Plato's 'gods'. Second, Euthyphro's dilemma also focuses more on the difficulty of *defining* what piety is without circularity; our dilemma is more about the coherence of the concept of God in relation to morality.

PLATO, *EUTHYPHRO*

In response to Socrates' questioning, Euthyphro's first formal definition of piety is 'that which is dear to the gods' or again 'what the gods love'. Socrates then asks whether something – an action, say – is pious because it is loved by the gods, or whether the gods love the action because it is pious. Euthyphro's definition is ambiguous. Which of these two does it mean?

Euthyphro answers that the gods love what is pious because it is pious. This makes piety independent of the gods' love – it would count as piety whether or not the gods loved it. It is pious and *so* the gods love it. That some action is dear to the gods doesn't *make* something an act of piety. If they love pious actions because they are pious, there must be something that qualifies them as pious independent of the gods' love.

Socrates objects that this can't be right. Whatever 'is dear to the gods is dear to them because it is loved by them, not loved by them because it is dear to them'. Since piety is dear to the gods, it must be dear to them *because* they love it. Curiously, Plato doesn't support this objection with any arguments. The thought is that what the gods value, they value because they love that thing. To accept this means accepting that piety isn't a *reason* for the gods loving what they do. Why do the gods love certain actions? Whatever the answer, it isn't piety. An action qualifies as pious simply because the gods love it. On this view, if the gods love something, doing that thing – whatever it is – is pious.

But suppose we persist in the face of this objection, and agree with Euthyphro that piety is independent of what the gods love. Then what is it? Euthyphro suggests it is justice in relation to the gods. But what is it to treat the gods justly? It is to please them in prayers and sacrifices. This doesn't bring them any benefit; it simply pleases them. But now, piety = justice = what is pleasing to the gods. And so, objects Socrates, piety once more becomes whatever pleases the gods – what is pious is pious because the gods love it. They happen to love prayers and sacrifices, and so these actions become pious. Euthyphro has found it impossible to say what piety is, independent of what the gods love.

> Outline and explain Euthyphro's struggle to define piety.

OMNIPOTENCE AND MORALITY

Having looked at the origin of the *Euthyphro* dilemma, we return to our version of it. On our best understandings of God and morality, should we think of morality as dependent on God or as independent of God?

First, can we defend (1), the independence of morality from God? Perhaps there are ways to show that what is morally good *must* be good and cannot be evil, that what is wrong cannot be right. If so, then God cannot turn good into evil or wrong into right but this is no limitation of God's omnipotence, since it is logically impossible for moral good and right to be other than they are. This thought is supported by the idea, mentioned above, that even if God commanded us to murder babies, it still wouldn't be right to murder babies, because such an action *can't* be right.

But if this is true, why is it true? It seems wrong to say that it is *logically* impossible. For instance, 'murdering babies is right' isn't (obviously) a contradiction in terms. What is morally right and wrong doesn't seem, at

The Israelites warring against the Canaanites.

Figure 2.3 According to some Old Testament stories (e.g. Deuteronomy 7:1–6), God *did* command people to kill babies. Would this make such actions morally right?

least, to be a matter of pure logic. We were able to argue that an omnipotent being can't do what is logically impossible, since what is logically impossible is nothing at all. But if 'murdering babies is right' isn't logically impossible, then why couldn't an omnipotent being make it true? Whatever makes moral wrong and moral right what they are must be something about the way the world is. Surely an omnipotent being can change the way the world is to be any way that is logically possible. Not being able to change the world does seem like a lack of power.

Put another way, if moral wrong can't become right, what explains why the world must be this way? If the explanation doesn't refer to logic, and it doesn't refer to God, then won't it refer to something that places a constraint on what God can do?

We can develop this thought by starting again from the concept of God. If the concept of God we are discussing is roughly right and God exists, then it would be very strange to think that morality (for human beings) is completely independent of God. Nothing that exists is independent of God. If God exists and is supremely good, then everything that is morally good must relate back to God as the ultimate reality. If it is impossible for what is good to be evil, for what is wrong to be right, this may be because what is good depends on God's nature, and it is impossible for God not to be God.

God's omnipotence, then, requires that we reject (1).

The discussion assumes that morality is not a matter of purely subjective human responses. If God exists and is supremely good, then in Moral Philosophy, we should probably assume some form of MORAL REALISM, p. 351.

So can (2), the claim that morality depends on God, be defended more successfully? We have already seen the objection that the view also entails that it would be right to murder babies if God willed it, and this doesn't seem right! Certainly, we would no longer think that God is good if God ordered such a thing, which suggests that we understand morality to be independent of what God wills.

Second, a challenge to the coherence of the concept of God begins to arise with this thought: if what is good or right is whatever God wills, then 'God is good' doesn't say anything substantial about God. *Whatever* God wills is by definition good – even murdering babies. So what can we mean by 'good' any longer if even this could be good? 'God is good' means no more than 'God wills whatever God wills'. It states a tautology. This empties the idea that God is good of any meaning.

We can develop this thought in a different direction. Saying that what is good is whatever God wills threatens to make morality arbitrary. *Why* does God will what he wills? There is no moral reason guiding what God wills because God *invents* morality. For example, the suffering of children is not yet a reason for God to think that it is morally wrong to command their death, because there is no moral right or wrong until God wills it to be so. The suffering of children could just as easily be a reason for God to think it morally right to command their death. It would not be against reason for God to will either the death of children or their care. In other words, facts about the suffering of children don't function as reasons at all, supporting one act of will over another. But if God has no reasons to will what he does, this means that there is no rational structure to morality. God's will is arbitrary.

Explain the claim that if morality depends on God's will, then morality is arbitrary.

These objections take us back to (1): there must be some independent standard we are implicitly relying on to say that what God wills is, in fact, morally good. But (1) is incompatible with God's omnipotence. The dilemma leaves us struggling to say that God is omnipotent or to say that God is good – we cannot, it seems, say both meaningfully. This challenges whether our concept of God is coherent.

Outline and explain the *Euthyphro* dilemma, giving one objection to each horn of the dilemma.

Discussion

One reply to the dilemma is to argue that although God's will does not respond to anything independent of it, it is not arbitrary. To defend this claim, we can appeal to God's other attributes, such as love. God's will is structured by God's love, and it is this that creates morality. God wills what he does because he loves.

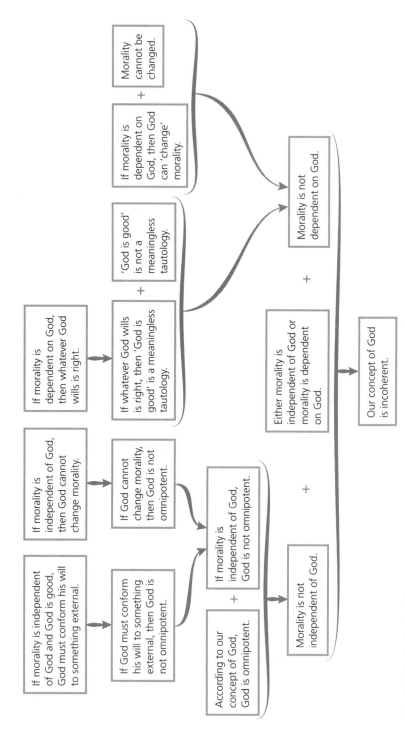

Map 2.2 The *Euthyphro* dilemma

Yet we may still ask: why does God love what he does? Is this arbitrary? If God loved something else, then morality would be different.

But could God love something different? For instance, suppose God loves all reality. Then there is nothing God doesn't love. Or again, given God's nature, could God love differently? If we can't form a clear conception of God loving differently and still being God, then the objection fades away.

Thinking harder: good is the same property as what God wills

One development of this position draws a distinction between *concepts* and *properties* to explain how morality is the same thing as what God wills, but 'God is good' is not a tautology. The thought is that 'God' and 'morally good' are different concepts. It is not an analytic truth that goodness is what God wills. However, goodness is the same property as what God wills.

A different example will help. 'Water' and 'H_2O' are different concepts, and before the discovery of hydrogen and oxygen, people knew about water. They had the concept of water, but not the concept of H_2O. And they didn't know that water is H_2O. So 'water is H_2O' is not analytically true. However, water and H_2O are one and the same thing – the two concepts refer to just one thing in the world. Water is *identical* to H_2O.

The same account can be given of 'good' and 'what God wills' – they are different concepts, and people can have and understand the concept of goodness without the concept of God. So 'God is good' is not an

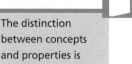

The distinction between concepts and properties is also used in arguments for MIND–BRAIN TYPE IDENTITY THEORY, p. 216, and in Moral Philosophy for MORAL NATURALISM, p. 354.

Figure 2.4 Water

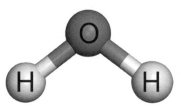

Figure 2.5 A water molecule

Explain the claim that what is good is identical with what God wills, yet 'God is good' is not a tautology.

Can the *Euthyphro* dilemma be solved? If so, how?

analytic truth. However, what is good is the same thing as what God wills. It is not something separate which provides a standard for God's will. Morality is dependent on God. This is a metaphysical truth (about what exists) but not a conceptual truth about morality.

But how can we establish that goodness and what God wills are the same thing? Unless we have an *independent* standard of goodness, we cannot claim that what God wills meets this standard and so can be identified with what is good.

This is true, but it only applies to how we *know* what is good, not what goodness turns out to *be*. We can only judge that water is H_2O if we have some independent idea of what water is. But that doesn't mean water is not H_2O. Likewise, to judge that what is good is what God wills, we need, *at least initially*, independent concepts of what is good and of what God wills. Which is fine, since we do form these concepts in distinct ways. But once we think that water is H_2O, we will say that whatever is H_2O is water. Likewise, once we come to believe that what is good is what God wills, we may use what we believe God's will to be to start judging what is good. Our understanding of God's will, we may argue, is our best source of knowledge about what is good.

Omniscience and free human beings

Can God know what we will do in the future? If God is eternal, existing outside time, the answer would seem to be 'yes'. Being outside time, God's knowledge of all events is 'simultaneous'. Past, present and future are all the same to God. God knows what happens in that period of time which we call 'future', just as he knows what has happened in the past. We can argue that this is part of what it is for God to be omniscient.

But if God knows what we will do in the future, are our actions *free*?

P1. For me to do an action freely, I must be able to do it or refrain from doing it.

P2. If God knows what I will do before I do it, then it must be true that I will do that action.

C1. Therefore, it cannot be true that God knows what I will do before I do it and be true that I *don't* do that action.

P3. If it is true that I will do that action, then nothing I can do can prevent it from coming true in the future that I am doing that action.

C2. Therefore, if God knows what I will do before I do it, then I cannot refrain from doing that action in the future.

C3. Therefore, if God knows what I will do before I do it, then that action is not free.

(P2) also follows from the claim that knowledge is always of true propositions. See Epistemology, TRUTH IS NOT A NECESSARY CONDITION OF KNOWLEDGE, p. 42.

The argument does not claim that we aren't free. It claims that *if* God knows what we will do before we do it, *then* we aren't free. If God is omniscient,

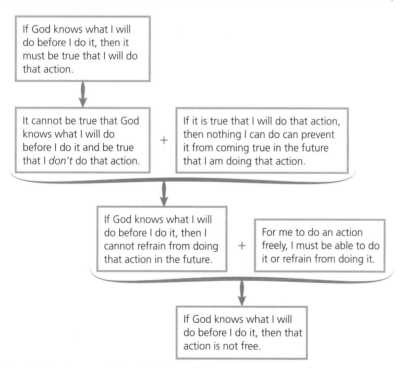

Map 2.3 The incompatibility of divine omniscience and human freedom

Explain the argument that if God knows my future actions, then my actions are not free.

We discuss free will and its moral importance in THINKING HARDER: MIDGLEY ON FREE WILL, p. 133.

as suggested in the first paragraph of this section, then the antecedent is true – God does know what we will do before we do it. In that case, the argument claims, the consequent follows – we aren't free.

We can also argue the other way around. If we *are* free, then this argument entails that God does *not* know what we will do before we do it. So there is something God does not know, and so God is not omniscient.

We could simply conclude that God is omniscient and we are not free. However, freedom – free will – is a great good that allows us to do good or evil and to enter willingly into a relationship with God or not. Without free will, we couldn't choose how to live or what kind of person to be, so our lives would not be meaningful or morally significant. As supremely good, God would want our lives to be morally significant and meaningful, so he would wish us to have free will. If we are not free, God is not supremely good.

Now it seems we have another dilemma concerning our concept of God. We are either free or we are not. If we are free, then God is not omniscient. If we are not free, then God is not good. So either God is omniscient or God is good, but not both. To avoid this conclusion, it seems that we need to understand how God's omniscience could be compatible with human free will. But is this possible?

If God does not know what we will do in the future, is God omniscient?

Thinking harder: three solutions

One solution is to argue that God is not eternal, but everlasting. We can then argue that it is *impossible*, even for God, to know the future, because of the existence of free will. And so God's not knowing what we will do before we do it is not a *restriction* on God's knowledge, since omniscience only involves knowing what it is possible to know. God still knows everything it is possible to know *at any given time*.

This reply accepts the argument above, but claims that the argument does not show that God isn't omniscient. The solution makes God's omniscience compatible with human free will, but we can question, first, whether this is a satisfactory view of omniscience, and second, whether it is a satisfactory view of the relationship between God and time.

A second solution is to argue that God knows what we will do before we do it, but this does not mean that we aren't free. (P2) is ambiguous. By definition, no one can know what is false, so it must be true that if God knows that I will do some action, then I will do that action. (The conditional is necessarily true.) However, while it *is* true that I will do that action, this doesn't mean that it *must* be true that I do that action. (The consequent is not necessarily true.) We can know lots of contingent truths, e.g. that Paris is the capital of France. Just because this *is* true doesn't mean that it *must* be true – the capital of France could have been some other city. Likewise, just because I will do some action in the future doesn't mean that I *must* do that action. I *won't* refrain from doing it, but that doesn't mean that I *can't* refrain from doing it. So for God to know what I will do in the future, it only needs to be the case that I *don't* do something else. It doesn't mean that I *can't*. So God can know what I will do, and I can still do what I do freely. So God's omniscience is compatible with free human beings.

We may object that this doesn't solve the problem. If I can refrain from doing what God knows I will do, then I *can* change what God knows (even if I *don't*). But, it seems, God *already* knows what I will do. So changing what God knows I will do means changing the past. And that's not something I can do. (Alternatively, if I can refrain from doing what God knows I will do, I can make God's belief false, and so not knowledge at all. But this means that I can make God not omniscient. And that's not something I can do.)

We can press the objection by asking *how* it is that God knows what I will do. Start by thinking about how we know what each one of us will do. For instance, perhaps you can accurately predict that a friend of yours will help this old lady across the street, because he is a kind person, in a good mood, and has just said that this is what he will do. In this instance, your belief is not only true, but justified as well, so we are happy to say that you know what your friend will do. Or again, if your beliefs about what your friend does are generally reliable, then you know what he will do. Clearly, simply having a true belief that someone will do something doesn't mean that they are not free.

But we cannot suppose that God's knowledge of what I will do is like this. Because God is omniscient, his beliefs are not merely reliable, but *complete and infallible*. How can there be complete and infallible knowledge of what someone will choose to do if that choice is not already

See Epistemology, NECESSARY/CONTINGENT TRUTH, p. 116.

See Epistemology, THE TRIPARTITE VIEW, p. 37, and RELIABILISM, p. 55.

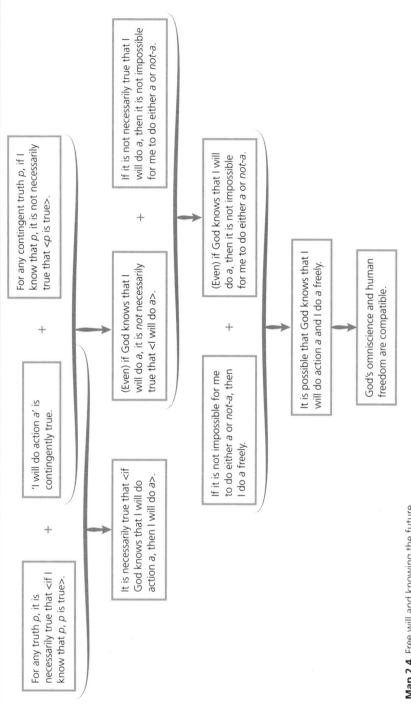

Map 2.4 Free will and knowing the future

For any truth *p*, it is necessarily true that <if I know that *p*, *p* is true>.

+

'I will do action *a*' is contingently true.

+

For any contingent truth *p*, if I know that *p*, it is not necessarily true that <*p* is true>.

It is necessarily true that <if God knows that I will do action *a*, then I will do *a*>.

(Even) if God knows that I will do *a*, it is *not* necessarily true that <I will do *a*>.

If it is not necessarily true that I will do *a*, then it is not impossible for me to do either *a* or *not-a*.

+

If it is not impossible for me to do either *a* or *not-a*, then I do *a* freely.

(Even) if God knows that I will do *a*, then it is not impossible for me to do either *a* or *not-a*.

+

It is possible that God knows that I will do action *a* and I do *a* freely.

God's omniscience and human freedom are compatible.

determined in some way? The justifications we offered above, e.g. knowing someone's character, might give you knowledge of the general shape of their choices and actions, but not every minute detail. And it certainly won't be enough for knowledge of what they will be doing in the distant future. If God knows now what I will be doing on 23 May 2026, this can't simply be because he knows my character well! For a start, God must know whether I will be alive then, and he could only know that if the future is fixed in some way. But if the future is fixed, can we act freely?

Our third solution argues that the discussion so far has misunderstood what it is for God to be eternal. Once we understand this correctly, and we understand the implications for what it means to say that God knows what we will do, we will see that God's omniscience is compatible with human freedom.

Construct an argument map for the objection presented in the last three paragraphs.

STUMP AND KRETZMANN, 'ETERNITY'

In their discussion of the nature of God's existence as eternal, Stump and Kretzmann also discuss a number of implications of their view. One of those concerns God's omniscience and human free will.

See THINKING HARDER: STUMP AND KRETZMANN ON ETERNITY, p. 32.

We said that because God's existence is atemporal, all of God's life, including all events in time, is 'present' to God, part of the eternal 'now'. Every moment in time is ET-simultaneous with God. This means that some event in the future to us is present to an eternal being. This isn't to say that the future 'pre-exists', as though the future was *now in time*, but simply that God is ET-simultaneous with both today and any date in our future. Both days are present to an eternal being, but in the sense of the eternal present, not the temporal present. God is atemporally aware of both 'at once'.

If we don't understand this correctly, then it can appear to lead to contradictions. For instance, take a future date after my death. God knows that I am 'now' alive and that I am 'now' dead. But how can I be both at once? The answer is that 'now' and 'at once' are ambiguous, between the temporal now and the eternal now. I am alive in the temporal present, but will be dead in the temporal future. So I am not both alive and dead in time. But nor am I both alive and dead in the eternal present. As a temporal being, I am only alive and dead in time. I am not a being that exists in the eternal present. However, both my life and my death are ET-simultaneous with the eternal present.

About God's knowledge, we should say this: God knows future events because all temporal events are present to God. But what this means is not that God knows now (in time) what will happen in the future. God's knowledge is *not in time*. God can't know anything 'now' in the temporal sense. God's knowledge is in the eternal, *atemporal* now. So God cannot *foresee* future events, i.e. God does not know about events in time *before* they happen. There is no 'before' for God. God's knowledge of events in time is ET-simultaneous with when they happen. In other words, God only ever knows what is happening as it is happening. God is aware of all events in time in the (eternal) present.

Once we understand this, we can see that (P2) on p. 48 contains a confusion. In talking about God knowing what we will do before we do it, it supposes God's knowledge is in time. But God can't know what we will do before we do it, since God's knowledge is not 'before' anything. God's

Explain the claim that God's knowledge of what we do is ET-simultaneous with our doing it.

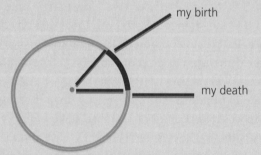

Figure 2.6 Every time in my life, and after my death, is ET-simultaneous with God's eternal present

omniscience consists in God knowing what we do, but God knows this ET-simultaneously with our doing it.

This doesn't cause any obvious difficulty for human free will. We and other people know what we are doing when we are doing it – our knowledge is T-simultaneous with our actions. But this doesn't stop those actions being free. The same can be said of God's knowledge of what we do.

?

Is God's omniscience compatible with human freedom?

Key points: arguments for the incoherence of the concept of God

- We face difficulties in saying coherently what God's individual attributes are, and in attempts to combine them.
- Can God create a stone that he can't lift? The answers 'yes' and 'no' both suggest that there is something God can't do, so God can't be omnipotent. One solution may be to say that 'a stone that an omnipotent being can't lift' is a contradiction in terms. Another is to say that God cannot create a stone that he cannot lift, because God can lift any stone. But because there is no limit on God's power to lift stones, there is no limit on God's power to create stones.
- Is morality independent of God or created by God's will? If the former, is God omnipotent? If the latter, what does it mean to say that God is good and would it be right to do *whatever* God commands?
- One reply is to say that God cannot change morality, but this is because it is logically impossible for moral truths to be different. Another is to say that morality is whatever God wills, but God's will is guided by love. A development of this position is to say that 'good' and 'God's will' are distinct concepts that refer to the same thing.
- Is God's omniscience compatible with free human beings? One response is to define omniscience as what it is possible to know, and then argue that God is everlasting and the future is impossible to know because we have free will.
- A second response is to argue that God's knowing what I will do doesn't mean that I *must* do what I do. We can object that it is difficult to

understand *how* God could know the future unless, in some sense, the future is already fixed.

- A third response argues that since God is eternal, God's knowledge is not in time. Every event is present to God, every temporal event is ET-simultaneous with God's knowledge of it, and so God does not know anything 'before' it happens.

Summary: the concept and nature of 'God'

In this section, we have considered what the concept of God is a concept of, i.e. what the nature of God is. We have looked at the following issues:

1. How should we best understand the attributes of omniscience, omnipotence, supreme goodness (omnibenevolence), and God's relationship to time?
2. Do these attributes make sense, e.g. can God know everything it is possible to know? Can God do everything it is possible to do?
3. Can these attributes be combined without incoherence, e.g. can God be omnipotent and supremely good?
4. Does the nature of God raise puzzles for our understanding of morality and human freedom?

II. Arguments relating to the existence of God

Philosophers have long been fascinated by the possibility of showing that God exists by rational argument. Almost all the most important philosophers in history have discussed such arguments, either to offer support or criticism. We will look at three main types of argument in support of God's existence, discussing variations of each and criticisms. We will then look at one type of argument against God's existence.

Throughout this section, it is important, for each variation of each argument, to think carefully about exactly how the argument works and what its conclusion is.

1. Some of the arguments we will look at are deductive, trying to prove the existence (or non-existence) of God from the premises. All the ontological

arguments and all the cosmological arguments (on one interpretation) take this form, as does one version of the problem of evil. Others – the arguments from design and a second version of the problem of evil – are inductive, trying to provide a case for thinking that the premises provide evidence for, or are best explained by, the existence (or non-existence) of God. This difference is important. For example, it is possible that deductive arguments for or against God's existence fail, but one or more of the inductive arguments succeed.

On deduction and induction, see PHILOSOPHICAL ARGUMENT, p. 5.

2. Some of the arguments in support of God's existence claim that God exists (the arguments from design and some cosmological arguments), while some claim that God *must* exist, i.e. that God's existence is 'necessary' (other cosmological arguments and the ontological arguments). Again, the difference is important, and one conclusion may succeed where the other fails.

3. Some of the arguments try to show that what exists is the most perfect possible being (ontological arguments). If they succeed, and our discussion in THE CONCEPT AND NATURE OF 'GOD' (p. 28) is correct, then God exists with all the attributes we discussed. Others argue that what exists is a being that caused, or sustains, or designed the universe (design and cosmological arguments). Even if these arguments succeed, they would not show that a being with the attributes of omnipotence, omniscience and omnibenevolence exists. We need additional arguments to get from their conclusions to existence of a being that matches the concept of God as we have discussed it.

A. Ontological arguments

Ontological arguments claim that we can deduce the existence of God from the concept of God. Both Anselm and Descartes argue that it is self-contradictory to say that God does not exist. Just from thinking about what God is, we can conclude that God must exist. Because it doesn't depend on experience in any way, the ontological argument is a priori.

The word 'ontological' comes from ontology, the study of (Greek, *-ology*) what exists or 'being' (*ont-*).

Ontological arguments have held a fascination for philosophers, and almost every major historical philosopher discussed them. We shall discuss two historical variations and a twentieth-century restatement. While the overall shape of the argument remains the same, the differences in detail can be philosophically important to the success of the argument.

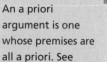

An a priori argument is one whose premises are all a priori. See Epistemology, A PRIORI/A POSTERIORI KNOWLEDGE, p. 115.

St Anselm's ontological argument

In GOD'S ATTRIBUTES (p. 28), we saw that the idea of God as the most perfect possible being has a long history. And perfection has also been connected to reality: what is perfect is more real than what is not. Anselm's argument makes use of both these ideas.

The *Proslogium* is also known as the *Proslogion*.

Explain why Anselm claims that God is a being 'greater than which cannot be conceived'.

Here and elsewhere, implicit premises needed to complete the argument are indicated in brackets.

ANSELM, *PROSLOGIUM*, CHS 2–4

In Ch. 2, Anselm starts from the concept of God as a being 'greater than which cannot be conceived'. Why define God like this? If we could think of something that was greater than the being we call God, then surely this greater thing would in fact be God. But this is nonsense – God being greater than God. The first being isn't God at all. We cannot conceive of anything being greater than God – if we think we can, we're not thinking of God.

Anselm then argues that if we think of two beings, one that exists and one that doesn't, the one that actually exists is greater – being real is greater than being fictional! So if God didn't exist, we could think of a greater being than God. But we've said that's impossible; so God exists.

P1. By definition, God is a being greater than which cannot be conceived.
P2. (We can coherently conceive of such a being, i.e. the concept is coherent.)
P3. It is greater to exist in reality than to exist only in the mind.
C1. Therefore, God must exist.

In Ch. 3, Anselm explains (P3) further. Conceive of two almost identical beings, *X* and *Y*. However, *X* is a being which we can conceive not to exist; *X*'s not existing is conceivable. By contrast, *Y*'s not existing is inconceivable. We can conceive of such a being, a being who *must* exist. This idea of *necessary* existence is coherent. *Y* is a greater being than *X*, because a being that must exist is greater than one who may or may not exist. Therefore, the greatest conceivable being is a being who, we conceive, must exist. It is inconceivable that the greatest conceivable being does not exist.

Of course, it can *seem* like we can think 'God does not exist'. In Ch. 4, Anselm notes that we can have this thought, we can think this string of words. But, he argues, in having this thought, we fail to understand the concept of God fully. We fail to understand that the greatest conceivable being is one that must exist. Once we fully understand the concept, we can no longer affirm the thought that God does not exist, because we recognise that it is incoherent.

Compare: you can have the thought 'there are male vixens', but once you understand the concept VIXEN as 'female fox' and understand that what is male is not female, then you recognise that your thought 'there are male vixens' is incoherent. Or perhaps, as another analogy, you can believe that '256 × 3,645 = 933,140'. But once you do the calculation again carefully, you'll discover that this is a mistake: 256 × 3,645 = 933,120, and there is no way that 933,140 = 933,120. If you understand the concepts of each number and multiplication correctly, and you are able to think clearly with these concepts, you'll recognise that 256 × 3,645 must be 933,120. There is no coherent alternative.

When a word refers to a concept, I put it in capital letters.

Outline and explain Anselm's version of the ontological argument.

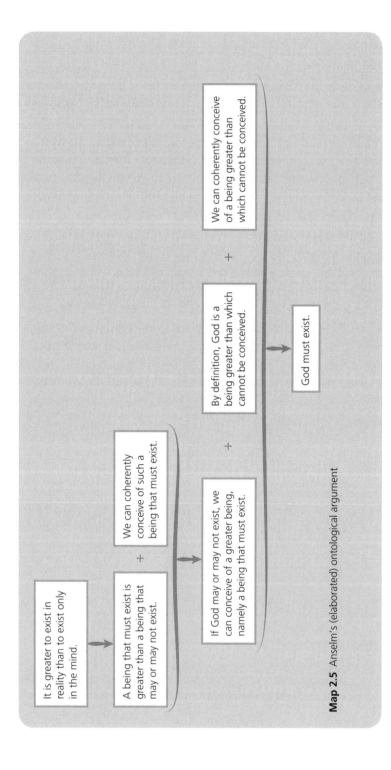

Map 2.5 Anselm's (elaborated) ontological argument

It is greater to exist in reality than to exist only in the mind.

+

We can coherently conceive of such a being that must exist.

A being that must exist is greater than a being that may or may not exist.

If God may or may not exist, we can conceive of a greater being, namely a being that must exist.

+

By definition, God is a being greater than which cannot be conceived.

We can coherently conceive of a being greater than which cannot be conceived.

God must exist.

GAUNILO'S 'PERFECT ISLAND' OBJECTION

GAUNILO, *IN BEHALF OF THE FOOL*

Anselm received an immediate reply from a monk named Gaunilo. The essence of his most famous objection is that the conclusion doesn't follow from the premises.

How great *is* the greatest conceivable being? Well, if it doesn't exist, it is not great at all – not as great as any real object! We can *conceive* how great this being *would be if it existed*, but that doesn't show that it *is* as great as all that and so must exist.

Gaunilo argues that Anselm's inference must be flawed, because you could prove anything which is 'more excellent' must exist by this argument. I can conceive of an island that is greater than any other island. And so such an island must exist, because it would be less great if it didn't. This is ridiculous, so the ontological argument must be flawed.

(Gaunilo slips from talking about the *greatest* conceivable being to talking about conceiving of a being that is *greater* than all other beings. So he talks of an island that is greater than other islands. But this doesn't work. It is possible to conceive of the being which, as it happens, is greater than all other beings as not existing. So let's correct Gaunilo here, and talk of 'an island greater than which is inconceivable'.)

Suppose we grant that, unlike the island, the non-existence of God is inconceivable. This still doesn't show that God actually exists. First, we need to establish that God does exist. And then from understanding his nature, we can infer that he must exist.

Outline and explain Gaunilo's perfect island objection to Anselm's ontological argument, first in prose, then using an argument map.

Thinking harder: Anselm's reply

Anselm, *Apologetic*

Anselm claims that the ontological argument works *only* for God, and so this is not a counterexample. Why? Anselm reasons that there is something incoherent in thinking 'the greatest conceivable being doesn't exist'. By contrast, the thought 'the greatest conceivable island doesn't exist' *is* coherent. When we have this thought, we are still thinking of an island. There is nothing in the concept of such an island that makes it *essentially* or *necessarily* the greatest conceivable island. Compare: an island *must* be a body of land surrounded by water. An island attached to land is inconceivable. But islands aren't essentially great or not. Instead, the thought of an island that is essentially the greatest conceivable island is itself somewhat incoherent. For example, what features would make it the greatest conceivable island?

By contrast, argues Anselm, God *must* be the greatest conceivable being – God *wouldn't be God* if there was some being even greater than God. So being the greatest conceivable being is an essential property of God. But then because it is greater to exist in reality than merely in the mind, if we think of God as not existing in reality, we aren't thinking of God at all. So to be the greatest conceivable being, God *must* exist.

However, even if Anselm is right about the island, it isn't clear that he has answered the essence of Gaunilo's objection. Gaunilo's point is that although we conceive of God *as* the greatest conceivable being, this doesn't show that God *is* the greatest conceivable being, because if God doesn't exist, God isn't any being at all. And if God isn't a being, then God isn't the greatest conceivable being. We can only say that *if* God exists or were to exist, then God is or would be the greatest conceivable being. So before we can say that God is the greatest conceivable being, we must first demonstrate that God exists.

If this objection is right, Anselm's ontological argument fails.

Does Anselm's ontological argument prove the existence of God?

Figure 2.7 What would make an island the greatest conceivable island? Why?

Descartes' ontological argument

Descartes' version of the ontological argument relies heavily on his doctrine of clear and distinct ideas and his claim that the idea of God is innate.

See Epistemology,
CLEAR AND DISTINCT IDEAS,
p. 156, and CESCARTES'
TRADEMARK ARGUMENT,
p. 161.

DESCARTES, *MEDITATION* V

Descartes opens *Meditation* V by explaining how we can explore our concepts in thought to gain knowledge. For example, you may think that there can be triangles whose interior angles don't add up to 180 degrees, but reflection proves this impossible. Once you make the idea of a triangle (the concept TRIANGLE) clear and distinct, you understand that the interior angles of a triangle add up to 180 degrees, and this shows that this is, in fact, true. Our thought is *constrained* in this way. The ideas we have determine certain truths, at least when our ideas are clear and distinct.

We can now apply this method to the concept of GOD. Descartes' argument is very brief:

The idea of God (that is, of a supremely perfect being) is certainly one that I find within me …; and I understand from this idea that it belongs to God's nature that *he always exists*.

We can understand this passage either in terms of rational intuition of the clear and distinct idea of GOD or as a very short deduction from such a clear and distinct idea.

Understood the first way, Descartes is arguing that careful reflection on the concept of GOD reveals that to think that God

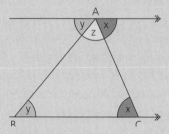

Figure 2.8 A proof that the interior angles of a triangle add up to 180 degrees

does not exist is a contradiction in terms, because it is part of the concept of a supremely perfect being that such a being has existence. Thus, we can know that it is true that God exists.

In fact, it shows that God must exist. A contradiction in terms does not just happen to be false, it *must* be false. So to say 'God does not exist' *must* be false; so 'God exists' must be true. As in the case of the triangle, it is not *our thinking it* that makes the claim true. Just as the concept TRIANGLE forces me to acknowledge that the interior angles of a triangle add up to 180 degrees, so the concept GOD forces me to acknowledge that God exists.

Furthermore, I cannot simply *change* the concept in either case; I can't decide that triangles will have two sides nor that it is no part of the concept of a supremely perfect being that such a being exists. I haven't invented the concept of GOD. I discover it in my mind, because it is *innate* (this was the conclusion of the Trademark argument).

One striking puzzle is why Descartes thinks that the concept of a supremely perfect being includes the thought that such a being exists. Spelling this out (P4 below) gives us a short deductive argument:

(P1. I have the idea of God.)
P2. The idea of God is the idea of a supremely perfect being.
P3. A supremely perfect being does not lack any perfection.
P4. Existence is a perfection.
C1. Therefore, God exists.

But why should we accept (P4)? In the main body of the *Meditations*, Descartes doesn't say. However, in an appendix to the *Meditations*, known as 'Objections and Replies', Descartes explains that God's existence is entailed by the other perfections of God. For example, a supremely perfect being is omnipotent, possessing all power it is logically possible to possess. An omnipotent being cannot depend on any other being for its existence, since then it would lack a power, namely the power to cause its own existence. An omnipotent being has this power and so depends on nothing else to exist. Such a being exists eternally, never coming into being or going out of being. As a supremely perfect being, God is omnipotent by definition, and so God must exist.

God is the only concept that supports this inference to existence, because only the concept of God (as supremely perfect) includes the concept of existence (as a perfection). We can't infer the existence of anything else this way.

Explain Descartes' ontological argument and construct an argument map for it.

Two objections to ontological arguments

EMPIRICIST OBJECTIONS TO A PRIORI ARGUMENTS FOR EXISTENCE

Empiricists claim that nothing can be shown to exist by a priori reasoning. It is not self-contradictory to say that God does not exist. Hume provides an example of this response. Hume's fork separates what we can know a priori – 'relations of ideas' – from claims about what exists, 'matters of fact'. Matters of fact can't be established by a priori reasoning, but require experience. So anything that can be established by a priori reasoning must be a relation of ideas.

See Epistemology, HUME'S FORK, p. 152.

HUME, *DIALOGUES CONCERNING NATURAL RELIGION*, PT 9

Hume applies his fork to the question of God's existence as follows:

P1. Nothing that is distinctly conceivable implies a contradiction.
P2. Whatever we conceive as existent, we can also conceive as non-existent.
C1. Therefore, there is no being whose non-existence implies a contradiction.

We can put the argument another way: If 'God does not exist' is a contradiction, then 'God exists' is an analytic truth. But this can't be right, because claims about what exists are matters of fact, synthetic propositions.

Explain how Hume's fork may be used to object to the ontological argument.

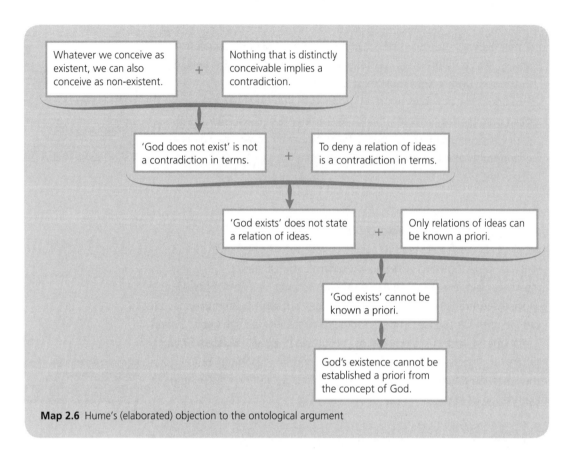

Map 2.6 Hume's (elaborated) objection to the ontological argument

Descartes could respond in either of two ways. He could claim that 'God exists' is a synthetic truth, but one that can be known by a priori reflection. In other words, he rejects Hume's fork. Or he could claim that 'God exists' is an analytic truth, though not an obvious one. Because he doesn't have the concepts 'analytic' and 'synthetic' (they were invented 150 years later, by Kant), he doesn't, of course, say either. Instead, he defends his claim as the product of rational intuition (and perhaps deduction). His epistemology rejects both Hume's fork and Hume's (P2).

Descartes would argue that not *everything* that we can conceive of existing can we also conceive of not existing. God is the exception. Because our minds are finite, we normally think of the divine perfections, such as omnipotence and necessary existence, separately and so we don't notice that they entail one another. But if we reflect carefully, we shall discover that we cannot conceive of one while excluding the other. It *is* a contradiction to deny that God exists.

However, this response faces Gaunilo's objection to Anselm: God's attributes only entail each other *in fact*, rather than merely conceptually, *if God actually exists*. If God doesn't exist, then God isn't (in fact) omnipotent (or anything else), so God's omnipotence doesn't entail his existence.

KANT'S OBJECTION: EXISTENCE IS NOT A PREDICATE

Kant presents what many philosophers consider to be the most powerful objection to any ontological argument. It is a development and explanation of Hume's objection. Ontological arguments misunderstand what existence is, or what it is to say that something exists. Premise (3) of Anselm's argument and premise (4) of Descartes' argument are both false. Things don't 'have' existence in the same way that they 'have' other properties. So existence can't be a perfection or make something 'greater'.

How does Kant argue for this claim? Consider again whether 'God exists' is an analytic or synthetic judgement. In claiming that 'God does not exist' is a contradiction, it seems that Anselm and Descartes take 'God exists' to be an analytic judgement. Now, an analytic judgement, such as 'A triangle has three sides', unpacks a concept. The concept in the predicate, THREE SIDES, is part of the concept in the subject, TRIANGLE. And so the analytic truth 'A triangle has three sides' tells you something about what triangles are. By contrast, saying '*x* exists' does *not* add anything to a concept of what *x* is. It doesn't tell you anything more about *x*. 'Dogs exist' doesn't inform you about what dogs are.

Figure 2.9 A dog; and a dog that exists

In fact, not only does it not unpack a concept, EXISTENCE doesn't add anything to the subject at all. Put another way, 'existence' isn't a real predicate. If I say 'The kite is red', I add the concept RED onto the concept KITE, and can create the new concept of a red kite. But if I say 'The kite exists' or 'The kite is', this adds nothing to the concept of the kite to create a richer or more detailed concept. The concept of existence is not a concept that can be added into the concept of something.

So what does 'x exists' actually mean? It simply claims that something corresponds to my concept in the world; 'x' is an object of possible experience.

Once we understand how 'x exists' works and how analytic statements work, we can see that the claim that x exists is not an analytic statement. It is, instead, a synthetic statement, one that will need to be verified against experience. But if 'x exists' is a synthetic statement, it is not contradictory to deny it.

This applies even in the case of God. 'God exists' is just 'God is'; it doesn't add anything to, or unpack, the concept of God. Suppose we try to add the concept EXISTENCE to another concept. This makes no difference to that other concept. For example, there is no difference between the concept of 100 real thalers (the money of Kant's day) and the concept of 100 possible thalers. Adding the concept of EXISTENCE to the concept of THALERS does not make the thalers exist. Likewise, we can't add the concept of EXISTENCE to GOD and draw the conclusion that God exists.

We can formalise Kant's argument like this:

P1. If 'God does not exist' is a contradiction, then 'God exists' is an analytic truth.
P2. If 'God exists' is an analytic truth, then EXISTENCE is part of the concept GOD.
P3. Existence is not a predicate, something that can be added on to another concept.
C1. Therefore, EXISTENCE is not part of the concept GOD.
C1. Therefore, 'God exists' is not an analytic truth.
C2. Therefore, 'God does not exist' is not a contradiction.
C3. Therefore, we cannot deduce the existence of God from the concept of God.
C4. Therefore, ontological arguments cannot prove that God exists.

Why does Kant claim that existence is not a predicate? Explain his argument by creating an argument map.

Outline and explain Kant's objection to ontological arguments.

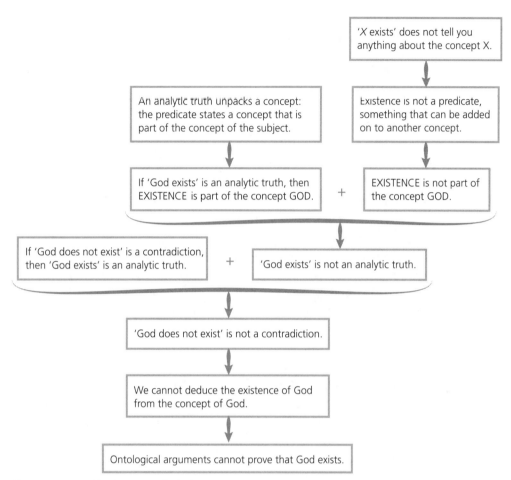

An analytic truth unpacks a concept: the predicate states a concept that is part of the concept of the subject.

'X exists' does not tell you anything about the concept X.

Existence is not a predicate, something that can be added on to another concept.

If 'God exists' is an analytic truth, then EXISTENCE is part of the concept GOD.

+

EXISTENCE is not part of the concept GOD.

If 'God does not exist' is a contradiction, then 'God exists' is an analytic truth.

+

'God exists' is not an analytic truth.

'God does not exist' is not a contradiction.

We cannot deduce the existence of God from the concept of God.

Ontological arguments cannot prove that God exists.

Map 2.7 Kant's objection to ontological arguments

Malcolm's ontological argument

Norman Malcolm agrees with Kant that we cannot think of existence as a property in the way that Descartes' and Anselm's first formulations of the ontological argument do. However, Malcolm argues that in Ch. 3 of the *Proslogium*, when Anselm takes himself to be explaining his argument (as represented in MAP 2.5, p. 60), in fact he provides a *different* argument. We should interpret Anselm's text in a different way than we did above.

MALCOLM, 'ANSELM'S ONTOLOGICAL ARGUMENTS'

Anselm says that a being whose non-existence is inconceivable (*Y* in our discussion in ST ANSELM'S ONTOLOGICAL ARGUMENT, p. 58) is greater than a being whose non-existence is conceivable (*X*). Here we aren't comparing what exists with what doesn't, but the concept of something that, by its nature, may or may not exist with the concept of something that, by its nature, must exist. So while *existence* is not a perfection, *necessary existence* is.

We can show that necessary existence is part of the concept of God. 'God is the greatest possible being' is a logically necessary truth – it is part of our concept of God. Therefore, God's existence cannot depend on anything – because a being that depends on something else for its existence is not as great as a being whose existence is completely independent of anything else. So God cannot depend on anything for coming into existence or staying in existence.

Suppose God exists. Then God cannot cease to exist – nothing can cause God to cease to exist. In that case, God's non-existence is inconceivable. So if God exists, God exists necessarily. Suppose God doesn't exist. Then if God came into existence, God's existence would then be dependent on whatever caused or allowed God to exist. This, we said, is impossible. So if God does not exist, then God's existence is impossible.

P1. Either God exists or God does not exist.
P2. God cannot come into existence or go out of existence.
P3. If God exists, God cannot cease to exist.
C1. Therefore, if God exists, God's existence is necessary.
P4. If God does not exist, God cannot come into existence.
C2. Therefore, if God does not exist, God's existence is impossible.
C3. Therefore, God's existence is either necessary or impossible.

Malcolm now adds two further premises to complete the form of ontological argument he finds in Anselm's *Proslogium*, Ch. 3:

Outline and explain Malcolm's argument that God's existence is either necessary or impossible.

P5. God's existence is impossible only if the concept of God is self-contradictory.

P6. The concept of God is not self-contradictory.

C4. Therefore, God's existence is not impossible.

C5. Therefore (from (C3) + (C4)), God exists necessarily.

One objection to Malcolm's argument is that he has not shown that (P6) is true; is the concept of God coherent? Malcolm admits that he can think of no general proof that it is. But there should be no presupposition that the concept is incoherent, so the argument is sound unless we can *show* that the concept of God is incoherent.

MALCOLM, 'ANSELM'S ONTOLOGICAL ARGUMENTS'

MALCOLM'S REPLY TO KANT

Malcolm agrees with Kant that *contingent* existence is not a property, but argues that Kant does not show that *necessary* existence is not a property. Kant discusses the claim 'God exists', but he doesn't satisfactorily distinguish it from the claim 'God exists necessarily'. The two claims are not equivalent. To say that 'God exists necessarily' *is* to unpack the concept of God. It tells us more about what the concept GOD is a concept of. So it is an analytic judgement, not a synthetic one. Not all claims about existence have the same kind of meaning. Or again, the concept NECESSARY EXISTENCE has a different logic from the concept EXISTENCE.

Kant accepts that it is part of our concept of the greatest possible being that such a being would exist necessarily. But what this means, he says, is that 'if God exists, then God exists necessarily'. And this doesn't entail that God exists. In other words, the claim 'if God exists, then God exists necessarily' is compatible with the possibility that God doesn't exist at all.

Malcolm responds that this is confused. If we accept that 'God exists necessarily' is an analytic truth, derived from our concept of God, then this rules out 'it is possible that God doesn't exist'. 'God doesn't exist' is necessarily false.

Outline and explain Malcolm's ontological argument.

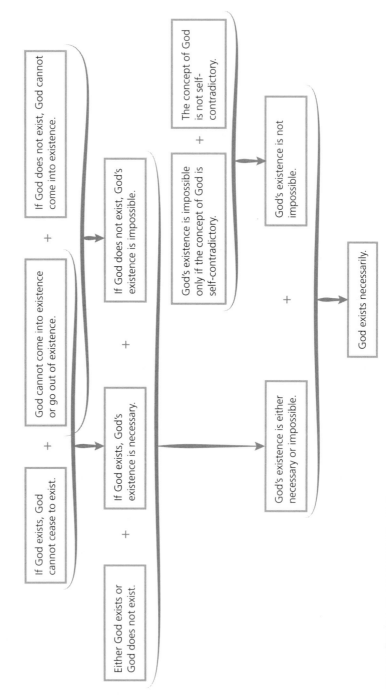

Map 2.8 Malcolm's ontological argument

Thinking harder: a response to Malcolm

But is Malcolm right? Is 'God exists necessarily' an analytic truth that we can derive from our concept of God? Or is the analytic truth that we can derive, only 'if God exists, God exists necessarily', as Kant claims?

Malcolm understands necessary existence as a property. It is the *type* of existence that God has if God exists. The concept of God entails that God's existence does not depend on anything. This means that if God does not exist, then God cannot be *brought* into existence (because then God's existence *would* depend on something). In *this* sense, if God does not exist, God's existence is impossible. But this impossibility is not the same as the existence of something logically impossible. So *(P5) is false*. If God does not exist, what makes God's existence impossible is not the self-contradictory nature of the concept of God, but the self-contradiction in the idea of bringing into existence something that does not depend on anything for existence.

This has implications for (C4). Let's allow that the concept of God is coherent. We still cannot conclude that God's existence is not impossible. If God does not exist, then God's existence *is* impossible. Given our concept of God, whether God's existence is impossible or not depends on whether God exists or doesn't. The problem is, we still don't know whether God exists or not!

The only conclusion that we can draw from Malcolm's argument is that 'if God doesn't exist, God's existence is impossible' and 'if God exists, God exists necessarily'. Not depending on anything characterises the nature of God's existence, if God exists; but existence does not characterise God. Or put another way, for it to be true that God exists necessarily, it must be true that God exists. Until we know whether God exists, all we can say is that God would exist necessarily if God were to exist.

Does any form of the ontological argument succeed in proving the existence of God?

Key points: ontological arguments

- Ontological arguments are a priori. They move from the concept of God to the claim that God exists. More precisely, they conclude that God exists necessarily.

- St Anselm's version states that God is the greatest conceivable being and that it is greater to exist in reality than to exist only in the mind. He concludes that God's non-existence is inconceivable, so God exists.
- Gaunilo objects that you could show that the greatest conceivable island must exist using this argument. Something's being the 'greatest conceivable' doesn't show that it does exist.
- Aquinas replies that the ontological argument only works for God. Nothing else exists in such a way that its non-existence is inconceivable.
- Descartes' version claims that it is impossible to think of God, a supremely perfect being, as lacking existence, because existence is a perfection.
- Empiricists such as Hume object to ontological arguments that 'God exists' does not state a relation of ideas, but a matter of fact. Therefore, it is not a contradiction to deny that God exists. Descartes can respond that God's attributes entail God's existence.
- Kant objects that existence is not a predicate, not a property that something can lack or possess. To say something exists is only to say that something corresponds to a concept we have; it is not to say anything further about that concept. Therefore, 'God exists' is not an analytic judgement, and can be denied without self-contradiction.
- Malcolm argues that while existence is not a perfection, necessary existence is. Because God's existence cannot depend on anything else, God's existence is either impossible or necessary. Since God's existence is not impossible, it is necessary, so God exists.
- We can object that Malcolm has only shown that God's existence is impossible if God doesn't exist, because God could not be brought into being. So in showing that God's existence is not impossible, Malcolm has not shown that God exists necessarily, only that if God exists, God exists necessarily.

B. Teleological/design arguments

It is common to feel wonder and amazement at the complexity and intricacy of living creatures. The way in which living things work requires a huge coordination of lots of tiny bits, each doing their specific job. The eye provides a common example. The eye is for seeing, and its parts work together to make this possible. For example, the muscles attached to the lens change its thickness so that it can focus light from different distances

Human Eye Anatomy

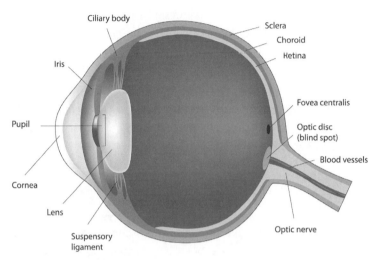

Figure 2.10 Diagram of an eye

onto the retina. Without the lens, the muscles and the retina, the eye wouldn't work properly. The parts serve the purpose of the whole.

The whole of life has this structure, with parts of cells working together to serve the purposes of cells, and cells working together as tissues, and tissues working together as organs, and organs working together to support the life of the organism. What we find is order, 'regularity', throughout nature. But it could have been very different – the universe could have had no order, no regularity. So what explains the order that we find?

The coordination and intricacy of interrelations between parts in living things working together for a purpose suggests that living things have been *designed*. If they are designed, then we can infer that there is a designer. Teleological or design arguments infer from the order and regularity that we see in the universe, the existence of a God that designed the universe. While life has been an important example of possible design in the debate, we will see that the order inherent in the laws of nature may provide more compelling evidence.

'Teleology' comes from the Greek word *telos*, meaning 'end' or 'purpose'.

There are two distinct questions that such arguments raise. First, is the order that we see really evidence of a designer? Second, if so, is that designer God? We will discuss each in turn.

The design argument from analogy

David Hume presents a version of the design argument that he goes on to criticise. We'll look both at the argument as he presents it, and then his reasons for thinking that it fails.

HUME, *DIALOGUES CONCERNING NATURAL RELIGION*, PTS 2, 8; *AN ENQUIRY CONCERNING HUMAN UNDERSTANDING*, §11

Hume expresses the argument like this:

> The intricate fitting of means to ends throughout all nature is just like (though more wonderful than) the fitting of means to ends in things that have been produced by us – products of human designs, thought, wisdom, and intelligence. Since the effects resemble each other, we are led to infer by all the rules of analogy that the causes are also alike, and that the author of nature is somewhat similar to the mind of man, though he has much larger faculties to go with the grandeur of the work he has carried out.

By 'the fitting of means to ends', Hume is talking about the intricate coordination of parts to achieve some purpose that we commented on above. As Hume says, we can draw an *analogy* with human design. So Hume's version of the argument is an argument from analogy.

P1. In 'the fitting of means to ends', nature resembles the products of human design.
P2. Similar effects have similar causes.
P3. The cause of the products of human design is an intelligent mind that intended the design.
C1. Therefore, the cause of nature is an intelligent mind that intended the design.

Explain Hume's version of the design argument, and construct an argument map for it.

Hume's objections

Objections to the analogy

Hume presents a series of objections attacking the analogy and its use. He begins by arguing that the analogy is not very strong. First, the products of human design, such as a house or a watch, are not much like nature or the universe as a whole. Second, the 'great disproportion' between a part of the universe and the whole universe also undermines the inference that something similar to human intelligence caused the universe. We cannot, therefore, reasonably infer that the cause of nature is anything like a human mind.

Even if we could infer from part to whole, there is no good reason to choose design by an intelligent mind as the explanation of the whole universe: 'why would we select as our basis such a tiny, weak, limited cause as the reason and design of animals on this planet seems to be?' Thought moves the bodies of animals – why take it to be the original cause of everything?

Draw up a list of analogies and disanalogies between human inventions and natural objects *without* referring to what causes them.

Whether a designer is the only or best explanation

Even if the analogy was stronger, the argument faces a further problem. In order to infer that there is a designer of nature, we have to rule out other possible explanations of the organisation of parts for a purpose. Suppose that matter is finite but that time is infinite. Given that there are only a finite number of possible arrangements of matter, over infinite time, all the arrangements of matter – including those we experience as design – would occur.

See HYPOTHETICAL REASONING, p. 8.

Is this a better explanation? There are problems with this proposal, such as why the arrangement of parts should *benefit* organisms. But this doesn't automatically make it a worse proposal, because there are problems with the proposal of a designer as well. For example, in all our experience, mind is joined to matter so that matter can affect mind (e.g. bodily processes can cause mental states, such as pain) just as much as mind can affect matter. Are we to suppose that the designer has a body? Or again, we have no clear concept of a mind that is eternal.

The right conclusion, then, is that neither explanation is clearly better. So the design argument doesn't show that there is a designer. Instead, Hume concludes, we should suspend judgement.

Explain Hume's argument that we cannot show that the best explanation of order in nature is the existence of a designer.

Thinking harder: arguing from a unique case

The argument makes an inference from an effect – the order and apparent purpose we find – to a possible cause, a designer. But we can't defend this inference, argues Hume, because it is at odds with our idea of causation.

The idea of causation is the idea of a relation between two objects or events, the cause and the effect: whenever you have the cause, you get the effect. Hume calls this 'constant conjunction'. Because causation involves *constant* conjunction, we cannot tell, from a *single* instance of some object or event, what its cause is. Think of one billiard ball hitting another and the second moving away. The second ball's movement could follow many, many events – your breathing, someone walking about the room, a light going on … How do you know which is the cause? We need *repeated* experience of the cause and effect occurring together in order to infer that one thing causes another. Our repeated experience shows us that the event followed by the second ball's movement is consistently the first ball hitting it. The second ball doesn't consistently move after a light goes on or someone breathes, etc. In general, then, we can only infer the cause of some effect when we have many examples of the effect and cause.

Here's the objection: the origin of the universe is unique. To make *any* inference about the cause of the universe, we would need experience of the origins of many worlds. We don't have this kind of experience, so we simply cannot know what caused the universe.

We can develop the point about restrictions on our knowledge of causation to the specific example of design. As just argued, we can only know the cause of some effect when we have repeated experience of the effect following the cause. In the case of products of human design, we have repeated experience of a designer bringing about the arrangement of parts for a purpose. But we don't have any such experience in the case of nature. What causes the arrangement of parts for a purpose in nature? We don't know

See Epistemology, MATTERS OF FACT, p. 153.

that it is a designer, since we have no experience of a designer bringing about this effect in natural things. The arrangement of parts for a purpose does not, *on its own*, show that the cause is a designer – because we can only know what causes what from experience. Without experiencing the cause as well as the effect, we don't know what brings about the effect. So we can't infer that the cause of order in nature is a designer.

In *An Enquiry concerning Human Understanding*, §11, Hume adds a further development of the objection. The inference of a designer is 'useless'. When we infer from a cause to an effect, we should only attribute properties to the cause that we need in order to explain the effect. Anything else is mere speculation. For example, if you find a squashed Coke can on the pavement, you can infer that it came under pressure from a force strong enough to squash it. But you can't infer whether that was a foot, a stone, or a car.

Now, in most cases, we learn more about a cause through other means. This allows us to make informative predictions about both the cause and its effects. In the case of human inventions, we can find out lots about human beings, so we can make predictions about their inventions, including ones we haven't encountered. But with the designer of nature, *all* we have to go on is what we already know – nature. We can't find out about other designers or other worlds to draw any useful conclusions about nature or the designer. So the hypothesis of a designer adds nothing to our knowledge.

> Explain Hume's argument that because we cannot infer the cause of a unique case, the design argument fails. Construct an argument map for it.

Paley's design argument

PALEY, *NATURAL THEOLOGY*, CHS 1–5

William Paley begins his version of the design argument by comparing our responses to finding a stone lying in a field and finding a watch lying in a field. If I wondered how the stone came

Figure 2.11 The complex machinery of a watch

to be there, I might rightly think that, for all I knew, it had always been there. But if I found a watch, I wouldn't feel that the same answer is satisfactory. Why not?

Because, says Paley, the watch has parts that are organised and put together for a purpose, and without the parts being organised as they are, the purpose would not be fulfilled. This property – having parts that are organised for a purpose – is the mark of design. We therefore conclude that the watch must have been designed and made according to that design.

Suppose now that after a while the watch, on its own, produces another watch (Ch. 2). It contains within itself all the robotic parts and tools for constructing a new watch. The second watch has been made by the first watch. Does this explain the *design* of the second watch? No, says Paley. The first watch simply mechanically constructs the parts of the second watch according to a design that it follows, but it doesn't come up with that design. The design of the watch is only explained by its being designed by a designer.

In Ch. 3, Paley argues that 'the works of nature' have the *same* property as the watch, namely parts organised for a purpose (he discusses the examples of the eye and the ear). In Ch. 4, he notes that living things create new living things (reproduction). But as with the watch, this doesn't explain the organisation of living things, including their ability to produce new living things. Plants don't design their seeds, and hens don't design their eggs. Rather, plants and hens simply mechanically produce seeds and eggs. Now,

? What is 'design', according to Paley?

we rightly infer from the fact that the watch has parts organised for a purpose, that the watch is designed. Thus, in Ch. 5, Paley argues that we are right to infer from the fact that the works of nature have parts organised for a purpose, that they also have a designer.

In Ch. 23, Paley makes two claims about the designer. First, to design requires a mind – consciousness and thought – because design requires that one perceive the purpose and how to organise parts to serve this purpose. So the designer is a mind. Second, the designer must be distinct from the universe, because everything in the universe bears the marks of design. To explain the design of things in the universe, we must appeal to something distinct from the universe.

So, Paley argues:

P1. Anything that has parts organised to serve a purpose is designed.

P2. Nature contains things which have parts that are organised to serve a purpose.

C1. Therefore, nature contains things which are designed.

P3. Design can only be explained in terms of a designer.

P4. A designer must be or have a mind and be distinct from what is designed.

C2. Therefore, nature was designed by a mind that is distinct from nature.

C3. Therefore, such a mind ('God') exists.

Outline and explain Paley's argument from design.

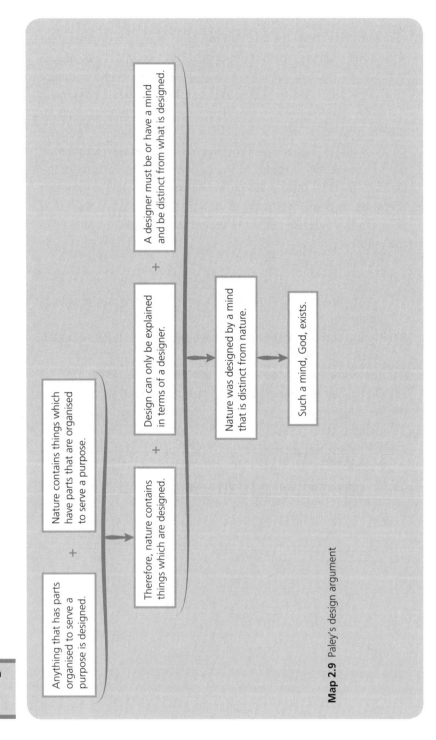

Anything that has parts organised to serve a purpose is designed.

+

Nature contains things which have parts that are organised to serve a purpose.

Therefore, nature contains things which are designed.

+

Design can only be explained in terms of a designer.

+

A designer must be or have a mind and be distinct from what is designed.

Nature was designed by a mind that is distinct from nature.

Such a mind, God, exists.

Map 2.9 Paley's design argument

Discussion

Does Paley's version of the design argument avoid Hume's objections? Paley claims that the organisation of parts for a purpose is evidence of design and that design can only be explained in terms of a designer. But, Hume argues, we can't know this to be true in the case of nature. (P1) and (P3) of Paley's argument are either false or unknown. How can Paley respond?

PALEY, *NATURAL THEOLOGY*, CHS 1, 5

Thinking harder: Paley, analogy and inferring causes

Hume's first set of objections are to drawing an analogy between the universe and human artefacts. Paley can escape these objections, because *Paley doesn't offer an argument from analogy*. He does not argue that natural things are *like* watches, so their causes are *like* the causes of watches. He is arguing that watches have a property – the organisation of parts for a purpose – which supports the inference of a designer. *Everything* that has this property has this cause. Natural things have *exactly this property* as well and so have *exactly that cause*. Thus, he says 'Every observation which was made … concerning the watch, may be repeated with strict propriety … concerning … all the organized parts of the works of nature'. 'With strict propriety', not 'by analogy'. Natural things have the same property, so they too have a designer.

According to Paley's argument, Hume's objections should apply just as much to our inference regarding the watch. If we found a watch in a field and had never previously experienced a watch, then if Hume were right, we cannot reasonably infer that it was designed.

But perhaps Hume *is* right. If we have never experienced a watch *or anything relevantly similar*, then, Hume argues, we cannot reasonably infer that it is designed. We can only make the inference from the organisation of parts for a purpose to a designer in those

Compare and contrast Paley's argument from design with Hume's version from analogy.

cases in which we have the relevant experience. With watches, in fact, we do; but in Paley's thought experiment, *we should assume that we don't*. In Paley's thought experiment, we don't know anything about watches or watchmakers. We only have the experience – our very first experience – of the watch to go on. In such a situation, Hume would say, then we can't infer a designer. And that is the situation we are in regarding the natural world.

What of Hume's objections concerning the problems of inferring that the universe is designed because it is a unique case? Suppose again we had never come across watches before. If Hume were correct, then if we found a watch in a field, this would be a unique case for us. And so we could not reasonably infer that it was designed.

But Paley argues, even if we had never seen a watch being made, even if we couldn't understand how it was possible, even if we couldn't tell if it could be done by a human being or not, we would still be perfectly correct to conclude, by examining the watch, that it was designed by some designer. We know enough about the causes of the organization of parts for a purpose to be able to infer, *whenever* we come across such organization, that it is the result of a designer.

We should say exactly the same in the case of nature. Paley rejects Hume's claim that we don't know enough to infer a designer. *All* we need to know is the organisation of parts for a purpose. This is sufficient to infer that something is designed, and hence a designer exists. We would say this in the case of the watch, and the case of nature is no different.

If you found a watch in a field, and knew nothing about watches, would you be justified in thinking that the watch was designed by someone?

Inference to the best explanation

Hume argues that to infer a designer of nature, we need to rule out alternative explanations of the order we see in nature. Paley does this. He considers and rejects alternative explanations. He accepts that it is *possible* that finite matter has taken all possible combinations over an infinite time. But, he argues, this is clearly a *worse* explanation than the proposal of the existence of a designer, because we have no evidence that matter constantly pushes into new forms or that all possible combinations of matter (plants, animals) have been tried in the past. (We may add that we now know that the universe began around 13.8 billion years ago, so time isn't infinite, and we know that matter doesn't organise itself randomly, but follows very particular laws of nature.) And, Paley claims, minds supply the only explanation of design we know of. Thus, the existence of a designer is the best explanation of the organisation of parts for a purpose.

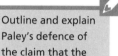

Outline and explain Paley's defence of the claim that the best explanation of order in nature is a mind.

THE PROBLEM OF SPATIAL DISORDER

We have so far looked at two design arguments. Both of them have appealed to regularities of 'spatial order', in which different things, e.g. parts of an eye, exist at the same time in an ordered way, e.g. being organised to serve a purpose. However, what we are supposed to explain is the whole universe. And that contains a great deal of spatial *disorder*, vast areas of space in which there is no organisation of parts, no purpose.

This observation can be used to argue against the inference to a designer or to argue that the designer is not God. We defer the second issue to IS THE DESIGNER GOD? (p. 92). For now, we may ask of both Hume's and Paley's design arguments, why should we take the order to be more striking or important than the disorder when considering the cause of the universe? What reasons are there to suppose that the order outweighs the disorder?

Paley's response questions the strength of the objection. He claims that the inference from the organisation of parts for a purpose to a designer is correct even if the watch sometimes went wrong or if some of the parts don't contribute to its purpose. Likewise, evidence of some imperfections and irregularities in nature does not undermine the inference that it, too, is designed. His point is that the *balance* of spatial order and disorder isn't crucial. We needn't weigh one against the other to tell that the organisation of parts for a purpose must be explained in terms of a designer.

EVOLUTION BY NATURAL SELECTION

Paley was wrong to say that the organisation of parts for a purpose *can only* be the effect of a mind. And if some other explanation is as good as or better than invoking the existence of a designer, then Paley's argument will fail. Neither Hume nor Paley knew or anticipated the explanation of the organisation of parts for a purpose that is now very widely accepted. Darwin's theory of evolution by natural selection provides an excellent account of how the *appearance* of design can come about without being the result of a designer.

Millions of alterations in the traits of living creatures randomly take place. Most disappear without a trace. But some trait that *coincidentally* helps a creature to survive and reproduce slowly spreads. That creature and its descendants reproduce more than others without the trait, so more and more creatures end up with it. It's not that the feature is 'selected' *in order for* the creature to live better and so reproduce more. Instead, the feature simply *enables* the creature to reproduce more, so its descendants also have that feature and they reproduce more, and so on. One very small change is followed by another. Over time, this can lead to great complexity, such as the eye. In time, creatures appear to be designed when they are in fact the product of coincidence. So we don't need to say that living things are actually designed by a designer.

This is a better explanation because it is simpler: we aren't inferring the existence of something new, but appealing only to what we already know exists.

Does the organisation of parts for a purpose in living things give us good reason to believe in the existence of a designer?

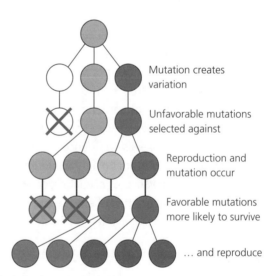

Figure 2.12 Evolution by natural selection

Swinburne's design argument

A third form of the design argument does not appeal to spatial order. Swinburne starts his argument from the observation that the universe contains regularities of 'temporal order' – an orderliness in the way one thing follows another, e.g. how if you let go of something, it falls to Earth (or more precisely, how any two masses exert gravitational attraction on each other). These temporal regularities are described by the laws of nature.

Explain the difference between spatial and temporal order.

Appealing to temporal regularities rather than spatial regularities as examples of design has two advantages. First, such laws are (nearly?) universal; there aren't parts of the universe that exhibit temporal 'disorder' even if they exhibit spatial disorder. Second, we haven't yet accounted for the order, the regularity, that *enables* matter to become organised into parts serving a purpose. Evolution works by the laws of nature, it doesn't explain them. The spatial order that evolution produces is a result of the temporal order that evolution relies upon. So what explains the temporal order?

Swinburne argues that the activity of a designer is the best explanation of the operation of the laws of nature. The design evident in nature, then, is in the laws of nature themselves.

SWINBURNE, 'THE ARGUMENT FROM DESIGN'

Swinburne argues that there is no scientific explanation for the operation of the laws of nature. For example, science explains why water boils when you heat it by appealing to the operation of the laws of nature on the initial state of the water and the application of heat. The explanation will be in terms of laws governing the effect of heat on the properties of molecules. If we want more, then a scientific explanation of these effects on these properties can be given in terms of other laws and properties – atomic and subatomic ones. Some further explanation of these may be possible, but again, it will presuppose other laws and properties. Laws can be explained in terms of more general laws, but that's all. How do the most fundamental laws, whatever they are, work? Their operation can't be explained by science (if they could, they wouldn't be the most fundamental laws).

Outline and explain Swinburne's argument that science cannot explain the operation of the fundamental laws of nature.

Explain and illustrate the difference between scientific and personal explanation.

Put another way, science must *assume* the fundamental laws of nature in order to provide any explanations at all. It can't explain why one thing succeeds another in accordance with these laws, because all scientific explanations presuppose laws. Therefore, scientific laws have no explanation unless we can find some other kind of explanation for them.

We use another type of explanation all the time, namely 'personal explanation'. We explain the products of human activity – this book, these sentences – in terms of a person, a rational, free agent. I'm writing things I *intend* to write. This sort of explanation explains an object or an event in terms of a person and their purposes. So we know of regularities in succession – things coming about because someone intentionally brings them about – that are caused by the activity of a person.

Can we explain the temporal order we find in laws of nature in this way? Yes – we can explain this temporal order, and so the laws of nature that describe this order, by supposing that there is a person that can act on the universe just as we can act by moving our bodies. This provides a personal explanation for the operation of the laws of nature, and so for the order of the universe. The regularities of temporal succession that the laws of nature describe are the actions of a person. We will call this person 'the designer' for now, understanding that the 'design' this person brings about is temporal order.

So Swinburne argues:

P1. There are some temporal regularities, e.g. related to human actions, that are explained in terms of persons.
P2. There are other temporal regularities, e.g. related to the operation of the laws of nature, that are similar to those explained in terms of persons.
C1. So we can, by analogy, explain the regularities relating to the operation of the laws of nature in terms of persons.
P3. There is no scientific explanation of the operation of the laws of nature.

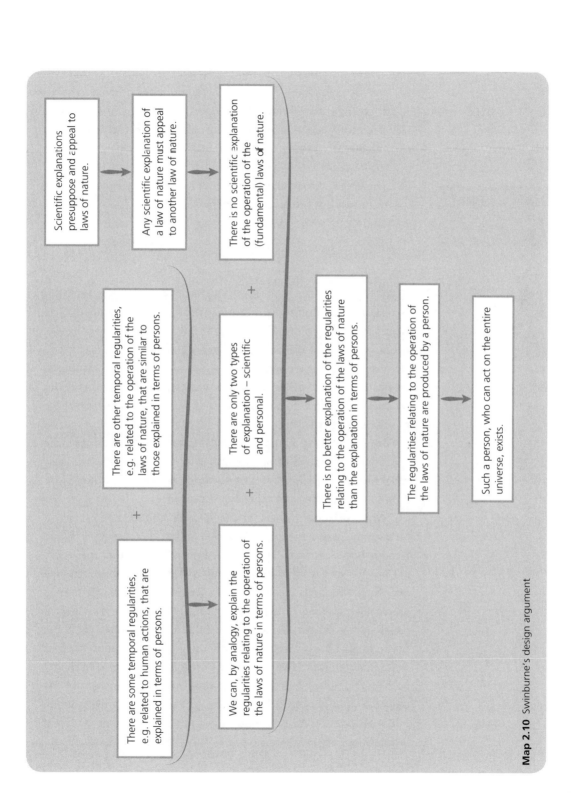

Map 2.10 Swinburne's design argument

P4. (As far as we know, there are only two types of explanation – scientific and personal.)

C2. Therefore, there is no better explanation of the regularities relating to the operation of the laws of nature than the explanation in terms of persons.

C3. Therefore, the regularities relating to the operation of the laws of nature are produced by a person.

C4. Therefore, such a person, who can act on the entire universe, exists.

Outline and explain Swinburne's design argument.

Swinburne's response to Hume

Like Hume, Swinburne has offered an argument from analogy. The argument depends on (P2) and with it, (C1). So we may ask, how strong is the analogy between human action and the designer's actions through the operation of the laws of nature? Swinburne grants that Hume's objections to the analogy *may* be successful. But we should ask how persuasive they are in the context of inference to the best explanation.

So, why choose human reason as a model for explaining the operation of the laws of nature, rather than anything else? Because other causes of order in the universe *rely on* the operation of the laws of nature which they don't themselves explain.

What of Hume's idea that spatial order could be the result of random changes in the distribution of matter? Could we apply that to temporal order as well? To do this, we need to say either that there are no laws of nature or that the laws of nature themselves change over time, randomly producing order or disorder. Both alternatives are problematic. We have no reason to say that there are no laws of nature and every reason to think that there are. But then, could the operations of the laws of nature themselves change randomly over time, sometimes producing regularity, sometimes producing chaos? Perhaps, but given the amount of order in the universe, and the universal applicability of laws of nature, this is a poor explanation of our experience. Thus, Swinburne argues that explaining temporal regularities in personal terms remains the best explanation.

Like Paley, Swinburne rejects Hume's argument that we can't reach conclusions about the causes of a unique object, such as the universe. As Swinburne notes, cosmologists have drawn all sorts of conclusions about the universe as a whole. Uniqueness is relative to how something is described. For example, many of the processes involved in the universe as a whole, e.g. its expansion, can be identified repeatedly in other contexts. (This is Paley's point about organisation of parts for a purpose – it is a property repeated in many instances.)

How successful is Swinburne's defence of the design argument against Hume's criticisms?

Thinking harder: is the existence of a designer a good explanation?

Even if the explanation in terms of a designer is technically the 'best' – because there is no other – we still might not accept it if it isn't a *good* explanation.

We discuss multiverse theory in extension material.

One important criterion for this is whether it is simple. Ockham's razor says 'Do not multiply entities beyond necessity.' Swinburne's explanation introduces a new entity – the designer.

But this is not yet an objection. If a designer is *necessary* to explain the laws of nature, then the explanation respects Ockham's razor.

Nevertheless, we might object that for the designer to be a satisfactory explanation of design in nature, we would in turn need to explain the designer. A mind is as complex and as ordered as nature, so if the order in nature requires an explanation, so does the order of the designer's mind. If we can't explain the designer, then it would be better to stop our attempts at explanation at the level of nature.

Swinburne argues that this misrepresents explanation. Science is full of examples of explanation that don't explain what is assumed in the explanation. Science will introduce an entity – like a subatomic particle – in order to explain something, e.g. explosions in a nuclear accelerator. However, these new entities now need explaining, and scientists don't yet know how to explain them. This is absolutely normal, and has happened repeatedly throughout the history of science.

If we will always have *something* we can't explain, why invoke a designer? Why not just say we can't explain scientific laws? Because invoking a designer explains one more thing, namely the operation of scientific laws, and we should explain as much as we can. This is a principle of science and philosophy. If you give up on this, you give up on pursuing these forms of thought. So we can still say that the designer is a good explanation for the operation of scientific laws even if we can't explain the designer.

Is it legitimate to introduce something you can't explain in order to explain something else?

Is the designer God?

The argument from design is intended as an argument for the existence of God. However, Paley, Hume and Swinburne all agree that even if we could infer the existence of a designer of the universe, it is an *extra step* to argue that the designer is God. Hume argues that, if we are drawing an analogy between human designers and the designer of the universe, this extra step faces new difficulties.

HUME'S OBJECTIONS

HUME, *DIALOGUES CONCERNING NATURAL RELIGION*, PT 5

If we are arguing for a designer on the basis of a similarity between human inventions and the universe (or even human actions and the operation of the laws of nature), then shouldn't we think that the designer is *more* similar to human beings than God is traditionally said to be? Hume presents six objections based on this idea.

1. The scale and quality of the design reflect the power and ability of the designer. The universe isn't infinite. So we can't infer that the designer is infinite. As God is thought to be infinite, we can't infer that the designer is God.
2. THE PROBLEM OF SPATIAL DISORDER (see also p. 85): the universe gives us no reason to say that the designer is perfect. Illnesses

and natural disasters could be evidence of mistakes in design. If so, we should say that the designer isn't fully skilled, but made mistakes. At best, we can't tell. By contrast, God is said to be omnipotent, omniscient and supremely good. So we can't infer that the designer is God.

3. Designers are not always creators. Someone who designs a car may not also build it. So we can't infer that the designer of the universe also created the universe. The creator could just be following someone else's designs. But God is said to be the creator of the universe; so we can't infer that the designer is God.

4. The design may have resulted from many small improvements made by many people. So we cannot infer that 'the designer' is just one person. More generally, we can't infer that the powers to design and create a universe are all united in one being, rather than being shared out between lots of different beings. But God is said to be one. We have no reason to believe in one God rather than lots of designers that are not divine.

5. We find mind always connected to body. There is no reason to think that the designer has no body. But God is thought to be just a mind, so we can't infer that the designer is God.

6. Designers can die even as their creations continue. So the designer may have designed the universe and then died. God is said to exist eternally, so again, we can't say the designer is God.

In summary, the argument from design doesn't show that the designer is omnipotent, omniscient, the creator of the universe, just one being, non-corporeal, or even still in existence. So it doesn't show that God – as a single omnipotent, omniscient, eternal creator spirit – exists.

See THE CONCEPT AND NATURE OF 'GOD', p. 28.

Explain three of Hume's arguments that the design argument cannot establish the existence of God.

SWINBURNE'S RESPONSE

SWINBURNE, 'THE ARGUMENT FROM DESIGN'

Swinburne accepts Hume's objections (1) and (2) – if the designer is God, many of God's traditional qualities will need to be established by some other argument.

In reply to (3) and (4), Swinburne invokes Ockham's razor. Simplicity requires that we shouldn't suppose that two possible causes exist when only one will do. If we can explain the design and creation of the universe by supposing that there is just one being capable of this, then we shouldn't suppose that there is more than one being unless we have positive evidence that there is. If, for instance, different parts of the universe operated according to different laws, then that could be evidence for more than one designer being involved. But the uniformity of nature gives us good reason to suppose that there is just one designer, who is also creator.

In reply to (5), the explanation requires that the designer *doesn't* have a body. Having a body means that one has a particular location in space and can only act on a certain area of space. If God's effects are the operations of the laws of nature, and these hold throughout the universe, then God can act everywhere in space simultaneously. So it is better to say that God has no body.

In reply to (6), Swinburne asserts that the objection only works if we are thinking about things in spatial order, such as inventions. But temporal order – regularities in 'what happens next' – requires that the agent is acting *at that time*. To bring about order in what happens next, I must act. If I don't act, then the operation of the laws of nature take over. But these operations of the laws of nature are exactly what we are explaining in terms of God's activity. So God acts wherever the laws of nature hold. So God must continue to exist.

Explain the claim that the operation of the laws of nature provide evidence that there is only one designer, who has no body.

Does any form of the design argument establish the existence of God?

Key points: the argument from design

- Teleological/design arguments use the order and regularity we find in life and the universe to infer the existence of a divine designer.
- Hume expresses the argument using analogy: artefacts created by humans exhibit purpose and order, and so do natural things. From purpose and order in artefacts, we infer that the artefact was designed. As natural things are similar, in exhibiting design, we may infer that a similar cause, an intelligent mind, explains their design.
- Hume objects that the analogy is weak – natural things aren't very like human artefacts, and human thought doesn't obviously provide a good model for explaining natural things. So we cannot infer that they have a similar cause.
- Paley identifies the property of having parts that are organised for a purpose as the property from which we infer that human artefacts are designed. He then claims that natural things have this same property, so the inference that they are also designed is equally valid, not an analogy at all.
- Hume also objects that to make any causal inference, we need repeated experience of the relation between cause and effect, but we don't have it regarding the origin of the universe, which is a unique case. Paley can respond that if Hume were right, we could not infer that human artefacts of which we have no experience have a designer.
- Hume argues that we have not shown that the cause of order and regularity could not simply be the chance arrangement of matter over infinite time. Paley responds that this is a much worse explanation than the existence of a designer.
- However, Darwin's theory of evolution by natural selection explains how living things can have parts organised for a purpose without being designed by a designer.
- The widespread occurrence of spatial disorder challenges the inference to a designer, as well as the claim that the designer is perfect, i.e. God.
- We can ask *why* nature is capable of producing apparently designed things, i.e. what explains the operation of the laws of nature that enable this. Swinburne argues that science cannot provide a satisfactory explanation of fundamental laws, since scientific explanations always

presuppose laws. So we need a personal explanation. Therefore, God is the only explanation of design, and so the best.

- Swinburne responds to Hume by arguing that the human mind provides the best (only) model of explaining the operation of the laws of nature.
- Swinburne argues that the fact that we can't explain God is no objection. Science is always postulating things that it cannot explain in order to explain other things.
- Hume objects that even if there is a designer, we can't infer that the designer is God. If similar effects have similar causes, then the designer is imperfect and finite, because natural things appear to be imperfect and finite. The designer may not be the creator, the design might be the collaboration of many people, and the designer might have died.
- Swinburne argues that the claim that there is just one designer who is also the creator is simpler, and so better than the other hypotheses. Finally, if the operation of the laws of nature are God's actions, God must continue to exist as long as the laws of nature hold.

C. The cosmological argument

The question at the heart of the cosmological argument is 'why does anything exist?' The argument is that unless God exists, this question is unanswerable. There are different forms of the argument. We will look at six – four from causation and two from contingent existence. We will explain each of the four arguments from causation before discussing objections to all four. Similarly, we will look at the two arguments from contingent existence together before looking at objections to both.

The Kalām argument

The Kalām argument is an argument that puts together ideas about causation, time and the world.

'*Kalām*' was medieval Islamic theoretical theology.

P1. The universe is composed of temporal phenomena – things that occur and exist in time – that are preceded by other temporal phenomena that are ordered in time.
P2. An infinite regress of temporal phenomena is impossible.

C1. Therefore, the universe must have a beginning.

P3. Everything that begins to exist has a cause of its existence.

C2. Therefore, there is a cause of the existence of the universe.

To get to the conclusion that God is the cause of the universe, we have to add further premises to the Kalām argument.

(P1) is obviously true – we live in a universe that is in time, not an atemporal world. Things that occur in time occur in an order in time – one happens before the next before the next, and so on.

(P2) and (P3) are more contentious. If we deny (P3), it seems we have to say that something can come out of nothing. There can be nothing, and then something just starts to exist. This is so strange that (P3) seems likely enough for now (we will discuss it further in HUME ON THE CAUSAL PRINCIPLE, p. 110).

That leaves (P2). Given that the universe is temporal, (P2) claims that the universe cannot have always existed. If the universe has always existed, there is an infinite sequence of things existing in time, each caused by and following earlier things existing in time. Such an infinite series would also mean that the universe is infinitely old. If this is impossible, we can infer (C1), that the universe must have a beginning. But should we accept (P2)? Why think it is impossible for the universe to be infinite in time or for there to be an infinite series of temporal phenomena?

Thinking harder: infinity

Infinite time is not a 'very long time', and an infinite series is not a very long series. Infinity is not a very large number. It is not a *number* at all. If the universe is infinite in time, then, quite literally, it has no beginning, ever.

Because the universe exists, to claim that the universe has always existed is to claim that an *actual* infinity – something that is in fact infinite – exists. This is quite different from talking about the *idea* of infinity. The idea of infinity makes sense; but does it make sense to think that something infinite actually exists?

Defenders of the Kalām argument think not, because it would lead to impossible paradoxes. Here's a popular example. Suppose there is a hotel with infinite rooms. Even when the hotel is completely full, it can still take more people! You cannot add any number to infinity and get a bigger number: $\infty + 1 = \infty$. Suppose, when the hotel is full, infinitely more people show up. They can all be accommodated! $\infty + \infty = \infty$. But it is impossible for the hotel to be full and still have room for more guests. So there cannot be an 'actual' infinity.

Applying this to the universe, we can generate other paradoxes. For example, the universe gets older as time passes, we naturally think. But this couldn't happen if the universe were infinitely old. If the universe is infinitely old, it is not getting any older as time passes! Or again, to have reached the present, an infinite amount of time would need to have passed. But it is not possible for an *infinite* amount of time to have passed, since infinity is not an *amount*. So if the universe was infinitely old, it could never have reached the present.

While the Kalām argument focuses on a series of events through time, the same point applies to an infinite series of causes. Each thing that begins to exist in the universe – stars, planets, people – is caused to exist by something before it, and whatever caused each thing is itself caused by something before it. But if there is an infinite chain of causes, bringing new things into existence, that series of causes never has a starting point. The process never gets started, because it has always been going on. So each new cause doesn't add one more cause to the series, since $\infty + 1 = \infty$. And we would never have reached the point in the series of causes at which we are now if it were an infinite series.

If these paradoxes show that an infinite sequence of temporal phenomena is impossible, then that establishes (P2).

Explain the argument that it is impossible for the universe to have always existed.

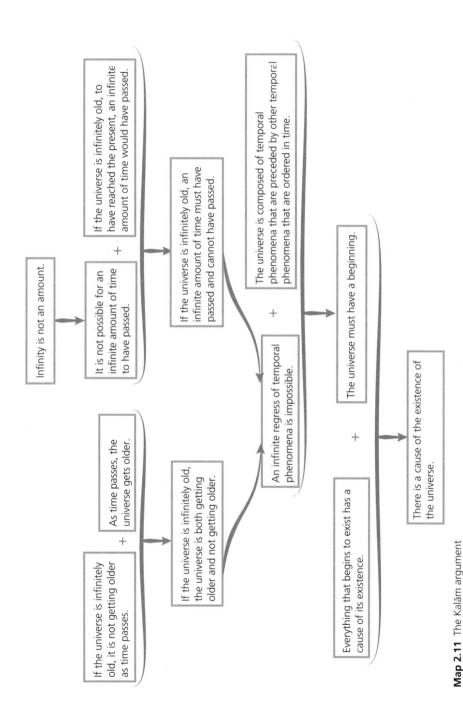

Map 2.11 The Kalām argument

Aquinas' First and Second Ways

The Kalām argument rests on rejecting the possibility of an infinite sequence of events through time. Aquinas didn't think it was possible to show whether or not time stretches back infinitely. So in his First and Second 'Ways' (of proving God's existence), he argues against an infinite regress of causes. To understand his arguments, we need to make a distinction between temporal causes and sustaining causes.

A *temporal cause* brings about its effect after it – the effect follows the cause in time – and the effect can continue after the cause ceases. For instance, the cause of my existence is my parents, and I can continue to exist after they die. Or again, if someone throws a ball, the ball continues to move after their action of throwing is finished.

A *sustaining cause* brings about its effect continuously, and the effect depends on the continued existence and operation of the cause. It operates continuously rather than at a time. That I am sitting on a chair is a *continuing state of affairs* that has causes, namely gravity and the rigidity of the chair. Should either of those sustaining causes change, then I would no longer be sitting on the chair. I'd either be floating (no gravity) or sitting on the ground (collapsed chair).

Here is another example, this time of a *process of change* that depends upon other processes to keep going. Plants grow by photosynthesis, and they need a continuous supply of various things to do this, e.g. sunlight and certain atmospheric conditions. So plant growth causally depends on the processes in the sun that produce sunlight and on a huge variety of factors that ensure that the Earth has an atmosphere with water and oxygen. These factors may in turn causally depend on other processes, e.g. in the sun, nuclear fusion that turns hydrogen into helium, emitting light.

In both his first two Ways, Aquinas is interested in the causal dependencies of sustaining causation, not a sequence of causes occurring over time. We shall look at Aquinas' Second Way first as it is easier to understand.

Explain two differences between a temporal cause and a sustaining cause.

Figure 2.13 Photosynthesis is an ongoing process that depends on other ongoing processes

AQUINAS' SECOND WAY

AQUINAS, *SUMMA THEOLOGICA*, PT 1, Q. 2, ART. 3

We can summarise Aquinas' Second Way as follows:

P1. We find, in the world, (sustaining) causes and effects.

P2. Nothing can causally depend on itself. (To do so, it would have to have the power to sustain its own existence, but for that, it would already have to exist.)

P3. (Sustaining) causes follow in (logical) order: the first causally sustains the second, which causally sustains the third, etc. (Think of nuclear fusion sustaining sunlight sustaining plant growth.)

P4. If you remove a cause, you remove its effect.

C1. Therefore, if there is no first cause, i.e. a sustaining cause that does not causally depend on any other cause, there will be no other causes.

P5. If there is an infinite regress of causes, there is no first cause.

C2. Therefore, given that there are (sustaining) causes, there cannot be an infinite regress of causes.

C3. Therefore, there must be a first cause, which is not itself caused.

P6. God is the first cause.

C4. Therefore, God exists.

Explain Aquinas'
Second Way.

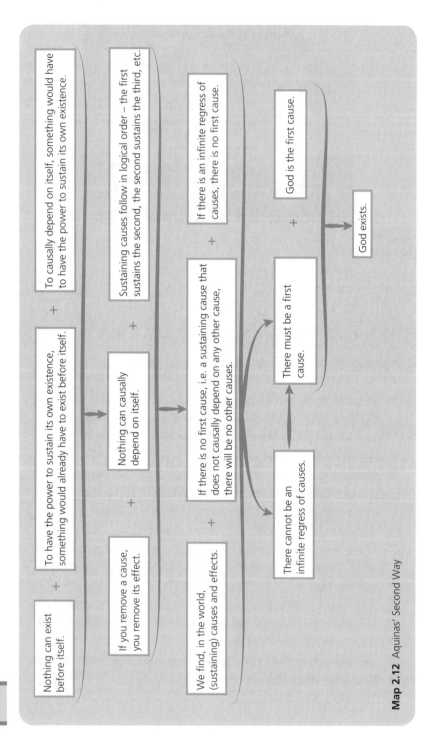

Nothing can exist before itself.

+

To have the power to sustain its own existence, something would already have to exist before itself.

+

To causally depend on itself, something would have to have the power to sustain its own existence.

If you remove a cause, you remove its effect.

+

Nothing can causally depend on itself.

Sustaining causes follow in logical order – the first sustains the second, the second sustains the third, etc.

+

We find, in the world, (sustaining) causes and effects.

+

If there is no first cause, i.e. a sustaining cause that does not causally depend on any other cause, there will be no other causes.

If there is an infinite regress of causes, there is no first cause.

There cannot be an infinite regress of causes.

There must be a first cause.

+

God is the first cause.

+

God exists.

Map 2.12 Aquinas' Second Way

See e.g. MALCOLM'S ONTOLOGICAL ARGUMENT, p. 69.

Why God?

The thought of (C1) is that any relations of causal dependency must come to an end with something that doesn't causally depend on anything else – not so much a cause that is first in time, but a cause that is 'ontologically first'.

But why think that this thing is God (P6)? Aquinas doesn't here try to spell out what he means by 'God'. But in claiming that the first cause is God, Aquinas is assuming a number of things about our concepts of God and of natural things. Our concept of natural things is that they are causally dependent. Their existence isn't 'self-sufficient' (see AQUINAS' THIRD WAY, p. 115, for development). By contrast, it is part of our concept of God that God does not depend on anything for his existence. This follows, for example, from his omnipotence. Are there any other concepts of things that exist and are not causally dependent in any way on something further? Not obviously. So God fits the bill as a first cause; nothing else does.

AQUINAS' FIRST WAY

Aquinas' First Way is said to be an argument from 'motion'. But by 'motion', Aquinas means *change*, how the properties of something change from one thing to another. Aquinas understood change in terms of 'actuality' and 'potentiality'. When a change happens, something that was only 'potential' becomes 'actual'. For instance, when I heat a pan of water, the water starts cold. Cold water has the potential to become hot, under the right conditions. With heating, it changes – its potential to be hot (and its actually being cold) is replaced by the water actually being hot.

Things can only change in ways in which they have the potential to change. Water can be hot or cold, it can be ice or steam, but it can't change into a rock! And something cannot have a property both potentially and actually at the same time. If water is hot, it makes no sense to say it has the potential to be hot. It *is* hot. (It now has the potential to be cold.) If something is stationary, it has the potential to move. But if it is moving, it doesn't have the potential to move.

Change can only be brought about by something that is actual. For instance, a pan of cold water sitting on a hob will not get hot unless the hob is turned on (or some other actual source of heat is applied). The hob has the potential to change the water, but its potential needs to become actual – it needs to be turned on – before it can change the water.

If 'motion' in Aquinas' argument means a change from potential to actual, then a 'mover' is what causes or brings about the change. Because

What does Aquinas mean by 'motion'?

change can only be brought about by something that is actual, a 'mover' must itself first be actual to bring about a change in something else from potential to actual.

AQUINAS, *SUMMA THEOLOGICA*, PT 1, Q. 2, ART. 3

Having clarified the concepts he uses, we can now state Aquinas' argument:

P1. Some things in the world undergo change.

P2. Whatever changes is changed by something, i.e. change is caused. The cause must be something else. Something potential can only be made actual by something that is already actual. A property can't cause itself to exist.

P3. If *A* is changed by *B*, and *B* is changed, then *B* must have been changed by something else again.

P4. If this goes on to infinity, then there is no first cause of change.

P5. To remove a cause is to remove its effect.

P6. Therefore, if there is no first cause of change, then there are no other causes of change, and so nothing changes.

C1. Therefore, there must be a first cause of change, i.e. something that causes change but is not itself changed.

P7. The first cause of change is God.

C2. Therefore, God exists.

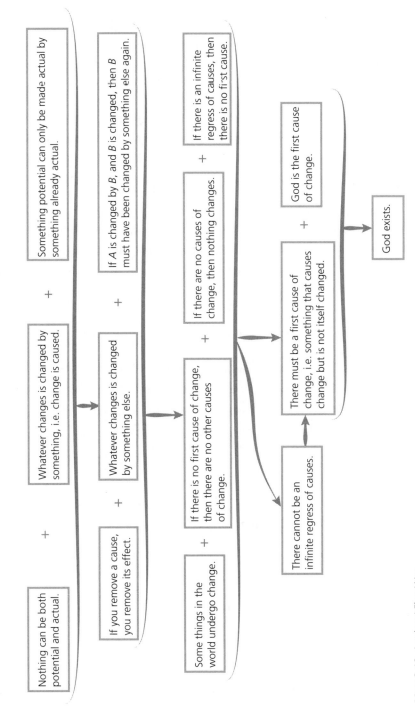

Map 2.13 Aquinas' First Way

Nothing can be both potential and actual.

Whatever changes is changed by something, i.e. change is caused.

Something potential can only be made actual by something already actual.

If you remove a cause, you remove its effect.

Whatever changes is changed by something else.

If A is changed by B, and B is changed, then B must have been changed by something else again.

Some things in the world undergo change.

If there is no first cause of change, then there are no other causes of change.

If there are no causes of change, then nothing changes.

If there is an infinite regress of causes, then there is no first cause.

There cannot be an infinite regress of causes.

There must be a first cause of change, i.e. something that causes change but is not itself changed.

God is the first cause of change.

God exists.

Discussion

In this argument, the idea of a 'first cause of change' is the idea of something that is actual and not potential – an 'unmoved mover'. This must be something that exists already and (unlike the hob) does not need to be changed in order to bring about changes in other things.

Although it is possible to read his argument as talking about temporal causes, this isn't the best understanding of Aquinas' thought. He isn't concerned with these dependencies of being changed from potential to actual as dependencies *in time*. Instead, the thought is that whatever is only potential must depend on what is actual. Each thing that changes was, at some point, only potential. So as long as we explain change in terms of other things that change, our account is incomplete. To explain how anything changes, we need to find something that does not – that is entirely actual, and never potential. The idea is not a first cause in time, but something that is ontologically prior – it is actual while other things are only potential.

Explain Aquinas' First Way.

Thinking harder: Descartes' cosmological argument

On his other proof, see Epistemology, DESCARTES' TRADEMARK ARGUMENT (p. 161). On his state of knowledge, see THE COGITO, p. 155.

In the *Meditations*, Descartes tries to bring into doubt all his beliefs. In *Meditation* III, he offers two proofs that God exists. The second is a cosmological argument. At this stage in the *Meditations*, he still doubts whether an external, physical world exists, but is certain that he exists. So Descartes asks what causes *his* existence, rather than the existence of the universe. Like Aquinas, he is concerned not so much with temporal causes, but sustaining causes.

DESCARTES, *MEDITATION* III, PP. 15–16

As the argument is long and complicated, I have divided it into sections.

P1. If I cause my own existence, I would give myself all perfections (omnipotence, omniscience, etc.).
P2. I do not have all perfections.
C1. Therefore, I am not the cause of my existence.

P3. A lifespan is composed of independent parts, such that my existing at one time does not entail or cause my existing later.

C2. Therefore, some cause is needed to keep me in existence. My existence is not uncaused.

P4. I do not have the power to cause my continued existence through time.

C3. Therefore, I depend on something else to exist.

P5. I am a thinking thing and I have the idea of God.

P6. There must be as much reality in the cause as in the effect.

C4. Therefore, what caused me must be a thinking thing and have the idea of God.

P7. Either what caused me is the cause of its own existence or its existence is caused by another cause.

P8. If its existence is caused by another cause, then its cause is in turn either the cause of its own existence or its existence is caused by another cause.

P9. There cannot be an infinite sequence of causes.

C5. Therefore, some cause must be the cause of its own existence.

P10. What is the cause of its own existence (and so, directly or indirectly, the cause of my existence) is God.

C6. God exists.

Descartes adds a further argument, picking up (C2).

C2. Some cause is needed to keep me in existence.

P11. There cannot be an infinite chain of causes because what caused me also causes my continued existence in the present.

See Epistemology, THINKING HARDER: DEGREES OF REALITY, p. 165, for discussion of (P6).

Outline and explain Descartes' cosmological argument.

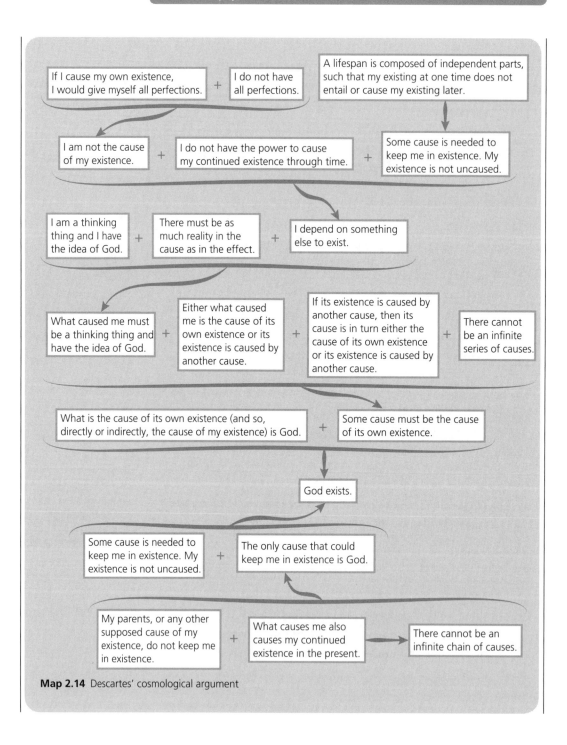

Map 2.14 Descartes' cosmological argument

> P12. My parents, or any other supposed (temporal) cause of my existence, do not keep me in existence. (They are not a sustaining cause.)
> P10. The only cause that could keep me in existence is God.
> C6. God exists.

Discussion

Like Aquinas, Descartes is discussing sustaining causes, a cause that *keeps* Descartes in existence. As the final additional argument makes clear, what brought him into existence, e.g. his parents, can't explain his continued existence. Does there need to be a cause of his continued existence? Yes, he says (P3): the mere fact that he exists at one moment doesn't entail that he continues to exist. So something must make it true, rather than false, that he continues to exist. As with all sustaining causes, whatever his continued existence is causally dependent on must itself continue to exist.

We might object, however, that his continued existence is simply dependent on the immediately preceding state of affairs. For instance, his bodily processes keep him alive at any moment. Descartes is wrong to say in (P3) that his existence at one moment doesn't cause his existence at the next.

But, first, this forgets that Descartes is talking about his *self*, which is his mind, not his body. Descartes has argued that he, his mind, is an entirely separate substance from the body. So what keeps a mind in existence through time? If it was something in his mind itself, he would know, he claims (C1). If he could cause his own existence at the next moment, he would give himself all perfections (P1). Second, even if we allowed that our bodily processes keep us alive from moment to moment, what are *they* causally dependent on? This line of thought triggers the argument from (P7). Bodily processes aren't the cause of their own continuation.

If Descartes' existence is causally dependent on something else, and an infinite regress of causal dependency is impossible, then, Descartes argues with Aquinas, that something must exist that is not causally dependent on anything else for its existence. This is God.

Explain why Descartes claims that his continued existence requires a cause.

Outline two similarities and two differences between Descartes' cosmological argument and Aquinas' Second Way.

Two issues for arguments from causation

All four cosmological arguments from causation share two claims. One is the universe (or just Descartes) has a cause – it does not exist uncaused (or again, things in the universe have causes and do not exist uncaused). The second is that an infinite series of causes is impossible, whether 'cause' means temporal cause (Kalām) or sustaining cause, and whether the sustaining cause is of existence (Aquinas' Second Way and Descartes) or a cause of a change from potentiality to actuality (Aquinas' First Way). We can raise doubts about both claims.

HUME ON THE CAUSAL PRINCIPLE

A Treatise of Human Nature, Bk 1, Pt 3, Ch. 3

The causal principle is the claim that everything has a cause. But is it true, whether we mean by 'cause' a temporal cause or a sustaining cause? Could some things come into existence without being caused? Or again, must everything be sustained in existence by causal dependency on something else?

See Epistemology, HUME's 'FORK', p. 152.

Explain Hume's objection to the causal principle, first in prose, then using an argument map.

Hume argues that the causal principle is not analytic; we can deny it without contradicting ourselves. (That every *effect* has a cause is analytic. But is everything an effect?) Without contradiction, we can assert 'something can come out of nothing' or 'I exist uncaused' or 'some natural things exist or change uncaused'. Logically, these claims may be true or false. That means that these claims are not only not analytic, they are also not *certain*. If they are not analytic, we can only know them through experience. Now, our experience supports these claims; they are probably true. But experience cannot establish that a claim holds *universally*, without exception. So we can't know (for certain) that everything, without exception, has a cause.

Applying Hume's objection to the Kalām argument, we may argue that we have no experience of such things as the beginning of the universe. Furthermore, the beginning of the universe is not an event like events that happen within the universe. For instance, it doesn't take place in space or time, since both come into existence with the universe. We cannot apply principles we have developed for events *within* the universe, such as 'everything has a cause', to the universe as a whole. So perhaps the universe began but was not caused to begin.

Applying Hume's objection to sustaining causes, do we even need to believe that everything that exists (except God) has a sustaining cause? For instance, perhaps at the most fundamental level of physical processes (e.g.

the nuclear fusion in the sun), there is no further sustaining cause. Fundamental physical particles are simply 'brute' – they exist, but nothing keeps them in existence.

Or again, perhaps there are no sustaining causes at all – there are only highly complex and rapid temporal causes, each of which brings about the immediately succeeding part of the process (e.g. some nuclear fusion occurs in the sun, immediately followed by the emission of light, followed – eight minutes later – by the arrival of that light on Earth, followed by a little bit of plant growth).

We will look at a response to these thoughts in Aquinas' and Leibniz's cosmological arguments from contingent existence (pp. 115–20).

For now, one response to Hume's objection to the causal principle is to accept that it shows that the cosmological arguments don't *prove* that God exists. However, even Hume accepts that we have *very good reason* to think that everything has a cause. So we have good reason to accept these premises. As long as the conclusions follow from the premises, we therefore still have good reason to accept the conclusion.

(A related aside: Descartes argues that the cause of his existence must be a mind which itself has the idea of God (C4). This depends on Descartes' principle that a cause must have as much 'reality' as its effect (P6). Hume would argue again that this is neither an analytic truth nor is it established by experience. Rather, 'anything may produce anything'. There is no a priori reason to think that matter cannot produce thought, and experience would indicate that matter does indeed produce thought. So we cannot infer that either the first cause or what sustains Descartes' continued existence as a mind must itself be a mind, let alone one that has the perfections attributed to God.)

Must everything have a cause?

Thinking harder: the possibility of an infinite series

The Kalām argument claims that there cannot be an infinite series of things that begin and exist in time. Infinite time and an infinite series of events in time are impossible. Before going further with this thought, can't we just cut it short by invoking science? We don't need to show that an infinite series of events in time is impossible to know that the universe has a beginning, because cosmology shows that it did – the Big Bang, just under 14 billion years ago.

Appealing to science, then, initially supports the claim of the Kalām argument, that the universe is not infinite but had a beginning. If we allow that the beginning of the universe has a cause, we can ask what caused the Big Bang? And at this point, the possibility of an infinite series arises afresh. Even if *this* universe has a beginning, perhaps it was caused by a previous (or another) universe, and so on, *infinitely*. Current speculation in physics suggests several different ways in which universes might be related to each other, including the idea that our universe is just one aspect of an infinite 'multiverse'. The Kalām argument would likely reject the idea that there could be an *infinite* series of universes, each causing another.

However, the Kalām argument is only concerned to reject an infinite *temporal* series of events. But physics also tells us that space-time exists as part of the universe. Therefore, whatever caused the universe doesn't exist in time – or rather, it doesn't exist in the time of *this* universe. One universe doesn't precede another 'in time' if each universe has its own time. It is very unclear whether the cause of the universe can be a temporal cause in the sense relevant to the Kalām argument. Once physics gets into more

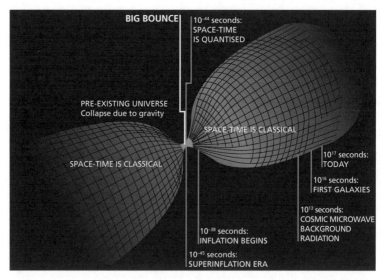

Figure 2.14 The 'Big Bounce': could our universe have been caused by a previous universe?

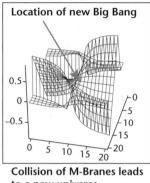

Location of new Big Bang

**Collision of M-Branes leads
to a new universe
from....NOTHING!**

Figure 2.15 Or perhaps it was caused by the collision of M-Branes?

'dimensions' than the four dimensions of space and time, our everyday ways of talking about how things exist tend to break down.

The Kalām argument uses the paradoxes of an actual infinity (THINKING HARDER: INFINITY, p. 97) to argue that there can't be an infinite temporal series of events. The paradoxes we discussed, e.g. the universe not becoming older, were related to an infinite series *in time*. Multiverse explanations of the beginning of the universe don't appeal to a single time line. So do the same problems arise when we are dealing with causes that aren't in the same time dimension?

We may argue that they do: the paradoxes support the idea that there can't be *any* kind of actual infinity. For instance, we saw that paradoxes arise for an infinite series of causes as well as an infinite series of temporal events. Think again of the hotel with an infinite number of rooms. All actual infinities raise paradoxes. So we have good reason to think that an infinity of causes – temporal or sustaining, within the universe or across universes – is impossible.

In response, we may appeal again to Hume's 'fork'. The claim 'there cannot be an infinite series of causes' is not an analytic truth, nor can we have experience of this matter. It seems conceivable, therefore, that something has always existed, and each thing has in turn caused the next.

But this is too quick. An actual infinity (of causes or hotel rooms or whatever) leads to paradoxes. If these paradoxes cannot be resolved, then they are genuine self-contradictions (e.g. that each new cause adds to the number of causes and that it does not). Anything that entails a contradiction must be false. So, if we cannot solve the paradoxes, Hume is wrong: we can deduce that there cannot be an infinite series of causes. We do not need experience to establish the claim.

But perhaps the paradoxes are the result of limitations on how we are thinking about infinity. Mathematicians (following Georg Cantor) argue that we are mistaken to apply intuitions about finite numbers to infinity, and new ways of thinking are needed (e.g. about different 'sizes' of infinity).

There might be some evidence of mistaken thinking about infinity in the arguments we've considered. For example, Aquinas argues, in both his First and Second Ways, that if we remove the 'first' cause, no other causes follow. But an infinite chain of causes isn't like a finite chain of causes with the first cause removed. It is simply a chain of causes in which every cause is itself caused. An infinite series of causes doesn't mean that there isn't a 'first cause' in the sense that some effect occurs without a cause (which would violate the causal principle). It sounds like Aquinas defends the impossibility of an infinite series of causes on the grounds of the causal principle, but this involves a mistaken idea of an infinite series of causes.

So what, if anything, is problematic with the idea of an actual infinite series of sustaining causes? Here are two possible responses.

The first we already saw in relation to the causal principle. We may grant that we cannot demonstrate the impossibility of an infinite series of causes. However, we may argue that an explanation for the universe on the basis of such an infinite series of causes is improbable. Cosmological arguments don't work deductively, but they may be good inductive arguments for a first cause (and hence God).

A second response claims that if there is not a first cause, we cannot explain the *whole series* of causes. This could be what Aquinas has in mind in thinking that all subsequent causes depend on the first cause. We can explain one cause in terms of the one before, but not why there is a series of causes at all. Hume dismisses this – 'uniting' the individual causes into a series is 'an arbitrary act of the mind'. The series doesn't have any separate existence that needs causing or explaining. All that explanation requires is that each cause in turn is explained.

To consider this further, we need to turn from cosmological arguments based on causation to ones based on the explanation of things that exist contingently.

Dialogues concerning Natural Religion, Pt 9, p. 39

?

Does the possibility of an infinite series refute the cosmological argument?

Aquinas' Third Way

Aquinas offers a third cosmological argument, from 'possibility' or 'contingency'. To understand the argument, we need to distinguish between contingent existence and necessary existence. Something exists contingently if it is possible for it to exist and for it not to exist. Something exists necessarily if it must exist, i.e. if it is impossible for it not to exist.

AQUINAS, *SUMMA THEOLOGICA*, PT 1, Q. 2, ART. 3

We can summarise Aquinas' argument like this:

P1. Things in the universe exist contingently.
P2. If it is possible for something not to exist, then at some time, it does not exist.
C1. If everything exists contingently, then it is possible that at some time, there was nothing in existence.
P3. If at some time, nothing was in existence, nothing could begin to exist.
C2. Since things do exist, there was never nothing in existence.
C3. Therefore, there is something that does not exist contingently, but must exist.
P4. This necessary being is God.
C4. God exists.

Explain Aquinas' cosmological argument from contingent existence.

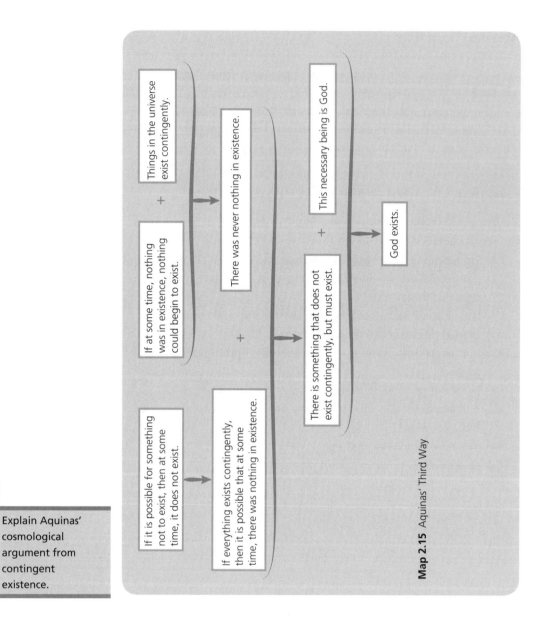

If it is possible for something not to exist, then at some time, it does not exist.

If everything exists contingently, then it is possible that at some time, there was nothing in existence.

If at some time, nothing was in existence, nothing could begin to exist.

Things in the universe exist contingently.

+

There was never nothing in existence.

+

There is something that does not exist contingently, but must exist.

This necessary being is God.

+

God exists.

Map 2.15 Aquinas' Third Way

Discussion

(P3) states the causal principle (see p. 110). The discussion of Hume's objection to this principle applies as much to Aquinas' Third Way as it does to the arguments from causation.

(P2) is puzzling, and looks false. Just because it is *possible* for something not to exist doesn't mean that it *actually* does not exist at some time. We have no reason to think that everything that is possible actually occurs. It may be that Aquinas is thinking of things that we have experience of, since he talks of our experience of things coming into existence and going out of existence. And of these things, it seems true of any of them, that at some time, they did or will not exist. Alternatively, Aquinas might reply that if there was something that *always* existed, then we would need a very peculiar explanation for how this could be so given that its existence is not necessary.

A similar point, however, may be made about the inference to (C2). We should agree that it is *possible* that, if everything exists contingently, then at some point, nothing exists. But, again, from the fact that it is possible, it doesn't follow that there *actually* was nothing in existence. It is equally possible that there has always been, and always will be, some contingent thing in existence. However, this response presupposes an infinite sequence of contingent things, and as such would face the difficulties of claiming that an actual infinity exists.

> Is Aquinas right to claim that everything contingent does not exist at some point?

Leibniz's argument from contingency

Leibniz refocuses the argument from contingent existence. We don't need the difficult premises in Aquinas' argument to make the argument work. We can put aside the question of whether nothing ever existed, and even whether the causal principle is true. Suppose, then, that the Big Bang was the beginning of the universe, and even that it was uncaused. Stopping there is unsatisfactory. We have no explanation of the Big Bang. As Aquinas says, everything in the universe – and we may want to add, the universe itself – exists contingently. It doesn't *have* to exist. So there is no reason why the Big Bang *had* to occur. It was possible that it never took place. So why did it occur?

LEIBNIZ, *MONADOLOGY*, §§32–9

Leibniz begins his argument with a commitment to the idea that there must be an answer to that question.

P1. The principle of sufficient reason: every true fact has an explanation that provides a sufficient reason for why things are as they are and not otherwise (even if in most cases we can't know what the reason is).

P2. There are two kinds of truth: those of reasoning and those of fact.

P3. Truths of reasoning (e.g. mathematical truths) are necessary, and their opposite is impossible. When a truth is necessary, the reason for it can be found by analysis. We understand the reason for it by understanding why it is necessary.

P4. Truths of fact (e.g. truths about physical objects) are contingent, and their opposite is possible. For contingent truths, reasons can be given in more and more detail, because of the immense variety of things in Nature. But all this detail only brings in other contingent facts. For example, if we want to explain why I am as tall as I am, we have to refer to many factors, such as genes and upbringing, but each of these truths is itself contingent.

C1. Each of these further contingent facts also needs to be explained. For example, why do I have the genes I do, why did I have the upbringing I did?

C2. Therefore, when we give explanations of this sort we move no nearer to the goal of completely explaining contingencies. The sequence of contingent facts doesn't contain the sufficient reason for any contingent fact.

C3. Therefore, to provide a sufficient reason for any contingent fact, we must look outside the sequence of contingent facts.

C4. Therefore, the sufficient reason for contingent facts must be in a necessary substance.

P6. This necessary substance is God.

P7. This necessary substance is a sufficient reason for all this detail, which is interconnected throughout.

C5. So there is only one God, and this God is sufficient.

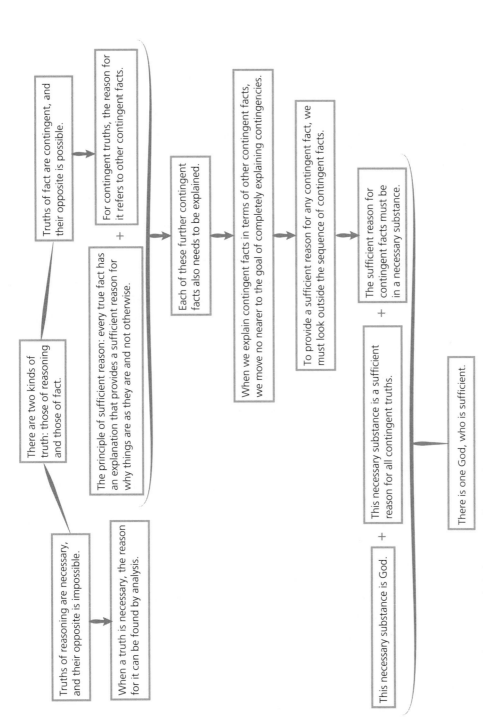

Map 2.16 Leibniz's cosmological argument from contingency

Discussion

Both arguments from contingency focus on the distinction between what is possible and contingent and what is necessary, between things which do not have to be the case and things which do. The belief that everything that exists is contingent leaves us with an inadequate idea of what exists, the argument claims. Only if there is something that must be the case – a necessary being – can we understand why there is anything at all. Again, why God? Because, as ONTOLOGICAL ARGUMENTS (p. 58) also claim, only God is the kind of being that exists necessarily.

Explain Leibniz's cosmological argument from contingency.

Two more issues for cosmological arguments

We saw in the discussion on p. 117 that Aquinas' Third Way, at least as we have phrased it, faces a possible objection to its use of the causal principle. Leibniz's argument does not, and neither argument appeals to the impossibility of an actual infinite series. However, these arguments face two new objections.

RUSSELL ON THE FALLACY OF COMPOSITION

We said (p. 117) that in Aquinas' Third Way, the inference to (C2) was puzzling. Even if we grant that each contingent thing does not exist at some point (P2), why think that this means that at some point, there were no contingent things at all? Aquinas could reply that because each contingent thing exists contingently, then all contingent things (e.g. the universe) *as a whole* exist contingently. Therefore, according to (P2), all contingent things did not exist at some point.

We can object that just because each thing exists contingently, it doesn't follow that the collection of all things exists contingently. Bertrand Russell presented a version of the objection.

Russell accepts that of any particular thing in the universe, we need an explanation of why it exists, which science can give us. But it is a mistake to think that we can apply this idea to the universe itself. Just because everything in the universe is contingent (and so needs an explanation), it doesn't follow that the universe is also contingent or needs an explanation. The universe, he says, is 'just there, and that's all'.

Russell is arguing that the argument commits the fallacy of composition. This fallacy is an inference that because the parts have some property, the

See FALLACIES, p. 15.

whole has the property, too. For instance, each tissue is thin, so the box of tissues is thin. Not true. Thus we can't infer from the contingent existence of each thing in the universe that the universe is contingent.

We can argue that Leibniz implicitly makes the same fallacy in (C2), which seems to say that in explaining one contingent thing in terms of another, we don't have a sufficient reason until we can explain *all* contingent things. To explain each contingent thing in turn is not to provide a sufficient reason for all of them.

We saw a similar point earlier (p. 113), when Hume objected that uniting individual causes into a single series that itself needs causing is 'an arbitrary act of mind'. We can apply that here to say that once we explain each thing in turn, we don't need a further explanation for the whole thing.

One reply is that the explanations of each part are in terms of other contingent things. So this will lead to an infinite regress of explanation, which is unsatisfactory. But why? Is an infinite regress of explanation any more (or less) problematic than an infinite series of causes?

Perhaps a better response is that inferring from parts to whole does not always commit the fallacy of composition. For instance, each part of my desk is wooden, so my desk is wooden. We can argue that the same applies in the cosmological argument. For instance, if every part of the universe ceased to exist, so would the universe. This shows that just as everything in the universe is contingent, so is the universe. As a contingent being, the universe requires an explanation. There is no other contingent being we can appeal to, since the universe comprises all contingent beings, so we must appeal to a necessary being.

But is the universe contingent? Is it possible for every thing in the universe to cease to exist at the same time? Perhaps, suggests Hume, if the argument shows that a necessary being must exist, then it is matter/energy (in some form) that is the necessary being, rather than God. For example, a fundamental law of physics is the conservation of energy: the total amount of matter/energy in the universe remains constant, it cannot be increased or decreased. If a version of this law applied even at the beginning and end of this universe and others, then matter/energy is a necessary being.

We can respond that we have no reason to believe that this law does apply at the beginning (and possibly the end) of the universe. The Big Bang theory suggests that matter/energy was created, along with time and space, i.e. the universe came into existence – so it is contingent.

Explain Russell's objection that the argument from contingency commits the fallacy of composition.

Dialogues concerning Natural Religion, Pt 9, p. 39

Does the argument from contingency commit the fallacy of composition?

If the argument doesn't commit the fallacy of composition, Russell needs to find some other objection to the principle that *all* contingent beings, including the universe, require an explanation for their existence. We could develop such an objection from Hume, applying Hume's fork to Leibniz's principle of sufficient reason (P1). It is not an analytic truth that all contingent beings *have* an explanation, any more than it is an analytic truth that everything has a cause. Thus, Russell remarks that while scientists will look for causes, that doesn't imply that they can find them everywhere. Likewise, we should leave open the possibility that the universe has no explanation.

As we found with each of the TWO ISSUES FOR ARGUMENTS FROM CAUSATION (p. 110), we can avoid the objection by giving up the deductive form of the cosmological argument, to claim that it is an inference to the best explanation instead. God's existence is certainly a better explanation than no explanation at all!

THE IMPOSSIBILITY OF A NECESSARY BEING

The arguments from contingency conclude that some being exists necessarily. The final objection we will discuss targets this conclusion, rather than the arguments for it. The objection doesn't try to show that the arguments don't work, but it provides an independent reason for rejecting the conclusion. And if the conclusion can't be true, then something must be wrong with the arguments, even if we don't know what that is.

On this distinction, see EVALUATING ARGUMENTS (p. 12) and EVALUATING CLAIMS (p. 13).

Both Hume and Russell argue that the concept of a being that necessarily exists is problematic. As we saw in EMPIRICIST OBJECTIONS TO A PRIORI ARGUMENTS FOR EXISTENCE (p. 65), Hume argues

P1. Nothing that is distinctly conceivable implies a contradiction.
P2. Whatever we conceive as existent, we can also conceive as non-existent.
C1. Therefore, there is no being whose non-existence implies a contradiction.

Russell agrees. If there were a being that exists necessarily, it would have to be self-contradictory to deny its existence. But it isn't self-contradictory to deny the existence of something. So the concept of a being that exists necessarily is confused – it is the concept of something that is logically impossible (like a square with three sides). So there can be no such being.

We can respond that Hume and Russell are wrong to think that the concept of a being that exists necessarily is confused. The concept of God is a concept of such a being. For example, both Descartes (p. 64) and Malcolm (p. 70) argue that God's omnipotence entails that God exists necessarily.

Now both Descartes and Malcolm think that this in itself shows that God exists (which is why they defend ontological arguments). We needn't accept that. All we need to respond to Hume and Russell is to show that the concept of God, as a being that exists necessarily, is *coherent*. In other words, we only need to argue that if God exists, then God exists necessarily. This helps us see where Hume and Russell go wrong.

Hume and Russell think that a being that exists necessarily is one whose existence we cannot deny without self-contradiction, i.e. they wrongly assume that 'God exists necessarily' means 'The sentence "God exists" is necessarily true.' But, following Malcolm, we should distinguish between existence and necessary existence. Hume and Russell are *right* that we can deny 'God exists' without self-contradiction. But, we may argue, we cannot deny 'if God exists, God exists necessarily' without self-contradiction. And this is enough to reject their conclusion that a being that exists necessarily is logically impossible.

'God exists necessarily' tells us not that God exists but what kind of existence God has – necessary, not contingent. And Hume and Russell have offered no reason to think that it is impossible for a being to have this kind of existence, if it exists at all. The cosmological argument from contingency then supplies a reason to think that such a being exists.

> **?**
>
> Does any cosmological argument from contingency succeed in proving the existence of a being that exists necessarily?

Key points: the cosmological argument

- The Kalām argument claims that an infinite regress of temporal phenomena is impossible, so the universe began to exist. Because everything that begins to exist has a cause, the universe has a cause. It rests on the claims that an actual infinity (such as the universe existing for an infinite time) is impossible and that something can't come out of nothing (the causal principle).

- A temporal cause brings about its effect after it and the effect can continue after the cause ceases. A sustaining cause brings about its effect continuously, and the effect depends on the continued existence and operation of the cause.

- Aquinas' Second Way argues that each thing is causally sustained by something else, and an infinite regress of causes is impossible, so there must be a first cause, a cause that is not sustained by anything else. This is God.

- Aquinas holds that when something changes, what was potential becomes actual. The cause of change must itself be actual.

- Aquinas' First Way argues that whatever changes is caused to change by something else, which is already actual. This cannot go on infinitely, so there must be a cause of change which itself does not change (it is never potential). This is God.

- Descartes argues that he depends on something else to exist, and as a thinking thing with the idea of God, his cause must also be a thinking thing with the idea of God. He also rejects the possibility of an infinite series of causes, and concludes that there must be something whose existence is not causally sustained by anything else – God.

- Hume objects that the claim that everything, or everything that begins to exist, has a cause is not an analytic truth. We cannot establish that it holds without exception.

- We can also object that it may be possible for an infinite series to exist. For instance, even if the universe began, the Kalām argument does not show that an infinite series of causes across universes is impossible. Or we may apply Hume's fork to argue that we cannot know that an infinite series of causes is impossible. Or we can argue that paradoxes of infinity arise from our lack of understanding.

- One response to these objections is to accept that cosmological arguments cannot *prove* that God exists, but still provide good reasons for thinking God exists, as the premises are likely to be true.

- Aquinas argues that contingent things do not exist at all times. Because this would lead to nothing existing, and so nothing ever existing, there must be something that exists necessarily.

- We can object that while this is possible, it is also possible that some contingent thing or other has always existed.

- Leibniz argues that every true fact needs a sufficient reason for why it is true. Explanations of contingent facts that refer to other contingent facts don't provide a sufficient reason, since these facts need explaining in turn. Therefore, what explains contingent facts must itself exist necessarily. This is God.

- Russell objects that arguments from contingency commit the fallacy of composition. While each contingent thing must be explained, the universe as a whole doesn't require an explanation.

- We can reply that the argument does not commit the fallacy of composition. If everything in the universe ceased to exist, so would the universe. So the universe exists contingently and requires an explanation.
- We can object that while we may search for such explanations, it is not an analytic truth that everything has an explanation of its existence. We can reply that the argument nevertheless works as an inference to the best explanation.
- Hume and Russell object that the concept of a being that exists necessarily is incoherent, so the conclusion that such a being exists must be false. We can respond that they misunderstand necessary existence.

D. The problem of evil

The problem of evil is widely considered to be the most powerful argument against the existence of God. The central issue is whether evil, as it occurs in this world, either proves that God, as traditionally conceived, does not exist or at least makes the belief in such a God unreasonable.

An outline of the problem

In THE CONCEPT AND NATURE OF 'GOD' (p. 28), we saw that God is traditionally understood to be supremely good, omnipotent and omniscient. The existence of evil causes problems for believing that such a being exists. Here's the argument:

P1. If God is supremely good, then he has the desire to eliminate evil.
P2. If God is omnipotent, then he is able to eliminate evil.
P3. If God is omniscient, then he knows that evil exists and knows how to eliminate it.
C1. Therefore, if God exists, and is supremely good, omnipotent and omniscient, then God will eliminate evil.
C2. Therefore, if a supremely good, omnipotent and omniscient God exists, evil does not exist.
P4. Evil exists.
C3. Therefore, a supremely good, omnipotent and omniscient God does not exist.

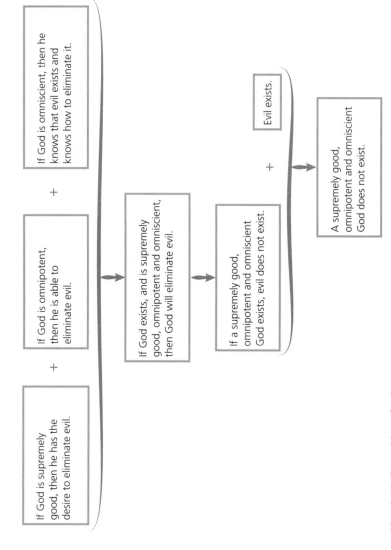

Map 2.17 The problem of evil

If God is supremely good, then he has the desire to eliminate evil.

+

If God is omnipotent, then he is able to eliminate evil.

+

If God is omniscient, then he knows that evil exists and knows how to eliminate it.

If God exists, and is supremely good, omnipotent and omniscient, then God will eliminate evil.

If a supremely good, omnipotent and omniscient God exists, evil does not exist.

+

Evil exists.

A supremely good, omnipotent and omniscient God does not exist.

There are two versions of this argument. The *logical problem of evil* claims that the mere existence of evil is logically incompatible with the existence of God. In other words, the following claims cannot all be true:

1. God is supremely good.
2. God is omnipotent.
3. God is omniscient.
4. God exists.
5. Evil exists.

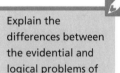

What is the problem of evil?

If any four of the claims are true, the fifth *must* be false. On this version, the argument above is deductive.

The *evidential problem of evil* makes a weaker claim. It claims that the *amount and distribution* of evil that exists is *good evidence* that God does not exist. On this version, the argument above is inductive, and we need to replace 'evil' with something like 'unnecessary evil'.

Explain the differences between the evidential and logical problems of evil.

Two types of evil

To understand the argument, we need to be clear on what 'evil' means in this context. 'Evil' usually refers to the morally wrong actions or motives of human beings. So we say that Hitler was evil in trying to eradicate the Jews from Europe or that ethnic cleansing is an evil policy. This is *moral evil*.

But this isn't the only kind of evil the problem of evil is talking about. There is also *natural evil*, which refers to *suffering* caused by natural events and processes, e.g. the suffering caused by earthquakes, diseases, the predation of animals on each other, and so on.

In the first instance, the two types of evil are distinct. What people choose to do to each other is not usually the result of natural events. Sometimes it is: famine may drive people to stealing and killing. And natural events are not usually the result of what people choose to do. Again, sometimes they are – the results of global warming could be an example.

We need to keep both types of evil in mind when we look at responses to the problem of evil. In particular, some responses may solve the problem of moral evil, but don't answer the problem of natural evil.

Explain the differences between moral and natural evil.

Thinking harder: Midgley on human evil

It is worth thinking in more depth about how we should understand the evil done by human beings. Why do people treat others very badly? Mary Midgley frames the question in terms of human nature. This approach connects natural evil to moral evil, and will provide a helpful resource when we come to discuss free will.

On choice, responsibility and character, see Moral Philosophy, VOLUNTARY ACTION, CHOICE AND MORAL RESPONSIBILITY, p. 301, and JUSTICE, p. 307.

MIDGLEY, *WICKEDNESS*, CH. 1

There are two ways of attempting to explain the evil that human beings do which are both much too simple. The first is to refer simply to free will. Someone does something evil because they choose to do so. If they make such a choice repeatedly, this shows that they are an evil person. The second is to think that people are only caused to do evil as a result of their environment and upbringing.

Midgley argues that neither takes proper account of human nature and the complex interaction between individual human choices and society. Suppose we say that evil only arises from social causes, such as bad teaching, upbringing, or examples available to children, or from certain kinds of social organization, such as tyranny or political repression. Then how do any of these causes start? How do they spread? Suppose we explain evil just in terms of free will. Would evil develop unless we were prone to such emotions as spite, resentment, envy and cruelty? Neither explanation is complete.

To understand evil in human beings, we need to think carefully about how it works through individual psychology. Three points are central. First, evil is not aggression. Some aggression is good, e.g. in friendly competition and in the protection of what one needs to live. And much evil is brought about through motives such as fear, greed or laziness.

Second, someone who does evil need not be thoroughly evil or think of themselves as evil. Very often, people do evil actions on the basis of intentions that they understand as good. And they can act in good ways in other contexts. Likewise, political movements that end up causing much suffering, even Nazism, are typically mixed in their motivation, and seek to do some good even if their conception of that good and how it can be brought about is very misinformed.

Third, Midgley argues that evil is the result of a failure to live as we are capable. It arises out of our natural capacities, which can give rise to both good and evil. Human beings are, by nature, concerned with power. This concern is expressed in our capacities for aggression, for defending our territory and possessions, our competitiveness and desire to dominate others. All of these 'animal instincts' have good aspects and can contribute to a flourishing human life. But each on their own does not aim at the overall good for a person, and the conflicts between people that they give rise to need to be carefully considered and resolved.

How is evil a 'failure' then? Our positive capacities for doing good logically entail the capacities for evil. For example, if we have a capacity for courage, then we have the capacity for cowardice. If we have a capacity to help others, we have the capacity to harm them. Evil is the absence of good. In fact, in our moral thinking, the idea of the evil comes first. Virtues are needed for a good life because of the dangers of vice. It is only because human beings have certain weaknesses (to self-indulgence, to greed, to fear) that certain traits of character – temperance, justice, courage – count as virtues and need to be actively developed.

Evil is often thought of as a positive force, something that motivates a person to act. And undoubtedly it can be powerful. But its motivating power does not make it positive – cold and dark are powerful motivators, yet they are also essentially negative, an absence of heat and light. Evil involves saying 'no' to what is good, as Goethe expresses it in the speech of the devil Mephistopheles:

> The spirit I, that endlessly denies
> And rightly too; for all that comes to birth
> Is fit for overthrow, as nothing worth;
> Wherefore the world were better sterilized;
> Thus all that's here as Evil recognized
> Is gain to me, and downfall, ruin, sin,
> The very element I prosper in.

Faust, Pt 1, Sc. 2

To argue that human beings have a 'nature' that inclines them to evil (and to good!) is not to deny that people have free will. Midgley argues that our motives concerned with power are natural, not that they are overwhelming. They don't make evil inevitable, but it is impossible to explain evil without referring to them. The fact that we are naturally inclined to aggression, say, does not mean that when someone acts aggressively, they cannot be held morally responsible. To act on one's motive is not to act involuntarily! There is an important moral difference between being hurt as a result of an accident and being hurt by someone's deliberately cruel action. But before we can discuss this point further, we will need to think more about what free will involves (p. 133).

Midgley's approach connects the two types of evil with which the problem of evil is concerned. 'Natural evil', we said, normally describes unavoidable, non-human disasters. 'Moral evil' describes deliberate evil-doing. But between the two is human nature. Human nature is natural, it is not chosen. And the natural impulses that can lead to evil cause great suffering. So moral evil has a 'natural history', a causal story about how and why it tends to occur in the species *Homo sapiens*. Being aware of this connection can enrich our understanding of the problem of evil.

Outline Midgley's understanding of evil in human psychology.

The logical problem of evil

We noted above (p. 127) that the logical problem of evil claims that the existence of an omnipotent, omniscient, supremely good God is logically inconsistent with the existence of evil.

One response to the logical problem is to give up one or other of the claims. For example, someone might deny that evil exists, arguing that what we call evil isn't really evil. If evil doesn't exist, then there is no problem of evil! An alternative is to deny that God is omnipotent. If God isn't omnipotent, then perhaps he can't prevent evil from occurring.

However, a more common response is to attempt to show that the existence of evil isn't logically inconsistent with the existence of God. We will start with responses based on free will.

A FREE WILL THEODICY

Why does God allow evil? If we try to answer this question, to give a reason why God allows evil, we offer a *theodicy*. Perhaps the most famous theodicy argues that the answer is free will.

Figure 2.16 If human beings didn't have free will, would we just be puppets and God the puppet-master?

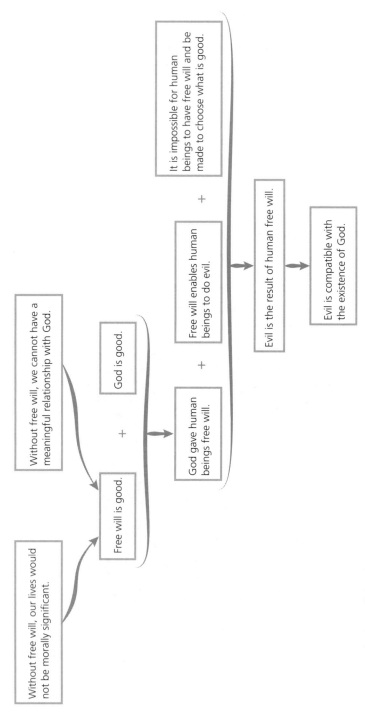

Map 2.18 The free will theodicy

Free will is a great good. Without it, our lives would not be morally significant, because we could not choose to do what is morally good or evil. Furthermore, we would be unable to have a meaningful, personal relationship with God, because any relationship would not be willingly and freely entered into. A world without moral significance is not as good as a world which has moral significance. Being supremely good, omnipotent and omniscient, God creates a world with moral significance – and so human free will.

Being morally imperfect, we do not always use our free will for good, but sometimes bring about evil. Evil is the price that must be paid for free will. A world without evil would be a world without free will, which would be a morally meaningless world. So the existence of evil isn't logically incompatible with the existence of God, since it is the result of free will, which is such a significant good that it outweighs the evil that we bring about.

Why, we may object, doesn't God just make us choose what is good? Why not create a world with free will, but without evil? Because, the theodicy responds, this isn't logically possible. To be free is for one's choices not to be determined. If God *made* us choose good, then our choices would be determined, so we wouldn't be free.

Of course, the theodicy only works if we *have* free will. Because many philosophers have argued that we do not, it is worth pausing to briefly consider a defence of the claim.

We discussed the objection that if God is omniscient, then we cannot have free will in OMNISCIENCE AND FREE HUMAN BEINGS, p. 48.

Explain the argument that free will defeats the logical problem of evil.

We discuss free will further in extension material.

Thinking harder: Midgley on free will

The most important argument against free will claims that free will is incompatible with determinism. Determinism is a view about causality. In its most common form, it holds that everything that happens or occurs has a cause ('universal causation'). Our idea of causality includes the idea of *regularity*, that the same cause will operate in the same way on different occasions. This allows us to formulate laws of nature. More controversially, many philosophers want to develop the idea of regularity into the stronger claim that, given a particular cause in a particular situation, only one outcome is *possible* ('causal necessity').

For example, suppose there is water on the kitchen floor. We assume that there is a causal explanation of how the water got there, even if no one knows what it is. If the mess was not caused at all, then we would consider it a miracle. Suppose a pipe burst. So we say 'The burst pipe caused the kitchen floor to become wet.' This claim is about this one occasion. But we expect that on other occasions if a pipe burst in the kitchen, the floor would be wet. This is the idea of regularity. The same cause will lead to same effect, and if the effect is different, then the cause must be different too. So if on another occasion, a pipe burst, but the floor remained dry, there must be something which is different between that situation and our original one. (For example, it might be that the whole house is well below freezing, so that the water in the burst pipe is and remains ice – so it stays where it is, and the floor remains dry.)

The idea of regularity can lead to the stronger thought that, given this cause – in exactly this situation – only one outcome is *possible*. In a different situation, a burst pipe might not lead to water on the floor; but in this situation, not only does the burst pipe lead to a wet floor, but it had to. For instance, it is not possible that in this situation, or any other situation exactly like it, the pipe could burst but the floor not become wet. The situation determines a unique effect. This is the idea of causal necessity.

It is worth pointing out that determinism is not an empirical discovery, something that science has proven true. As discussed in HUME ON THE CAUSAL PRINCIPLE (p. 110), we can't show that every event has a cause. It isn't an analytic truth and we can't investigate every event to establish that the event does, indeed, have a cause. However, as science has progressed, it has explained more and more events, and discovered more and more general regularities in how the world works. Determinism is best understood as a commitment or an assumption that we make in doing science.

How does determinism threaten free will? Determinism is a completely general doctrine, which could be just as true of human beings, our choices and actions, as it is of physical objects. The argument runs something like this:

P1. Determinism is true.

C1. Therefore, our choices have causes. (For instance, those causes might be part of human nature, part of the external environment, our upbringing or social situation, or even previous states of the brain.)

C2. Therefore, each choice we make has a particular set of causes and takes place in a particular situation.

C3. Therefore, given those causes and situation, no choice is possible other than what we actually choose.

P4. If we couldn't make any other choice, then we do not have free will.

C4. Therefore, we don't have free will.

On the understandings of determinism and free will here, free will requires us to be able to choose and act outside or independent of causation. If our choices are caused, then they are not free.

    If determinism is true and incompatible with free will, then the free will theodicy doesn't succeed. One defence of free will is to accept that free will and determinism are incompatible in this way, but to reject determinism. However, Midgley argues that 'incompatibilism' misunderstands both free will and determinism.

> Explain the argument that determinism and free will are incompatible, first in prose, then as an argument map.

MIDGLEY, *WICKEDNESS*, CH. 5

Determinism and fatalism

We can and should accept determinism if we understand it properly, says Midgley. Determinism says we should view events as intelligibly connected and occurring according to laws. As a result, events are predictable in principle in advance, given suitable evidence. But determinism should not be understood as claiming that events are *forced* to happen. Saying that 'only one outcome is possible' can encourage a false picture of the regularity that connects events. It can lead us mistakenly from determinism to 'fatalism'.

    Fatalism, as the term is being used here, is the belief that human action is useless – that whatever one does, the outcome

> In a different sense of fatalism, the term means a resigned acceptance of things that one cannot change. This can be rational, e.g. accepting that one will die.

will be the same. It is the thought that human choices and action have no influence on how things are or future events. If we think determinism is incompatible with free will, we turn determinism into fatalism. We shift our responsibility onto the laws of nature – 'There was nothing else I could do, I was made to do it, it wasn't me but the laws of nature.'

It is true that we cannot change the laws of nature, but if we understand them, we can use them. Through our actions, things become possible that would not be possible otherwise. For example, a farmer who lives by the Nile cannot change the regular flooding of his land, but he can use the flooding to his advantage. By planning when to plant, he can grow more crops rather than having the crops destroyed. The regularities of nature enable human action. This is not fatalism, but its opposite.

The confused fatalist interpretation of determinism has appeared in various forms in Western thought. An early debate concerned God's omniscience. If God knows the future, then God knows what we will do. But – and here is a direct implication for the problem of evil – God created us, knowing that we would do evil. And so God is responsible for the evil that we do. 'God' is later replaced with various forms of scientific determinism – natural laws, evolutionary theory and human nature, history and the external social environment. In each case, the implication is drawn that we are helpless in the face of such forces (natural, evolutionary, historical or social). But, once again, Midgley argues, the fact that we cannot change some law or situation does not mean that we have lost all ability to choose how to act in response to it.

Prediction and free will

The argument so far shows that Midgley does not accept that free will involves acting outside causation. So how is free will compatible with determinism?

Explain Midgley's distinction between determinism and fatalism.

Midgley's understanding of free will is close to Aristotle's idea of VOLUNTARY ACTION in Moral Philosophy, p. 301.

The opposite of free will, she says, is slavery to external forces or internal constraints on our capacity to choose. Free will doesn't require omnipotence, nor is it random. We expect normal people to act in ways that stem from their life and character so far. Not to do so, to act in a way that doesn't grow from one's previous life, is a kind of psychological disorder. Even as people change, we expect them to change in ways that result from their previous motives and to preserve some form of continuity with who they already are. Free will is rational – it involves understanding and overcoming difficulties, whether they are external or psychological. To be free is to think and act in this way.

All this shows that we assume psychological regularities as well as physical ones. We should not try to defend free will by thinking that human actions are unpredictable. Without accepting that we have a nature, we would have no idea how people would be in other cultures or epochs. We could make no general claims about people; and history and social science would be impossible. Being able to predict what someone will do is compatible with free will if the prediction rests on good reasons for acting in a certain way and/or appeals to general truths about human nature.

Someone who holds that determinism and free will are incompatible can try another line of argument. If determinism is true, then each state of someone's brain can be predicted in advance. Assuming that their thoughts and choices depend on the physical states of their brain, this means that we can predict their thoughts and choices in advance, not on the basis of their reasoning, but by using neurophysiological laws. This isn't compatible with free will.

Midgley replies that things are more complicated than this. Take the example of Pythagoras coming up with his famous theorem. Here's the problem he's thinking about: how long is the hypotenuse of a right-angled triangle? From

The relation between mind and brain is discussed in Metaphysics of Mind. See, in particular, MIND–BRAIN TYPE IDENTITY THEORY, p. 216.

knowing the state of his brain, could we predict his solution, that the square of the hypotenuse equals the sum of the squares of the two other sides? Midgley argues that

> *even if we could make the physical prediction* [of what brain state followed next] we would still not be able to read off the theorem from it, unless we had a complete account of the relation between brain-states and thought. But if we had that, we would already have a complete description of Pythagoras' thoughts, as well as of his brain-states. And this is what we should have to use to discover the theorem, because accounts of brain-states simply do not mention matters like triangles and hypotenuses at all. In trying to predict thought, we should have to use existing thought as our only possible starting-point. And in order to do this, we should have to drop the attempt at prediction and start instead to work out the problem for ourselves. Given all Pythagoras' data, we might even come up with his solution. But this would be quite a different feat from predicting that *he* would come up with it ... In this way, we would have become colleagues in his enterprise, instead of mere predictors. If we had stuck only to the physical data, we would have made no headway with his problem at all.

There are two key points in this passage. First, the physical processes of the brain do not 'force' our thoughts to occur as they do, as though thoughts are only along for the ride and contribute nothing. Rather, mind and brain (if we think of them as distinct at all) are interdependent – we can predict physical states of the brain on the basis of thought and thoughts on the basis of the brain. Thinking – the process of one thought leading to another – is not an illusion. Second, when it comes to reasoning – which is where free will shows itself – we can only understand it if we move from trying to predict it to joining in with it. The creativity of Pythagoras in discovering his theorem is a creativity we all share in every decision we make, albeit usually in a lesser degree. This individual creativity isn't at odds with the general regularities discovered by science.

What is free will?

PLANTINGA'S FREE WILL DEFENCE

Midgley's argument may convince us that we have free will. Nevertheless, we may still doubt whether free will is the reason why God allows evil to exist. Perhaps, we think, we don't – or even can't – know why, in fact, God allows evil. Plantinga argues that to solve the logical problem of evil, we don't need to discover and defend *the true explanation* for why evil exists. All we need to do is show that the existence of God *is consistent* with evil. Two (or more) claims are consistent if they *can* both (or all) be true together. To show this, we don't need to show that the claims *are* true. Plantinga calls this approach a 'defence' rather than a theodicy.

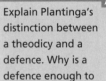

Explain Plantinga's distinction between a theodicy and a defence. Why is a defence enough to defeat the logical problem of evil?

PLANTINGA, *GOD, FREEDOM, AND EVIL*, PP. 29–34

Plantinga begins his argument by clarifying his terms:

1. To be *free* is to be able to do or refrain from some action, not to be causally determined to act in one way or another. (Depending on what Plantinga means by 'causally determined', he could be agreeing with Midgley or defending incompatibilism. If Midgley is right, we can be free and yet determinism is true.)
2. A *morally significant action* is one which it is either right or wrong to perform. (An action that is permissible to do or omit, e.g. to have a banana for breakfast, is not morally significant.)

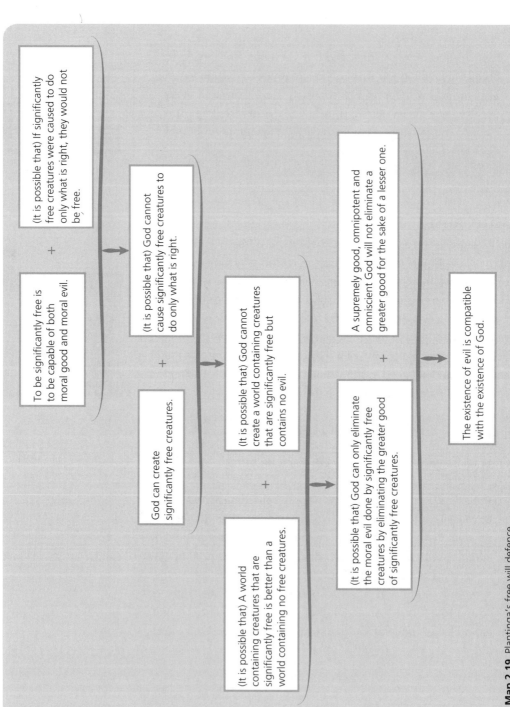

Map 2.19 Plantinga's free will defence

The boxes in the map contain the following text:

(It is possible that) If significantly free creatures were caused to do only what is right, they would not be free.

+

To be significantly free is to be capable of both moral good and moral evil.

→ (It is possible that) God cannot cause significantly free creatures to do only what is right.

+

God can create significantly free creatures.

→ (It is possible that) God cannot create a world containing creatures that are significantly free but contains no evil.

+

(It is possible that) A world containing creatures that are significantly free is better than a world containing no free creatures.

+

(It is possible that) God can only eliminate the moral evil done by significantly free creatures by eliminating the greater good of significantly free creatures.

+

A supremely good, omnipotent and omniscient God will not eliminate a greater good for the sake of a lesser one.

→ The existence of evil is compatible with the existence of God.

3. A creature is *significantly free* if it is free to do or refrain from morally significant actions.
4. Moral evil is evil resulting from the actions of significantly free creatures. (This contrasts with natural evil.)

Plantinga then offers the following argument:

P1. A world containing creatures that are significantly free is better than a world containing no free creatures.
P2. God can create significantly free creatures.
P3. To be significantly free is to be capable of both moral good and moral evil.
P4. If significantly free creatures were caused to do only what is right, they would not be free.
C1. Therefore, God cannot cause significantly free creatures to do only what is right.
(C2. Therefore, God cannot create a world containing creatures that are significantly free but which contains no evil.)
C3. Therefore, God can only eliminate the moral evil done by significantly free creatures by eliminating the greater good of significantly free creatures.

If the conclusion, (C3), is asserted as a true claim, this argument is a form of the free will theodicy. The free will defence, however, only claims that (C3) is *possible* – it *could* be true. If it could be true, and assuming that a good God would not eliminate free will in order to eliminate evil, then the existence of evil is logically consistent with the existence of God. So the logical problem of evil does not prove that God does not exist.

> Explain Plantinga's free will defence.

NATURAL EVIL

In the form we have discussed it so far, the free will theodicy and free will defence only address moral evil. We may grant that moral evil is compatible with the existence of God. But natural evil doesn't seem to have much to do with free will. So can we make the existence of natural evil consistent with the existence of God?

One response, that Plantinga presents, is that natural evil is the result of the free will of Satan and demons. The traditional story goes that the Devil was an angel, created by God, endowed with free will. But he rebelled against God, and since then has sought to bring evil into the world. Natural evil is actually a form of moral evil, the result of Satan's choices. Again, Plantinga does not claim this story is true, but that it is possible.

A different response is this. The logical problem of evil assumes that God has the desire to eliminate *all* evil. But this isn't true if some evil is *necessary for a greater good*. Just as we argued that moral evil was the price that has to be paid for the greater good of free will, we can say the same about natural evil. In particular, there are virtues, such as sympathy, benevolence and courage, that require suffering to exist. Without danger, we don't need or develop courage; without illness and poverty to respond to, we don't need benevolence; without suffering, we don't need sympathy. A universe without suffering would be a universe without these virtues; and a universe without either suffering or virtue would be a worse universe than one in which there is both suffering and virtue. The evil of suffering makes the good of virtue possible.

We may give a similar argument regarding human nature, which disposes us to evil. As we discussed in THINKING HARDER: MIDGLEY ON HUMAN EVIL (p. 128), we only develop virtues in the face of temptation and weakness. If we had no fear, while we would act 'well' in the face of physical danger, we wouldn't develop courage as we know it. It would take no more psychological effort than feeding ourselves when we are hungry. Likewise, if we were not tempted by selfishness, benevolence would not be the virtue it is.

Is this persuasive? If not, the theist can retreat from a theodicy to a defence. It is *possible* that what has been said is right, and that shows that natural evil is not logically incompatible with the existence of God. Because the logical problem of evil makes such a strong claim, this is all we need to show to defeat it.

Of course, these arguments don't yet address the *evidential* problem of evil, which we turn to next.

> **Is the existence of God logically compatible with the existence of evil?**

The evidential problem of evil

The responses to the logical problem of evil claim that the existence of evil (moral and natural) is logically compatible with the existence of an

Figure 2.17 Would a good God make a world in which a tsunami kills 230,000 people?

omnipotent, omniscient and supremely good God. Let us grant that this claim is correct. The evidential problem of evil does not challenge this claim. Rather, it argues that the amount of evil, the kinds of evil, and the distribution of evil are good evidence for thinking that God does not exist. Put another way, we can grant that evil as we know it does not make it *impossible* that God exists. But the fact that it is possible doesn't show that it is *reasonable* to believe that God exists. Planets made of green cheese are logically possible; but it isn't reasonable to think they exist. The evidential problem of evil tries to show that belief in an omnipotent, omniscient, supremely good God is unreasonable, given our experience of evil.

The discussion of the logical argument has been very abstract. But the problem of evil more naturally arises, as a challenge to belief in God, when we consider specific examples of evil. In wars and ethnic cleansing, people kill each other in the millions, perhaps the worst example being the Holocaust of the Second World War. People who have already suffered terribly may suffer more, without reprieve. Innocent children suffer agonising deaths. Natural disasters – such as the tsunami of December 2004 – kill hundreds of thousands of people. Who suffers and how much, whether as a result of moral evil or natural evil, is very unfair. Animal suffering is also an issue, as they are eaten alive or develop chronic debilitating illnesses.

The examples are intended as illustrations of the kind, amount or distribution of evil that an omniscient, omnipotent, supremely good God would eliminate. Even if certain evils are necessary for certain goods, such as free will and virtue, are *all* these evils necessary? It seems that a better world is possible, one that contains free will, virtues and some evil, but less – and less terrible – evil than exists. This is a good reason to believe that God does not exist.

Outline and explain the evidential problem of evil, first in prose, then as an argument map.

PLANTINGA'S FREE WILL DEFENCE AGAIN

> ### PLANTINGA, *GOD, FREEDOM, AND EVIL*, PP. 59–64
>
> Plantinga argues that the free will defence can deal with the evidential problem. To recap, according to Plantinga, the free will defence shows that it is *possible* that most of the evil in this world is moral evil (because it is possible that natural evil is the result of the moral evil of Satan). Or again, developing our previous argument, if important virtues depend on the existence of natural evil, it is *possible* that God could not create a world with less evil without reducing the good. It is *possible* that there is no better balance of moral good and moral evil than the one that exists. The evidential problem accepts that it is possible, but is very unlikely. But, Plantinga asks, why think this? How are we to assess how *probable* it is that there is no better balance between good and evil? Do we really have any evidence *against* the claim that evil cannot be reduced? Plantinga argues that we don't. In particular, the amount of evil that exists, on its own, neither supports nor opposes the claim that a better balance of good and evil is possible. Therefore, it does not make it less likely that God exists.

Explain Plantinga's response to the evidential problem of evil.

Discussion

Plantinga's argument only considers the *amount* of evil, and in a very abstract way – the total amount in the universe. But the evidential problem also appeals to the kinds and distribution of evil. We may object that these are more difficult to dismiss as not providing evidence that a better balance of good and evil *is* possible.

In particular, we can consider whether free will is so good that it outweighs all the evil that exists. In the discussion of the logical problem of evil, we compared a world with creatures that are free with a world without such creatures. We can object that this leaves out other possibilities. Even if free will is a great good, that doesn't mean we should never interfere with it. For example, if we see someone about to commit murder and do nothing about it, it is no defence to appeal to how wonderful it is that the murderer has free will. To eliminate some evils, one has to eliminate certain instances of free will. But this type of selective interference is compatible with the existence and goodness of free will; it doesn't eliminate a greater good. So God would interfere in this way.

We can challenge this. If God always interfered to prevent us from causing evil, then this is equivalent to his causing us to do good. In that case, we don't have free will at all.

We can refine the objection. God could interfere just on those occasions on which we would bring about terrible evil. Or again, God could have given us free will without giving us the power to commit terrible evil. The point is that free will doesn't seem *such* a good thing that each occasion of choosing freely is a good thing. *Some* choices are better eliminated. Wouldn't a limited kind of free will have been better?

One response, from John Hick, is that the value of free will depends on what one can do with it. A world in which we couldn't harm each other – either because we didn't have the power to do so or because God always interfered to stop us – would also be one in which we would have very little responsibility for each other's well-being.

Hick, *Evil and the God of Love*, Ch. 16, §3

Whether or not this justifies the moral evil that human beings do, we can raise the objection again regarding natural evil. Appealing to free will to justify all the suffering not caused by human beings requires us to accept the story of Satan. But is the free will of Satan so good that it outweighs all the natural evil that he has caused? Surely a world without Satan would be a better world, and a world that God could have created. When it comes to natural evil, we can argue that appeals to free will fail against the evidential problem of evil.

Can appealing to free will successfully answer the evidential problem of evil?

HICK'S 'SOUL-MAKING' THEODICY

In seeking to explain why evil exists, theodicies seek to justify it in terms of some greater good that evil enables, such as free will or the development of virtue. John Hick develops the argument that the existence of evil is necessary for us to become good people, for us to grow morally and spiritually.

HICK, *EVIL AND THE GOD OF LOVE*, CHS 13–17

The value of soul-making

In Ch. 13, Hick argues that we shouldn't think that God has finished creating human beings. We are unfinished. The first stage of our creation is given by evolutionary history, which brings into existence creatures – us – who are capable of conscious fellowship with God. The second stage of our creation is both individual and more difficult. It involves bringing each person freely towards personal, ethical and spiritual virtues and a relationship with God. This work of perfection is individual, rather than collective. It does not entail that the world as a whole is getting better, morally speaking.

The response to the problem of evil – in both logical and evidential forms – is that such virtuous development is impossible unless there is evil to respond to and correct. For example, we can't be courageous unless there is danger, we can't be benevolent unless people have needs, we can't learn forgiveness unless people treat us wrongly, and so on. Through struggles and suffering, not only with natural disasters and illness, but also with our own motives and the actions of other people, we mature and develop spiritually. Both natural and moral evil are necessary. Defenders of the problem of evil often assume that God would seek to maximise pleasure and minimise pain. Such an environment *may* be suitable for perfected creatures, but it is no good for helping unperfected creatures like us develop. We can understand this world, then, as a place of 'soul-making'.

God does not seek to reduce suffering. Instead, God seeks our development of virtues, and this requires suffering. Because God is good, he wants us to become good, and so he wants a world in which this is possible. It turns out that such a world must contain evil. And so the existence of evil is compatible with the existence of God.

God could have created creatures that had some version of the virtues immediately. But the virtues we achieve that result from challenges, discipline, and overcoming of temptation are 'good in a richer and more valuable sense' than the qualities of someone simply created good. In addition, Hick argues (Ch. 14, §4), there are some attitudes that God *could* not create, but must come through freedom. It is impossible to create free human beings that can be guaranteed to respond to God in authentic faith and love. Setting up human nature in this way would be tantamount to a form of manipulation, and so the attitudes would be inauthentic.

Outline and explain Hick's soul-making theodicy.

Challenges from the evidential problem

We may object that the argument addresses the logical problem, but hasn't yet offered a response to the amount, kind or distribution of evil. In essence, the theodicy only justifies *all* evil if *all* evil leads to spiritual growth. So we can object:

1. What about animal suffering? Animals don't grow spiritually, so how is the natural evil that they suffer justified?
2. Is it plausible that terrible evils are really necessary for our moral and spiritual growth?
3. A great deal of evil doesn't (appear to) contribute to spiritual growth. Many people suffer terribly in a way that breaks their spirit, e.g. children who never recover from being abused; others suffer at the end of their lives when there is little time to develop further; people die prematurely, before they have a chance of spiritual growth; people who need to grow spiritually don't suffer much at all; others who are already leading good and mature lives suffer a great deal.

Hick discusses each objection in turn. But we first need to understand the value of pain and its distinction from suffering. Physical pain is valuable not primarily in the information it provides when we are ill, but in the lessons we learn about how to preserve ourselves, about risks and dangers (Ch. 15, §3). Life without pain would not be better – it would not be life as we know it at all, and it certainly would not be a life in which we were able to develop morally and spiritually. Pain and suffering are not the same thing. We endure pain without suffering in experiences of adventure, triumph over obstacles, etc. Much of our suffering – in its self-centredness, self-pity, desire to avoid weakness and mortality – is a result of our response to pain. Our response to pain needn't be like this (which is not to say it is easy to respond differently!), and these aspects of our response can be understood as a result of our going wrong morally (Ch. 16, §1).

Bearing these points in mind, we can now turn to the objections.

Animals: We shouldn't misrepresent the experience of animals (Ch. 15, §5). They live in the present without fear of death or of future pains or dangers. And, as just argued, to be alive is to be subject to pain. But why, if they don't have souls to be perfected, should they exist (and so feel pain) at all? Wouldn't a world without animals and their pain be better? Hick's reply is that if we were the only living things or clearly set apart from the rest of nature, we would lose some of our *cognitive freedom* (Ch. 15, §5). If God proved that he exists, we would not really be free to choose whether or not to develop a relationship with him. For us to develop the best form of faith and love, there must be 'epistemic distance' between us and God. So the world needs to be one which we can understand as though God did not exist. The existence of animals and our close relationship to them serves that purpose. We have an account of our origin and place in nature independent of God. This provides the justification of animals and their pain – it is a necessary part of a world in which our souls may be perfected.

Terrible evils: Terrible evils are terrible in contrast to more 'ordinary' evils (Ch. 16, §4). If we remove the terrible ones, the next-to-terrible ones will seem exceptional and we will wonder why those are permitted. If we continue to remove the worst evils, eventually we arrive at a world in which there is little evil but also very little human freedom, moral responsibility, or the development of moral and spiritual virtues.

Pointless evil: What about the distribution of evil, evil that seems to fail to contribute to the purpose of soul-making? We cannot rationalise such evils, says Hick. They must remain a challenge and a

Explain Hick's argument that animal pain is not something that God would eliminate, first in prose, then as an argument map.

mystery (Ch. 16, §6). However, we can understand that the existence of such irrational evils is part of the process of soul-making. Imagine a world in which we knew, on every occasion when someone suffered, that it was for the best. This would leave us without deep sympathy, the kind that is evoked precisely in response to suffering that is unjust and excessive. We may add that we would need neither faith nor hope, both of which depend on uncertainty and unpredictability. But faith and hope are two central virtues, two ways in which souls grow spiritually. So for our souls to grow spiritually, it *must* look like the distribution and amount of evil are unfair or unjustified.

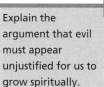

Explain the argument that evil must appear unjustified for us to grow spiritually.

None of Hick's theodicy succeeds as a response to the problem of evil unless our souls *are* perfected. But we can object that this is frequently not the case. People die undeveloped, morally and spiritually immature or corrupt. Hick accepts the point. The theodicy only works if we also believe in a life after death (Ch. 17, §1). Indeed, we must believe in universal salvation as well: if there are wasted lives or unredeemed sufferings, he claims, then either God is not supremely good or not all-powerful.

In light of the existence of evil, can belief in an omniscient, omnipotent, supremely good God be reasonable?

Key points: the problem of evil

- The problem of evil is this: if God is supremely good, then he has the desire to eliminate evil. If God is omnipotent, then God is able to eliminate evil. If God is omniscient, then he knows that evil exists and knows how to eliminate it. Evil exists, so an omniscient, omnipotent, supremely good God does not.
- The logical problem: the existence of evil is logically incompatible with the existence of God.
- The evidential problem: the amount and distribution of evil makes the existence of God very unlikely.
- 'Evil' means moral and natural evil. Moral evil is that caused by beings with free will. Natural evil is suffering caused by natural processes, e.g. drought and predation.

- Midgley argues that we cannot understand why people do evil by appealing either to free will or their environment alone. Human nature provides capacities for good, but we can fail to live as we are capable, and evil is the result of this failure.

- The free will theodicy argues that evil is the result of human free will. It is impossible for God to give us free will and make us choose what is good all the time. This shows that the existence of evil and of God are not logically incompatible.

- We can object that we don't have free will, because our choices and actions are caused deterministically. Midgley responds that this misunderstands both determinism and free will. The regularity of nature does not mean that we lose the ability to choose how to act. Free will isn't the absence of causation, nor the impossibility of prediction, but to rationally consider and overcome difficulties.

- Plantinga distinguishes between a theodicy – an account of why God allows evil – and a defence, which only tries to show that the existence of both God and evil is consistent.

- Plantinga's free will defence argues that the world is better with free creatures, but free creatures cannot be caused to do what is right. It is therefore *possible* that God can only eliminate the moral evil done by significantly free creatures by eliminating the greater good of significantly free creatures. So the logical problem does not show that the existence of God and evil is logically inconsistent.

- We can object that this doesn't cover natural evil. Plantinga claims that it is possible that natural evil is the result of moral evil by Satan. Alternatively, we can argue that natural evil is necessary for greater goods, such as the development of virtues.

- We can object that the free will defence doesn't answer the evidential problem of evil. Plantinga responds that we don't have any evidence against the claims that God can only eliminate evil by eliminating free will, and that natural evil is the result of moral evil caused by Satan.

- However, we can argue that God would prevent some, or the worst, evil actions, including those of Satan. Even if free will is a great good, this does not mean it should not be interfered with.

- Hick presents the soul-making theodicy, which says that evil is necessary for moral and spiritual growth. This world is not intended to achieve the greatest balance of pleasure over pain, but to provide an environment in which our souls can develop.

- We can object that this doesn't deal with animal suffering. Hick responds that pain is necessary for life, and animals are alive so that we have cognitive freedom, i.e. the existence of God is not forced on us.
- Terrible evils are justified by understanding that they are 'terrible' in comparison – however much or little evil there was, whatever is worst will look terrible.
- To the objection that not all evil contributes to spiritual growth, Hick responds that unless it appeared this way, we would not develop deep sympathy for each other (and, we can add, faith and hope).
- To the objection that people's souls are not developed, Hick argues that the theodicy only succeeds if there is an afterlife in which we are perfected.

Summary: arguments relating to the existence of God

In this section, we have looked at three forms of argument for the existence of God:

1. ontological arguments, from the concept of God alone;
2. arguments from design, from the order and regularity in the universe;
3. cosmological arguments, from the existence of things.

We have also discussed how the existence of evil raises a challenge to the existence of an omniscient, omnipotent, supremely good God.

In our discussion, we have looked at the following questions and issues:

1. How do Anselm, Descartes and Malcolm try to prove the existence of God from the concept of God alone?
2. What does it mean to say that God is the greatest possible or conceivable being?
3. What does it mean to say that something exists or exists necessarily? Is either existence or necessary existence a predicate?
4. Is the apparent purpose found in living creatures and the organisation of their parts evidence of design?
5. Does an analogy between human inventions and the natural world support the claim that there is a designer of the natural world?

6. What is the best explanation of the regularity that we find in the laws of nature?

7. If there is a designer of the natural world, is that designer God?

8. Must the universe have a 'first cause' or a 'sufficient reason' for its existence?

9. Is an actual infinity possible?

10. Does anything that exists contingently need an explanation for its existence?

11. What is the logical problem of evil? How does it differ from the evidential problem of evil?

12. What is the difference between a theodicy and a defence?

13. What is the free will defence and does it solve the logical problem of evil?

14. Does the fact that we need to face evil in order to grow spiritually justify the amount and distribution of evil in the world?

III. Religious language

> Because religious language is based on talk about God, I shall use the phrases to mean the same thing.

What are we doing when we are talking about God? Are we stating truths, facts, how things are? Or is religious language meaningful in some other way, e.g. expressing an attitude or commitment toward the world, rather than trying to describe it? Is talk about God meaningful at all?

> This distinction is drawn regarding ethical language as well. See Moral Philosophy, THE DISTINCTION BETWEEN COGNITIVISM AND NON-COGNITIVISM, p. 350.

The distinction between cognitivism and non-cognitivism

We can draw a distinction between two families of answer to the question of whether and how religious language is meaningful. Cognitivism claims that religious language expresses beliefs. Beliefs can be true or false, so religious claims can be true or false. To believe that God exists is to believe that the sentence 'God exists' is true. Religious language aims to describe the world. Cognitivists do not have to claim that this is *all* that religious language does. But they argue that it is how religious language is meaningful.

Non-cognitivism claims that religious language does not express beliefs, but some other, non-cognitive mental state. And so religious claims do not try to describe the world and cannot be true or false. They express an attitude toward the world, a way of understanding or relating to the world. (We may still want to talk of religious 'beliefs' but this is better understood as 'faith' or 'belief in God' than as 'belief that God exists'.)

Discussion

The arguments concerning the existence of God that we have discussed in this chapter assume that cognitivism is true. First, they assume that the statement 'God exists' is, in some sense, a statement of fact. If the arguments establish their conclusion, then 'God' refers to a being that exists, and 'God exists' is a belief that is objectively true. Second, they assume that the belief – or knowledge – that God exists is something that *could* be supported, or established, by reasoning. In other words, the existence of God can be deduced or inferred as the best explanation from premises that are more certain or plausible than God's existence. Third, they assume that God is a being that exists independently of (and prior to) human beings and religious beliefs. For example, to be the cause of the existence of the universe *in a literal sense*, God must exist independently of the universe.

However, these are not assumptions that all philosophers of religion – or all people who believe in God – accept. Non-cognitivists point out that people don't normally acquire religious beliefs by argument or testing evidence. Instead, they come to an understanding of the world that is expressed in values and a way of living. When someone converts to a religion, what changes isn't so much intellectual beliefs, but their *will*, what they value and how they choose to live. This supports the claim that 'God exists' is not a statement of fact, but has meaning as an expression of a non-cognitive attitude or commitment. These attitudes – which include attitudes towards other people, nature, oneself and human history – present the world in a certain light and support commitments to act in certain ways and to mature as a spiritual being.

However, we can raise two important objections to non-cognitivist accounts of religious language. First, an important implication of these theories is that we can't criticise or support religious beliefs by using *evidence*. Religious beliefs cannot be criticised on the grounds that they are *not true* or highly *improbable*, because this presupposes that religious language makes factual claims, and it does not. So, for example, both TELEOLOGICAL/DESIGN ARGUMENTS (p. 74) and THE PROBLEM OF EVIL (p. 125) are irrelevant as attempts to prove or disprove the existence of God. 'God exists' is not a claim that is true or false, and so it cannot be shown to be true or false. This, we can object, cuts religious belief off from reason too severely.

Outline and explain three differences between cognitive and non-cognitive accounts of religious language.

We discuss Wittgenstein's non-cognitive theory of religious language in extension material.

Explain the claim that religious language expresses an attitude.

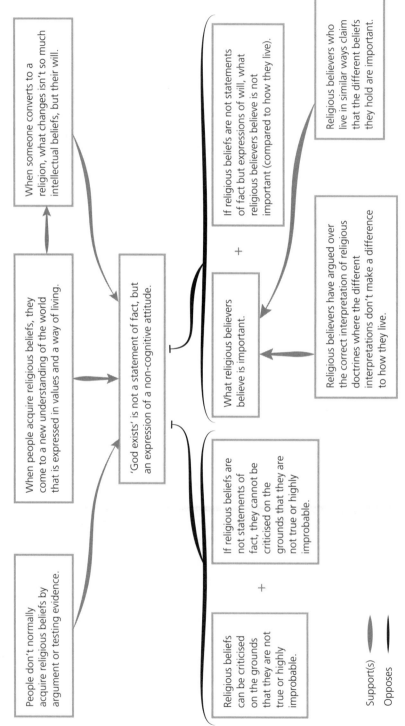

When someone converts to a religion, what changes isn't so much intellectual beliefs, but their will.

When people acquire religious beliefs, they come to a new understanding of the world that is expressed in values and a way of living.

People don't normally acquire religious beliefs by argument or testing evidence.

'God exists' is not a statement of fact, but an expression of a non-cognitive attitude.

If religious beliefs are not statements of fact but expressions of will, what religious believers believe is not important (compared to how they live).

Religious believers who live in similar ways claim that the different beliefs they hold are important.

What religious believers believe is important.

Religious believers have argued over the correct interpretation of religious doctrines where the different interpretations don't make a difference to how they live.

If religious beliefs are not statements of fact, they cannot be criticised on the grounds that they are not true or highly improbable.

Religious beliefs can be criticised on the grounds that they are not true or highly improbable.

Support(s)

Opposes

Map 2.20 Non-cognitivism in religious language

A non-cognitivist can respond that, as part of human life, religious belief still needs to *make sense* of our experiences. The problem of evil could be relevant here. Not any set of attitudes and commitments makes sense in light of our experience. The difficulty now, however, is to know what it is for a non-cognitive attitude to 'make sense', given that it doesn't make any claims about what is true and what is not.

A second objection is that non-cognitivism conflicts with how many believers think of God and their faith. For example, it makes *what you believe* much less important, as if religious faith is only about how we live. Yet many religious believers who act in similar ways and hold similar values argue that there is something distinctive and important about the different beliefs they hold. Furthermore, within the history of any religion, there have been heated arguments about how to interpret a particular doctrine (e.g. in Christianity, the Incarnation), when it is very difficult to see how the different interpretations could make any impact on different ways of living. All this suggests that religious language is intended to be true, i.e. fact-stating, and not just expressive.

We can allow that non-cognitivists are right that religious language is expressive of people's emotions and attitudes. However, just because religious beliefs express attitudes, this does not show that they cannot *also* be cognitive. There is no reason to think that they cannot be *both*. After all, religious believers *do* think they are saying something factual when they say 'God exists'. But this fact has enormous significance to people's lives, and so our emotions and attitudes to the world respond to it and are expressed in our talk about it.

Verificationism

If we reject non-cognitivism about religious language, we must say that religious language is cognitive if it is meaningful at all. But are there limitations on what we can meaningfully talk about? For instance, can we meaningfully talk about what is 'true' unless we can somehow establish that truth? This is a challenge posed by verificationism.

Compare this objection with the objection made against non-cognitivism in Moral Philosophy, THINKING HARDER: DISAGREEMENT AND MORAL ARGUMENT, p. 392.

Can the view that religious language is non-cognitive make sense of religious belief?

The verification principle and objections to it were discussed in Moral Philosophy, A. J. AYER'S VERIFICATION PRINCIPLE, p. 363, but are repeated here for convenience. See ISSUES FOR MORAL REALISM, p. 362, generally for further empiricist challenges to moral language that may also be applied to religious language.

AYER, *LANGUAGE, TRUTH AND LOGIC*, CHS 1, 6; AYER, *THE CENTRAL QUESTIONS OF PHILOSOPHY*, PP. 22–7

In the 1930s, a school of philosophy arose called logical positivism, concerned with the foundations of knowledge. It developed a criterion for when a statement is meaningful, called the principle of verifiability, also known as the verification principle. On A. J. Ayer's version, the verification principle says that a statement only has meaning if it is either analytic or empirically verifiable. He explains and defends the principle in *Language, Truth and Logic*, Ch. 1, and discusses it further in *The Central Questions of Philosophy*, pp. 22–7. The verification principle is a cognitivist view of language generally. It says that language is only meaningful if it is cognitive.

A statement is analytic if it is true or false in virtue of the meanings of the words. For example, 'Bachelors are unmarried' is analytic and true; 'Squares have three sides' is analytic and false. A statement is empirically verifiable if empirical evidence would go towards establishing that the statement is true or false. For example, if I say 'The moon is made of green cheese', we can check this by scientific investigation. If I say 'The universe has 600 trillion planets', we can't check this by scientific investigation in practice, but we can do so *in principle*. We know how to show whether it is true or false, so it is 'verifiable' even though we can't actually verify it. Furthermore, we don't need to be able to *prove* that an empirical claim is true or false. For empirical verification, it is enough for empirical evidence to raise or reduce the probability that a statement is true.

The principle can be understood as a development of Hume's 'fork'. However, while Hume's fork provides an account of what we can *know*, the verification principle is an account of what statements have *meaning*. But the verification principle defines meaning in terms of *how we can know* whether a statement is true or false. Unless there is some way of showing, at least in principle, that a statement is true or false, then it doesn't really say anything, it doesn't make a meaningful claim. The verification principle claims that the only alternative to knowing something analytically is to use empirical experience. So like Hume's fork, it defends a form of empiricism.

See Epistemology, ANALYTIC/SYNTHETIC PROPOSITIONS, p. 115.

What is the verification principle?

See Epistemology, HUME'S FORK, p. 152.

So what can we say about the proposition 'God exists' and other claims about God? Despite the best attempts of the ONTOLOGICAL ARGUMENTS (p. 57), Ayer argues in Ch. 6, we cannot prove 'God exists' from a priori premises using deduction alone. So 'God exists' is not analytically true. On the other hand, if 'God exists' is an empirical claim, then it must be possible to imagine the conditions under which we would say that it was or was not a fact. But we cannot empirically test whether God exists or not. If a statement is an empirical hypothesis, it predicts that our experience will be different depending on whether it is true or false. The claim 'God exists' makes no predictions about our experience. So it is not empirically verifiable.

P1. The verification principle: all meaningful claims are either analytic or empirically verifiable.
P2. 'God exists' is not analytic.
P3. 'God exists' is not empirically verifiable.
C1. Therefore, 'God exists' is not meaningful.

Because most religious language depends on 'God exists' being meaningful, we can argue that most religious language is also meaningless.

Some philosophers argue that religious language attempts to capture something of religious experience, although it is 'inexpressible' in literal terms. Ayer responds that whatever religious experiences reveal, they cannot be said to reveal any facts. Facts are the content of statements that purport to be intelligible and can be expressed literally. If talk of God is non-empirical, it is *literally* unintelligible, hence meaningless.

> Explain Ayer's argument that religious language is meaningless, first in prose, then as an argument map (include his reasons for (P2) and (P3)).

OBJECTIONS

'Eschatological verification'

One response to Ayer's argument is to question whether he is right that religious claims cannot be verified empirically. John Hick understands verification to involve removing rational doubt, ignorance or uncertainty

> Hick, 'Theology and verification'

about the truth of some proposition through experience. An empirically verifiable claim makes some prediction about how our experience would be under certain conditions, e.g. 'There is a table next door' can be verified by sight or touch, but it requires us to go next door. Hick agrees with Ayer that 'God exists' is not a claim that we verify through our current experience. The disagreement between theist and atheist is not about what to expect in life.

However, this isn't enough to show that religious language is meaningless. Hick develops the idea of 'eschatological verification', verification in the afterlife or at the end of time. In believing that God exists, the (traditional Christian) theist believes that there will be unambiguous experiences of God in life after death. The atheist denies this.

Does this show that 'God exists' is meaningful? First, it must be meaningful to speak of an afterlife. All empirically verifiable statements are conditional – they predict what we will experience under certain conditions of observation. However, for this to apply to the afterlife, the concept of personal existence after death must be logically possible. Second, we must be able to form some conception of what an experience of God could be. Hick argues that we already have *some* sense of this, since we are aware that our experience in this life is ambiguous – it doesn't establish or disprove God's existence. He suggests that an experience of our personal fulfilment and relation to God could serve as verification.

Rejecting the verification principle

Hick's response to Ayer's challenge accepts the verification principle in some amended form. But a more common response is to reject it. According to the verification principle, the principle itself is meaningless. The claim that 'a statement only has meaning if it is analytic or can be verified empirically' is not analytic and cannot be verified empirically. But if the principle of verification is meaningless, then what it claims cannot be true. So if the principle is true, it is meaningless, and so not true. Obviously, if it is false, it is false. Either way it is not true. Therefore, it does not give us any reason to believe that religious language is meaningless.

Ayer claims that the principle is intended as a *definition*, not an empirical hypothesis about meaning. In other words, it is intended to reflect and clarify our understanding of 'meaningful' uses of words. Ayer accepts that the principle isn't obviously an accurate criterion of 'literal meaning', but that is why he provides arguments in specific cases, such as religious language, which support it.

Eschatology is the study (-*ology*) of the 'last things' (Greek *eskhatos*) – death, the final judgement, and the ultimate destiny of human beings.

Explain Hick's concept of eschatological verification, and his argument that it establishes the meaningfulness of religious language.

Figure 2.18 Does the meaningfulness of religious language depend on possible experiences in an afterlife?

But in that case, the verification principle is only as convincing as the arguments that are intended to show that it is the right definition of 'meaningful'. If we do not find the arguments convincing, the principle provides no independent support. However, the challenge remains: if religious language is cognitively meaningful, how is this so?

> Does the verification principle show that religious language is meaningless?

Thinking harder: verification and falsification

One response to the difficulties facing the verification principle is to replace it with a 'falsification' principle. A claim is falsifiable if it is logically incompatible with some (set of) empirical observations. We can suggest, then, that a claim is meaningful only if it rules out some possible experience. For example, 'There is a fork there' is incompatible with – rules out – the experience of reaching out and grasping nothing but thin air where we see the fork.

One apparent advantage of falsification is how it deals with generalisations. A claim such as 'All swans are white' threatens to be meaningless according to the verification principle, because no experience

Figure 2.19 A perfect hologram could falsify a belief about what exists

will prove it true – there might always be a swan out there somewhere which isn't white. However, it is easy to prove false – observing a single non-white (black) swan will do it!

However, this advantage is balanced by distinct disadvantages. Hick notes that there are particular claims that are easy to verify but impossible to falsify, such as 'There are three successive 7s in the decimal determination of π', 3.141592 … . As soon as we find three 7s in a row, we have verified the claim. But because the decimal determination of π is infinitely long, we can never show that it is false (if it is false), because there may always be three 7s together later in the series. Or again, as Ayer notes, existence claims are very difficult to falsify. 'There is a yeti' is easier to know how to prove true than false. So are claims about the future, e.g. 'The sea will one day encroach on this land.' And so are probability claims. 'There is a one-in-six chance the rolled die will show a six' is not falsified by twenty 6s in a row, since the probability of one-in-six may be restored over a larger number of throws. And this is always true, no matter how many times you roll the die.

So a falsification principle that requires a meaningful statement to entail some decisive, refuting empirical experience is unacceptable. Many meaningful statements do not clearly entail an observation with which they are logically incompatible. If, on the other hand, we weaken falsification to talk about evidence which would 'count against' the truth

The Central Questions of Philosophy, p. 29

of some claim, then this is not different from Ayer's version of the verification principle. As explained above, for a statement to be 'verifiable', we know what experiences will support *or reduce* the probability of a claim. It is already part of Ayer's theory that we need to know what empirical experiences would lead us to reject a claim as well as what experiences support it.

> Does a falsification principle for meaning improve on the verification principle?

The University *debate*

In a debate published in the journal *University*, Anthony Flew, Richard Hare and Basil Mitchell discussed the meaning of religious language.

FLEW, HARE AND MITCHELL, 'THEOLOGY AND FALSIFICATION'

Flew's challenge

Flew opened the debate with a story from John Wisdom's article 'Gods'. Two explorers come across a clearing in the jungle in whichboth flowers and weeds grow. One claims that the clearing is the work of a gardener; the other disagrees. They try to detect the gardener by various means – first keeping watch, then an electric fence, then dogs – but never discover him or her. At each stage, the 'believer', however, rejects the claim that their failure is evidence that the gardener doesn't exist, saying first that the gardener must be invisible, then intangible, then leaves no scent and makes no sound. The 'sceptic' finally asks how the claim that there is such a gardener differs from the claim that the gardener is imaginary or doesn't exist at all.

Flew's point is that for a claim to be meaningful, for it to be asserting something, there must be something it is denying. In other words, there must be some way of establishing that it is false, something that leads us to withdraw the claim. If we know what the claim rules out, we can understand what the claim means. But if

> Flew presents a kind of falsification principle for truth claims. He is arguing that assertions must be cognitive to be meaningful. But, unlike the verification principle, he doesn't present a *general* theory of meaning.

Figure 2.20 Is this the work of an undetectable gardener?

there is nothing it rules out, then the claim is not a genuine attempt to say something true. What would lead the believer to say that there is no gardener? If nothing would, then saying that there is a gardener doesn't say anything. Another example: the theory of evolution by natural selection rules out aliens coming to Earth and demonstrating that they had planted 'fossils' (which they had made) for us to find. If this happened, we would give up the theory of evolution.

If 'God exists' is a real claim, then there should be some possible experience that would lead us to accept that it is false. Something should be able to 'count against it', e.g. the existence of evil. If religious believers are not prepared to accept that anything could show that God doesn't exist, then saying 'God exists' states nothing at all. Flew objects that this is the case – many religious believers refuse to accept that anything could show that God doesn't exist. Instead, they keep *qualifying* what it means to think that 'God exists'. For example, they might argue that the existence of evil only shows that we don't understand God's plans. This deprives religious claims of meaning.

See THE PROBLEM OF EVIL, p. 125.

P1 For a truth claim to be meaningful, there must be some possible state of affairs it denies or rules out.

C1. To meaningfully assert a claim, someone must accept that it rules out some possible state of affairs.

P2. The occurrence of a state of affairs that a claim rules out demonstrates that the claim is false.

C2. To meaningfully assert a claim, someone must be willing to withdraw it if the state of affairs it rules out were to occur.

P3. Religious believers refuse to specify which state of affairs would lead them to withdraw the claim that 'God exists'.

C3. When religious believers say 'God exists', they do not rule out any state of affairs.

C4. The claim that 'God exists', when made by religious believers, is meaningless.

Explain Flew's argument that religious language loses its meaning if we cannot falsify religious claims.

Mitchell's response

Mitchell accepts Flew's cognitivism and his argument that for a truth claim to be meaningful, we must allow something to count against it – (P1). But he disagrees with Flew's claim that an assertion is only meaningful if we are willing to *withdraw* it as false in light of certain experiences – (C2).

Suppose there is a war in which someone's country has been occupied, and he joins the resistance movement. One day, this partisan meets a stranger who tells him that he is the leader of the resistance. The partisan is very impressed by the stranger and trusts him deeply. However, the stranger later acts in ambiguous ways, sometimes seeming to help the resistance and other times apparently helping the enemy. But the partisan, because he trusts the stranger, continues to believe that the stranger is on the side of the resistance, and so must have some good reason for his ambiguous behaviour.

If the partisan refused to count the ambiguous actions of the stranger even as *evidence* against the claim that the stranger is on the side of the resistance, this would be irrational. Such a view would empty religious language of its meaning. But while recognising that there is evidence against his belief, the partisan is not rationally required to simply relinquish it. His trust sustains his belief in the stranger, and we cannot say, in the abstract, just how much evidence against his belief is needed before his belief becomes irrational and should be given up as false.

Likewise, religious language makes assertions, but these claims are not simply provisional hypotheses, to be discarded in the face of contrary experiences. They involve a certain commitment as well. A claim can be meaningful without us being able to say what experiences would lead us to relinquish it, as long as we recognise that experiences can count against it.

Flew accepts Mitchell's response. However, he argues, that THE LOGICAL PROBLEM OF EVIL (p. 131) is insoluble. We are unable to find any justification of evil that is compatible with an omniscient, omnipotent, supremely good God, and the only way out for religious believers is to qualify what they mean by God or his purpose for us.

We can now object, though, that this is now no longer an argument about whether religious claims are meaningful, but about whether they are either true or coherent.

Outline and explain Mitchell's theory of religious language.

Hare's 'bliks'

Hare responds to Flew in a very different way. He rejects Flew's form of cognitivism. Religious beliefs are not like assertions that can be shown to be true or false. Instead, they are part of someone's attitude toward or view of the world (or some aspect of it), which Hare calls a 'blik'.

Hare gives a number of examples of bliks. First, someone may be paranoid that university lecturers want to murder him. He doesn't count anything as evidence against this view (this is a normal feature of delusions). But the difference between his view and the view of the rest of us is meaningful, important and makes a difference to how we live. Another example is someone who trusts the properties of steel or the continued ability of a road to support cars v. someone who doesn't; or someone who thinks everything happens by chance v. someone who believes in laws of nature. A disagreement in bliks can't be decided by empirical experience, and two people who disagree may not assert anything different about what to expect from experience. Yet the disagreement is meaningful. To hold that God exists is a blik, as is the view that God does not exist.

It is unclear whether Hare thinks bliks – and so religious language – are cognitive or not. On the one hand, there is a truth of the matter (whatever one believes) whether university lecturers are trying to kill you or not or whether everything happens by chance or not. So it seems bliks can be true or false, which suggests that they are cognitive. On the other hand, because bliks can't be falsified, Hare claims that they work more like attitudes or commitments than beliefs. This would suggest that they are non-cognitive. But notice that *any* empirical claim which would normally be held as a (cognitive) belief (about the motives of university lecturers, the properties of steel, the explanations of science) could be held as a (non-cognitive) blik. The difference is how the person thinks about it.

When someone holds a blik about some claim, while the rest of us just hold falsifiable beliefs, we tend to think that the person is *irrational* in some way. Does Hare's analysis entail that religious believers are irrational? If not, why not? Hare doesn't say. As Flew objects, Hare's theory that religious belief is a blik is very unorthodox and fails to make sense of what religious believers actually say. If religious claims aren't assertions, then a claim such as 'You ought to do it because it is God's will' becomes 'You ought to do it' (since 'it is God's will' is not an assertion, but the expression of a blik). But this is not what religious believers mean.

> What, according to Hare, is a 'blik'?

> 1) Is religious belief a blik? 2) Is religious language meaningful? If so, how? If not, why not?

Key points: religious language

- A cognitivist account of religious language argues that religious claims describe how the world is, can be true or false, and express factual beliefs.
- A non-cognitivist account of religious language argues that religious claims do not describe the world, cannot be true or false, and express an attitude toward the world.

- We can object to non-cognitivism that if religious language is not cognitive, religious beliefs can't be criticised or supported by reasoning.
- We may also object that many religious believers think religious language is partly cognitive. Religious language can both express attitudes and describe the world.
- The verification principle claims that only statements that are analytic or empirically verifiable are meaningful. Empirical verification does not require proof, but being able, in principle, to provide evidence that makes an empirical claim more or less probable.
- Ayer argues that 'God exists' is neither analytic nor empirically verifiable, and is therefore meaningless.
- Hick argues that eschatological verification – provided by experiences after death – is relevant to showing whether God exists. Therefore, religious language is not meaningless.
- We can object that the verification principle is self-defeating: it is neither analytically true nor empirically verifiable. By its own standard, it is meaningless. It therefore cannot show that religious language is meaningless. Ayer argues it is a definition. But it will only be convincing as a definition if his arguments for its implications are convincing.
- The falsification principle claims that a statement is meaningful only if it is logically incompatible with some empirical experience. This faces difficulties, as some meaningful claims, such as existence and probability claims, cannot be falsified.
- Flew argues that for a claim to be meaningful, it must rule out some possible experience. 'God exists' is meaningless because religious believers do not accept that any experience shows they are mistaken.
- Mitchell argues that religious language is cognitive, but religious belief also involves commitment. Therefore, experiences can count against religious claims without the believer withdrawing the claim.
- Hare argues that religious beliefs are part of a 'blik', an attitude to or view of the world that is not held or withdrawn on the basis of empirical experience. Disagreements in bliks are, nevertheless, meaningful.
- We can object that Hare's analysis cannot help us distinguish between rational and irrational bliks and fails to make sense of how religious believers actually use religious language.

Summary: religious language

In this section, we have discussed the meaning of religious language, and looked at challenges to the view that it is meaningful at all. In our discussion and evaluation of these claims, we have looked at the following questions:

1. What is the difference between a cognitivist and non-cognitivist account of religious language?
2. Does religious language express a non-cognitive attitude toward life?
3. Does the verification principle show that 'God exists' is a meaningless statement?
4. Must a religious claim, such as 'God exists', rule out certain possible experiences in order to be meaningful?

Chapter 3

Metaphysics of mind

Please see the INTRODUCTION (p. 1) for an explanation of the different kinds of marginal boxes and what they mean. Please see CHAPTER 1 HOW TO DO PHILOSOPHY (p. 5) for explanations of philosophical argument and how to understand argument maps.

What are you? I mean, what is it to be you? What kind of thing is a human being? What makes a person a person? People have given surprisingly different answers to these questions. You might think, in light of evolutionary theory, that the answer is that we are animals. But sometimes, when someone is in an irrecoverable coma or brain-dead, we say that they no longer exist, that they've 'gone'. But the body lying there is still the same animal. So our *minds* seem particularly important to who or what we are. Without a mind, I am not a person at all and I'm not 'me'.

This raises the metaphysical question, of course, what is 'a mind'? Is it a 'thing', a thing that has its own existence, e.g. that could survive the death of the body? Or is it simply another word for the brain or what the brain does? Or something else again?

In this chapter, we begin by discussing what we mean by 'mind', i.e. what kinds of phenomena we are talking about. We identify thought and consciousness as central. Then we turn to examine six philosophical theories that answer the questions 'what is the mind?' and 'how does the mind relate to the body?' These six theories fall into three categories. First, dualist theories argue that there is *some* sense in which what is mental is quite different and independent of what is physical. Second, physicalist theories claim that what is mental can be understood in terms of what is physical. 'The mind' is not a 'thing', but can be explained in terms of either neurological processes or behaviour. Third, functionalist theories claim that thought and consciousness are not a matter of *what exists*, but of *how things work* or 'function'.

In discussing these theories, we examine a wide variety of topics, such as the nature of consciousness, how we know that other people have minds, how the mind can cause bodily movements, how to understand scientific progress, and whether philosophical thought experiments are useless. By the end of the chapter, you should be able to argue for and against the six theories of the mind, and evaluate them in relation to different topics.

Metaphysics asks questions about the fundamental nature of reality. *Meta-* means above, beyond or after; physics enquires into the physical structure of reality – which may or may not be the fundamental nature of all reality.

Syllabus checklist ✓

The AQA syllabus for this chapter is:

I. What do we mean by 'mind'?

Features of mental states:

✓ All or at least some mental states have phenomenal properties
  - Some, but not all, philosophers use the term 'qualia' to refer to these properties, where 'qualia' are defined as 'intrinsic and non-intentional phenomenal properties that are introspectively accessible'
✓ All or at least some mental states have intentional properties (i.e. intentionality)

II. Dualist theories

A. Substance dualism

Minds exist and are not identical to bodies or to parts of bodies
✓ The indivisibility argument for substance dualism (Descartes)
  - Responses, including:
    - The mental is divisible in some sense
    - Not everything thought of as physical is divisible
✓ The conceivability argument for substance dualism (expressed without reference to God) (Descartes)
  - Responses, including:
    - Mind without body is not conceivable
    - What is conceivable may not be metaphysically possible
    - What is metaphysically possible tells us nothing about the actual world

B. Property dualism

There are at least some mental properties that are neither reducible to nor supervenient upon physical properties

- ✓ The 'philosophical zombies' argument for property dualism (David Chalmers)
  - Responses, including:
    - ○ A 'philosophical zombie'/a 'zombie' world is not conceivable
    - ○ What is conceivable may not be metaphysically possible
    - ○ What is metaphysically possible tells us nothing about the actual world
- ✓ The 'knowledge/Mary' argument for property dualism (Frank Jackson)
  - Responses, including:
    - ○ Mary does not gain new propositional knowledge but does gain ability knowledge (the 'ability knowledge' response)
    - ○ Mary does not gain new propositional knowledge but does gain acquaintance knowledge (the 'acquaintance knowledge' response)
    - ○ Mary gains new propositional knowledge, but this is knowledge of physical facts that she already knew in a different way (the 'New Knowledge/Old Fact' response)

C. Issues

Issues facing dualism, including:
- ✓ The problem of other minds
  - Responses, including:
    - ○ The argument from analogy
    - ○ The existence of other minds is the best hypothesis
- ✓ Dualism makes a 'category mistake' (Gilbert Ryle)

Issues facing interactionist dualism, including:
- ✓ The conceptual interaction problem (as articulated by Elisabeth, Princess of Bohemia)
- ✓ The empirical interaction problem

Issues facing epiphenomenalist dualism, including:

✓ The challenge posed by introspective self-knowledge
✓ The challenge posed by the phenomenology of our mental life (i.e. as involving causal connections, both psychological and psycho-physical)
✓ The challenge posed by natural selection/evolution

III. Physicalist theories

A. Physicalism

Everything is physical or supervenes upon the physical (this includes properties, events, objects and any substance(s) that exist).

B. Philosophical behaviourism

✓ 'Hard' behaviourism: all propositions about mental states can be reduced without loss of meaning to propositions that exclusively use the language of physics to talk about bodily states/movements (including Carl Hempel)
✓ 'Soft' behaviourism: propositions about mental states are propositions about behavioural dispositions (i.e. propositions that use ordinary language) (including Gilbert Ryle)

Issues, including:

✓ Dualist arguments applied to philosophical behaviourism
✓ The distinctness of mental states from behaviour (including Hilary Putnam's 'super-spartans' and perfect actors)
✓ Issues defining mental states satisfactorily due to a) circularity and b) the multiple realisability of mental states in behaviour
✓ The asymmetry between self-knowledge and knowledge of other people's mental states

C. Mind–brain type identity theory

All mental states are identical to brain states ('ontological' reduction) although 'mental state' and 'brain state' are not synonymous (so not an 'analytic' reduction)

Issues, including:

✓ Dualist arguments applied to mind–brain type identity theory
✓ Issues with providing the type identities (the multiple realisability of mental states)

D. Eliminative materialism

Some or all common-sense ('folk psychological') mental states/properties do not exist and our common-sense understanding is radically mistaken (as defended by Patricia Churchland and Paul Churchland)

Issues, including:

✓ Our certainty about the existence of our mental states takes priority over other considerations
✓ Folk psychology has good predictive and explanatory power (and so is the best hypothesis)
✓ The articulation of eliminative materialism as a theory is self-refuting

IV. Functionalism

Functionalism: all mental states can be characterised in terms of functional roles which can be multiply realised

Issues, including:

✓ The possibility of a functional duplicate with different qualia (inverted qualia)
✓ The possibility of a functional duplicate with no mentality/qualia (Ned Block's China thought experiment)
✓ The 'knowledge/Mary' argument can be applied to functional facts (no amount of facts about function suffices to explain qualia)

I. What do we mean by 'mind'?

Features of mental states

Many philosophers think that the mind has two important features, 'thought' and 'consciousness'. These terms pick out the two most important aspects of what we mean by 'having a mind'. We can talk about 'minds' or about 'mental properties', to include mental states, like beliefs, and mental events, like thinking a thought or feeling a pain. What distinguishes things that have minds or mental properties from things that don't is that things with minds have a 'point of view', a 'perspective', on the world. Things with a point of view experience the world, there is a 'subjectivity' to their existence, they are not just objects. And this involves ideas of being conscious and of being able to experience and think about things, to have beliefs and desires.

INTENTIONALITY

Thoughts are 'about' something, objects or events in the world. For example, I might have a belief *about Paris*, a desire *for chocolate*, be angry *at the government*, or intend *to go to the pub*. In all these cases, my state of mind is 'directed' towards an 'object', the thing I'm thinking about (Paris, chocolate, the government, going to the pub). This idea of 'directedness' is known as 'Intentionality'.

> From the Latin *intendere*, meaning 'to aim at'.

Intentionality is not about intentions (to mark the difference, I shall use a capital 'I' for 'Intentionality'). If I have an intention, I am 'aiming at' *doing* something. With Intentionality, it is the thought or mental state which 'aims at' its object, what it is about, and no 'doing' needs to be involved. Beliefs, desires, emotions all have Intentionality; they are all about or concern some object or other. They are all 'Intentional mental states'.

Whenever we think of, have a belief about, or desire something, we always conceive of it in a certain way, under a particular description. For example, in Sophocles' famous play *Oedipus Rex*, Oedipus kills his father and marries his mother. He doesn't want to do this. But he doesn't know who his (biological) parents are. On his journeys, he meets an old man in the road who gets in his way. Oedipus becomes very angry, and kills the old man. In fact, the man was his father, Laius. Oedipus was angry at the old man. Was he angry at his father? From his point of view, he wasn't – he didn't think of the old man as his father. So Intentional states represent the world in particular and partial ways. It's like seeing something – a desk, say – from a particular aspect; you can see it, but not all of it.

[handwritten: aspectual shape = perspective of thought]

What Intentional states represent – Paris, chocolate, the government, going to the pub, an old man – is called the 'Intentional object'. The way they represent that object we can call the 'aspectual shape' of the object. The Intentional object + the aspectual shape comprise the Intentional content of a mental state. The Intentional content of a mental state is the

Figure 3.1 Intentionality is a relation between a thought and what the thought is about

What is Intentionality?

answer to 'what are you thinking (about)?' The way the person answers the question will also tell us how they are thinking about it, e.g. 'I'm angry at the old man.'

We can now say that an Intentional mental state is a mental state with Intentional content. But we can add to this. We can have different mental states with the same Intentional content if we take different 'attitudes' to that content. For example, I can believe I'm arriving late; I can want to be arriving late; I can fear I'm arriving late; I can be pleased I'm arriving late. An Intentional state, then, comprises a particular 'attitude' or 'mode' towards a particular Intentional content. (Many philosophers call these mental states 'propositional attitudes', because the Intentional content is (usually) expressed as a proposition.)

There is a debate in the philosophy of mind whether *all* mental states have Intentionality and whether there are *other* mental properties besides the properties of Intentionality. One aspect of that debate concerns how we should best understand the second feature of the mind, consciousness.

PHENOMENAL PROPERTIES/QUALIA

Consciousness, especially the sort of consciousness involved in perception, sensation and emotion, has a 'feel' to it, a distinctive 'experiential quality'. The phrase often used to try to capture this experiential quality is 'what it is like'. There is something it is like to taste beer, to see a red rose, to feel sad.

'What it is like' here isn't meant to compare the experience to other experiences, it is meant to pick out how the experience is for the subject. When we make comparisons between experiences (e.g. 'Seeing a red rose is like seeing a ripe tomato'), we do so *in virtue of* what it is like to see a red rose in the sense meant here. It is the experience of redness that allows us to compare roses and tomatoes; and there is something it is like to experience redness. Similarly, there is something it is like to feel sad. I don't mean by this that feeling sad is like feeling some other emotion. I mean that there is a distinctive 'feeling' to sadness.

We can call the properties of an experience which give it its distinctive experiential quality 'phenomenal properties'. We are aware of these properties through consciousness and introspection, by turning our attention to our conscious experiences themselves.

> What are 'phenomenal properties'?

Some philosophers call phenomenal properties 'qualia'. However, to do this usually means that the philosopher has a particular *theory* of phenomenal properties in mind. Phenomenal properties are only qualia if they are *intrinsic*, *non-Intentional* properties of experience. What does this mean?

An intrinsic property is one that its possessor (in this case, the experience) has in and of its own, not in virtue of its relations to anything else. Think of the smell of coffee. It is the smell 'of coffee' because of its relation to the substance of coffee. That it is 'of coffee' is not an intrinsic property. But consider: something else could cause the *same* smell as the smell caused by coffee. So, what makes that smell the smell that it is, someone who believes in qualia would argue, is not the fact that it is caused by coffee. How that smell smells is an intrinsic property, because it would be that smell even if it wasn't caused by coffee. The smell can't be analysed just in terms of what causes it. Another example: pain wouldn't be pain if it didn't *feel* painful, whatever it is or isn't caused by. Phenomenal properties of experience, then, are intrinsic, and their identity is fixed not by what causes the experience (or what the experience causes) but by how the experience is in itself. Or so people who believe in qualia argue.

Intentional properties, we saw above, are properties of a mental state that enable it to be 'about' something, to represent what it does. So Intentional properties are a matter of how the mental state 'hooks up' to the world. So they are relational rather than intrinsic properties. That a belief is about Paris is a property it has in virtue of its relation to Paris; that a desire is for chocolate is a property it has in virtue to chocolate; and so on. So qualia, because they are intrinsic properties, are non-Intentional properties.

The syllabus adds that qualia are, by definition, 'introspectively accessible'. Introspection is just turning your attention to your own mind. Because qualia are properties of consciousness, they are properties we are consciously aware of. What it is like to smell coffee is something that we can know by being conscious of the smell of coffee. So we can 'access' qualia

What are qualia?

through introspection, by consciously turning our attention to our own conscious experiences.

But do qualia, in this more specific sense, exist? Or put another way, are phenomenal properties of consciousness qualia? Are they intrinsic and non-Intentional, or can they be analysed in terms of their Intentionality? For example, isn't the smell caused by coffee the smell *of* coffee? Doesn't this smell represent, isn't it 'about', coffee? People who believe in qualia would argue that it isn't. The smell that is caused by coffee isn't – in and of itself – *about* coffee, because exactly the same smell could be caused by something else. When we say that it is the smell *of* coffee, we add to the experience itself a thought about what caused the smell – and it is this thought, not the smell itself, that has Intentional content that links the smell to coffee. Our conscious experiences have an element of Intentional content, they also have an element – qualia – that is non-Intentional and intrinsic. We cannot, for instance, understand and explain how red looks to us or what it is like to feel pain just in terms of what these mental states are about, how they are related to the world.

This claim about the relationship between phenomenal properties and Intentional content is controversial. And that is why the debate over whether phenomenal properties are qualia – i.e. whether phenomenal properties are intrinsic, non-Intentional properties, or whether they are properties of Intentional content – continues. We won't try to resolve that debate, but we will look at the implications for saying that phenomenal properties are qualia for the metaphysics of mind, in particular towards the end of the chapter in the ISSUES for functionalism (p. 276) and the arguments supporting PROPERTY DUALISM (p. 291).

Overview of the six theories

Philosophy of mind is a branch of metaphysics, and different theories in philosophy of mind disagree on metaphysical questions about *what* exists and its nature. Questions about what exists are questions about ontology. In this section, I give a brief overview of the positions that we shall examine in this chapter. Not everything will be clear right away, as some of the terms will require further explanation. But it is worth having a sense of the different theories and how they relate to each other at the most general level. You may want to keep returning to this overview as you learn more about each theory.

'Ontology' comes from *ont-*, 'being', and *-ology*, 'study of'.

According to a traditional metaphysics, a substance is an entity, a thing, that does not depend on another entity for its continued existence. It has 'ontological independence'. For example, this book is a (physical) substance. Substances are also understood by contrast with properties.

1. Substances are what possess properties. The chair (substance) is solid (property). Properties can't exist without substances – they depend on substances to exist. Solidity depends on things being solid; the property 'being 1 metre long' depends on something being that long; and, Descartes claimed, thoughts can't exist without a thinker.

   ← Agree ?

2. Substances persist through changes in properties – something can change from being 1 metre long to being 1.1 metres long, e.g. by growing. Obviously, its property of 'being 1 metre long' does not persist through this change. It loses that property and gains another. Or again, a thinker can think a series of thoughts – the thinker persists, the thoughts do not.

Explain and illustrate the difference between substances and properties.

A central question in metaphysics of mind is 'is the mind a substance?' Can your mind exist on its own, independently, or is it dependent on something else in order to exist? In particular, is your mind dependent on your body, perhaps especially your brain, in order to exist at all? Many people believe, and many religions teach, that your mind can exist after death, i.e. the death of your body. This can mean many things, which we can't review here, but one common interpretation is that your mind is a separate substance from your body. If the mind is a substance, then the end of your body's existence is not the end of your mind's existence.

See the flow chart on page 179.

The view that the mind and the body are separate substances is known as *substance dualism*. Substance dualism claims that there are two fundamental *kinds* of substance – mental and physical. We can contrast substance dualism with idealism, the view that minds are the *only* kind of substance, and so whatever exists is either a mind or depends on a mind. However, the most popular alternative to dualism is the view that the only kind of substance is physical. On this view, because the mind is not a separate *thing*, it is more accurate to talk about mental *properties*. We have seen that these are properties of Intentionality and consciousness. Mental properties include mental states, such as beliefs, and mental events, such as having a thought or feeling pain. If the only kind of substance is physical, then mental properties are properties of a physical substance. You can think of the

See Epistemology, BERKELEY'S IDEALISM, p. 96.

physical substance that has such properties as either the person or the brain. If substance dualism is right, then mental properties are possessed by mental substances.

Suppose there is only physical substance. Our question about the mind now becomes a question about mental properties and their relation to physical properties. Are thoughts and conscious experiences themselves types of physical property (physical states and events)? There are many different types of physical property, e.g. size, shape, motion, mass, various forms of energy, chemical properties such as molecular structure, biological properties such as genetic code, and many others. Are mental properties, such as thinking about snow or feeling sad, also physical properties? One might argue, for instance, that they are simply neurological properties, e.g. to think about snow *just is* for certain neurons to fire in one's brain. This view is known as the *mind–brain type identity theory*.

Alternatively, one might argue that mental properties are not physical properties and can't even be understood or explained in terms of physical properties. (Neurons firing is just a physiological process, like food being digested. How can consciousness *be* neurons firing any more than it could be digestion?) Although mental properties are possessed by physical substances, they are completely different from any of the other properties physical substances possess. This view is *property dualism* – there is only one kind of substance but two radically different kinds of property.

There is a parallel between the metaphysics of property dualism and MORAL NON-NATURALISM (p. 357) in Moral Philosophy.

On the other hand, if we can't say that mental properties are physical properties, then perhaps we should question whether there are any mental properties as we usually think of them. *Eliminative materialism* claims just this. Our whole common-sense way of thinking about 'the mind' and mental properties is mistaken. This is very counter-intuitive – no such things as having a thought or feeling a pain? But we shall leave the arguments for the view for when we discuss it properly.

Another approach argues that all the views above are misled in their metaphysics. Mental 'properties' aren't like physical properties, 'only different'. Instead, talk of the mind, of thought and consciousness, should be understood in terms of behaviour and dispositions to behave. Wanting to go for a drive, feeling cross, thinking about your mother – these are each a matter of being disposed to behave in certain, perhaps highly complex, ways. This view is *philosophical behaviourism*.

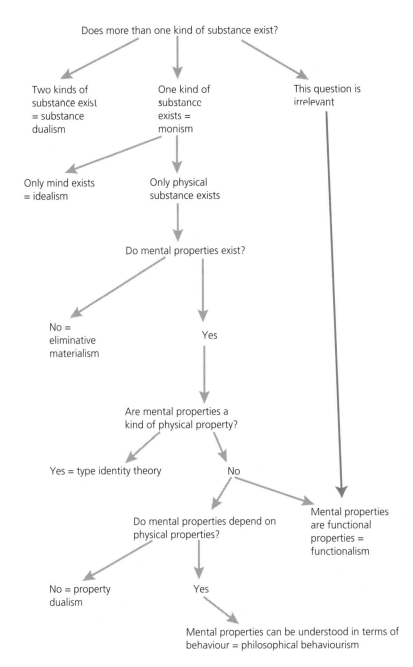

Figure 3.2 Flow chart of positions in metaphysics of mind

Our final theory follows this lead, but argues that thinking of mental properties just in terms of behaviour is too restrictive. We can talk more broadly in terms of the contribution of mental properties to how the person (or brain) functions, including the interactions of mental properties with each other, such as how one thought leads to another, how desires lead to emotions and vice versa, as well as how any and all of these lead to behaviour. This view is *functionalism*.

Key points: what do we mean by 'mind'?

- To have a mind or mental properties is to have a 'point of view' on the world, to have 'subjectivity'. This can be understood in terms of Intentionality and consciousness.
- Intentionality is the property that mental states have in being 'about' something. The Intentional content of a mental state is the answer to the question 'what are you thinking?'
- One central feature of consciousness is its experiential quality, 'what it is like' to undergo a particular experience. This is given by a mental state's phenomenal properties.
- Qualia are phenomenal properties, understood as intrinsic and non-Intentional properties. Whether this understanding of phenomenal properties is correct is an important debate in the metaphysics of mind.
- A substance is ontologically independent, not characterising or depending upon another entity for its existence. Substances possess properties and persist through change. A central question in metaphysics of mind is 'is the mind a substance?' Substance dualism claims that minds and bodies are distinct substances.
- If the mind is not a substance, and the only kind of substance is physical, then 'the mind' is composed of mental properties (properties of Intentionality and consciousness) possessed by a physical substance, such as the brain or person.
- Mind–brain type identity theory claims that mental properties are actually types of physical property, namely neurological properties. Property dualism claims that mental properties are not physical properties, and are not dependent on physical properties. Eliminativist materialism claims that some mental properties, as we usually think of them, don't exist.

- Philosophical behaviourism claims talk of the mind should be understood in terms of behaviour and dispositions to behave. Functionalism argues that mental properties are to do with how the mind or brain or person 'works', not to do with what they are made of.

II. Dualist theories: substance dualism

A. Substance dualism

Substance dualism claims that both minds and bodies – physical objects – exist. It is common in contemporary philosophy of mind to assume that bodies exist, and since we are not discussing idealism, we shall share that assumption. Substance dualism is controversial, therefore, in claiming that the mind is an ontologically distinct substance.

Substance dualism holds that there are two fundamentally different types of substances. In traditional dualism, these two types of substances are physical substances ('bodies', physical objects) and mental substances (minds). Minds are distinct from bodies – they are not bodies, they are not parts of bodies, and because they are substances, they are not properties of bodies either. Cartesian dualism – the form of substance dualism defended by Descartes, and the only form of substance dualism that we will discuss – also claims that minds do not depend on bodies in order to exist, i.e. minds can exist separated from any body. People who believe that the mind is the soul, and the soul can continue to exist without a body after death, are usually substance dualists.

If mental substances exist, they will be very unlike physical substances. For instance, we shall see that Descartes argues that they do not have any parts and do not even exist in space.

For a more detailed discussion of Descartes on mind and body, see extension material available on the companion website.

Descartes' indivisibility argument

DESCARTES, *MEDITATION* VI

In *Meditation* II, Descartes argues that mind and body have different essential properties – thought and extension. He understands thought in terms of consciousness and Intentionality; extension is the property having a size and taking up space. In *Meditation* VI, Descartes claims that this provides an argument that mind and body cannot be the same thing: if they were the same thing, they would have the same properties.

Leibniz later formalised this claim in his principle of the indiscernibility of identicals: if two things are identical (i.e. are just one thing), then they share all their properties. Why? Because one thing cannot have different properties from itself. So if two things have different properties, that proves that they cannot be one and the same thing.

But why think that the mind has different properties from the body? Descartes argues that, unlike physical objects, the mind does not have any parts and cannot be divided, and so it is not extended:

> When I consider the mind – i.e. consider myself purely as a thinking thing – I can't detect any parts within myself; I understand myself to be something single and complete ... the faculties of willing, of understanding, of sensory perception and so on, these are not *parts* of the mind, since it is one and the same mind that wills, understands and perceives.

Willing, understanding and perceiving are properties of the mind, different ways of thinking. By contrast, the body does have parts. You can literally lose part of your body, e.g. a hand. So the body (physical substance) is divisible into parts, but the mind (mental substance) is not. So mind and body are distinct types of thing.

Explain Leibniz's principle of the indiscernibility of identicals.

All quotations from Descartes' *Meditations* are from the translation by Jonathan Bennett available at www.earlymoderntexts.com.

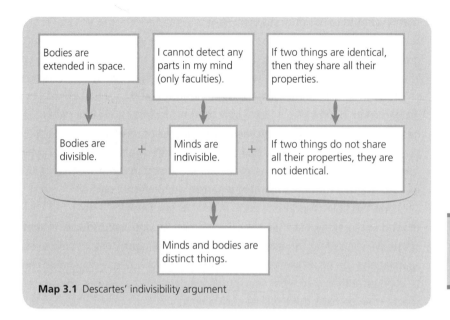

Map 3.1 Descartes' indivisibility argument

Outline and explain Descartes' indivisibility argument.

THE MENTAL IS DIVISIBLE IN SOME SENSE

Descartes' claim that we will, think, imagine, with the whole of our minds, not a literal part, is appealing. However, cases of mental illness, e.g. multiple personality syndrome, might be used to suggest that the mind can be divided. In such cases, it seems that some 'parts' of the person's mind are unable to communicate with other 'parts'. Theories of the unconscious suggest something similar: people may believe or desire one thing consciously and the opposite thing unconsciously. So it makes sense to talk about 'parts' of the mind.

Briefly explain the objection to the indivisibility argument that the mental is divisible.

However, Descartes could respond that *the way* in which the mind is 'divisible' is entirely different from the way in which the body is. Bodies are *spatially* divisible, while minds are only *functionally* divisible. The different 'parts' do different things, but they aren't in different spatial locations. So his argument that mind and body are different because they have different properties is unchallenged.

NOT EVERYTHING THOUGHT OF AS PHYSICAL IS DIVISIBLE

Is it true that physical substances are always divisible? When Descartes argued that extension is the *essential* property of physical objects, and that what is extended is divisible, was he right? We may question whether this theory of physical objects is correct. It was a matter of some debate in the seventeenth and eighteenth centuries whether physical objects are infinitely divisible. If you cut something up, can you always cut it into smaller pieces? The question is not whether we can actually do this right now, with the technology we have, but whether there are physical things that cannot be divided even in principle. If, for example, the smallest physical particles are best understood as packets of energy or force fields, then we can't further divide these – you can't have half a force field! Or again, perhaps not only force fields but also processes or waves or something else that can't be divided spatially form a fundamental part of the physical universe.

One possible response is that even if force fields or waves can't be divided in reality, we can still conceive of them having *half the size*. In that sense, we can still talk of spatial 'parts'. There is no *logical* limit to how small spatial parts can be. However, whether this is true or not may depend on the best physical theory of what space is. If we need to change our concept of space, then perhaps there will be such a limit.

The implication of these reflections is that it may not be an *essential* or *defining* property of every physical substance that it is divisible. There are some indivisible things, such as force fields, that are physical. In that case, the fact that the mind is not divisible does not entail that it is not physical. It could be a form of non-divisible physical thing. So even if Descartes is right that the mind isn't divisible, this doesn't prove that it isn't physical.

This line of thought does not show *how* the mind could be a non-divisible physical thing. After all, the mind is very different from subatomic particles! The objection only seeks to show that Descartes' indivisibility argument, as it is stated, fails.

Explain how the claim that not everything physical is divisible forms an objection to Descartes' indivisibility argument.

For Descartes' argument that the mind is a substance, which derives from his *cogito*, see extension material.

Thinking harder: is the mind a substance?

Perhaps a more conclusive objection to Descartes' indivisibility argument is that the argument *assumes* that minds exist as substances, and then argues that they are not physical substances. But suppose that minds are not 'things', not substances at all. Then minds are not divisible or indivisible – they simply don't exist. Instead, there are only mental properties – thoughts, desires, pains, etc. Perhaps they are properties of the brain. It is true that these properties are not spatially divisible, but that is because properties *in general* are not divisible. It is only substances that literally have parts. For example, while the brain has spatial parts, the temperature of the brain does not have parts, and yet it is a physical property of a physical substance. Properties themselves don't 'take up space' in the way that physical substances take up space, and so they can't be divided into spatial parts. But a substance that is spatially divisible can nevertheless possess properties that are not divisible.

In his argument, Descartes cannot assume that the theory of the mind supposed here is false. He needs to *show* that it is false. To do that, he first needs to show that the mind is a substance, not simply a way of talking about mental properties, and then he can use the indivisibility argument to show that it is not a physical substance.

Briefly explain the objection that the indivisibility argument only succeeds if we assume that the mind is a substance.

Descartes' conceivability argument

DESCARTES, *MEDITATION* VI

In *Meditation* VI, Descartes presents a second argument for substance dualism:

P1. I have a clear and distinct idea of myself as something that thinks and isn't extended.

P2. I have a clear and distinct idea of body as something that is extended and does not think.

P3. If I have a clear and distinct thought of something, God can create it in a way that corresponds to my thought.

C1. Therefore, God can create mind as something that thinks and isn't extended and body as something that is extended and does not think.

C2. Therefore, mind and body can exist independently of one another.

C3. Therefore, mind and body are two distinct substances.

See Epistemology, CLEAR AND DISTINCT IDEAS, p. 156.

Relies on God

See Epistemology, THE COGITO, p. 155, and THE CONCEPT OF A PHYSICAL OBJECT, p. 175.

In (P1) and (P2), Descartes appeals to the concepts of mind and body that he argued for in *Meditation* II. We can understand (P1) and (P2) to entail the claim that it is conceivable that mind can exist without body. Nothing in our concepts rules this out.

In *Meditation* VI, Descartes adds (P3). Assuming that God is omnipotent, the only reason for thinking that God cannot make something is that the concept of it is contradictory. The concepts of mind and body aren't self-contradictory. So God can create the mind and the body just as Descartes conceives of them – a thinking thing and an extended thing. We can summarise (P3), (C1) and (C2) in terms that don't refer to God: it is possible that mind can exist without body.

Finally, a quick reminder helps in understanding the inference from (C2) to (C3). A substance, we said above, is something that does not depend on another thing in order to exist. In other words, a substance can exist independently, on its own.

We now have a simpler form of this argument:

P1. It is conceivable that mind can exist without body.
C1. Therefore, it is possible that mind can exist without body.
C2. Therefore, mind and body are distinct substances.

vry fallible assumption

It is important for Descartes' argument that our clear and distinct ideas of mind and body are *complete* and *exclusive*. The mind is *nothing but* thought; the body is *nothing but* extension. We know this to be true, he says, because the ideas of mind and body are clear and distinct.

Outline and explain Descartes' conceivability argument.

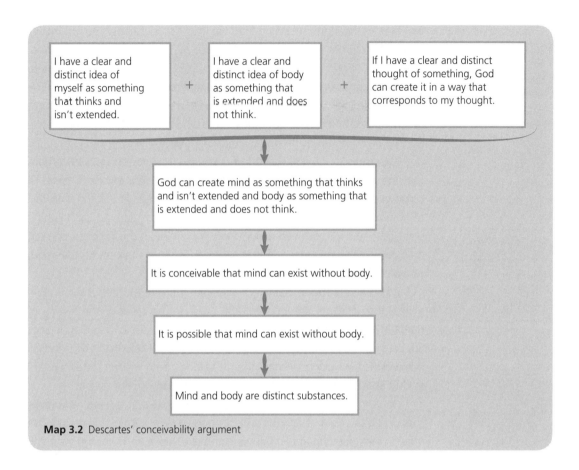

I have a clear and distinct idea of myself as something that thinks and isn't extended.

+

I have a clear and distinct idea of body as something that is extended and does not think.

+

If I have a clear and distinct thought of something, God can create it in a way that corresponds to my thought.

God can create mind as something that thinks and isn't extended and body as something that is extended and does not think.

It is conceivable that mind can exist without body.

It is possible that mind can exist without body.

Mind and body are distinct substances.

Map 3.2 Descartes' conceivability argument

MIND WITHOUT BODY IS NOT CONCEIVABLE

Many philosophers believe that Descartes' conceivability argument doesn't work. Objections to an argument either challenge the truth of one of the premises or they challenge an inference. On the simplified version of the argument, there is only one initial premise, (P1) 'It is conceivable that mind can exist without body.' There are then two inferences. First, Descartes infers possibility from conceivability, (C1): because it is conceivable that mind can exist without body, it is possible that mind can exist without body. The second inference is (C2), from the possibility that mind can exist without body to substance dualism. We will look at an objection to each stage of the argument. We start by challenging (P1).

Is Descartes right that we can conceive of mind and body as separate substances, that we can conceive of mind existing without body? Or more

This and the next two responses introduce some very difficult material. We will return to them in greater depth in RESPONSES TO THE ZOMBIE ARGUMENT, p. 311.

flying pigs

precisely, is he right to claim that we can do so clearly and distinctly? Descartes assumes that he can identify what it is to think from introspection. But what is thinking, *really*? What is its nature? If we knew the answers to these questions, we might find that we cannot clearly and distinctly conceive of thought (mind) without the body. Descartes may *think* that it is conceivable that mind and body are distinct substances when, in fact, it isn't conceivable. He may be confused or simply lack relevant information.

For example, we will see that PHILOSOPHICAL BEHAVIOURISM (p. 239) argues that the mind – mental states and events – should be analysed in terms of behaviour. To talk of beliefs, thoughts, desires, choices and so on is to talk of how something behaves. Now, without a body, something can't exhibit behaviour; and without behaviour, there is no mind. If this theory is correct, then once we've understood what we mean when we talk about the mind, we will realise that mind without body is inconceivable.

This is a very strong claim. For example, if it is right, then disembodied minds, such as God, are inconceivable. And yet for most of the history of humanity, people have claimed to be able to make sense of the idea of God. So, we may object, defending Descartes, that it is likely that philosophical behaviourism is wrong to think that in talking about mental states, we are talking about behaviour. And so mind without body is conceivable.

However, philosophical behaviourism provides just one argument supporting the claim that mind without body is inconceivable. There may be others. The general point is that we can make mistakes over what we think is conceivable.

Descartes accepts this. We can make mistakes, which is why we must get our ideas clear and distinct first. His claim is that we can't make mistakes with clear and distinct ideas. So to object to the first premise of the conceivability argument, what we actually need to argue is one of two things. Either we cannot *clearly and distinctly* conceive of the mind as separate from the body – as the analysis of philosophical behaviourism claims – or we can challenge Descartes' theory of clear and distinct ideas guaranteeing truth. Perhaps we can make mistakes concerning even what we conceive clearly and distinctly.

Explain the objection that we cannot clearly and distinctly conceive of the mind existing without the body.

Thinking harder: what is conceivable may not be metaphysically possible (I)

(11)–313

Let us suppose that we can conceive of our minds and bodies as distinct substances. Just because we can, this doesn't mean that our minds and bodies really *could be* distinct substances. Perhaps to exist at all, minds must depend on bodies in some way that we don't know about. This objection challenges the first inference in Descartes' (simplified) argument.

To understand the objection, we first need to clarify what it is for something to be 'metaphysically possible'. And to do that, we first need to understand physical possibility and logical possibility.

Physical possibility: Call the world we live in, as it is in fact, the 'actual world'. This world has particular laws of nature, such as the law of gravity and $e = mc^2$, and physical constants, such as the speed of light. These laws and their application to physical objects define what is physically possible. For instance, it is not (physically) possible for human beings to fly unaided (on Earth), because the upward thrust they can generate using their bodies cannot exceed the force of gravity. What is physically possible is what is possible given the laws of nature as they are in the actual world.

Logical possibility: Logical possibility is easiest to understand by relating it to analytic and synthetic propositions. All meaningful synthetic propositions describe what is logically possible. True analytic propositions describe what is logically necessary (what must be the case). False analytic propositions describe what is logically impossible (what cannot be the case). For example, it is logically impossible for there to be a square with three sides. The phrase 'a square with three sides' is conceptually incoherent, i.e. the meanings of the terms contradict each other, and so no such thing can exist. Anything that is not logically impossible is logically possible (or logically necessary).

So, we can think of logical possibility as conceptual possibility – what our concepts allow as making sense. We can argue that this is the same as what is conceivable – what we can imagine without self-contradiction.

The laws of nature seem contingent, i.e. it seems possible that they could have been otherwise. Light could have gone faster or slower; the ratio of mass to energy could have been $e = mc$, and so on. Of course, these things aren't *physically* possible. But they are, it seems, logically

See Epistemology, ANALYTIC/SYNTHETIC PROPOSITIONS, p. 115.

See Epistemology, NECESSARY/CONTINGENT TRUTH, p. 116.

possible. Nothing in the *concept* of light entails that it *must* travel at 299,792 kilometres per second. Or again, it isn't *logically* impossible that human beings can fly unaided, just physically impossible.

Everything that is physically possible is logically possible (unless our concepts are terribly muddled!), but not everything that is logically possible is physically possible.

Metaphysical possibility: Some philosophers want to stop there, with two types of possibility – physical and logical. But debates in metaphysics, including the metaphysics of mind, over the last forty years have led many philosophers to argue that there is a third type of possibility, metaphysical possibility. The reason is that analytic truths and necessary truths may come apart.

For example, 'WATER' and 'H$_2$O' are different concepts, and before the discovery of hydrogen and oxygen, people knew about water. They had the concept of WATER, but not the concepts of HYDROGEN and OXYGEN, and so not the concept of H$_2$O. And so they didn't know that water is H$_2$O. Even after hydrogen and oxygen were discovered, someone may have thought 'I wonder whether water is made of hydrogen and oxygen or something else.' So 'water is H$_2$O' is not analytically true. On this understanding, it is *conceivable*, or *logically* possible, that water is not H$_2$O.

When a word refers to a concept, I put it in capital letters.

analytic relying on synthetic?

See also THINKING HARDER: GOOD IS THE SAME PROPERTY AS WHAT GOD WILLS, p. 47.

Figure 3.3 Water

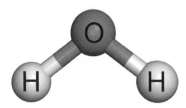

Figure 3.4 A molecule of H$_2$O

But water and H_2O are one and the same thing – the two concepts refer to just one thing in the world. Water is *identical* to H_2O. Now, nothing can be what it is not. So if the property of being water and the property of being H_2O are *one and the same* property, you can't have 'one' without 'the other'. If *A* is the same thing as *B*, then *A* and *B* can't be separated – there is just one thing here. So while we have two concepts – WATER and H_2O – there is only one property that they both pick out in the world.

— different chemical states?

What this is means is that, although it is logically possible for water not to be H_2O, it is *metaphysically* impossible for water to be anything other than H_2O. It seems that not everything that is logically possible is metaphysically possible.

Why don't we just say that it is physically impossible for water to be anything other than H_2O? This claim is certainly true, but it isn't strong enough. If the laws of nature are contingent, then perhaps they could be different. Light could still be light but travel at a different speed, couldn't it? The claim with water and H_2O is stronger. Water wouldn't be water if it wasn't H_2O. If the laws of nature changed, so that hydrogen and oxygen never bonded and there was no such thing as H_2O, then there would be no such thing as water. There couldn't be water, but with a different chemical composition.

— why?

We now have a sense of what metaphysical possibility is, and how it is different from both physical possibility and logical possibility. What is metaphysically possible is constrained by the real nature or identity of things. We also have an example of how something could be conceivable but not metaphysically possible, namely thinking that water is not H_2O but something distinct.

Another example is often used to try to make the point that what we *think* is distinct may not always be distinct. Suppose I believe that the Masked Man has robbed the bank. I also believe that my father has not robbed the bank. Clearly, I conceive that the Masked Man is not my father. It is logically impossible for one and the same person both to rob the bank and not to rob the bank. Does this entail that it is metaphysically possible that the Masked Man is not my father?

In one sense, we might say that the Masked Man could be anyone – nobody knows who he is. But we also rightly think that whoever the

Explain the differences between physical, metaphysical and logical possibility.

Masked Man is can't be someone else. No one can be somebody else. I can't be you, and you can't be me. So if my father is not the Masked Man, it is metaphysically impossible that my father is the Masked Man. And if my father is the Masked Man, then it is metaphysically impossible that my father is not the Masked Man. (You can run the same argument with Batman and Bruce Wayne …)

Now I can conceive that my father is not the Masked Man (it is logically possible). But this doesn't show that it is metaphysically possible that my father is not the Masked Man. If the Masked Man *is* my father, then it is metaphysically impossible for my father to be a different person from the Masked Man. From my conceiving that 'two' people are distinct, we cannot infer that it is metaphysically possible that they are distinct.

We can now apply these ideas to Descartes' argument. Descartes argues that it is possible for the mind to exist independently of the body, because he can conceive of it existing without the body. In other words, he argues that because it is logically (conceptually) possible for the mind to exist without the body, it is also metaphysically possible. But this doesn't follow. Perhaps unknown to him, the mind is not an ontologically independent substance, and it is metaphysically impossible for it to exist separately from the body (just as it is metaphysically impossible for water to exist without H_2O).

Explain the objection that Descartes mistakenly infers what is metaphysically possible from what is conceivable.

Reply

However, Descartes is happy to grant that we cannot *in general* infer what is (metaphysically) possible from what we think. But in the case of *clear and distinct ideas*, the inference is justified. For example, we may *rightly* claim that it is impossible for a triangle to have interior angles that don't add up to 180 degrees just because it is inconceivable that they should. Likewise, because he can *clearly and distinctly* conceive that mind and body are distinct substances, Descartes argues, it follows that it is possible that they are.

This provides a contrast with the Masked Man. My conceptions of my father and the Masked Man are not clear and distinct in the way that Descartes requires. It is only while we do not know who we are thinking

false analytic?

could do the opposite in response to show he's wrong

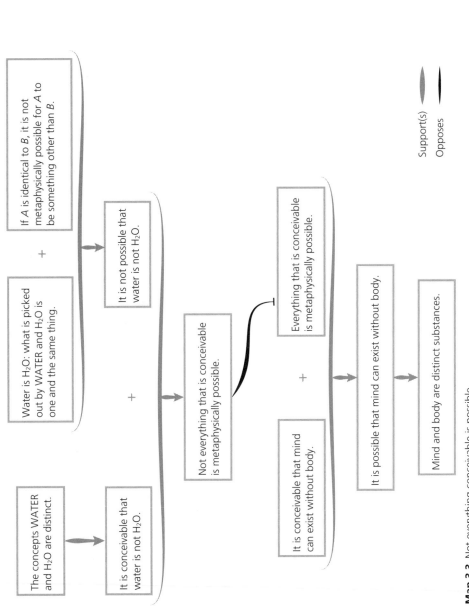

The concepts WATER and H₂O are distinct.

It is conceivable that water is not H₂O.

Water is H₂O: what is picked out by WATER and H₂O is one and the same thing.

If A is identical to B, it is not metaphysically possible for A to be something other than B.

It is not possible that water is not H₂O.

Not everything that is conceivable is metaphysically possible.

It is conceivable that mind can exist without body.

Everything that is conceivable is metaphysically possible.

It is possible that mind can exist without body.

Mind and body are distinct substances.

Support(s)

Opposes

Map 3.3 Not everything conceivable is possible

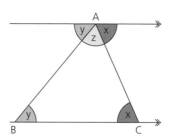

Figure 3.5 The interior angles of a triangle add up to 180 degrees

of when we think of the Masked Man that we can think that the Masked Man could be anyone. And so, Descartes would argue, the Masked Man fallacy cannot be used as an objection to his argument.

Does this response work against the case of water and H_2O as well? Were people who wondered about whether water is H_2O simply not thinking clearly and distinctly? Descartes could argue that they were not – our sense experience, e.g. of water, doesn't tell us what water really is. By contrast, he holds, introspection does tell us clearly and distinctly what mind is. We fully understand what the mind is by reflecting on our own mind, and we fully understand what bodies are by reflecting on our experience of bodies. Because we have this understanding, we can know that minds do not depend on bodies to exist, and are therefore separate substances.

See Epistemology,
THE CONCEPT OF A
PHYSICAL OBJECT, p. 175.

WHAT IS METAPHYSICALLY POSSIBLE TELLS US NOTHING ABOUT THE ACTUAL WORLD

Suppose that it is metaphysically possible that the mind can exist as a distinct substance. Does it follow that the mind *does* exist as a distinct substance?

Let us assume, for the purposes of argument, that we conceive of mind as something that thinks and of body as something that is extended. From this, it does not follow that the mind exists as something that thinks *and isn't extended* or that body exists as something that is extended *and does not think*. There is nothing in the initial conceptions of mind and body that oppose each other. There is no contradiction in conceiving of mind as something that is extended and thinks, or again as the thinking part of something that is extended. Likewise, there is no contradiction in conceiving of body as something that is extended, but which may, in some instances, also think. If this is right, then we can conceive of mind and body as distinct substances, or we can think of thought and extension as properties of the same substance.

Assume that whatever we can clearly and distinctly conceive is metaphysically possible. Therefore, if Descartes is right about clear and distinct ideas, it is metaphysically possible that mind and body are distinct substances. But equally, given what was just argued, it is metaphysically possible that thought and extension are two properties of a single substance. What we need to know is *which option is true in the actual world*. Simply knowing what is metaphysically possible does not tell us which possibility correctly describes reality. So just because it is metaphysically possible for mind and body to be separate substances doesn't show that they are separate substances.

However, we should accept that what is metaphysically *impossible* does tell us something about how things actually are in the world, because what is metaphysically impossible cannot exist. If Descartes could show that it is metaphysically impossible for mind and body to be the same substance, that would show that they must be separate substances. So he could argue that we cannot clearly and distinctly conceive of mind and body as *anything other* than separate substances – just as we cannot clearly and distinctly conceive of a triangle not having interior angles that add up to 180 degrees. Something about our concept of mind, e.g. its indivisibility, means that we cannot conceive of it as extended; and something about our concept of body (what?) means that we cannot conceive of it as having thought. But is this right?

> Explain the objection that what is metaphysically possible does not tell us about the actual world, first in prose, then using an argument map.

> Do Descartes' arguments succeed in establishing substance dualism?

Key points: substance dualism

- Substance dualism holds that there are two types of substances, mental substances (minds) and physical substances (bodies). It holds that minds are not bodies, parts of bodies or properties of bodies. Cartesian substance dualism also claims that minds can exist independently of bodies.
- Descartes argues that bodies are divisible into spatial parts, but minds have no such parts. Therefore, the mind is a distinct substance from the body. (This relies on Leibniz's principle of the indiscernibility of identicals: if two things are identical (i.e. are just one thing), then they share all their properties.)

- We can object that not everything that is physical is divisible. Therefore, showing that the mind isn't divisible doesn't show that it isn't physical. We can also object that Descartes' indivisibility argument assumes that minds exist as substances.
- Descartes argues that he has clear and distinct ideas of mind and body as separate substances, and that God can create whatever Descartes has a clear and distinct idea of. Therefore, mind and body can exist as, and therefore are, separate substances.
- We can question whether it is conceivable that the mind can exist without the body. This thought may be confused or uninformed.
- Many philosophers distinguish between physical, metaphysical and logical possibility. What is physically possible is possible according to the laws of nature as they happen to be in the actual world. What is logically possible is anything that it is not conceptually self-contradictory. What is metaphysically possible is what is logically possible, constrained by the real nature or identity of things.
- We can object that Descartes is wrong to infer that, because he can conceive of the mind existing without the body, it is metaphysically possible for it to exist without the body. Descartes replies that the inference is justified if our conceptions are clear and distinct.
- We can object that not only can we conceive of mind and body as distinct substances, we can also conceive of them as distinct properties of the same substance. Both are metaphysical possibilities. So we cannot infer from how it is metaphysically possible for the mind and body to be to what they are in the actual world.

PROPERTY DUALISM and issues facing it are discussed on pp. 291–333.

B. Issues facing substance dualism

Issues facing interactionist substance dualism

Descartes claimed that mind and body causally interact with one another. Walking, talking and other bodily movements are caused by thoughts, decisions and feelings, and we feel pain from physical causes and acquire beliefs from our sense experience. Cartesian substance dualism is most often rejected because it cannot give an adequate account of the causal role of the mind. The objection focuses on explaining the causation of physical events by mental events.

THE CONCEPTUAL INTERACTION PROBLEM

Nothing seems more obvious than that the mind and the body interact with each other, e.g. I decide to phone a friend and move my body to do so. But how is it that a mental substance, which is not in space and has no physical force, can affect a physical substance, which is in space and moved by physical forces? This puzzle was expressed to Descartes by Elisabeth, Princess of Bohemia.

THE CORRESPONDENCE BETWEEN PRINCESS ELISABETH OF BOHEMIA AND RENE DESCARTES, LETTERS FROM MAY 1643

Princess Elisabeth of Bohemia posed this objection in terms of pushing and movement.

P1. Physical things only move if they are pushed.
P2. Only something that is extended and can touch the thing that is moved can exert such a force.
P3. But the mind has no extension, so it can't touch the body.
C1. Therefore, the mind cannot move the body.

In fact, as Descartes points out in his reply (letter of 21 May 1643), this isn't an accurate understanding of how things are moved. For example, we might explain why something falls in terms of its weight. But weight doesn't 'push' the object whose weight it is! Weight is the result of the force of gravity on the mass of an object, and gravity is a force of attraction that operates without needing contact between the two physical objects.

> Explain Elisabeth's objection to causal interaction between mind and body.

But this is all a matter of details. We can generalise from the force of pushing to force more generally. If the mind is just thought, it has no physical force of any kind. In that case, how could it possibly affect the body? (We can understand how something very refined, like a gas, can have causal effects, but the mind is not a kind of very insubstantial matter.) And the mind is *not in space* at all. If causation is thought to involve any kind of spatial relationship between cause and effect, the problem is particularly pressing. Clearly nothing can come into a spatial relationship with a mind which occupies no space.

Hume - no such thing as causation

P1. The movement of a physical object is only initiated by some physical force, exerted at some point in space.

P2. If dualism is true, then the mind is not in space and cannot exert any physical force.

C1. Therefore, if dualism is true, the mind cannot cause any physical object to move.

C2. Therefore, either dualism is false or the mind cannot cause (any part of) the body to move.

In a later letter (1 July 1643), Elisabeth says that she accepts, from her own experience, that the mind *does* cause the body to move. The problem is that experience gives us no indication of *how* this happens. She continues, 'This leads me to think that the soul has properties that we don't know – which might overturn your doctrine … that the soul is not extended …. Although extension is not necessary to thought, it isn't inconsistent with it either.' So, we can continue the argument:

P3. The mind can cause the body to move.

C3. Therefore, dualism is false.

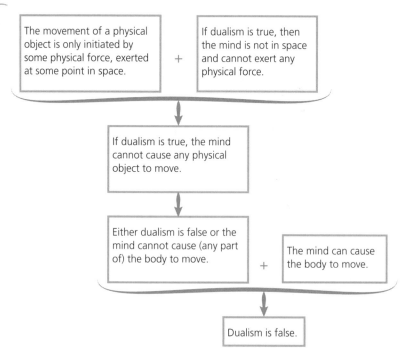

Map 3.4 The conceptual interaction problem

But perhaps it is a mistake to try to understand the mind's power to act on physical objects in terms of how physical objects act on each other. We have a tendency to conceive of *all* causation in terms of the causation of physical events by other physical events. But perhaps this is mistaken.

Then how *should* we think about mental causation? Certainly, we can reflect on the fact that we can move our bodies at will. But as Elisabeth points out, the question remains *how*, according to dualism, this is possible.

The challenge is just as daunting when thinking about how physical objects could cause changes in the mind. How can something which is *not* thought or consciousness bring about changes in a substance that is entirely thought and consciousness? Physical causation operates, as we said, through the exertion of forces at particular points in space. But it seems impossible to exert a physical force on a mental substance which has no spatial location.

> Explain the conceptual problem regarding mental causation that faces interactionist dualism.

THE EMPIRICAL INTERACTION PROBLEM

Interactionist (substance) dualism also faces some empirical challenges. The first is very general. The law of the conservation of energy states that in any closed system, the total amount of energy in that system remains unchanged. The energy can only change forms, e.g. movement can produce heat. A 'closed system' is simply one that doesn't interact with anything outside itself. The (physical) universe is usually understood as a closed system, because there is nothing 'outside' the universe that it can interact with. So the total amount of energy in the universe can't change. If something in the universe, such as your body, moved without that energy coming from some other physical source, the law of the conservation of energy would not be true of the universe. So:

P1. If the mind, as a non-physical substance, moved the body, the total amount of energy in the universe would increase.

the energy comes from food?

P2. If the total amount of energy in the universe increased, the law of the conservation of energy would not apply to the universe, and the universe is not a closed system.

C1. Therefore, if the mind moved the body, the law of the conservation of energy would not apply to the universe, and the universe is not a closed system.

C2. Therefore, because the mind, which changes the physical energy in the universe, is not itself physical, physics cannot give us the complete, correct account of physical energy in the universe.

While we may want to say that physics doesn't tell us everything about what exists, interactionist dualism entails that physics isn't even the correct account of what exists *physically*. We can make this more specific to link it to the conceptual issues above: physics is wrong to think that physical movement can only be caused by a physical force.   *true*

The second empirical challenge is much more specific. Current science indicates that movements of the body are caused by physical events in the brain. So, if the mind moves the body, it does so by changing what happens in the brain. We may object that we have no evidence of the mind changing what happens in the brain.

That is true, but we have no evidence that the claim is false either. This is because, while neuroscience is making good progress, we still have no clear account of the very complicated causation involved in something like making a choice. But we may think that neuroscience could discover the complete story in time. If interactionist dualism is true, then it seems that what neuroscience must discover is that some events in the brain *have no physical* cause, because they are caused by the mind.

It is common, but perhaps a mistake, to think that there is empirical *evidence* against substance dualism. The issues are so complex – How does the brain work? Is the universe a closed system? – that we don't yet have definitive evidence one way or another. So both the objections presented focus instead on the incompatibility between interactionist dualism and empirical science.

how would they discover them?

> ?? ?
>
> **Can interactionist dualism solve the problems of interaction between mind and body?**

Issues facing epiphenomenalist substance dualism

> **An 'epiphenomenon' is a by-product, something that is an effect of some process, but with no causal influence.**

example?

We could accept that the objections above show that, if substance dualism is true, then mental causation is impossible. But this doesn't undermine substance dualism if we accept epiphenomenalism, the view that the mind has no causal powers. On this view, the mind does not cause any physical events, so there is no problem of how they do so. But nor do mental events cause other mental events. (For example, the theory of 'occasionalism' claimed that nothing has causal powers except God. Whenever it seems like a thought causes me to say something, or a desire causes me to act, what actually happens is that God brings about the effect – my having the thought or the desire is merely the 'occasion' for God's action.)

Phenomology–consciousness objects of direct perception

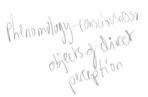

While it is more common for property dualists than substance dualists to be epiphenomenalists, it is worth briefly considering two objections that can be raised against epiphenomenalist theories at this point.

The first is that epiphenomenalism simply doesn't accord with our experience. Surely we *experience* causal connections between our mental states, and between our mental states and our behaviour. It is part of my experience that whether I feel pain makes a difference both to what I think (e.g. that I'm in pain) and to what I do (e.g. jump around shouting). Similarly, when I say what I think, it is part of my experience that my thought is the cause of what I say. It is part of the 'phenomenology of our mental life' that we interact with the physical world outside us, that mental processes unfold over time, that our thoughts, feelings, etc., respond to one another and have effects. Epiphenomenalism has to argue that my experience is completely misleading in this respect, because there are no causal connections between my pain, thoughts, and other mental states or events and anything that follows them.

Second, epiphenomenalism makes it hard to understand how we have knowledge of our own mental states. How do I know that I am in pain when I am? The obvious answer is that my belief that I am in pain is caused by my pain itself. I can tell that I am in pain just from introspection. But if epiphenomenalism is true, pain doesn't cause anything, even my belief that I am in pain. This threatens a natural account of our knowledge of our mental states. If my thoughts and feelings don't cause my beliefs about my mind, then I could have those beliefs whatever my mental states, just as long as the causes of my beliefs (whatever they are – perhaps brain processes, perhaps God) operate in the same way. In other words, whatever causes me to believe that I am in pain could cause me to have this belief even when I am not in pain. And so my beliefs about my mind are unjustified and unreliable. So I can't know my own mind.

For a fuller discussion of these issues, see ISSUES FACING EPIPHENOMENALIST PROPERTY DUALISM (p. 325).

would Hume be this?

Outline and explain two challenges facing epiphenomenalist dualism, first in prose then using argument maps.

The problem of other minds (I)

The problem of other minds is the question of how we can know that there are minds other than our own. We each experience our own minds *directly*, from 'within'. We can each apprehend our sensations and emotions in a way that is 'felt'. We can know what we want or believe through introspection (at least, if epiphenomenalism is false!). But our knowledge of other people's

Figure 3.6 Can you tell from her behaviour whether she has a mind?

minds is very different, it seems. We cannot experience other people's mental states. It seems that all we have to go on is other people's *behaviour*, what is expressed through their bodies.

This raises an important challenge for substance dualism. If minds and bodies are entirely independent, then how can I infer from seeing a body that there is a mind 'attached'? The two things exist independently of one another. So other 'people' – other bodies – could all be machines, programmed to behave as they do, but with no minds. How can I know otherwise?

THE ARGUMENT FROM ANALOGY

The argument from analogy claims that we can use the behaviour of other people to infer that they have minds too.

Explain the argument from analogy for the existence of other minds.

P1. I have a mind.
P2. I know from experience that my mental states cause my behaviour.
P3. Other people have bodies similar to mine and behave similarly to me in similar situations.
C1. Therefore, by analogy, their behaviour has the same type of cause as my behaviour, namely mental states.
C2. Therefore, other people have minds.

The argument is perhaps the 'common-sense' position on how to solve the problem of other minds. But we can object to its use of induction. The conclusion that other people have minds is based on a single case – mine. This is like saying 'that dog has three legs; therefore, all dogs have three legs'. You can't generalise from one case, because it could be a special case. Perhaps I am the only person to have a mind. And we can't get around this by first checking that other people have minds to show that I am not a special case!

However, instead of talking about the causal relation in the single case of my behaviour and my mind, we can formulate the argument to cite many instances of behaviour which we know to have a mental cause.

P1. This behaviour has a mental cause.
P2. That behaviour has a mental cause.
P3. That third behaviour has a mental cause.
P4. Etc.

C1. Therefore, many behaviours have a mental cause (I know this from my own experience).
P5. Other people exhibit the same types of behaviour as cited above.
C2. Therefore, those behaviours also have mental causes.
C3. Therefore, other people have minds.

However, this faces two objections. First, although many behaviours of which I have experience have mental causes, not all of them do. Sometimes I do something without being aware of a mental cause. So while (C1) is correct, it isn't strong enough to support the claim that the behaviour of other people also has mental causes – perhaps, like some of my own behaviour, it does not. Second, the argument relies on the contentious claim that similar effects (behaviour) have similar causes (mental states). But sometimes similar effects can have different causes. Perhaps those instances of other people's behaviour that are similar to my behaviour have different (non-mental) causes.

> Can I justifiably infer the existence of other minds from the fact that my mental states often cause my behaviour?

THE EXISTENCE OF OTHER MINDS IS THE BEST HYPOTHESIS
Rather than inferring from one's own case to other minds, we may employ a standard form of theoretical scientific reasoning, inference to the best explanation. This argument doesn't appeal to the first-personal experience of having a mind nor does it draw an analogy between my behaviour and that of other people. Instead, the question is entirely third-personal. Why do human beings behave as they do? What hypothesis best explains people's behaviour in general? The claim is that the best explanation is that people have minds, and that their mental states cause them to behave as they do. And if people in general have minds, then obviously people other than me have minds.

> See HYPOTHETICAL REASONING, p. 8.

Why think that the best hypothesis for explaining human behaviour is that people have minds that cause their behaviour? In particular, why think that it is a better hypothesis than the claim that people are machines without minds?

One way philosophers have developed the argument is to analyse mental states as the 'inner' states of an organism that respond to the environment and cause behaviour – this is what mental states *are*. This claim is defended by FUNCTIONALISM (p. 268). Pain makes you respond quickly to prevent further damage; desire makes you pursue something you want; belief gives you information you need in order to pursue desires – and so on.

The theory that there are such 'inner' states that cause behaviour is then said to be the best explanation of behaviour. (A substance dualist can then argue that these 'inner' states are states of a distinct mental substance, rather than, say, states of the brain.)

This line of argument faces three challenges. First, it depends on functionalism being the right account of what mental states are. We will leave that objection for when we discuss functionalism.

Second, if we understand the mind in terms of its causal relations to behaviour, then we need to solve the problem of how the mind can cause physical events. As we saw in ISSUES FOR INTERACTIVE SUBSTANCE DUALISM (p. 196), substance dualism has difficulties in explaining mental causation. However, the dualist can respond that to solve the problem of other minds, we only need the claim *that* behaviour is caused by mental states, not an explanation of how.

Third, we can object that the belief that people have minds is *not a hypothesis*, nor do we infer, on the basis of evidence, that they have minds. Consider: have you ever *seriously* wondered whether people have minds and then used their behaviour as evidence that they do? This whole way of understanding the way we think about minds is mistaken. We will see this thought developed by PHILOSOPHICAL BEHAVIOURISM (p. 239).

In Epistemology, a similar line of objection was presented by direct realism in arguing that THE EXISTENCE OF MIND-INDEPENDENT OBJECTS IS NOT A HYPOTHESIS, p. 90.

Thinking harder: Avramides on Descartes' solution

The problem of other minds seems particularly challenging to substance dualism, because it claims that mind and body are completely separate things. So a human body, it seems, really could be just a machine, programmed to behave in certain ways but with no thought or consciousness, because these properties belong to something entirely different to a body. So what did Descartes say about how we know that other people have minds? Many philosophers have thought that he offers a version of the argument from analogy, but Anita Avramides argues that this is a misinterpretation.

AVRAMIDES, *OTHER MINDS*, CH. 2

At the end of *Meditation* II, Descartes says 'if I look out of a window and see men crossing the square … I say that I **see** the men themselves … Yet do I see more than hats and coats which could conceal robots? I judge that they are men.' This can sound like he is entertaining the idea that what we 'see' when looking at other people could either be men, i.e. with minds, or machines, i.e. without minds. But we infer – 'judge' – that they are men.

But, argues Avramides, there are two objections to understanding Descartes in this way. First, the argument from analogy uses two separate observations and two separate judgements, namely that others behave as I do, and so (by analogy) others must have a mind as I do. By contrast, Descartes suggests there is just one judgement in observing another mind.

Second, the context for this passage in Descartes is the relation between perception and judgement. Using an example of wax that undergoes changes when heated, Descartes has argued that our sense experience doesn't give us knowledge of what physical objects are. The sensory qualities of the wax change, but we judge that the wax remains the same thing. It is our judgement, not our perception, that gives us knowledge that the wax exists. Although we say we 'see' the wax (through vision), in fact we judge (through understanding) that it is present from what we see. Similarly, we ordinarily say that we see men, but we really see hats and coats, and from this, judge that what we see are men. Descartes does not say we see the body of a man and then judge that this body has a mind. And unlike the argument from analogy, he does not proceed from his own case – that he has a mind is not a premise in his argument. He is simply not discussing the problem of other minds.

See Epistemology, THE CONCEPT OF A PHYSICAL OBJECT, p. 175.

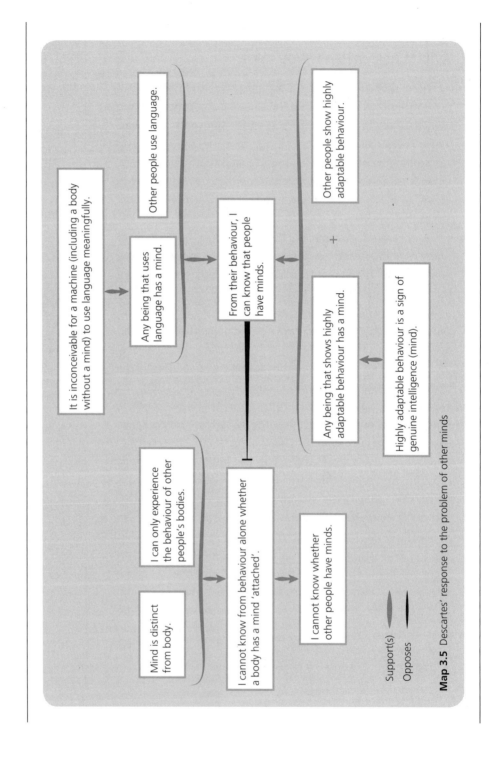

Map 3.5 Descartes' response to the problem of other minds

In fact, Descartes *never* discusses the problem of other minds as such. However, we can find his solution to the problem by looking at what he says about people and animals. Descartes believes that, unlike people, animals are machines, without minds. All bodies, insofar as they are bodies alone, are machines. Their functions and their behaviour can be seen to follow from the arrangement of their parts. This can seem to raise the problem of other minds in a very acute form: how do we know that other people aren't simply like other animals, without minds?

Descartes' answer is that there are two differences between animals (without minds) and people (with minds). First, people use language, while animals don't use language. It is inconceivable for a machine to answer questions meaningfully, Descartes claims, so our use of language shows that we have a mind while they do not. Second, people are capable of highly adaptable behaviour, and while some animals can show adaptable behaviour in some situations, they lack adaptability in others. If they had genuine intelligence (mind), there would be no such asymmetry.

So, a person is both mind and body, united. What distinguishes a person is language and adaptable behaviour. When we encounter others, we observe not just their hats and coats, but their use of language and adaptable behaviour. On this basis, we judge that this other is a real man (i.e. with a mind), not a machine.

yes they do

? How do we know that other people have minds?

Substance dualism makes a 'category mistake'

We have seen that the metaphysical framework for Cartesian dualism understands the mind in terms of substances and properties. It claims that mind and body are different substances, and that just as there are physical properties and processes, so there are mental properties and processes. Gilbert Ryle argues that this way of understanding the mind is mistaken.

RYLE, *THE CONCEPT OF MIND*, CH. 1

Ryle calls substance dualism 'the dogma of the Ghost in the Machine'. The mistake that it makes, he argues, is a 'category mistake'. What does that mean? Suppose someone is shown around Oxford University – they see the colleges, the buildings with the different faculties and departments, the administrative buildings. But then they ask, 'I've seen the colleges, the faculties, the administration. But where is the university?' They have misunderstood the concept of 'university', thinking that the university is another thing, alongside the colleges, faculties and administration. The person has made a category mistake. The university is not like this; it is how everything that the person has seen is organised.

Or again, suppose someone is having a game of cricket explained to them. The bowler, batters, wicketkeeper and fielders are all pointed out and their tasks explained. But then the person says, 'I've heard a lot about the importance of team spirit. Who does that?' They have misunderstood the concept and made a category mistake. The exercise of team spirit is not another task like bowling or fielding, nor is someone who is bowling and exercising team spirit doing two separate things. Team spirit is about *how* the players play the game together.

Concepts belong to different logical categories – different ways in which it makes sense to use a concept. A category mistake is to treat a concept as belonging to a different logical category from the one it actually belongs to.

According to Ryle, substance dualism makes the category mistake of thinking that the mind is like the body – another 'thing', a distinct, complex, organised unit subject to distinct relations of cause and effect. The mistake is to think that physical and mental concepts operate in the same way, in the same logical framework of 'things' and 'causes', 'substances' and 'properties'. But to 'have' a mind is not to be in possession of a thing, so that if you have a mind and a body, you have two things. (And 'losing your mind' isn't like losing your keys!) Similarly, talk of mental states and processes

?

What is a category mistake?

understands 'states' and 'processes' along the lines of physical states and processes. But believing something is not a state in the same sense as the physical state of being solid, and doing mental arithmetic is not a process in the same sense as the physical process of a log burning.

Around the time of Descartes, science reached the stage of plausibly claiming that all physical processes could be explained in non-rational, mechanical terms. So the question arose, what is the place of the mind? Ryle argues that people mistakenly inferred that mental concepts, if they don't characterise physical processes, must refer to non-physical, non-mechanical processes which occur in non-physical substance. He calls this the 'para-mechanical hypothesis'. But just as 'Oxford University' doesn't refer to another thing alongside the buildings and faculties, and 'team spirit' doesn't refer to another activity alongside bowling, batting and catching, mental concepts aren't like physical concepts, only applied to a separate thing called 'the mind'. Instead, we need to think again about the logical analysis of mental concepts – what do they mean, how do we use them? We will look at Ryle's theory in RYLE'S 'SOFT' BEHAVIOURISM (p. 245).

Explain Ryle's objection that substance dualism rests on a category mistake, first in prose, then using an argument map.

Key points: issues facing substance dualism

- Interactionist dualism claims that the mind can cause physical (and other mental) events. It faces the problem of explaining how the mind can cause physical events, given that it is not in space and exerts no physical force.
- The conceptual problem is understanding how this is possible. The empirical problem is that it conflicts with the presuppositions of empirical science.
- Epiphenomenalist dualism claims that the mind has no causal powers. We can object that we experience the causal connections between our mental states and behaviour, and that to argue that these experiences are mistaken is very counter-intuitive.

- We can also object that epiphenomenalism makes it difficult to understand how we can gain knowledge of our minds from introspection, since according to epiphenomenalist dualism, our beliefs about our mental states are not caused by those mental states.
- Substance dualism faces a further challenge of showing that we can know other minds exist. If minds are logically independent of bodies, then no evidence from someone's bodily behaviour can prove that they have a mind.
- The argument from analogy claims that I can infer other people have minds, because they behave as I do, and I have a mind. We can object that we cannot base an inference on one case. I could be a special case.
- A stronger form of the argument claims that I know from experience, for many types of behaviour, that they have a mental cause. I can generalise this to the behaviour of other people. So I know they have minds. But we can object that we are not always aware of a mental cause of our behaviour, and so the behaviour of others may also not have a mental cause.
- Rather than draw an analogy with our own case, we can argue that the hypothesis that people in general have minds is the best explanation for their behaviour. For example, behaviour is caused by inner states of the person, and these inner states just are mental states.
- We can object that this solution presupposes that minds cause physical events, and substance dualism has difficulty establishing this claim.
- We can also object that the belief that other people have minds is not a hypothesis based on evidence at all.
- Avramides argues that Descartes distinguishes between animals without minds and people with minds on the basis of language and adaptable behaviour. When we encounter other people, we observe these features of their behaviour and judge that they are people, i.e. bodies and minds, not bodies alone.
- A category mistake is treating a concept as belonging to a logical category that it doesn't belong to. Ryle argues that substance dualism rests on the category mistake of treating mental concepts as though they are concepts of substances and causal processes when they are not.

Summary: substance dualism

In this section on substance dualism, we have looked at Descartes' two arguments for substance dualism (from indivisibility and conceivability), objections to those arguments, and three objections to substance dualism itself (difficulties concerning mental causation, other minds, and a category mistake). In our discussion and evaluation of these arguments, we have looked at the following issues:

1. What does it mean to claim that the mind is a separate substance from the body?
2. Is the mind distinguished from the body by not being divisible?
3. Is it conceivable for the mind to exist separately from the body?
4. Is it possible for the mind to exist separately from the body? If so, does this show that mind and body are distinct substances?
5. If the mind is a distinct substance, can mental states cause bodily movements?
6. Do mental states have any causal powers at all?
7. If substance dualism is true, how can I know that other minds exist?
8. Is it a mistake to treat mental concepts as similar to physical concepts in referring to substances and causal processes, just non-physical ones?

III. Physicalist theories

The most common alternative to substance dualism is the view that there is only one kind of substance, which is matter. Thus the mind is not a distinct substance; it is not 'ontologically distinct' from what is material, not a separate thing from the body. The claim that there is only one kind of substance, physical substance, is often called 'materialism'. In recent years, talk of 'materialism' has been supplanted by talk of 'physicalism'. The most important reason for this is that physics has shown that 'matter' is too crude an identification of the most basic substance that exists, e.g. matter can be changed into energy. But in rethinking materialism, philosophers have also refined the claim from being just about what type of substance exists to include other conditions as well. It is not enough that the only *substance* is physical. The fundamental *nature* of the universe is physical, and this covers events and properties as well.

Physicalism

As a first attempt, we could define physicalism as the view that everything that exists – every substance, every property that substances have, every event that occurs – is either physical or completely depends upon something that is physical. 'Physical' means something that comes under the laws and investigations of physics, and whose essential properties are identified and described by physics.

But we should be more precise. Physicalism claims that what is physical is metaphysically fundamental. So physicalism says:

1. the properties identified by physics form the fundamental nature of the universe;
2. physical laws govern all objects and events in space-time;
3. every physical event has a physical cause that brings it about in accordance with the laws of physics. (This is known as the 'completeness of physics' or 'causal closure'.)

It is worth saying more about the first and third claims.

The third claim states that all physical events have sufficient physical causes. Of any event involving a change in physical properties (e.g. every movement of your body), that event can be brought about by something physical alone. No other, non-physical causes are necessary. So if there are non-physical causes, they don't contribute anything *in addition* to physical causes to the way the physical world changes over time.

The first claim states that the properties identified by physics are ontologically 'basic'. Other properties, in particular mental properties, are ontologically dependent on the properties identified by physics (or more broadly, the natural sciences). Mental properties, therefore, if they exist at all, are not part of the *fundamental* nature of the universe, but ontologically dependent on other properties.

There are three different ways in which this could be true.

1. Elimination: mental properties don't exist. ELIMINATIVE MATERIALISM (p. 225) claims that at least some mental properties, as we usually think of them, don't exist. At least some of our basic concepts of mental properties, such as CONSCIOUSNESS or INTENTIONALITY, are fundamentally

mistaken – these concepts don't refer to anything that exists. (And any other mental properties that do exist are physical properties.)

2. Identity: mental properties are, in fact, just types of physical properties. For example, they could be neurological properties. This is the view of MIND–BRAIN TYPE IDENTITY THEORY (p. 216). Neurological properties of the brain, such as what brain cells are made of, the connections they form with each other, the chemicals they exchange, are physical properties. They depend on other more fundamental physical properties to do with molecules and atoms that physics investigates. So mental properties are neurological properties, which are physical properties that depend on more fundamental physical properties.

3. Dependent but distinct: mental properties are not physical properties of the brain, but they completely depend upon physical properties (perhaps even just physical properties of the brain). But what is it to say that mental properties 'depend' upon physical properties? Philosophers spell this out in terms of the idea of 'supervenience'.

SUPERVENIENCE

The essence of supervenience is this: properties of type *A* supervene on properties of type *B* just in case any two things that are exactly alike in their *B* properties cannot have different *A* properties.

For example, a painting has various aesthetic properties, such as being elegant or balanced. It also has various physical properties, such as the distribution of paint on the canvas. The aesthetic properties supervene on the physical ones, because we cannot change the painting's being elegant or balanced without changing the distribution of paint on the canvas. There can be no change in aesthetic properties without a change in physical properties. And two paintings exactly alike in their physical properties (i.e. duplicates) will have the same aesthetic properties. If two paintings are completely identical in terms of how the paint is arranged – if they look exactly the same – then they must also be identical in terms of their aesthetic properties. Of two physically identical paintings, one can't be graceful while the other is awkward. Any differences in their aesthetic properties entail that there is a difference in their physical properties.

We need to notice the strength of this claim. For physicalism, it is not enough to say that if the paintings are physically identical, then they *are* aesthetically identical. Suppose we say simply that in this case, as it happens, they are both graceful. This allows that in another case, one could be graceful

What is
supervenience?

and one not. But that means that aesthetic properties would be able to vary even as the physical properties remained the same. It allows that the physical properties don't *fix* the aesthetic properties.

This isn't right. We want to say that if the paintings are physically identical, then they *must be* aesthetically identical. It is not merely false but *impossible* that one is graceful while the other is awkward, if they both look exactly the same. Put another way, once the physical properties of a painting are finalised – when the painting is finished – there is no further work to be done to 'add' the aesthetic properties. They are already part of the painting. To change the aesthetic qualities, you *must* change the physical properties.

According to physicalism, physical properties 'fix' *all* the other properties in such a way that it is *not possible* for the other properties to change without changing the physical properties. This is what physicalism means by claiming that everything 'depends on' what is physical.

We can picture this with the idea of 'levels' of existence that correspond to the different sciences. At the bottom is physics, investigating elementary particles and atoms. Molecules involve complex organisations of atoms, and cells involve complex organisations of molecules. Multicellular organisms involve complex organisations of cells, including organs such as the brain. Physicalism understands psychology as the next level of complexity, relating to the workings of the brain and the interactions of living things.

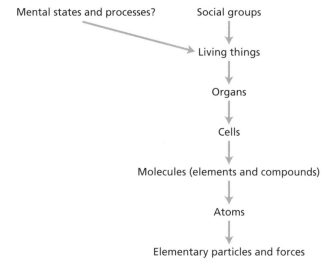

Figure 3.7 'Levels' of existence, each supervening on the ones below

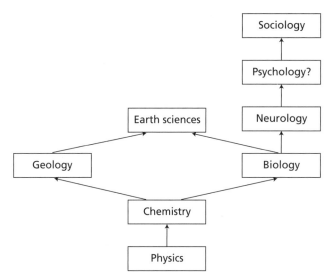

Figure 3.8 A simple hierarchy of the sciences

If mental properties supervene on physical properties, then they are fixed by physical properties such that it is impossible for two things to have the same physical properties and different mental properties. According to physicalism, just as two paintings with an identical distribution of paint must have the same aesthetic properties, two people with identical properties of their brain, say, must have identical mental properties.

Someone who denies this, who argues that what someone thinks or believes or feels is not completely dependent on their physical properties denies physicalism. They claim that (whether or not it happens) it *is* possible for two beings to have identical physical properties but different mental properties. They may argue, for instance, that physicalism is false because the mind is a separate substance (substance dualism), or because mental properties are somehow independent of physical properties (PROPERTY DUALISM, p. 291).

Physicalism claims that what is physical is metaphysically fundamental. In talking about what is 'possible' and 'impossible', physicalists mean not just physical possibility, but metaphysical possibility (see THINKING HARDER: WHAT IS CONCEIVABLE MAY NOT BE METAPHYSICALLY POSSIBLE (i), p. 189). Applying this to the mind, this means either that mental properties don't exist at all, or that they are identical with certain physical properties, or that they supervene on physical properties. We start our discussion of physicalist theories with the claim that mental properties are identical with certain physical properties.

What is physicalism?

- Physicalism claims that everything that exists is physical or depends upon something that is physical. More precisely, it claims that the fundamental nature of the universe is physical, so that the properties identified by physics are ontologically 'basic', physical laws govern all objects and events in space-time, and every physical event has a sufficient physical cause.
- Physicalist theories in philosophy of mind make one of three claims about mental properties. Either such properties do not exist or they are identical with physical properties or they supervene on physical properties.
- Supervenience is a relation between two types of property. Properties of type A supervene on properties of type B just in case any two things that are exactly alike in their B properties cannot have different A properties.
- If mental properties supervene on physical properties, then they are 'fixed' by physical properties – two things with the same physical properties must have the same mental properties.

A. Mind–brain type identity theory

Type identity theory

'Type identity theory' claims that mental properties *just are* physical properties. If we say that these physical properties are properties of a brain, then the theory is the mind–brain type identity theory. So this theory claims that thinking a thought or feeling an itch is *exactly the same thing* as certain neurons firing, say, and having a belief is the same thing as, say, certain neural connections existing. Any particular type of mental state is a particular type of brain state.

If we understand 'physical property' to cover all the properties investigated by the natural sciences (physics, chemistry, biology, geology, etc), then there are lots of different kinds of physical property. For instance, a swan is a bird and (usually) white – but what makes it a bird (a biological property) and what makes it white (a colour property) are different properties, though both are physical properties in the broad sense intended here. Just as being a swan and being white are physical properties, mental properties are also physical properties, probably highly complex neurophysiological properties, claims mind–brain type identity theory. Just as brains have physical properties of size and weight, their neurophysiological properties – synaptic connections, neurochemistry, the structure and organisation of neurons – are also physical properties. And some of these neurophysiological properties are thoughts, or pains, or desires … The mind is certain patterns of brain processing interacting with other patterns of brain processing.

Mind–brain type identity theory was developed in the 1960s as neuroscience gathered pace. The evidence is that mental events and states are very closely dependent on the brain, so many people now think that 'the mind' is just 'the brain', and everything mental is actually neurophysiological. The theory is called 'type' identity, because it claims that mental 'types' of thing (mental properties, states and events) are physical 'types' of thing (physical properties, states and events). Mental 'things' turn out to be physical 'things'; i.e. mental properties are actually physical properties of the brain, mental states are brain states.

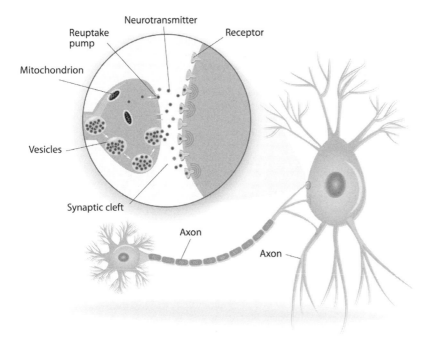

Figure 3.9 Neurones

Mental and neurophysiological properties may not *seem* the same, but, argues the type identity theorist, that's because we have different ways of knowing about these properties – through experience and through neuroscience. As we investigate the world through science, many things turn out to be something they don't seem to be; e.g. solid objects are mostly empty space, water is just hydrogen and oxygen (who'd have guessed?).

SMART ON CORRELATION, IDENTITY AND REDUCTION

Type identity theory needs to be distinguished from the claim that mental states are *correlated* with brain states. For example, having a heart is correlated with having kidneys – every animal that has a heart has kidneys and vice versa. But hearts and kidneys are not the same thing! Or again, having a size and having a shape are correlated – everything that has a size has a shape and vice versa. But size and shape are distinct properties. *(defined by same atoms?)* So simply pointing out that everything that has a particular brain state also has a particular mental state doesn't show that mental states and brain states are the same thing. They could be two distinct things that occur together. Correlation is not identity.

Suppose that neuroscience shows that thoughts, feelings, etc., are correlated with what happens in the brain. Why go on to argue that they are identical? J. J. C. Smart replies, because that is simpler.

?
What is the difference between correlation and identity?

> ### SMART, 'SENSATIONS AND BRAIN PROCESSES', PP. 141–8
>
> Smart claims that '[s]ensations are nothing over and above brain processes' – not correlated, but identical. While he defends the mind–brain type identity theory for sensations, the theory can be generalised to other mental states and occurrences. The motivation for the theory, Smart says, is simply Ockham's razor. If there are no overwhelming arguments in favour of dualism, then we should reject the idea of distinct non-physical substances or properties. Science indicates that the neurophysiological properties of the brain are a good candidate for what mental properties are.
>
> To understand the theory, it is important to get clear on the identity claim. It is not a claim about language or concepts, but about reality. So the claim is not, for example, that the concept

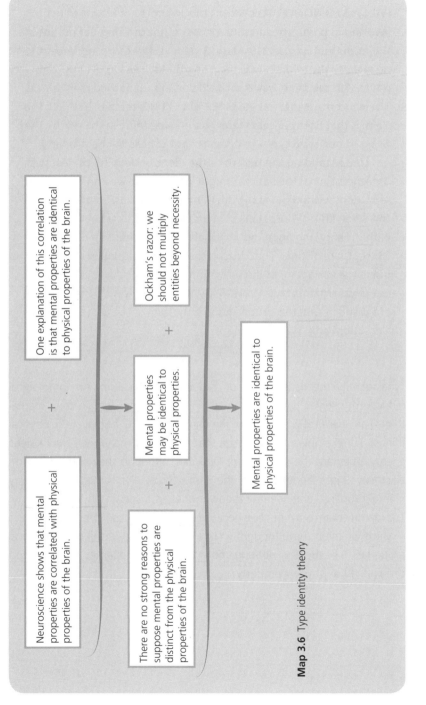

Map 3.6 Type identity theory

PAIN *means* NOCICEPTOR FIRING (nociceptors are a type of neuron involved in pain). The identity theorist is not offering definitions of the terms that we use. The identity claim is, therefore, not meant to be *analytically* true. 'Pain is the firing of nociceptors' (if it is true) is not true in the same way that 'bachelors are unmarried men' is true. The concepts PAIN and NOCICEPTOR FIRING remain distinct. The claim is that both concepts refer to *the same thing* in the world. The firing of nociceptors is what pain is. Two concepts, one property.

Understanding the nature of the identity claim helps deal with objections. In particular, we might object that we can talk about sensations without knowing anything about brains. So they can't be the same thing. But, replies Smart, we can talk about lightning without knowing anything about electrical discharge – because the concepts are distinct. That doesn't show that lightning isn't electrical discharge. Or again, as discussed in THINKING HARDER: WHAT IS CONCEIVABLE MAY NOT BE METAPHYSICALLY POSSIBLE (I) (p. 189), water is H_2O. The concepts are distinct, but the properties are the same. The same is true of 'sensation' and 'brain process'.

like naturalistic fallacy?

Explain the nature of the identity claim in the mind–brain identity theory.

ontological reduction

Explain why the mind–brain type identity theory is a reductive theory of the mind.

Type identity theory is a type of 'reductive' physicalism. An 'ontological reduction' involves the claim that the things in one domain (e.g. mental things) are identical with some of the things in another domain (e.g. physical things). For example, we can argue that heat is just mean molecular kinetic energy. They are the same thing. Or again, although they seem different, electricity and magnetism are the same force, electromagnetism. Every mental property, type identity theory argues, is a certain physical property. The identity claim is a reduction because we have 'reduced' mental properties – which we might have thought were a different kind of thing – to physical properties. I.e. there is *nothing more* to mental properties than being a certain kind of physical property.

Issues

PUTNAM AND THE MULTIPLE REALISABILITY OF MENTAL STATES

PUTNAM, 'THE NATURE OF MENTAL STATES', §3

The most famous objection to the type identity theory was developed by Hilary Putnam. He argues that mental properties are not *identical* to physical properties because the *same* mental property can be related to or supervene on *different* physical properties. For example, the brain states that relate to pain may well be different in different species, in humans and birds, say, but pain is the same mental state. If this is true, there are creatures who, when they are in pain, have different physical properties from us when we are in pain. Therefore, 'being in pain' cannot be exactly the same thing as having a particular physical property. This is the argument from 'multiple realisability'.

The term 'realise' here means 'to give actual form to' or 'to bring into reality'. For instance, we can talk of a design for a dress being beautifully realised in the final product. Similarly, in metaphysics, philosophers talk of one property 'realising' another. To say that a particular neurophysiological property 'realises' pain in human beings is to say what pain is, the form of existence it has, is given by that neurophysiological property.

Putnam's argument is that many different neurophysiological properties could realise pain, and so pain can't be the same thing as any one of those properties. Why not? Well, suppose pain is identical to some neurophysiological property in humans, call it N_1. Pain = N_1. If they are one and the same thing, then whatever has N_1 is in pain, and whatever is in pain has N_1. Now suppose pain is identical to some neurophysiological property in dogs, call it N_2. Pain = N_2. If they are one and the same thing, then whatever has N_2 is in pain, and whatever is in pain has N_2. If pain = N_1 and pain = N_2, then N_1 = N_2 (pain = pain). N_1 and N_2 must be the same neurophysiological property. But what if dogs' brains process pain in a different way from human brains, so that N_2 is a different neurological property from N_1? If $N_2 \neq N_1$, and pain = N_1, then the dog is not in pain. But

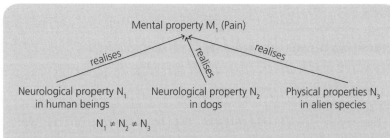

Figure 3.10 Multiple realisability: different physical properties can each realise the same mental property, such as pain, but as a result, none of them can be identical to it

Explain Putnam's objection from the multiple realisability of mental states, first in prose, then using an argument map.

the dog is in pain! So if both the human being and the dog are in pain, but they have different neurological properties, then pain can't *be* exactly the same thing as either N_1 or N_2. (This still allows that pain can be *correlated* with or *realised* by N_1 in human beings and N_2 in dogs.)

As Putnam presents it, this is an empirical argument, but it is a very plausible one. It becomes yet more plausible when we consider other mental states and non-terrestrial species. If there are aliens, given that they evolved completely separately from us, if they have mental states, it is extremely unlikely that they will have the same physical states as us. But according to type identity theory, to have a particular mental state just is to have a particular physical state. So the theory is making a very implausible prediction.

The argument can also be rephrased as an a priori argument from conceivability:

Explain the differences between the empirical and a priori forms of the argument from multiple realisability.

P1. It is conceivable, and therefore *logically?* possible, for a being with quite a different physical constitution from us to have the same thoughts or sensations.

P2. But it is inconceivable, and therefore impossible, for something both to have and not have a certain property.

C1. Therefore, mental properties can't be the same as physical properties.

The identity theorist could respond that we should talk about 'human pain', that this is a different property from 'dog pain'. Or again, if there are intelligent aliens who have thoughts, but different brains, we should talk of 'human thoughts' and 'alien thoughts'. But this doesn't seem plausible – pain is pain because of *how it feels*; thought is thought because of *what is thought*. A dog and a human being in pain share something in common, which we identify as the mental property 'being in pain'. If an alien believes that snow is white, and so do I, we have the same type of thought, whatever our physiology.

(Again, this is not to say that there is *no* relation between mental and physical properties. It is just to argue that the relation is not identity. For instance, we can accept that mental states are correlated with brain states in human beings, while also allowing that in different species, the same type of mental state is correlated with a different type of physical state.)

DUALIST ARGUMENTS

The syllabus lists four dualist arguments, two for substance dualism and two for property dualism, to be considered as objections to other theories. We will discuss the implications of the arguments for property dualism for type identity theory when we discuss property dualism. What can we say about the objections to type identity theory raised by DESCARTES' INDIVISIBILITY ARGUMENT (p. 182) and DESCARTES' CONCEIVABILITY ARGUMENT (p. 185)?

See THE KNOWLEDGE ARGUMENT, p. 293, and THE 'PHILOSOPHICAL ZOMBIES' ARGUMENT, p. 301.

The indivisibility argument

Descartes' indivisibility argument provides grounds to object to the mind–brain type identity theory. The mind cannot be identical to the brain because the mind is not divisible while the brain is.

However, type identity theorists can present the objection that we considered previously, namely that the indivisibility argument assumes that the mind is a 'thing' which can be divisible or not. This assumption begs the question against the type identity theory, which maintains that the 'mind' should be understood in terms of mental properties possessed by the brain. There are many properties that it does not make sense to talk of as literally spatially divisible or not. For instance, the brain has a particular temperature. 'Being 35 degrees Celsius' is not a spatially divisible property, yet it is a physical property. So even if mental properties are not spatially divisible, they could still be identical with physical properties of the brain.

The conceivability argument

We can express the thought behind the argument from multiple realisability in terms of Descartes' conceivability argument.

? P1. It is conceivable that, for any type of mental state, someone has a particular type of mental state without having the brain state with which, the identity theory claims, it is identical.

no P2. What is conceivable is metaphysically possible.

C1. Therefore, it is metaphysically possible that for any type of mental state, it can exist in the absence of the brain state with which the identity theory claims it is identical.

P3. If one thing can exist in the absence of a second thing, they are not the same thing.

C2. Therefore, mental states cannot be brain states.

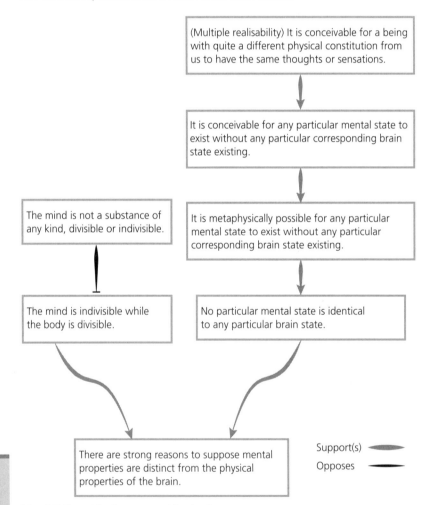

(Multiple realisability) It is conceivable for a being with quite a different physical constitution from us to have the same thoughts or sensations.

It is conceivable for any particular mental state to exist without any particular corresponding brain state existing.

The mind is not a substance of any kind, divisible or indivisible.

It is metaphysically possible for any particular mental state to exist without any particular corresponding brain state existing.

The mind is indivisible while the body is divisible.

No particular mental state is identical to any particular brain state.

There are strong reasons to suppose mental properties are distinct from the physical properties of the brain.

Support(s)
Opposes

? Are mental states nothing over and above brain states?

Map 3.7 Two objections to type identity theory

Key points: mind–brain type identity theory

- The type identity theory claims that not only is there just one kind of substance, that identified by physics, but that mental properties are, in fact, physical properties. This identity claim reduces mental properties to physical ones; i.e. what it is to be a particular mental property is to be a particular physical property.
- The identity claim is not that mental concepts mean the same as physical concepts, but that two distinct mental and physical concepts pick out one and the same property.
- The appeal of the theory is that it is simpler than other theories. It explains the mind without appealing to anything beyond physical properties.
- However, the argument from multiple realisability says that it is (empirically or conceptually) possible for two creatures to have the same mental property, e.g. 'being in pain', but have different physical properties. Therefore, the mental property is not (or cannot be) identical to any physical property.

B. Eliminative materialism

Eliminative materialism (also known as eliminativism) argues that future scientific developments, especially in neuroscience, will show that the way we think and talk about the mind is fundamentally flawed, at least in some very important respects. At least some of our mental concepts are so mistaken that they refer to things that neuroscience will show don't exist. We noted in FEATURES OF MENTAL STATES (p. 172) that central to our normal understanding of the mind are phenomenal properties and Intentionality. Eliminative materialism argues that neuroscience will revolutionise our understanding of each so that we may question whether they exist at all as we think of them now.

Mind–brain type identity theory, as we have discussed it, did not question the properties of Intentionality or consciousness. Its form of ontological reduction accepts that there *are* mental properties (as we think of them) but that they are neurophysiological properties. It assumes our usual understanding of mental life, in terms of beliefs, desires, emotions, sensations and so on. Eliminative materialism argues that things are not that straightforward. As neuroscience proceeds, it will show that at least some of our central psychological concepts don't refer to anything – nothing exists that corresponds to some mental terms, e.g. 'belief', 'desire' or 'pain' or even 'Intentionality' and 'consciousness'.

This last claim moves beyond reduction to elimination. It is most closely associated with the work of Patricia and Paul Churchland.

Patricia Churchland on reduction and elimination

PATRICIA CHURCHLAND, *BRAIN-WISE*, INTRODUCTION, §§1, 3, 4

Reductive explanation

So far, we have understood reduction in terms of identifying one property with another, more basic or fundamental kind of property, e.g. heat and molecular motion or mental properties and neurophysiological properties. Smart's argument for reduction is Ockham's razor – to say that mental properties are physical properties is simpler than saying that mental properties exist in addition to physical properties.

But how does science ever come to make such a claim? Patricia Churchland argues that what is involved is not just a simpler metaphysics (the claim that fewer things exist) but a more powerful explanatory theory. Inference to the best explanation goes beyond Ockham's razor. If identifying two properties enables you to explain something that you can't otherwise explain, that is the best reason for thinking they are the same thing. Otherwise, we can't move beyond the claim that they are merely correlated.

Ontological reduction is part of reductive causal explanation: 'a reduction has been achieved when the causal powers of the macrophenomenon are explained as a function of the physical structure and causal powers of the microphenomenon. That is, the macro-properties are discovered to be the entirely natural outcome of the nature of the elements at the microlevel, together with their

See HYPOTHETICAL REASONING, p. 8.

dynamics and interactions.' For example, we can explain everything about water – why it is liquid at certain temperatures, why it is transparent, why cars skid on it, why we can't breathe in it but fish can, etc. – in terms of the nature of molecules of H_2O, how they are structured and how they interact with each other and other things (such as car tyres or our lungs). To 'reduce' water to H_2O is just to be able to explain all the causal powers of water – the effects it has on other things and the effects other things have on it – in terms of the causal powers of H_2O molecules.

As Smart noted, the identity claim doesn't mean that the *concepts* of the macro-theory mean the same as those referring to the micro-properties. WATER doesn't mean H_2O, and THOUGHT doesn't mean 'neurophysiological firing pattern *x*'. However, what Smart and type identity theory *didn't* say is that in science, when one theory offers a reductive explanation of things in another theory, it often happens that the meanings of the concepts *change* in light of new empirical discoveries. For example, the term ATOM meant 'indivisible fundamental particle', but then physicists became able to split the atom. So the meaning of 'atom' changed to mean 'the smallest existing part of an element consisting of a dense nucleus of protons and neutrons surrounded by moving electrons'.

Beyond reduction to elimination: the example of heat

However, sometimes empirical discoveries indicate that, rather than changing the meaning of the concept, we should give up on that concept and what it refers to completely. In other words, the concept should be eliminated because nothing exists in the way it supposes.

A good example is given by the history of the science of heat. What do you think heat is, just from everyday experience? Well, hot things have more of it than cold things. Heat passes from hot things to cold things. Hot things 'give off' heat. So how about this suggestion: heat is a kind of fluid that makes things hot and can be passed from one thing to another. This was the theory of heat in the late eighteenth century, and the fluid was called 'caloric' (as in 'calories').

Ok, so if hot things have more caloric fluid than cold things, they should weigh more. So, when you heat something up, it should get heavier. Scientists tested this. Heating something up doesn't increase its weight. Ok, so maybe caloric is a fluid that doesn't have any weight? A rather unusual physical substance ...

Here's another puzzle: you can make two cold things hotter by rubbing them together, i.e. friction generates heat. How? Where does the caloric fluid come from? Well, perhaps caloric can be trapped between atoms and rubbing something releases its caloric, so it is now hot? Ok, but if that's true, then there will only be a finite amount of caloric fluid trapped between the atoms, so eventually it will run out and the thing you rub will no longer get hot. Scientists tested this. It's not true – friction never stops generating heat. So is caloric fluid not only weightless but also infinite? A very, very unusual physical substance ...

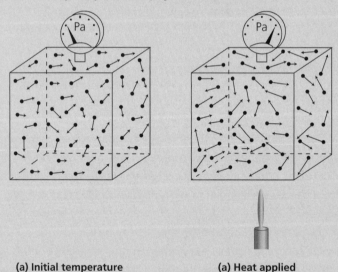

(a) Initial temperature   **(a) Heat applied**

The container on the left is cooler, the molecules move slower (have less kinetic energy) and exert a smaller pressure on the container walls compared to the molecules of the warmer container on the right.

Figure 3.11 Heat is the motion of molecules

In 1798, Benjamin Thompson, Count Rumford, suggested a different theory: heat is the motion of micro-particles (molecules, atoms). Over time, with other scientific developments on the movement of molecules and atoms, this became accepted. Heat is the kinetic energy of molecules that can be passed from one thing to another.

The theory of caloric fluid turned out be very mistaken. Heat isn't a kind of fluid at all, but something quite different. So we shouldn't say that actually, we have reduced caloric fluid to kinetic molecular energy, just changing the meaning of CALORIC FLUID along the way. Instead, we have eliminated caloric fluid – there is no such thing – and explained the phenomena of heat in different terms. Churchland says, 'the nonexistence of something [e.g. caloric fluid] is established as highly probable … through the acceptance of an explanatorily powerful framework that has no place for it'.

> Explain what 'elimination' means in the context of scientific theory.

could be like racism - still wrong

Complexity: genes and mental states

The reduction of heat to kinetic energy and the elimination of caloric fluid were fairly straightforward. It is unlikely that finding a neuroscientific explanation of thought or consciousness will be anything like as simple. It is worth bearing in mind, then, that scientific reductions can be very messy. In light of the objection from multiple realisability (p. 221), we should note that a reductive explanation doesn't have to identify one macro-level thing with one micro-level thing to succeed.

same mental properties span on different physical properties

Genes provide a good example. Genes are the fundamental 'units of heredity' that give rise to the observable characteristics of living things. Biologists talked about genes before they knew about DNA. But now we are all told that our genes are 'in' our DNA. However, a gene is not necessarily a single stretch of DNA (although genes are often misleadingly thought of this way). What we think of as a 'single' gene, relating to a characteristic that is inherited from one generation to the next, can involve many distinct segments of DNA (called 'exons'). It even turns out that the same DNA segment can contribute to different observable characteristics, depending

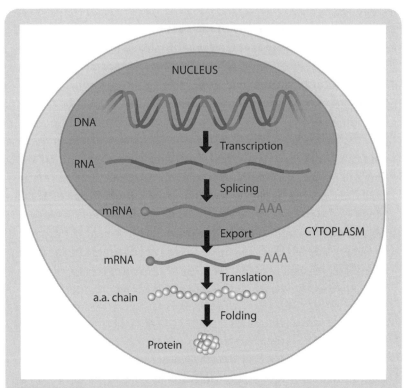

Figure 3.12 Gene structure

on the stage of development and the environment of the cell in which the DNA is located. Should we say that a gene, or part of a gene, 'for' one trait can simultaneously be the gene 'for' a different trait, or that the same strand of DNA is part of two different genes? Despite all this complexity, biologists accept that DNA – its structure and how it interacts with other things – provides a *reductive* explanation of genes. We can trace a line of cause and effect from DNA sequences to bodily traits, and no one thinks of genes as something *in addition* to DNA.

Understanding reductive explanations in science helps us understand what reductive explanations of mental properties in terms of neurological properties may involve. They may be very messy and complex. There may not be just *one* physical property that we can identify with a particular mental property, but this doesn't mean we can't reduce the mental property. The important point is that we can explain mental properties, such as Intentionality and consciousness, in terms of physical properties.

Elimination and mental properties

Unlike genes, but like caloric fluid, not all mental properties may survive the process of reductive explanation. The way we think about the mind now may be completely changed as neuroscience progresses. But we can't predict how. Reduction can threaten elimination.

Importantly for eliminative materialism, we aren't going to get reductive explanations of the mind just working from our everyday psychological concepts of 'belief', 'desire', 'emotion' and so on. These concepts are part of a theory about human behaviour (more on this below). Compared to the workings of the brain, human behaviour occurs over long periods of time (seconds, minutes, days), involves huge complexity and a far wider range of things in space, including other people. A theory of how the mind works can't reduce a theory of human behaviour to the very fast and tiny processes of neuroscience. An intermediate theory will be needed, e.g. how people process information, what happens when one desire conflicts with another, what processes are involved in a single emotion, how does imagination work, etc.

A good part of this intermediate theory will be developed by cognitive science. Before we can reduce mental properties to neurophysiological properties, we need a much better scientific theory of how the mind works. This will develop *side-by-side* with neuroscience. Only after cognitive psychology and neuroscience have 'co-evolved' will reductive explanations be possible. By this point, we can expect that our usual categories for thinking about how the mind works – beliefs, desires, emotions – will have changed and neuroscientific reduction will change them further. We have already rejected many psychological theories from the past, and we can expect this to continue.

Why does Patricia Churchland think explanation is more important than one–one identities in reduction?

Explain Patricia
Churchland's
argument that
developments in
neuroscience will
threaten to
eliminate some
mental properties.

For example, it turns out that some people are more easily addicted to substances (food, alcohol, smoking, drugs) than others. We might, commonsensically, say that they have less 'will-power'. But it turns out that they have different dopamine systems (dopamine is a neurochemical that relates to motivation and a sense of pleasure or 'reward' when you get what you want). So now what should we think about 'will-power'? What is it? Is there really any such thing?

Paul Churchland on why 'folk psychology' might be false

We consider Paul
Churchland's
explanation of
elimination in
extension material.

PAUL CHURCHLAND, 'ELIMINATIVE MATERIALISM AND THE PROPOSITIONAL ATTITUDES', §2

We mentioned above that we have a common-sense theory about why people behave as they do. For example, if someone is thirsty, they will – under normal conditions – look for something to drink. If someone believes it is raining outside, and doesn't want to get wet, they will – under normal conditions – pick up an umbrella or other covering to keep them dry. And so on. With claims like these, we are able to understand, explain and sometimes predict each other's behaviour very successfully. We do this by referring to each other's beliefs, desires, emotions, intentions and so on. Call this body of knowledge 'folk psychology'.

According to Paul and Patricia Churchland, folk psychology is an empirical theory. As such, it may turn out false, and the central concepts that it uses may, like CALORIC FLUID, turn out not to refer to anything that exists. So far, however, the claim has only been that this *may* happen. Paul Churchland argues that there are three good reasons to think that it *will* happen.

1. There are many aspects of mental life that folk psychology cannot explain, such as mental illness, the nature of intelligence, sleep, perception and learning. Explanations of these phenomena will need concepts that folk psychology lacks.

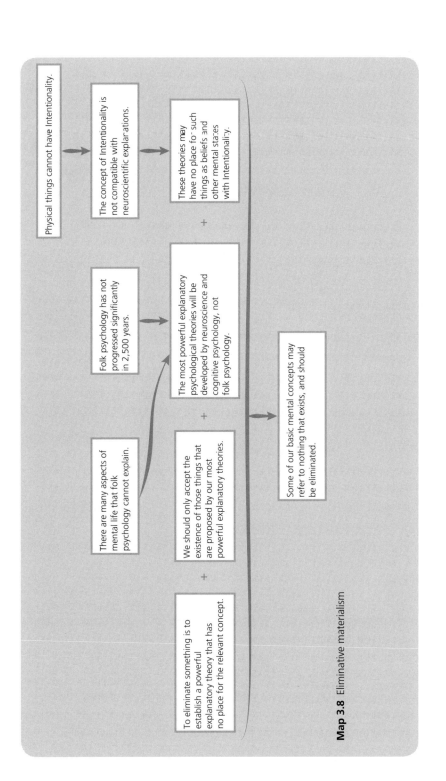

Map 3.8 Eliminative materialism

2. If we look at the history of folk psychology, it reveals no progress since the ancient Greek authors, 2,500 years ago. By contrast, neuroscientific explanations are constantly growing in scope and power.
3. We cannot make folk psychology coherent with other successful scientific theories. In particular, the central idea of INTENTIONALITY (p. 173) is highly problematic.

This third objection requires some unpacking. Why think that Intentionality can't be reduced by other scientific theories, but has to be eliminated? The reason is that it is very puzzling how anything physical could have Intentionality. Physical things are never 'about' anything. A particular molecular structure or physical process, described in physical terms, is not 'about' anything. For example, digestion is a chemical process, in which acids in your stomach break down food. What is that process 'about', what does it represent? Nothing – the question itself is puzzling! But the states and processes of your brain are just chemical states and processes, just like the states and processes of your stomach. So how could brain processes or states ever be about anything? So how could Intentional mental states be states of your brain?

Churchland concludes that folk psychology, with its explanations in terms of Intentional mental states like beliefs and desires, does not fit in with empirically robust theories, such as neuroscience, and so we have reason to abandon it.

Explain the argument for eliminativism.

Issues

Explain the claim that the argument for eliminativism cannot be as certain as the existence of our mental states.

OUR CERTAINTY ABOUT THE EXISTENCE OF OUR MENTAL STATES TAKES PRIORITY OVER OTHER CONSIDERATIONS

We can object that eliminativism is simply very counter-intuitive. What could be more certain – indeed, what could be more immediately and directly obvious – than that we have thoughts, desires, emotions, beliefs and so on? Descartes took 'I think' to be his first certainty, and for good reason. Nothing, it seems, could be more certain to me than the fact that I have mental states. So no argument could be strong enough to justify giving up such a belief.

But appeals to what is obvious are problematic in the history of ideas. For instance, isn't it just obvious that the sun moves round the Earth? Just look. And yet it is false. Descartes took it as obvious that there can be no thoughts without a thinker, so he was certain that he was a thinking *substance*. And yet there are good reasons to believe that there are no substances whose essence it is to think, and many philosophers have argued, along with Buddhists, that there is no 'self'. Similarly, my 'mental states' may not be what they appear to be.

More significantly, the objection misunderstands the Churchlands' claim. They do not deny the existence of psychological phenomena as such. They accept that the phenomena that we conceptualise as 'thinking' occur or again that we experience pain; they deny that folk psychology is the correct theory of their nature. Thinking is not defined by Intentionality as folk psychology understands it, and pain is not a matter of qualia. Instead, they claim that neuroscience will provide the correct account of what these are. As a result, there will be a revolution in our mental concepts. But we won't cease to feel pain just because we understand what it is in neurophysiological terms. While this revolution is difficult to predict, Paul Churchland argues that explanation will have no place for concepts like 'Intentionality', and whether we understand 'consciousness' as we do now is also something we may doubt.

All we can be 'certain' of is the existence of the phenomena we want to explain. But, the Churchlands argue, appealing to beliefs and desires, Intentionality and consciousness, is not appealing to the phenomena, but to a particular explanation or understanding of them. These concepts are all part of a theory, folk psychology, and we should reject these concepts if the theory that replaces folk psychology has no place for them. We can't reject unorthodox new ideas just because they are unorthodox.

surely they just want us to reword everything?

?

What does eliminativism eliminate?

FOLK PSYCHOLOGY HAS GOOD PREDICTIVE AND EXPLANATORY POWER (AND SO IS THE BEST HYPOTHESIS)

Paul Churchland criticises folk psychology for its explanatory failures concerning mental illness, sleep, learning, etc. But we can object that this is unfair. Folk psychology is not *intended* to be a theory of these aspects of mental life, so it is no criticism that it does not explain them. It is only meant to explain human behaviour; or even more specifically, human action. Here, it is incredibly successful. If I know what you want and what you believe, I can predict whether you'll study hard for your exams. If someone asks me why you went to the cinema last night, I will answer by talking about your love of films and so on. By contrast, neuroscience is almost useless at predicting whether you'll study hard for your exams or explaining why you went to the cinema last night.

Furthermore, folk psychology is the basis of developments in psychology that have extended its predictive and explanatory power. For instance, ideas about unconscious beliefs and desires have become part of folk psychology. The Greeks used an idea of fixed and unchanging 'character', whereas now we tend to appeal more to the situation someone finds themselves in. The importance of situation is a finding in recent empirical psychology, and there are many such findings and theories that use folk psychological concepts and ideas. To eliminate the concepts of beliefs, desires and other Intentional mental states would do away with much scientific psychology as well as folk psychology.

What this shows is that we don't have good reasons to think that folk psychological concepts, and especially the concept of Intentionality, will be eliminated as neuroscience develops. We can accept the Churchlands' insistence that we should only retain concepts that are part of the most powerful explanatory theory, but argue that folk psychology is and will continue to be part of such a theory. The hypothesis that we have Intentional mental states remains the best hypothesis for explaining human behaviour, and won't be replaced in favour of a neuroscientific theory that eliminates Intentionality.

Eliminativism could reply that these objections are not very strong. First, we need to know how human action or behaviour relate to the rest of mental life. To have very different *sorts* of theories – folk psychology, neuroscience – explaining different aspects of the mind is unsatisfactory. Second, the developments in folk psychology are relatively superficial. Our folk psychological explanations of behaviour are still far less powerful than the kinds of explanations we find elsewhere in the sciences. The only way to address this problem is to look to neuroscience. Finally, the challenge of explaining how physical states and processes can have Intentionality remains.

Explain the argument defending the explanatory power and importance of folk psychology, first in prose, then using an argument map.

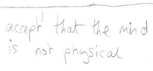
accept that the mind is not physical

Thinking harder: the articulation of eliminative materialism as a theory is self-refuting

The Churchlands' claim that folk psychology and our common-sense mental concepts comprise an empirical theory. This is why we can think about proving that it is false and eliminating its concepts in light of scientific progress. But there is good reason to suppose that they misunderstand folk psychology. We can argue for this indirectly, focusing again just on the case of beliefs and their Intentional content.

Eliminativism presents arguments, which are expressions of beliefs and rely on beliefs about what words mean and how reasoning works, in order to change our beliefs about folk psychology. Yet, if we turn Paul Churchland's prediction into a solid claim, eliminativism claims that *there are no beliefs*. But if that is true, what does eliminativism express and what is it trying to change? If there are no beliefs, including no beliefs about meaning, no beliefs linked by reasoning, then arguments for eliminativism are meaningless. An argument for eliminativism refutes itself – it concludes that there are no beliefs but it must presuppose that there are beliefs.

Eliminativists reply that this objection begs the question. It presupposes that the correct theory of meaning and reasoning is the one that folk psychology gives (in terms of Intentionality). Compare the nineteenth-century argument between people who thought that to be alive required some special energy, a 'vital force', and those who said there was no such force. The vitalists could argue that if what their opponents said was true, they would all be dead! Yet now we know there is no special 'vital force', that life arises from ordinary chemical reactions. Life just *is* certain processes, not some special property that living things have in addition to these processes. Eliminativism simply claims that we need a new theory of what it means to assert a claim or argument. What meaning is may turn out to be certain neurological processes.

But we can press the objection. Eliminativism predicts that Intentional content will be eliminated. The very ideas of meaning, or 'making sense', of 'true' v. 'false' belief, or 'reasoning' itself, are to be rejected, as they all rest on Intentional content. Claims and arguments are all 'about' something. This idea can't be eliminated in favour of some alternative. The analogy with vitalism fails. Anti-vitalists accepted that they needed to be alive to make their claims, but offered an alternative account of what 'life' is. Eliminativists claim that they do *not* need Intentional content to make their claims. Without having some *alternative* account of meaning which doesn't use Intentional content, this is what is inconceivable. We *cannot conceive* that folk psychology is false, because that very idea, 'folk psychology is false', presupposes the folk psychological concept of Intentional content. At least until we have another, better theory of meaning, the assertion that eliminativism is true undermines itself.

On this view, folk psychology – or at least, the central concept of Intentionality – turns out not to be an empirical theory (which might or might not be wrong), but a condition of intelligibility, a condition for thinking, reasoning and making claims at all. So we can't eliminate it. That means that Intentional mental states and properties must exist. They are therefore either reducible or irreducible to neuroscience. If Paul Churchland is right that we cannot reduce Intentional content to neuroscience, this isn't an objection to Intentional content. It is an argument in favour of the irreducibility of mental properties.

can't be no Intentionality so could be in support of non-reductive

> **? 1)** Is eliminative materialism self-refuting? **2)** Do we have good reason to think that folk psychological concepts will be eliminated by neuroscientific progress?

Key points: eliminative materialism

- Eliminativism argues that neuroscientific progress will show that some or all of our mental concepts are radically mistaken, and so some or all mental properties as we usually understand them do not exist.
- Patricia Churchland argues that in science, one theory (and the properties it refers to) is reduced to another when the second explains the causal powers of the phenomena identified by the first. In the process, the concepts in the first theory may change their meaning (e.g. atom), and in some cases, be eliminated entirely (e.g. caloric fluid).
- Reductive explanations can be 'messy' and complex, and don't need one–one identity claims (e.g. genes and perhaps mental states).
- Eliminativism claims that 'folk psychology' is an empirical theory of human behaviour. If it is false, it should be replaced by a better theory, e.g. neuroscience. However, we can't reduce folk psychology to neuroscience directly, but will need intermediate theories, such as cognitive science to connect the two.

- Paul Churchland argues that we have good reason to think that folk psychology is false. It does not explain many mental phenomena, has not progressed in over 2,500 years, and because of its central concept of Intentionality, it cannot be made consistent with scientific theories that we know to be true.
- We can object that we can be more certain that we have mental states than that eliminativism is true. Eliminativists can respond that our mental concepts refer to theoretical entities that explain our experience, and we cannot be certain that these explanations are correct.
- We can object that folk psychology does not intend to explain more than people's behaviour and that many developments in psychology use its concepts, including Intentionality.
- A more fundamental objection is that eliminativism cannot be true because any arguments for it are self-refuting. One cannot argue that a theory is false without presupposing Intentional content. Eliminativism offers us no alternative way of making sense of the idea of meaning. Folk psychology is therefore not an empirical theory, but a condition of saying anything meaningful at all.

C. Philosophical behaviourism

The two physicalist theories that we have discussed – mind–brain type identity theory and eliminative materialism – argue that mental properties can be reduced to physical properties or will be eliminated. But both theories agree that mental concepts, what we *mean* by 'thought', 'belief', 'desire', 'pain' and so on, are not explained by physical concepts. The reduction they defend is an *ontological* reduction – an account of properties, not concepts.

By contrast, philosophical behaviourism is a family of theories that claim that we *can* analyse mental concepts in terms of concepts that relate to the body, and in particular, the concept of 'behaviour'. While type identity theory and eliminativism focused on questions of metaphysics and whether mental properties 'exist' independently of physical properties, philosophical behaviourism focuses on questions of philosophy of language, and what it means to talk about mental properties in the first place. Once we get clear on this, philosophical behaviourism claims, we will see that metaphysical debates around 'reduction' and 'elimination' can be avoided. Before we try to do the *metaphysics* of mind, we need to do some *conceptual analysis*.

The term 'behaviourism' (without the adjective 'philosophical') refers to a theory of how psychology should conduct itself to achieve the status of a science. Science, behaviourism claims, can only investigate what is publicly accessible. Hence psychology can and must aim only at the explanation and prediction of bodily behaviour, as any talk of or appeal to 'inner', inaccessible mental states cannot be scientific. There is no scientific way to establish their existence or nature. This theory, of how psychology should proceed, is *methodological* behaviourism. It makes claims about the methods of science and about *how we can know* about mental states.

By contrast, philosophical behaviourism claims that *what we are talking about* when we are talking about the mind and mental states is behaviour – what people do and how they react. On this view, the mind is not a 'thing'. Rather, we can talk about organisms 'having minds', or better, having mental states, on the basis of how they behave.

There are different kinds of philosophical behaviourism. We will look at two theories, associated with Carl Hempel and Gilbert Ryle. We will see that, although they both agree that we can analyse mental concepts in terms of behaviour, their arguments for philosophical behaviourism, and indeed what they mean by 'behaviour', are very different.

See VERIFICATIONISM, p. 155.

Hempel's 'hard' behaviourism

Confusingly, the term 'logical behaviourism' is sometimes also used to mean 'philosophical behaviourism', the whole family of theories, and not just Hempel's original version. We will use the syllabus terms of 'hard' and 'soft' behaviourism to distinguish Hempel's and Ryle's theories.

Carl Hempel was a member of the 'Vienna Circle', the founders of logical positivism who developed and defended the verification principle. Just as the verification principle can be applied to the question of what religious language means, it can be applied to the question of what psychological language means. Hempel calls his resulting theory 'logical behaviourism'. Other philosophers sometimes call it 'analytical' behaviourism, while the syllabus calls it 'hard' behaviourism.

HEMPEL, 'THE LOGICAL ANALYSIS OF PSYCHOLOGY'

The meaning of scientific statements

Hempel starts with the general question of what the meaning of a scientific statement is. The answer, he claims, is that to know the meaning of a statement is to know the conditions under which we would call it true and those under which we would call it false. So 'the meaning of a statement is established by the conditions of its verification'. The 'conditions of its verification' are simply the observations that we can make to check its truth. For example, the meaning of the statement 'the temperature in the room is 21°C' is given by the (many different) ways in which we can establish whether this is true, e.g. by observing whether 'the level of mercury in the thermometer in the room is at the mark "21" on the Celsius scale'.

From this account of meaning, we can draw several conclusions. First, if we can't say what the conditions of verification for a statement are, i.e. if, in principle, we cannot empirically check or test the truth of the statement, then it is meaningless.

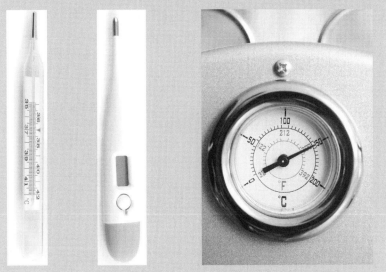

Figure 3.13 Three different conditions of verification

Second, two statements have the same meaning if they are both true or both false in the same conditions, i.e. if they have the same conditions of verification. If the meaning of the first is given by its conditions of verification, and the meaning of the second is given by its conditions of verification, and the two conditions of verification are the same, then the meaning of the two statements is the same. So 'the temperature in the room is 21°C' means the same as 'the level of mercury in the thermometer in the room is at the mark "21" on the Celsius scale and/or …', where we fill in the dots by all the other ways we can measure temperature. The statement 'the temperature in the room is 21°C' is really just an *abbreviation* of all the statements about its conditions of verification.

Third, this means that we can *translate* a statement into a series of statements that simply describe the conditions of verification. A translation is a statement with the same meaning, but expressed in different words or concepts. We can translate a statement with the concept 'temperature' into a series of statements describing the observations we make to establish whether the first statement is true. These statements don't use the concept 'temperature', but concepts of observation and measurement.

The meaning of psychological statements

Let's apply these results to statements in psychology. First, unless we can say how to check whether a statement like 'Paul has a toothache' is true or false, it will be meaningless. Second, its meaning is given by its conditions of verification. What might these be? That's an empirical matter, thinks Hempel, and the list below could be continued, but the conditions of verification will include claims like these:

a.   'Paul weeps and makes gestures of such and such kinds.' (Bodily behaviour)
b.   'At the question "What is the matter?", Paul utters the words "I have a toothache."' (Linguistic behaviour)

Explain Hempel's verificationism.

c. 'Closer examination reveals a decayed tooth with exposed pulp.' (Physical bodily states)
d. 'Paul's blood pressure, digestive processes, the speed of his reactions, show such and such changes.' (Physiological changes)
e. 'Such and such processes occur in Paul's central nervous system.' (Brain processes)

What is important about these first two points about the meaning of psychological statements is that psychological statements cannot be about private or inaccessible states of the person. The only way that they could have meaning is if there is some way that we could check whether or not someone has the mental state we say they do. All these means of checking have to be public, so they must relate to physical and behavioural states or changes.

The third implication is that the statement 'Paul has a toothache' *means* these claims. It can be translated without loss of meaning into these claims. These are not only ways of checking the truth of the statement, as though such behaviour is a (fallible) guide to what is privately going on in Paul's mind – to talk about Paul's mental states is to talk about Paul's behaviour and bodily states.

Fourth, these claims describing the conditions of verification don't use the concept of 'toothache' or 'pain' or any other mental concept. They only use physical concepts, concepts concerning physical, bodily behaviour and processes. We can generalise the point. All psychological statements can be translated, without changing the meaning of what is said, into statements that only use physical concepts of this kind.

Explain Hempel's 'hard' behaviourism.

Implications

Central to Hempel's theory is the thought that just as other scientific statements are really abbreviations for statements that describe their conditions of verification, the same is true of psychological statements. This may seem controversial, since we tend to think of psychological and physical concepts as quite distinct. But according to his theory, we can translate statements using psychological

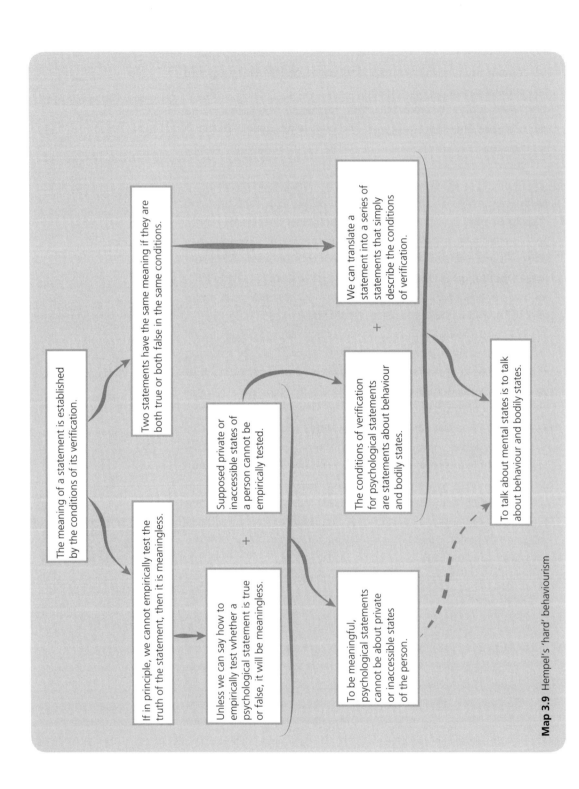

The meaning of a statement is established by the conditions of its verification.

Two statements have the same meaning if they are both true or both false in the same conditions.

If in principle, we cannot empirically test the truth of the statement, then it is meaningless.

We can translate a statement into a series of statements that simply describe the conditions of verification.

Unless we can say how to empirically test whether a psychological statement is true or false, it will be meaningless.

Supposed private or inaccessible states of a person cannot be empirically tested.

The conditions of verification for psychological statements are statements about behaviour and bodily states.

+

To be meaningful, psychological statements cannot be about private or inaccessible states of the person.

+

To talk about mental states is to talk about behaviour and bodily states.

Map 3.9 Hempel's 'hard' behaviourism

concepts into statements using physical concepts. There is no 'essence' to mental states and events (e.g. consciousness or Intentionality) that distinguishes them from what is physical. As a result, there is no genuine question about how mind and body relate to one another or interact with one another. Once we correctly understand the logic of mental concepts, such problems disappear.

This isn't because we have *eliminated* mental states. Hempel's behaviourism doesn't say that mental states don't exist but nor does it say that they do. Instead, the question of their 'existence' isn't a real question. To say that someone is in pain isn't to say that 'pain exists'. It is to say that there are certain observations we can make about the behaviour and physical state of the person. The person exists, their body exists, and they behave in certain ways. There is no further question about whether mental states exist.

We will look at objections to Hempel's theory in ISSUES, p. 251, after first discussing Ryle's theory.

Ryle's 'soft' behaviourism

Like Hempel, Ryle argues that statements using mental concepts, such as 'belief', 'think', 'pain', can be understood in terms of behaviour. However, his theory is different from Hempel's in a number of important ways.

1. He does not make this argument by appealing to the verification principle, or any other general theory of meaning. He presents arguments that are specifically concerned with mental concepts.
2. He does not claim that psychological statements can be translated or 'reduced' without loss of meaning into statements that refer to behaviour.
3. His understanding of the term 'behaviour' is not the same as Hempel's. He keeps our common-sense concept – how a person behaves, including what they say. The language we use to describe behaviour is our ordinary language, rather than Hempel's descriptions of bodily movements in physical terms, physiological changes or brain processes.
4. He places an explicit emphasis on the idea of *dispositions* to behave.

We start with this last point.

DISPOSITIONS

Hempel's list of the conditions of verification all describe actual, current behaviour and physical states – Paul weeps, Paul says 'I have a toothache', etc. While he allows that his list is incomplete, we can suppose that all statements about the conditions of verification will have to describe actual behaviour. Since these statements give us the meaning of psychological statements, Hempel must claim that when I say 'Paul is in pain', I am saying something about how Paul is *actually* behaving. The same is true for claims such as 'Paul believes that Paris is the capital of France' and 'Paul wants chocolate.' But this is very implausible.

First, we can, to some extent, control our behaviour, e.g. I might stop myself from showing that I am in pain. Second, many mental states, such as knowledge, are dispositions, rather than occurrences. They don't occur at a time, like actual behaviour does. For example, someone who knows French knows French even when they are talking or reading in English.

So we need to understand 'behaviour' not just in terms of actual behaviour, but behaviour that someone would display under different conditions. I want to say that someone *now* understands French (even when *now* they don't meet Hempel's conditions of verification), because e.g. if I *did* ask them whether they speak French, they would answer 'yes', or if they *were* in France, they would converse with people there in their own language, and so on. Ryle argues that to talk of mental states and processes is to talk not only of actual behaviour, but also of 'dispositions' to behave in certain ways.

RYLE, *THE CONCEPT OF MIND*, CH. 2

Central to Ryle's argument is his observation that we often speak of mental states in action, in their expression in behaviour. To know how to play chess is something demonstrated in actually playing chess, and we attribute this knowledge to someone on the basis of what they do. Or again, to do something intelligently or thoughtfully – playing, reading, cooking, arguing, etc. – is to be able to regulate what you do. So some of our mental concepts identify skills. A skill isn't an act – you can't tell from one piece of behaviour whether it is skilful or just lucky or something else again. But a skill isn't some invisible, non-spatial thing either (nor, we may add, a physical property of the brain). It is a disposition or complex of dispositions.

What is a disposition? A disposition, in its simplest form, is simply how something will or is likely to behave under certain circumstances. For instance, sugar is soluble. Solubility is the disposition to dissolve when placed in water. Having a disposition is not the same as behaving in a certain way *now*. Sugar is soluble even when it isn't actually in water. We can express dispositions using 'if ..., then ...' statements – hypothetical conditionals. To say that sugar is soluble is to say that *if* sugar is placed in water, *then* it will dissolve.

Solubility is a 'single-track' disposition – it is 'actualised' or 'manifest' in just one way, namely dissolving in water. Other dispositions, such as being hard, have many different ways in which they are actualised. We can infer many different facts from knowing that something is hard, e.g. about whether we can pass other things through it, what sound it will make when hit, whether we can change its shape easily, and so on. We need a series of hypothetical (if ..., then ...) statements to express the disposition of being hard.

Many mental concepts are also concepts of dispositions, so that when we talk of someone having a certain mental state, like being proud or believing that the earth is round, we are talking of what they would do, could do, or are liable to do, in particular situations or under particular conditions, including conditions that they are not in at the moment. Mental concepts can refer to very complex dispositions, dispositions which are 'indefinitely heterogenous'. For example, in saying that someone is proud, consider the many different and subtle ways in which people can manifest pride (Ryle refers to Jane Austen's novel *Pride and Prejudice*).

Whether someone has a particular disposition is a matter of whether certain statements about what they could or would do are true or not. These are hypothetical statements, conditional statements of the form 'if circumstances *c* occur, the person will do *x*'. They are not 'categorical' statements that say how things actually are; e.g. many of those circumstances may never arise. They don't describe actual states of some mental substance. So 'the mind is not

What is a disposition?

Explain the claim
that many mental
concepts are
dispositional
concepts.

Compare and
contrast Hempel's
'hard' behaviourism
and Ryle's 'soft'
behaviourism.

the topic of sets of untestable categorical propositions [as substance dualism must hold], but the topic of sets of testable hypothetical and semi-hypothetical propositions'.

Unlike Hempel, Ryle does not think that statements using a mental concept, such as 'he is proud' or 'he knows French', can be 'reduced' in meaning to a series of hypothetical statements about what the person will do in different situations (or what his physical state is). The mental concept can be analysed in terms of such statements – this is what it means – but we can never give a complete translation, so that we can replace the mental concept by physical ones. Dispositional statements are 'open'. They support and justify certain inferences, explanations and predictions. To say that someone is proud enables us to draw inferences about how he will behave in certain situations. But we cannot draw all possible inferences and replace the concept 'proud' with this set of inferences.

A note on other minds

According to philosophical behaviourists, talking about mental states is just talking about actual behaviour and dispositions to behave in certain ways. From how someone behaves, we can infer what behavioural dispositions they have. But from this, we don't then *infer* that they have a mind. The link between behaviour and minds isn't based on evidence, it is logical (conceptual). To say someone behaves in certain ways and has certain behavioural dispositions *just is* to say that they have certain mental states. To understand what others say and do is to understand that they have minds. We can know that other people have minds, because we can know directly that they behave in particular ways. Thus, philosophical behaviourism solves the problem of other minds (see THE PROBLEM OF OTHER MINDS (I), p. 201).

How does logical
behaviourism solve
the problem of
other minds?

THINKING AND OTHER MENTAL PROCESSES

Philosophical behaviourism is on its strongest ground when talking about the mind in action. But what, we may object, about *just* thinking, without acting (which is where Descartes started)?

RYLE, *THE CONCEPT OF MIND*, CHS 2, 5

Ryle's response to this challenge is first to note that there isn't just one kind of 'thinking'. Again, thinking is often done in, with and through action. When we act thoughtfully or intelligently, the thinking isn't a separate process from the doing, so that the thinking takes place in the mind and the doing in the physical world. There is one process – behaving (reading, driving, conversing …) intelligently – and what makes it an expression of thinking is that it has a certain manner which can be expressed by dispositional statements about what we can, could and would do in certain situations.

But there is also the matter of thinking quietly 'to oneself'. Ryle's central claim here is that this is *internalised speaking*: 'Much of our ordinary thinking is conducted in internal monologue or silent soliloquy.' Speaking is, of course, an overt behaviour, and we only acquire the ability to think – to speak silently to ourselves – with effort. The silence, and the fact that we are speaking only with ourselves, is *inessential* to the nature of thinking. To think through a maths problem, one can do so either with pen and paper, articulating the steps as one goes, or silently, 'in one's head'. Whether a process is public or private is irrelevant to whether it is thinking. 'The phrase "in the mind" can and should always be dispensed with.' Mental processes only sometimes and only contingently take place 'in the mind'. Processes that do, as it happens, take place silently don't define thinking any more than those that take place as publicly observable behaviours.

Dispositions and occurrences

Thinking is something that happens at a time and takes time. It is a process, it 'occurs', it is a mental 'occurrence'. So we can't say that thinking is *just* a matter of dispositions. The same is true of other mental occurrences and processes, such as being conscious of (paying attention to) what you are doing, feeling or thinking (what Ryle calls 'heeding'). What's the relation between occurrences and dispositions?

> Explain Ryle's claim that there is nothing essentially 'private' about thinking.

> We will say more about Ryle's theory of consciousness in THE ASYMMETRY BETWEEN SELF-KNOWLEDGE AND KNOWLEDGE OF OTHER PEOPLE'S MENTAL STATES (p. 259).

To understand this, compare 'it is dissolving'. This states that something is happening, but does so in dispositional terms. From 'it is dissolving', we know that it is soluble, and so dissolves in water. So it would do just what it is doing in this situation, given that it has that disposition.

Likewise, to say that someone is paying attention to what they are doing is to attribute dispositions about what they could say if you asked them, but also to add that they are 'in the mood or frame of mind' to do just what it is that they are doing. This is what Ryle means by a 'semi-hypothetical' statement – it both explains an actual occurrence and enables us to make inferences.

Thinking harder: a note on physicalism and the category mistake

In SUBSTANCE DUALISM MAKES A 'CATEGORY MISTAKE' (p. 207), we saw that Ryle argues that dualism misunderstands the logic of mental concepts. It understands the mind as another 'thing', like the body in fitting into a metaphysical framework of substances, properties and causation. We can extend his criticism to the physicalist theories of type identity theory and eliminative materialism.

While these theories reject the idea that the mind is a separate substance, they understand mental properties and physical properties in the same way. Mental properties *are* physical properties, according to type identity theory. According to eliminative materialism, mental properties are part of an empirical theory that offers causal explanations, just like other scientific theories of the physical world. However, unlike dualism, which infers that mental concepts refer to non-physical, non-mechanical processes, these physicalist theories infer that mental concepts must refer to the same physical, mechanical processes that our physical concepts refer to.

Ryle's philosophical behaviourism rejects both options. An analysis of our mental concepts shows that they don't work like physical concepts.

While physical explanations use categorical concepts, mental concepts are dispositional.

How, then, is philosophical behaviourism a form of physicalism? Because, according to philosophical behaviourism, there is no distinct psychological 'reality' – no distinct psychological substances or properties. This isn't because the theory eliminates them, but because questions about the mind aren't questions about what exists. What exists is given by natural science. Categorical facts about substances, their properties and causes belong here, in the descriptions of the world that natural science provides. Dispositions depend on such categorical facts – sugar's disposition to dissolve depends on its physical properties, and our dispositions to behave as we do depend on our physical properties. But dispositions, for Ryle at least, aren't additional 'properties' (at least, of the same kind as physical properties). Dispositions are expressed in hypothetical statements, not categorical ones. And saying 'if this happens, then this will happen' doesn't state anything about what exists.

Explain why philosophical behaviourism is a form of physicalism.

Issues

DUALIST ARGUMENTS

How can philosophical behaviourism respond to DESCARTES' INDIVISIBILITY ARGUMENT (p. 182) and DESCARTES' CONCEIVABILITY ARGUMENT (p. 185)?

The indivisibility argument claims that the mind cannot be the body because the mind is not spatially divisible while the body is. But philosophical behaviourism can respond that 'the mind' is not spatially divisible because it is not a thing at all. To talk of 'divisibility' and 'indivisibility' in relation to the mind is a category mistake. According to Ryle, mental states are dispositions; according to Hempel, statements using mental concepts are abbreviations for statements about physical conditions of verification.

What of the conceivability argument, which claims that we can conceive of the mind and body existing as distinct substances? As noted in MIND WITHOUT BODY IS NOT CONCEIVABLE (p. 187), it seems that if philosophical behaviourism provides the correct analysis of mental concepts, then it is inconceivable for there to be a mind without a body. A mind is not a thing, it does not 'exist' in the same way as bodies exist only with different properties. Again, to

We will discuss the implications for philosophical behaviourism of the arguments for property dualism when we discuss property dualism. See THE KNOWLEDGE ARGUMENT AS A DUALIST ARGUMENT AGAINST OTHER THEORIES, p. 296, and THE ZOMBIE ARGUMENT AS A DUALIST ARGUMENT AGAINST OTHER THEORIES, p. 310.

think of the mind as a thing (and hence something that could exist in its own right) is a category mistake, and category mistakes are misconceptions. As dispositions to behave, mental states can only be had by creatures that can behave in certain ways. Or again, as statements about behaviour, psychological statements can only be true of creatures that can behave in certain ways. And whether we use Ryle's ordinary concept of behaviour or Hempel's physical one, to behave requires a body.

See SUBSTANCE DUALISM MAKES A 'CATEGORY MISTAKE', p. 207.

Given this, if we can succeed in showing that it *is* conceivable for the mind to exist without the body, then it seems that philosophical behaviourism must be false. Now, many people have thought that mind without body is conceivable – belief in God and the existence of one's soul in the afterlife demonstrate this. Shouldn't the analysis of our mental concepts make such common thoughts coherent rather than incoherent? Aren't our concepts defined by how we use them?

Ryle argues that such beliefs *don't* actually reflect how we use our concepts in everyday life. The 'official doctrine' conflicts 'with the whole body of what we know about minds when we are not speculating about them'. The belief in mind without body is not part of everyday use, but the result of theological and philosophical theorising. We cannot have a clear and distinct idea of ourselves as 'minds' only, and we are mistaken if we think that we can. 'Many people can talk sense with concepts but cannot talk sense about them.'

Hempel would agree. For our mental concepts to have genuine meaning, we must be able to provide the conditions of verification for statements that use such concepts. These conditions of verification must refer to behaviour, since the only information we can have about other people's mental states is from their behaviour.

Is a mind without a body conceivable?

ISSUES DEFINING MENTAL STATES SATISFACTORILY

Philosophical behaviourism claims that we can understand our concepts of what mental states are in terms of behaviour and dispositions to behave. But to provide such an understanding, we need to successfully identify the behaviour that provides the conditions of verification for saying that someone has a particular mental state (Hempel), or say just what behaviour the mental state disposes us toward (Ryle). Or more precisely, even if we don't need to be able to actually do this, we need to think that, in principle, such an analysis is possible. But is it? There are two reasons to think that it is not.

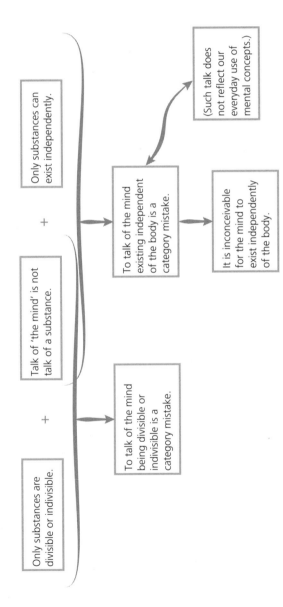

Map 3.10 Ryle's response to dualist arguments

Only substances are divisible or indivisible.

+

Talk of 'the mind' is not talk of a substance.

+

Only substances can exist independently.

To talk of the mind being divisible or indivisible is a category mistake.

To talk of the mind existing independent of the body is a category mistake.

(Such talk does not reflect our everyday use of mental concepts.)

It is inconceivable for the mind to exist independently of the body.

The multiple realisability of mental states in behaviour

The first is the 'multiple realisability' of mental states in behaviour. A mental state might be expressed in quite different behaviours not only in different situations, but even in very similar situations by different people. In fear, faced with a lion, I might freeze, you might run. But then again, in fear, faced with a snake, I might run, you might freeze. Or again, on one occasion, I run, and on another, I don't. 'Multiple realisability', in this context, just means that there are many ways in which the disposition (the mental state) can be actualised (expressed in behaviour).

For a different but related meaning of 'multiple realisability', see PUTNAM AND THE MULTIPLE REALISABILITY OF MENTAL STATES, p. 221.

How can we possibly give a list of the conditions of verification for all the ways in which people might behave when afraid? The list will be indefinitely long, especially if we have to specify all the different conditions under which people show fear. There is no way we can complete the sentence 'A person is afraid = if they are in situation x, they will do action A, or if they are in situation y, they will do action B, or if they are in situation z, they will do action C, or …'

The objection from multiple realisability can be understood in two ways. First, it shows that the analysis of mental states in terms of behaviour is not possible. There is no finite set of statements about behaviour which provides an account of the meaning of a mental concept. So philosophical behaviourism does not give an adequate account of what our mental concepts mean.

P1. People with the same mental state behave differently, both in different circumstances and even in the same circumstance.
P2. It is not possible to draw up a finite list of hypothetical conditionals or statements of the conditions of verification that describe all the ways someone with that mental state may behave.
C1. Therefore, the claim that mental states can be analysed in terms of behaviour is false.
C2. Therefore, philosophical behaviourism is false.

Second, if different people with the same mental state have dispositions to do different things in similar situations, how can we say that these *different* dispositions are actually the *same* mental state? What is it that makes it the same mental state, given that the dispositions are different? The objection shows that what makes any mental state the mental state that it is – what makes a pain pain, what makes the fear of snakes a fear of snakes, what makes the belief that Paris is the capital of France the belief that Paris is the capital of France – cannot be *simply* how someone behaves or is disposed to behave. The conditions of verification and/or behavioural dispositions don't express the identity conditions for mental states.

P1. People with the same mental state behave differently, both in different circumstances and even in the same circumstance.
C1. Therefore, what makes it true that two people have the same mental state is not that they have the same behavioural dispositions.
C2. Therefore, philosophical behaviourism is false.

Explain the objection to philosophical behaviourism from the multiple realisability of mental states in behaviour, first in prose, then using an argument map.

Circularity

The second difficulty in analysing mental states in terms of behaviour and behavioural dispositions is that how someone behaves in a particular situation depends not on just one mental state, such as being afraid, but on how this interacts with *other mental states*. Suppose I am afraid of dangerous snakes. Does this dispose me to run when I see one? That depends. Do I *believe* the snake is dangerous? Do I *believe* that this type of dangerous snake is one you shouldn't run away from? Am I able to *recognise* the type of snake? Do I *want* to avoid being bitten? And so on.

We can't specify the conditions of verification for fear, or again, what set of dispositions fear is, without mentioning other mental states. That's a problem for the claim that we can analyse mental states in terms of behaviour. Suppose I want to define the concept 'furniture'. I say 'furniture is tables, chairs, bookcases, and other pieces of furniture'. This is an awful definition, because the term 'furniture' appears in my definition of what 'furniture' means. The definition is circular, because the term we want to define appears in the definition.

The same challenge faces philosophical behaviourism. If we try to say what fear of snakes is by including sentences like 'if someone recognises a snake and believes that the snake is dangerous, then they will run', while this doesn't mention 'fear', it mentions other mental states. If we then provide a further analysis of these mental states, such as the belief that the snake is dangerous in terms of dispositions as well, we will have to mention other mental states again. What behaviour my belief that the snake is dangerous disposes me towards will depend on other mental states. In fact, it will depend on whether or not I am also afraid of snakes!

For a discussion of definitions, see Epistemology, THE DEFINITION OF KNOWLEDGE, p. 32.

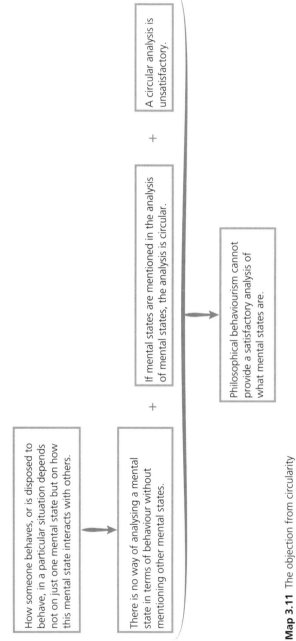

Map 3.11 The objection from circularity

How someone behaves, or is disposed to behave, in a particular situation depends not on just one mental state but on how this mental state interacts with others.

There is no way of analysing a mental state in terms of behaviour without mentioning other mental states.

+

If mental states are mentioned in the analysis of mental states, the analysis is circular.

+

A circular analysis is unsatisfactory.

Philosophical behaviourism cannot provide a satisfactory analysis of what mental states are.

The objection is that there is no way of analysing a mental state in terms of behaviour (either in terms of conditions of verification or in terms of dispositions) without mentioning other mental states. And so the analysis will be circular. A circular analysis, like a circular definition, is unsatisfactory. Philosophical behaviourism aims to tell us what mental states are, but can't do so without talking about mental states in the analysis! So it doesn't provide an analysis of what mental states are after all.

> Explain the objection that the analysis of mental states in terms of behaviour cannot avoid circularity.

Hempel's response to multiple realisability and circularity

The objections from multiple realisability and circularity are particularly forceful against Hempel's hard behaviourism, since he claims that the conditions of verification give a complete translation of statements using mental concepts in terms of statements about behaviour. For the translation to be complete, then we need a finite list of the conditions of verification. But multiple realisability suggests that there can be no such list. And for it to be a translation, then we must avoid using mental concepts in stating the conditions of verification. But circularity suggests that we cannot eliminate mental concepts in this way.

One response Hempel could make is to emphasise the importance of statements about physiology and brain processes. While people may behave in many different ways in different situations, their physiology and brain processes will be the same, he could argue. And it is these, not the many varied statements about how people might act, which are central to identifying what mental concepts really mean.

not necessarily

> See PATRICIA CHURCHLAND ON REDUCTION AND ELIMINATION, p. 226.

However, this response would move his theory closer to a form of type identity theory, since 'behaviour' turns out not to be as important as physical properties of the body. As a form of type identity theory, it doesn't avoid the problem of multiple realisability, since type identity theory faces its own version of this problem (p. 221)! The physiology and brain processes of different people (or certainly, of different species) could well be very different, even though they have the same mental state.

In fact, Hempel eventually abandoned his theory. He gave up the claim that we can define mental concepts in terms of behavioural conditions of verification; indeed, he gave up verificationism. Instead, he accepted that scientific statements as a whole, including psychological ones, may introduce 'hypothetical entities', e.g. beliefs, genes, atoms and so on. Claims about such entities cannot be understood just in terms of how we verify them; the relationship between talk of such things and testing the truth of claims about them is more complicated than that.

> Can philosophical behaviourism reduce talk of mental states to talk of behaviour and behavioural dispositions?

Ryle's response to multiple realisability and circularity

While Hempel's theory must answer the objections, Ryle's theory may escape them, because they misunderstand what he is claiming. In essence, he accepts both points, and builds them into his theory.

First, in accordance with circularity, Ryle argues that disposition statements are 'open', and cannot be replaced by a complete set of hypothetical statements linking particular matters of fact (such as a situation and a behaviour). Therefore, Ryle accepts that it is impossible to *specify* mental states in terms that replace mental concepts with behavioural ones alone in our thought and language. Second, in accordance with multiple realisability, Ryle argues that mental concepts are concepts of 'indefinitely heterogenous' sets of dispositions. Nothing that is 'indefinite' can be exhaustively characterised – no finite list is possible. The objections are correct, but they are not objections, since his philosophical behaviourism doesn't aim to offer finite translations of psychological claims.

However, this response doesn't address the second interpretation of the objection from multiple realisability. If mental states are so 'heterogenous', what makes a mental state the mental state that it is? Is there any stable correlation (let alone identity) between a mental state and behavioural dispositions? It seems that, given circularity, a particular mental state could be (compatible with having) a disposition to just about *any* behaviour, depending on a person's other mental states at the time. My fear of dangerous snakes could dispose me to say 'Well, hello there, Mr Muggins!' if I also believe that this phrase effectively prevents snake attacks!

If mental states are behavioural dispositions, then mental state *x* = behavioural disposition *x* and mental state *y* = behavioural disposition *y*. A different behavioural disposition is a different mental state, and the same mental state must give us the same behavioural disposition. But according to multiple realisability, you and I could have mental state *x*, but I have behavioural disposition *x* while you have behavioural disposition *y*, given our other mental states – we are both afraid of the snake, but I am disposed to say 'hello there, Mr Muggins' and you are disposed to run! Leibniz's law of the indiscernibility of identicals says that if two things are identical (i.e. are just one thing), then they must share all the same properties. So if we have the same mental state but different behavioural dispositions, by Leibniz's law, mental states can't be behavioural dispositions.

Ryle can reply that we shouldn't focus on individual 'pieces' of behaviour that may differ, as this again misunderstands the theory. Ryle's analysis

On Leibniz's law, see
DESCARTES' INDIVISIBILITY
ARGUMENT FOR SUBSTANCE
DUALISM, p. 182.

[handwritten margin note: not actually identical. Must accept that mental states are reliant on each other]

allows that we can't tell what disposition, if any, is being expressed in a single piece of behaviour. What makes the behaviour the expression of the disposition that it does in fact express depends on whether certain hypothetical statements about *other* situations are true or not. So whether or not I feel afraid of the snake isn't fixed only by what I actually say or do, but by a whole host of dispositions to other behaviour in other circumstances, e.g. what I would do if the snake comes swiftly towards me after I said 'hello there, Mr Muggins', and so on.

Once we recognise this, we can say that while mental states involve 'indefinitely heterogenous' dispositions, we shouldn't overstate the case. *On the whole*, people in the same mental state have very similar dispositions. Many of these similarities hold even when there are some things they do differently. For example, for fear, there are similarities in how they answer 'are you scared?', their facial expressions, etc. There is sufficient overlap for us to say that they are in the same mental state.

Furthermore, Leibniz's law is about identity in metaphysics, and so it doesn't obviously apply to Ryle's theory. His claim that mental states are behavioural dispositions isn't a claim of identity between two 'entities', but a logical analysis of what we mean when we are talking about mental states. Despite not being able to reduce mental concepts to statements about behaviour, Ryle argues that a concept of a mental state *is* a concept of a set of behavioural dispositions. Ryle's philosophical behaviourism provides an analysis of the meaning of mental concepts, but it does not justify the claim that we could replace talk of mental concepts with talk of specific behavioural dispositions. Mental concepts work at *a higher level of generality* that can't be reduced to sets of individual hypothetical statements about behaviour.

Can't have exceptions!

> **?**
> How should philosophical behaviourism respond to challenges concerning the definition of mental states in terms of behaviour?

THE ASYMMETRY BETWEEN SELF-KNOWLEDGE AND KNOWLEDGE OF OTHER PEOPLE'S MENTAL STATES

Ryle observes that it is part of the 'official doctrine' of substance dualism that the ways in which we gain knowledge of our own and others' mental states are very different. We are directly aware of our own mental states, but we can only infer those of others. Our self-knowledge comes from our *consciousness* of our mental states and our *introspection* of that consciousness. We cannot be conscious of anyone else's mental states in the same way. Furthermore, we are aware of our mental states in such a way that we cannot make mistakes, but this is not true of our beliefs about other people's minds.

Now if mental states were dispositions to behaviour, or again if what it means to say that someone has a particular mental state is given by conditions of verification, all this wouldn't be true. Given that what I am saying when I say 'I am in pain', or 'I believe that Paris is the capital of France', is that I behave or am disposed to behave in certain ways, then it seems that I would have to infer what mental states I have from how I behave, or how I think I am disposed to behave.

But, we can object, this isn't right. I can know what I believe, what I want or fear or hope, directly, without inference and without thinking about how other people would verify whether I have these mental states. Furthermore, if I am thinking to myself, I know what I am thinking in a way that no one else can.

Explain the objection to philosophical behaviourism from an asymmetry between self-knowledge and knowledge of other people's mental states, first in prose, then using an argument map.

P1. The analysis of mental states in terms of behavioural dispositions (or conditions of verification) rules out an asymmetry between self-knowledge and knowledge of other people's mental states.

P2. Yet it seems obvious from experience that there is such an asymmetry.

C1. Therefore, philosophical behaviourism is false.

Thinking harder: Ryle on consciousness

Self-knowledge is not an issue that Hempel addresses in his explanation of behaviourism. However, one response he could make is that he is only interested in discussing the meaning of statements in psychology, which as a science, deals only with knowledge of other people's mental states. But this response is unsatisfactory, since we obviously do use mental concepts when talking about our own mental states. The challenge remains how Hempel's behaviourism can understand and explain self-knowledge.

Ryle's response is to argue that consciousness, understood as giving special self-knowledge through introspection, is a myth. He argues that self-knowledge and our knowledge of other minds is on a par, gained in the same way in each case – by paying attention. This enables us to make reliable dispositional claims about our own or other people's behaviour, whether this is overt or silent. The main difference is simply that we have more evidence available to ourselves.

RYLE, *THE CONCEPT OF MIND*, CH. 6

Central to Ryle's argument is that being conscious of something is to pay attention to it (to 'heed' it, he says). We can pay attention to what we are doing and to what we have just felt or said silently to ourselves. But we can also pay attention to what someone else is doing and what they say out loud to us. To know what we are thinking or feeling is not to stand in some special, inner private relation to certain mental 'objects' ('thoughts', 'feelings'), but for us to be ready to say what we think or feel and be unsurprised by the occurrence of the thought or feeling.

Compare *not* knowing a process in one's mind: you make a joke spontaneously or come up with a solution to a problem. How did you do it? You can't say – the joke or solution comes as a 'surprise' to you. Knowing what you are thinking or doing is just to be continuously prepared for what comes next in that process.

Hence consciousness provides the same kind of knowledge in cases of knowing our own mental states and knowing the mental states of others. The main difference is that in our own case, we have more to go on, because we are the audience of our silent, inner speech – our thinking – and others are not.

Knowing what you are thinking is not different in *kind* from knowing what someone else is thinking, since we can know just as directly what someone else thinks when they speak, at least when they speak in an unguarded, unembarrassed and uncalculated way, which is the most natural way to speak. When we talk like this – whether to others, or silently to ourselves – we are directly expressing our mental states. So when we pay attention to what we say, we gain knowledge of the mind of whoever is talking. Introspection is not a form of perception of special mental objects. It is just to pay this kind of attention to ourselves.

Explain Ryle's theory of consciousness.

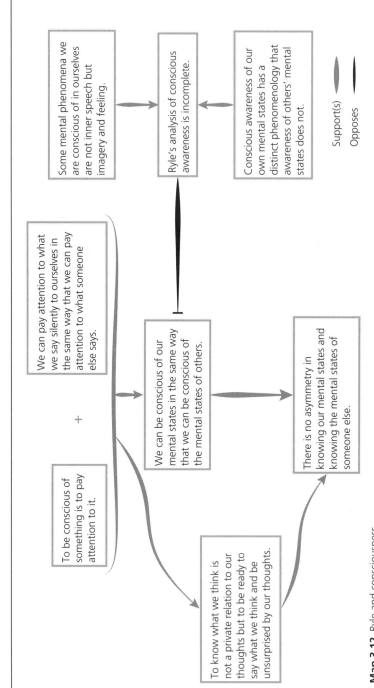

Map 3.12 Ryle and consciousness

Objections to Ryle's theory of consciousness

We can make two objections to Ryle's analysis of consciousness and self-knowledge. First, can thinking be adequately understood in terms of inner speech, and can internalised speech form the model for mental processes generally? What about non-linguistic mental processes or changes in feeling and mood? Here we aren't saying anything to ourselves.

Second, Ryle seems to miss out the subjective, experiential aspect of mental states and processes. The distinctive quality of certain experiences, e.g. how a sensation or emotion feels to the person experiencing it, is central to our mental lives. I have an awareness of this aspect of mental states and processes for my own mental states, but not for anyone else's. How does philosophical behaviourism account for this aspect of self-knowledge and the asymmetry between self-knowledge and knowledge of other people's mental states?

It may be that these objections don't themselves re-establish a strong asymmetry between self-knowledge and knowledge of others' mental states. But they attack Ryle's rejection of it.

> See PHENOMENAL PROPERTIES/QUALIA, p. 174.

> Compare and contrast substance dualism and philosophical behaviourism on self-knowledge.

THE DISTINCTNESS OF MENTAL STATES FROM BEHAVIOUR

It seems that many mental states and processes have an 'inner' aspect that can't be captured by behaviour and behavioural dispositions. We should agree that to be in pain often involves doing certain things, such as wincing, recoiling from the cause of pain, nursing the damaged part of the body, etc. (call all this 'pain behaviour'). But this doesn't capture the 'essence' of pain, which is that it *hurts*.

More generally, we can argue that statements about behaviour or conditions of verification only tell us about how to know about mental states. They don't give us the 'intrinsic nature' of mental states, what they are 'in themselves', so to speak. Mental states are not the same as these conditions of verification or behavioural dispositions, but are something distinct or something more than them. (For instance, perhaps they cause this behaviour, and that is why they are correlated with it.)

In his discussion of this objection, Hempel responds that our understanding of people in terms of their mental states, e.g. that they are in pain or that they want chocolate, is tied up with their physical state and their behaviour. We can't understand what it is for them to be in such-and-such a mental state without referring to such physical conditions. What would it be for someone to want chocolate but never seek it or express this in language? What is a 'desire' if not something that motivates behaviour? The behaviour isn't just evidence of their mental state, it gives us the meaning of the concept. Furthermore, our understanding of them is based on the information we have about them – and all the information we get concerns their bodily behaviour. Because meaning is given by conditions of verification, we can only meaningfully talk about things that we can gain information about, and the meaning of a concept is given by the ways in which we can check the truth of claims that use it.

But what, we may object, about perfect actors? Someone can pretend to be in pain, and may do so utterly convincingly, and yet not be in pain. Or again, someone may 'live a lie', pretending to have certain beliefs and desires without actually doing so.

Ryle might respond that mental states aren't just *doing* certain things, but to have the *disposition* to do them. The actor doesn't have the same dispositions that someone who really feels pain has. There are 'if …, then …' statements that are true of the actor that are not true of the person who is really in pain. And similarly with someone pretending to believe or want what they do not, in fact, believe or want.

This response may be convincing for Intentional mental states such as beliefs and desires. But we can object that, at least when it comes to phenomenal properties of consciousness, this analysis misses an important point. Pain isn't just a disposition to shout or wince; there is also *how pain feels*, 'what it is like' to experience pain. *This* is what distinguishes the person in pain from the actor. It is highly counter-intuitive to argue that this aspect of experience is constituted entirely by behavioural dispositions.

To make the point, Hilary Putnam asks us to imagine a community of 'super-spartans'. (The Spartans were an ancient Greek community who were very tough and discouraged demonstrations of pain.) These are people (or creatures) who so completely disapprove of showing pain that all pain behaviour has been suppressed. They aren't acting; this is how they are in everyday life. They no longer have any disposition to demonstrate pain in their behaviour. Yet, they could still be in pain. Pain is conceivable without any associated pain behaviour. Pain can't be understood just in terms of dispositions to pain behaviour, it is distinct from such behavioural dispositions. So philosophical behaviourism is false.

See FEATURES OF MENTAL STATES, p. 172.

'Brains and behaviour'

Explain the argument that at least some mental states are distinct from behaviour, first in prose, then using an argument map.

Handwritten margin notes: Still happens — no

Hempel argues in response that actors meet only some of the conditions of verification for pain, those based on directly observing their behaviour in the ordinary sense of the word. But his behaviourism claims that 'behaviour' covers physiological and neurological states and processes as well. And here there will be a difference between actors and people who are genuinely in pain. The physiology and brain activities of actors will be different. He gives the example of mental illness. No one can have *all* the symptoms of being mentally ill and yet not be mentally ill. If they could, then there would be no difference between being mentally ill and not being mentally ill. There must be something that distinguishes people who are mentally ill from those who are not (including actors).

We can apply his response to Putnam's example of super-spartans. There will be conditions of verification for saying that a super-spartan is in pain. Given that they do not show pain in their overt behaviour, the conditions of verification will have to prioritise statements about their physiology and brain processes (or whatever physical processes underlie their pain response).

Such a response would accept that mental states are distinct from behaviour in the ordinary sense of the word, but not distinct from the physical states of the body. In our discussion of the multiple realisability of mental states in behaviour, we made a similar proposal (p. 254). However, we noted that if Hempel prioritises the physiological and neurological conditions of verification over overt behaviour, then his theory starts to sound more like a kind of type identity theory (though one that proposes an analytic reduction of mental states to physical states rather than an ontological one).

> **?**
> Does any form of philosophical behaviourism provide a successful account of mental states?

Key points: philosophical behaviourism

- Philosophical behaviourism argues that the meaning of mental concepts can be analysed or understood in terms of 'behaviour'. It is a form of physicalism because it rejects the idea of a distinct psychological reality, arguing that talking about mental states is not talk about what exists.
- Hempel argues that the meaning of a statement is established by the conditions of its verification. This entails that statements using mental concepts can be translated, without any loss of meaning, into statements about the conditions of verifying such claims in terms of behaviour,

where 'behaviour' includes not only bodily movements, but also physiological and neurological states and processes, described by physical concepts.

- Dispositions are how something will or is likely to behave under certain circumstances.
- Ryle defends a non-reductive form of philosophical behaviourism, arguing that mental states can be understood as behavioural dispositions, where 'behaviour' has its usual meaning in ordinary language. A disposition is how something will or is likely to behave under certain circumstances, and can be expressed in hypothetical conditionals.
- The dispositions that are mental states are 'indefinitely heterogenous' and 'open'. Statements using mental concepts work at a higher level of generality than individual statements about behaviour. As disposition statements, they support and justify inferences, explanations and predictions of behaviour.
- Philosophical behaviourism avoids the problem of other minds. To say someone behaves in certain ways and has certain behavioural dispositions just is to say that they have certain mental states.
- Ryle argues that thinking is either part of what it is to act thoughtfully or internalised speaking. It is no part of the nature of thinking that it is 'private'.
- We can object that it is conceivable for minds to exist without bodies. Philosophical behaviourists can reply that this claim rests on a category mistake. Once we clarify what mental concepts mean, we will see that it is inconceivable.
- The multiple realisability of mental states in behaviour indicates that the same mental state in different people can involve different behavioural dispositions or again, that given such diversity of behaviour, a complete list of the conditions of verification for a mental state is impossible. So mental states can't be understood in terms of behaviour.
- Hempel could reply that while overt behaviour varies, physiology and brain processes will not. Ryle can reply that the objection misunderstands his theory. When we analyse the whole pattern of behaviour, not just individual instances, we will see that the same mental state involves very similar dispositions in different people.
- The circularity objection argues that we cannot eliminate references to mental states when trying to analyse what behaviour a mental state is a disposition towards, or when providing its conditions of verification.

How someone behaves, when they have a particular mental state, depends on the other mental states they have.

- Hempel abandoned the claim that we can reduce statements about mental states to statements about behaviour. Ryle can reply that his theory does not try to do this in the first place. Mental concepts are ineliminable because they work at a higher level of generality.
- We can object that philosophical behaviourism rejects the asymmetry between self-knowledge and knowledge of other people's minds.
- Ryle defends this rejection by arguing that 'consciousness' and 'introspection' are simply a matter of paying attention to ourselves, especially our internalised speech, just as we can pay attention to others and their speech. So we learn about our mental states and theirs in the same way.
- However, we can object that mental states have an 'inner', qualitative aspect, such as how they feel, their phenomenal properties. Perhaps all mental states are distinct from behaviour, but certainly at least this aspect of consciousness cannot be completely analysed in terms of behavioural dispositions.

Summary: physicalist theories

In this section on physicalist theories, we have looked at three theories:

1. Mind–brain type identity theory: mental states are identical with brain states.
2. Eliminative materialism: some or all mental properties as we usually understand them do not exist, because some or all of our mental concepts are radically mistaken. Those mental properties that do exist can be reduced to physical properties.
3. Philosophical behaviourism: all statements using mental concepts can be translated, without loss of meaning, into statements about the conditions of verification using only physical concepts of behaviour ('hard' behaviourism), or mental states are dispositions to behave in certain ways under certain circumstances ('soft' behaviourism).

In our discussion and evaluation of these theories, we have looked at the following issues:

1. What is physicalism, and why is it committed to the supervenience of mental properties on physical ones?
2. How does reduction in science work, and can mental properties be reduced to physical ones, e.g. neurological properties?
3. What is folk psychology, and are there good reasons to think that it is false?
4. Is it coherent to argue that our mental concepts are radically mistaken?
5. Is it conceivable or possible for the mind or mental states to exist independently of the body?
6. Are mental states 'multiply realisable', either in the brain or in behaviour?
7. Can we analyse mental states in terms of behaviour without circularity?
8. Is there something about what it is like to have conscious experiences that cannot be analysed in terms of behaviour?
9. How do we know our own minds?

IV. Functionalism

DUALIST THEORIES (p. 181) and PHYSICALIST THEORIES (p. 211) propose accounts of the mind in relation to claims about what exists. Physicalism claims that the only substance that exists is physical, and all properties, including mental properties, depend upon physical properties (if they exist at all). Substance dualism denies this, and argues that the mind is a distinct substance. Functionalism argues that we can and should understand what the mind and mental states are without making any claims about what kinds of substance exist. It is a theory about the mind that is compatible with both physicalism and dualism.

Functionalism claims that mental states are 'functional' states. We will need to understand what a 'function' is in more detail, but as a first definition, functionalism is the view that each mental state consists of a disposition to behave in particular ways and to have certain other mental states, given certain inputs from the senses and certain other mental states. In other words, we can give an analysis of what mental states are in terms of their 'inputs' and 'outputs'. The inputs are inputs from the senses and other mental states; the outputs are behaviour and other mental states. The complete description of the mental state's outputs for each possible set of inputs is the description of its *function*. It describes what the mental state does.

What is a function?

CAUSAL ROLE FUNCTIONALISM

Most functionalists understand the relations between inputs, mental states and outputs causally. Any functional state can be described in terms of what typically causes it, and what it typically causes in turn. We will call this 'causal role' functionalism.

There are many kinds of functional state – states that fulfil a functional role. For example, in biology, 'being an eye' can be understood in terms of functional role. There are lots of different types of eyes that work in different ways and have different physical properties – human eyes, fish eyes, fly eyes, etc. What makes them all eyes is what they do – convert light waves into *blind people?* neural signals to enable an organism to navigate its environment. In biochemistry, 'being a poison' is also a functional property. There are lots of different sorts of poisons that work in different ways and are made of different chemicals. But what makes them poisons is their harmful chemical effect on living creatures. In engineering, 'being a carburettor' is a functional property. A carburettor is that part of an internal combustion engine that mixes air and fuel. They can be different sizes and shapes and made out of different materials. And there are lots of other examples. In all these cases, we can define what something is – an eye, a poison, a carburettor – in terms of its causal functional role.

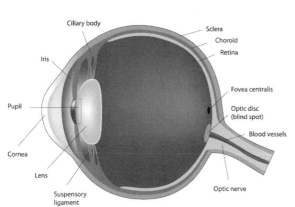
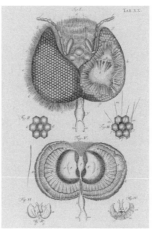

Figure 3.14 Two types of eye

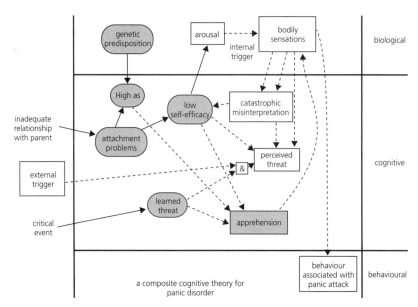

Figure 3.15 A functional analysis of panic disorder

Functionalism argues that the same is true of mental states and properties. What it is to be a mental state is just to be a state with certain typical causal relations to stimuli, behaviour and other mental states. Different mental states differ in their typical inputs and outputs. For example, the typical causes and effects of pain are quite different from the typical causes and effects of a belief that snow is white.

Of course, the causal roles of mental states will be very complicated, and functionalists disagree on how we should discover them. Some claim that their causal roles are described by 'folk psychology', so what we really need is conceptual analysis (as philosophical behaviourism argues). Others claim that their causal roles must be discovered by empirical scientific investigation (just as mind–brain type identity theory claims is needed for identifying brain states and mental states).

On folk psychology, see p. 232.

Explain causal role functionalism.

Thinking harder: a computational notion of function

In fact, functionalist theories began in the 1960s with a different notion of function, related to computers. On this view, the mind essentially works like a computer. Mental states can be compared to software – the instructions for how the machine operates.

PUTNAM, 'THE NATURE OF MENTAL STATES', §2; BLOCK, 'TROUBLES WITH FUNCTIONALISM', §1.1

Putnam first explained what he meant by 'function' in terms of how simple computers work. The functioning of a computer can be described by a 'machine table'. As Block explains, this is a long list of conditional statements of the form 'if the machine is in state S_1 and receives input I_1, then it produces output O_1 and goes into state S_2', 'if the machine is in state S_2 and receives input I_2, then it produces O_2 and goes into state S_3', and so on. For example, a drinks dispenser that sells drinks at 70p would have a machine table that includes 'if the machine is in state S_1 and receives input of 20p, it should output the message "Insert 50p" and go into state S_2'; 'if the machine is in state S_2 and receives input of 50p, it should output a drink and go into state S_1'. The machine table lists every possible combination of state and input, and assigns each combination an output.

Machine tables describe the operations of software. And software can be implemented by different systems. For instance, Microsoft Word is a programme that runs on desktop computers, tablets and phones. These machines have different physical constructions, different hardware. But that doesn't matter, says functionalism. The 'states' referred to in machine tables are defined just in terms of inputs, outputs and other states. All that matters, then, is that the hardware – *whatever it is* – can perform the functions that the machine table describes.

Explain the difference between defining 'function' in terms of causal role and in terms of machine tables.

> Putnam claims that mental states are simply machine table states. Any mental state, such as being in pain or believing that Paris is the capital of France can be completely described by a set of states and range of inputs within the machine table. Anything that can receive those inputs and have the functional states described by the machine table has the relevant mental state.

Functionalism and behaviourism

Functionalism can be understood as a descendant of PHILOSOPHICAL BEHAVIOURISM (p. 239), replacing 'behaviour' by 'function'. This has several advantages.

PUTNAM, 'THE NATURE OF MENTAL STATES', §4; BLOCK, 'TROUBLES WITH FUNCTIONALISM', §1

The first advantage, Putnam and Block argue, is that functionalism avoids the objection from CIRCULARITY (p. 255). Instead of talking of dispositions to behave in certain ways in certain circumstances, functionalism talks of dispositions to behave *and have other mental states*, given certain sensory inputs *and other mental states*. It explicitly recognises that what behaviour a mental state will cause depends on other mental states. So the definition of one mental state will have to mention other mental states.

Second, even apart from issues of circularity, there are other reasons to think that mental states cannot be understood just in terms of behaviour. For example, mental states often cause other mental states, e.g. pain normally causes the belief that one is in pain. Or again, if someone had the nerves to their muscles damaged, they might not be able to move, but this wouldn't mean they didn't have mental states. So behaviour doesn't, on its own, define what mental states are.

Are pain & believing you're in pain the same thing?

Third, Putnam argues that we think that mental states *cause* behaviour, e.g. your desire to eat causes you to look for food. According to Hempel and Ryle, your desire is simply a matter of looking for food, or being disposed to look for food. Mental concepts are not, for them, causal concepts, but abstract ways of describing what people will do under certain circumstances. This, thinks Putnam, is a mistake. The mental state is not the behavioural disposition, but the 'inner state' (see below) that causes your behaviour.

How does functionalism differ from behaviourism?

Functionalism and multiple realisability

INNER STATES

Whether it understands functions in terms of causal roles or in terms of machine tables, functionalism claims that for something to have functional states, it must have a complex internal organisation. If a functional state is a state with a particular causal role, that causal role will need to be filled by an inner state of whatever possesses the function. For example, to fulfil its function, an eye has to have parts that enable it to convert light waves into nerve firings. Different types of eye have different parts, different structures, but they must all have *some* structure or they couldn't enable the creature to see. Or again, a machine that implements a machine table must have a number of distinct physical states that it moves between in response to various inputs and that produce distinct outputs. Again, we need not know what these inner states are, what they are made of, or exactly what mechanisms make them work as they do, but there must be inner states that match each of the functions described by the machine table. *like computer circuitry*

This applies just as much to mental states, since mental states are functional states. For something – whether it is a machine or an animal or a human being – to have mental states, it must have a complex organisation of inner states that work in ways that fulfil the necessary functional roles. These inner states could be states of the brain, but they don't have to be. Things without brains could have mental states, as long as the relevant functions are performed by some part of them.

Functionalists say that the inner state 'realises' the function – it has that functional property. Using our earlier examples, for each eye, some arrangement of light-sensitive and other cells realises the functional property of being an eye; for each poison, some chemical state or other realises 'being a poison'. In each instance, the causal role that defines what it is to be an eye or a poison is played by some biological or biochemical state or other. What this is can vary from one case to another. The state will be whatever state fulfils the functional role. The nature of the inner state that realises the function isn't important.

The functionalist argues that each mental property, e.g. 'being in pain', is also a functional property. There may be lots of different states, e.g. different brain states, that have this functional property. The states can vary from one species to another. But as long as some state of the creature has the function that defines pain – given certain inputs, it causes certain outputs – then the creature is in pain.

What does it mean to say that a state 'realises' a functional role?

See PUTNAM AND THE MULTIPLE REALISABILITY OF MENTAL STATES, p. 221.

MULTIPLE REALISABILITY

Functionalism explains the multiple realisability of mental states, which gives rise to an objection to mind–brain identity theory. Mental properties are multiply realisable because functional properties *in general* are multiply realisable. As we've seen, 'being an eye' is multiply realisable. What identifies the property 'being an eye' is a particular causal role. In humans, in fish, in flies, the occurrence of a particular arrangement of cells fulfils this causal role, and so has the functional property of being an eye.

Functionalism avoids the objection that troubles type identity theory because it identifies mental properties not with the physical properties of brain states, but with what brain states can *do*. And what one brain state can do may be something that a different brain state, or even a state of something that isn't a brain, e.g. a computer, can also do. Things with very different states – different constitutions or internal organisation – can realise the same mental states as long as they are states with the same causal roles (or that realise the same machine table). The nature of the state – biological, electronic, etc. – doesn't tell us anything essential about the mental state, which is purely a matter of functional role.

This also explains why functionalism is compatible with both dualism and physicalism. The metaphysical nature of the state that plays the functional role could be anything. Mental states are mental states in virtue of what they do, not in virtue of the nature of the *substances* or *properties*

how does a junction begin to exist? Where do they begin?

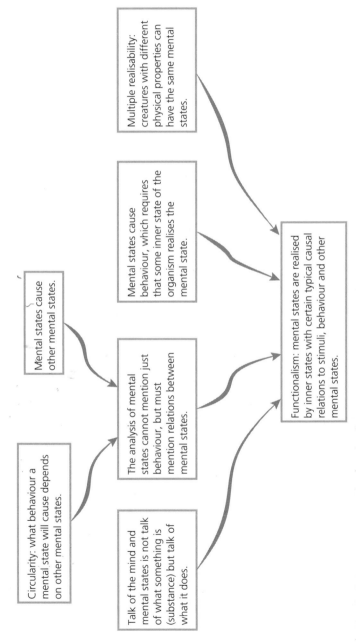

Map 3.13 Arguments supporting functionalism

that realise those mental states. Mental states could be realised by physical states, e.g. of the brain, or they could be realised by states in a distinct mental substance, or they could be realised by a creature composed of both mental and physical substances. However, while functionalism is compatible with dualism, most functionalists are physicalists.

Functionalism is compatible with physicalism because functional properties in general supervene on physical properties. As we've seen, functional properties occur throughout science, e.g. being an eye. Once something has a certain internal complexity and organisation and can receive certain inputs and produce certain outputs, then it can have the functional property of being an eye. All this – its internal structure, inputs and outputs – can be described and explained in terms of its physical properties. Nothing more is needed. Its physical properties fix its functional properties. These functional properties are not themselves physical properties, according to functionalism, because there are lots of different ways in which eyes can be constituted physically. However, functional properties are properties which are realised by physical properties operating in causal relationships. And what is true of 'being an eye', functionalism claims, is true of 'being a pain' or 'being a belief'. If physicalism is true, then it is a physical substance and its physical states, e.g. the physical states of a brain, that realise mental states.

See SUPERVENIENCE, p. 213.

Explain how functionalism can be a physicalist theory.

Issues

We discuss an objection concerning Intentionality in extension material.

Objections to functionalism take the form of arguments that we cannot reduce mental properties to functional properties. Objections can focus on either of the two FEATURES OF MENTAL STATES (p. 172), Intentionality or consciousness. Following the syllabus, we will look only at objections that concern consciousness.

We ended the last objection to philosophical behaviourism, THE DISTINCTNESS OF MENTAL STATES FROM BEHAVIOUR (p. 263), by talking about the difficulties of accounting for phenomenal properties in terms of behavioural dispositions. Functionalism faces a similar challenge in trying to analyse them as functional properties.

Take time to understand these claims by re-reading the discussion in PHENOMENAL PROPERTIES/ QUALIA, p. 174.

Phenomenal properties, we said, are properties which give an experience its distinctive experiential quality, 'what it is like' to undergo that experience. According to some philosophers, phenomenal properties are intrinsic and non-Intentional. If they are, then they are 'qualia'.

The objection to functionalism is this: if phenomenal properties are qualia, then they cannot be completely understood in terms of their causal roles (or inputs and outputs on a machine table), because these are relational properties, not intrinsic properties. It is not what causes them and what they cause in turn that makes pain or the smell of coffee or the visual sensation of red what it is. What it is like to experience these mental states – how pain feels, how red looks, how coffee smells – can't be analysed in terms of functions. Yes, of course, how pain feels is important to what it causes, e.g. it causes you to cry out or withdraw your hand from the fire. But the feeling of the pain isn't *just* these causal relations. So functionalism can't explain phenomenal properties.

> Could a functional analysis of panic disorder (FIGURE 3.15, p. 270) tell us what it is like to feel panic?
>
> *no*

P1. Qualia, by definition, are intrinsic, non-Intentional properties of conscious mental states.

P2. Intrinsic, non-Intentional properties cannot, by definition, be completely analysed in terms of their causal roles (or as machine-table states).

C1. Therefore, if qualia exist, some mental properties cannot be analysed in terms of their causal roles (or as machine-table states).

P3. Functionalism claims that all mental properties are functional properties which can be completely analysed in terms of their causal roles (or as machine-table states).

C2. Therefore, if qualia exist, functionalism is false.

P4. Qualia exist.

C3. Therefore, functionalism is false.

Valid, not yet sound

The controversial premise is (P4). In what follows, we will look at two thought experiments that try to establish this, before ending with a general discussion on the nature of consciousness from David Chalmers.

Thought experiments are designed to test a hypothesis or philosophical claim through imagining a hypothetical situation and coming to a judgement. In philosophy of mind, the most common kind of thought experiment is one in which we are asked to judge whether the hypothetical situation is possible or not. Thought experiments are used when actual experiments are either practically or physically impossible, or when the judgements concern matters that cannot be investigated by empirical means, e.g. the correct application of concepts or metaphysical questions of identity.

> We looked at thought experiments in Epistemology in GETTIER'S OBJECTION, p. 47, and AM I A BRAIN IN A VAT?, p. 185.

(DESCARTES' CONCEIVABILITY ARGUMENT (p. 185) and the a priori version of THE MULTIPLE REALISABILITY OF MENTAL STATES (p. 254) can be understood as thought

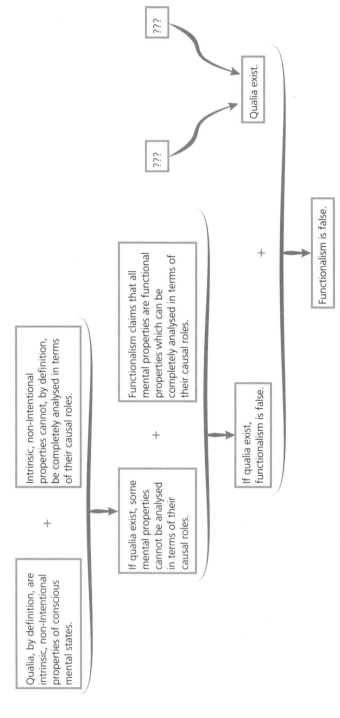

Map 3.14 The objection to functionalism from qualia: but what goes in the empty boxes?

Qualia, by definition, are intrinsic, non-Intentional properties of conscious mental states.

\+

Intrinsic, non-Intentional properties cannot, by definition, be completely analysed in terms of their causal roles.

If qualia exist, some mental properties cannot be analysed in terms of their causal roles.

\+

Functionalism claims that all mental properties are functional properties which can be completely analysed in terms of their causal roles.

If qualia exist, functionalism is false.

???

???

Qualia exist.

\+

Functionalism is false.

experiments if we add imaginary detail, e.g. 'imagine being (or communicating with) a mind without a body' or 'imagine having a conversation with an alien who turned out not to have a brain'.)

THE POSSIBILITY OF A FUNCTIONAL DUPLICATE WITH DIFFERENT QUALIA (INVERTED QUALIA)

We can show that phenomenal properties cannot be understood just in terms of their functions if we can show that it is possible for two people to have states with identical functions but different phenomenal properties. The most popular version of this objection is known as the case of 'inverted qualia'.

Suppose that you and I are looking at ripe tomatoes and fresh grass. Because we have grown up in the same linguistic community, we have learned to use the word 'red' to describe the tomatoes and 'green' to describe the grass. So we both say that the tomatoes are red, the grass is green. But the particular way that tomatoes seem to me is the way that grass looks to you, and vice versa. Functionally, we are identical, and yet we have different colour experiences. 'The way grass looks to you' and 'the way grass looks to me' are functionally identical; both are caused by the same inputs (grass) and cause the same outputs (e.g. saying 'grass is green'). But they are not identical in terms of their intrinsic properties. They refer to different qualia.

Of course, we might not *know* whether this is true or not. But that is irrelevant. The objection is that inverted qualia are *possible*. If functionalism were true, inverted qualia would be impossible. So functionalism is false.

> We will discuss a third thought experiment which is used to object to functionalism when we look at THE KNOWLEDGE ARGUMENT, p. 293.

> Briefly explain the objection to functionalism from inverted qualia, first in prose, then using an argument map.

Thinking harder: Patricia Churchland on inverted qualia

The functionalist can reply that in the case described, you and I are *not*, in fact, functionally identical. There are going to be small, but very important, differences, because the causal relations of phenomenal properties are very complex. Patricia Churchland argues that we have no good reason to think that qualia can be inverted in the way the thought experiment describes.

PATRICIA CHURCHLAND, *BRAIN-WISE*, CH. 4, §2.2

In presenting her argument, Churchland is defending eliminative materialism rather than functionalism. But because she argues that phenomenal properties are not intrinsic properties, her defence works for both theories.

She starts by making the objection from inverted qualia clearer. The main claim in the objection is that you and I – or our brains – could function in exactly the same way, but we would have different qualia. This is not being proposed as an empirical hypothesis, e.g. that you and I really do see red and green differently. Why not? Because empirical hypotheses are tested against the evidence. First, we have no evidence from neuroscience that identical brain functioning gives rise to different conscious experiences in different people. Second, as an empirical hypothesis, it is poor, since it proposes that there could be empirical differences (in our conscious experience) that are *undetectable*, since they make no functional difference. But science does not proceed by supposing undetectable facts! So if the inverted qualia objection were empirical, then it is either false or bad science.

So in saying that you and I could function in exactly the same way, but have different qualia, 'could' must mean 'it is conceivable'. So the argument is like other arguments from conceivability, and faces the same objections as other arguments from conceivability. We can question whether it is conceivable; whether, even if it is conceivable, it is possible; and whether its possibility tells us anything about whether there actually are qualia (i.e. whether phenomenal properties are intrinsic and non-Intentional).

Churchland then points out that the thought experiment is much too simple. First, every colour that we can discriminate has unique similarity and dissimilarity relations to all surrounding colours. For instance, red is more similar to

[handwritten margin note: Processing same info should = same output]

[handwritten margin note: Conceivable ≠ possible]

See DESCARTES' CONCEIVABILITY ARGUMENT, p. 185, and THE 'PHILOSOPHICAL ZOMBIES' ARGUMENT, p. 301.

orange than green is, while green is more similar to blue than red is. So we can't simply switch red and green without messing this up. If you and I saw red and green 'switched', then we wouldn't agree on whether red was more similar to orange or blue. And this is a functional difference.

One response would be to change the thought experiment – it is not just red and green that are inverted, but the whole spectrum. This could keep all the similarity relations as well. Someone who sees red as green also sees orange as blue, and so they say that red is similar to orange, but what they see is what I see when I look at green and blue.

But this meets another problem. Human beings can make much finer discriminations in green, yellow and orange than we can in blue. If we inverted everything, this would be apparent from behaviour, as whoever sees the inverted colours would be able to make finer discriminations in blue than the rest of us can, and fewer discriminations in green, yellow and orange. And so it is empirically impossible for someone to have inverted qualia without functional differences.

But isn't it still conceivable that we could correct for this as well? The person with inverted qualia has the same objective discrimination abilities as the rest of us, even if subjectively, they are discriminating between blue qualia in ways that we can't. This is conceivable, but, asks Churchland, *should we say that this person really sees the same colours as us*? The colours that they see bear new similarity relations to every other colour, and they have different powers of discrimination. What is essential to a colour being the colour it is?

The qualia theorist argues that phenomenal properties are intrinsic – they are essentially what it is like to experience them. In other words, it is conscious introspection that identifies whether two colours are the same or not. But is this right?

See the companion website for a diagram of 3D colour space.

We can offer an explanation of our experience of colour in terms of our physical constitution and how it functions. For example, why does colour have the three dimensions of red, green and blue? The answer has to do with types of colour-sensitive cells, 'cones', in our retinas and the way they are wired up to the brain. If we say that our experience of qualia *is* the way the brain processes this information, we can explain our colour experience – similarities and dissimilarities, what colours we can see and what we can't, etc. But if qualia are something distinct, we have no explanation for why we see colour as we do. What colour experience *is* should be decided by who has the best explanatory theory of colour experience, and not by thought experiments.

Are inverted qualia possible?

BLOCK ON THE POSSIBILITY OF A FUNCTIONAL DUPLICATE WITH NO QUALIA

The second objection to a functional analysis of consciousness tries to show that phenomenal properties cannot be understood just in terms of their functions because it is possible for two systems to have states with identical functions, but one system (you, say) has phenomenal properties while the other does not. The most popular version of this objection is Ned Block's China thought experiment.

BLOCK, 'TROUBLES WITH FUNCTIONALISM', §1.2

Block frames his argument in terms of machine-table functionalism. Suppose we have a complete functional description of your mental states. For each and every one of your mental states, we have an input–output analysis, giving us a machine table for your mind. Now imagine that a human body, like yours, is connected up via its sensory and motor nerves not to a brain but, through electronic transmitters, to the whole population of China. The Chinese are linked up to each other by two-way radios, and some of these are linked up to the input and output nerves of the body. (Block picks

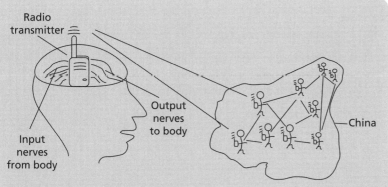

Figure 3.16 Block's China thought experiment

China because the population of China is 1 billion, which may be enough to fulfil the functions that comprise your mental states). Then, for a short time, the Chinese population realizes the same machine table that describes the functions of your mental states.

According to functionalism, this should create a mind; but even if we could accept that this set-up could have Intentional mental states such as beliefs or thoughts, it is especially difficult to believe that there would be a 'Chinese consciousness'. If the Chinese system replicated the functioning of my brain when I feel pain, would something be in pain? What? Is there something it is like to be this system? The objection is that the Chinese system, although it duplicates your functioning, can't duplicate your mind, because some mental states are qualia, and the system can't have qualia because they are not functional states.

Functionalists can reply that the Chinese system won't be functionally identical to you. For instance, it could be disrupted by things that your mind isn't disrupted by, e.g. the radios running out of batteries or the system being disrupted by bad weather.

True, but irrelevant, says Block. First, although this *could* happen, if it doesn't, then we have functional duplication, and the functionalist must say that the Chinese system is conscious. Second, these disruptions don't count as inputs or outputs, any more than having a brain tumour counts as an 'input' to our mental states. It is not part of their functioning – that's why they are disruptions.

Explain the objection to functionalism from Block's China thought experiment.

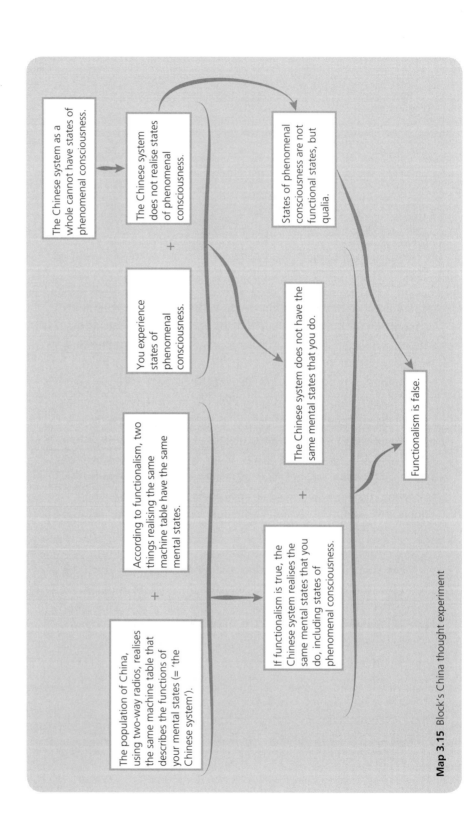

Map 3.15 Block's China thought experiment

Functionalists can object that the Chinese system is much slower than our brains. But, replies Block, why should this matter for whether it has mental states? Couldn't there be much slower minds than ours? In any case, this is just an objection about what is physically possible. A Chinese system that operated as fast as our brains is still metaphysically possible.

Can functionalism give a satisfactory analysis of phenomenal properties?

A physicalist response

If Block's objection works, then not *everything* about the mind can be explained in terms of functions. But perhaps we can combine functionalism and the type identity theory to argue as follows.

If the Chinese system can have Intentional mental states, then functionalism provides an accurate account of all mental states except for consciousness of phenomenal properties, which involves qualia. Why should this be? We could argue that the intrinsic properties of qualia depend on the specific *physical* properties of the system that realises the functional states. We saw this type of argument in Patricia Churchland's response to the objection from inverted qualia above. How colours look to us isn't (just) a matter of what causes the colour experience and what effects it has, it also depends on our physiology – the types of cones we have and the way our brains are wired. So what mental states something has depends on its functional properties *and* its intrinsic physical properties. Mental states are still nothing more than physical states playing a functional role. A physical, functional duplicate of a person with consciousness will have the same conscious states.

Are all mental states functional states?

Thinking harder: Chalmers on explaining consciousness

It is worth reflecting further on the debate over consciousness and phenomenal properties. Consciousness is, we said, one of the FEATURES OF MENTAL STATES (p. 172) intimately connected to the idea of 'subjectivity' and undergoing experiences. David Chalmers argues that this aspect of consciousness, the subjective quality of experience, is very different from anything else in the world, anything else that can be investigated by science, that we think of as objective.

CHALMERS, *THE CONSCIOUS MIND*, CH. 1

Chalmers begins by identifying consciousness in terms of phenomenal properties. Consciousness is not the same thing as the mind, since there can be unconscious mental states (beliefs or desires that someone isn't aware that they have) and even unconscious processes, such as thought and even unconscious perception. Consciousness is characterized by a subjective quality of experience, so that some being is conscious if there is something it is like to be that being, and some mental state is conscious if there is something it is like to be in that mental state.

This sense of 'consciousness' needs to be distinguished from the ability to introspect and report on what one thinks or believes or wants. It also needs to be distinguished from the ability to focus one's attention on something or to voluntarily control one's behaviour. In all these senses, one is 'conscious of' an object (e.g. by looking at it or listening to it) or 'conscious of' what one is doing. These are Intentional mental states, being 'conscious of' something in the sense of knowing about it.

Cognitive science has investigated a great deal about the mind, including the nature of consciousness in the sense just described. It has and continues to make progress on what it is for something to be conscious in these ways, including being awake, introspection, reporting mental states, self-consciousness, attention, voluntary control and knowledge. But cognitive science has had very little to say about consciousness in the first sense, the subjective quality of experience.

Chalmers argues that we really need two concepts of mind. The first is a 'phenomenal' concept, where minds or mental states are characterized by the subjective quality of experience. The second is a 'psychological' concept, characterized by what the mind does and how we explain behaviour. The phenomenal concept deals with first-person aspects of mind, the mind as experienced by the subject; the psychological concept, with third-person aspects, the mind as accounted for by others and in scientific theories. Cognitive science has said little about the mind as phenomenal because, as a scientific discipline, it deals just with those states relevant to the causation and explanation of behaviour, and not subjectivity as such.

The two concepts are complementary, but distinct. In particular, the phenomenal concept can't be reduced to or explained in terms of the psychological concept. For example, while the brain is very complex, there is no *deep* mystery about the idea of brains processing information, reacting to stimuli and exhibiting complex cognitive capacities like learning, memory and language. We can offer plausible evolutionary explanations of why such functions should emerge through natural selection, and plausible physical explanations of how they occur (although lots of the details are still missing). But why does subjective conscious experience occur? If we only knew facts of physics and information processing, there would be no reason to suggest that such a thing exists at all. It seems, Chalmers suggests, like a *new feature* of the world; it is surprising. Only our first-personal experience gives us reason to think it exists.

Functionalism argues that the analysis of mental states in terms of causal functional role can be applied not just to psychological states, but to all mental states, including phenomenal ones. But, says Chalmers, while we can understand how some state could have a certain causal role, it remains mysterious why it should have phenomenal properties. Functionalism gives a good account of psychological

Chalmers' distinction of phenomenal v. psychological is similar to, but not the same as, the distinction of the features of mental states as consciousness and Intentionality. First, he allows that there is a psychological concept of consciousness. Second, he allows that Intentionality may depend upon both phenomenal and psychological aspects of the mind.

PROPERTY DUALISM, p. 291, defends this claim, that consciousness is new or distinct from what is physical.

properties, including Intentionality, but not conscious experience. After we have explained the physical and computational functioning of a conscious system, we still need to explain why this system has conscious experiences.

Just as we can talk of phenomenal and psychological concepts of mind, we can also talk of phenomenal and psychological concepts of mental states. For example, we can distinguish a phenomenal concept of pain – how it feels – from a psychological one, that it is caused by damage and leads to aversive behaviour. We don't normally distinguish the two concepts, because the two properties usually go together. In the human mind, (phenomenal) conscious experience always also involves (psychological) cognitive processing. And so we don't have the words for describing phenomenal qualities independent of their psychological, functional properties. We tend to pick out phenomenal properties in terms of their external qualities or causal role, e.g. we define 'a sensation of green' in terms of being typically caused by grass, trees, etc. But 'a sensation of green' isn't just 'a state caused by grass, trees, etc.' We are talking of the phenomenal quality that typically occurs when we undergo a visual experience caused by grass, trees, etc. We can draw similar distinctions in our concepts of emotion, desire and other mental states.

As long as we recognise that there are two distinct concepts here, we don't need to argue over which is more essential to pain or colour experience or emotion … itself. But we should recognise that the co-occurrence of the two properties is not a conceptual truth. This is shown by the kind of thought experiments we looked at above – we can coherently imagine the phenomenal and the psychological properties coming apart.

Thus, we can talk of 'psychological consciousness' and 'phenomenal consciousness'. Many philosophical theories and psychological studies account for psychological consciousness

Explain Chalmers' distinction between the phenomenal and psychological concepts of mind.

but not phenomenal consciousness. As with other mental concepts, phenomenal consciousness involves some psychological processing, especially 'awareness' – having access to some information and being able to use it in controlling behaviour, e.g. to give a verbal report of what one sees. But while awareness may be necessary for phenomenal consciousness, as a purely psychological phenomenon, it isn't sufficient – it is possible to be aware of some fact without undergoing an experience with a particular subjective quality.

We can also talk of two 'mind–body problems'. The easy problem is how a physical system could have psychological properties, e.g. learning and memory. This is technical, but as we said above, it is not mysterious, since it is an account of causal roles and functions. The hard problem is how a physical system could have phenomenal properties. It is significant that the progress of cognitive science with the first problem has shed little light on the second.

necessary & sufficient

The second person?

It is worth noting that Chalmers claims that the two concepts of mind are reflections of first-person experience and third-person explanation of behaviour. These two concepts, he says, cover all mental phenomena. But, we may object, there is a number between 1 and 3. How should philosophy of mind and psychology think of *second*-person interaction, i.e. thinking of 'you' as someone with whom I interact as a person, rather than as an experimental subject to be explained? Of all the theories we have discussed so far, it is RYLE'S 'SOFT' BEHAVIOURISM (p. 245) that comes closest to recognising this natural way of thinking about other people. Descartes starts with the first person, physicalist theories (apart from Ryle) take a scientific, third-personal approach. Could beginning with the second person, looking at our experience of interacting with each other as people, open new ways of thinking about consciousness, Intentionality and what it means to have a mind?

Key points: functionalism

- Functionalism claims that mental properties are functional properties, defined in terms of their typical inputs and outputs (which may include other mental states). A mental state is just a state with a particular functional role. Functionalism can be understood as a descendant of philosophical behaviourism, replacing 'behaviour' in the analysis of mental states by 'function'.

- Causal role functionalism interprets 'function' as the role played in a network of causes and effects. Machine-table functionalism interprets 'function' in terms of a machine table that lists a series of conditional statements linking inputs, states and outputs.

- According to functionalism, mental states can be multiply realised. A functional property (and so mental properties) can be realised by various physical or even non-physical states, as long as they fulfil the relevant causal role (or machine table). Thus, functionalism is compatible with both physicalism and substance dualism.

- Some philosophers argue that phenomenal properties are qualia, i.e. intrinsic, non-Intentional properties of experience. If they are, then functionalism cannot be a complete theory of the mind, as qualia are not functional properties.

- The thought experiments of inverted qualia and Block's 'China mind' are designed to show that phenomenal properties are not functional properties.

- Patricia Churchland argues that the inverted qualia thought experiment fails. Empirically, it is not possible to invert qualia without a functional difference. Conceptually, it is unclear whether completely inverted colour experience would be experience of the same colours. The best explanation of colour experience rejects the claim that phenomenal properties are intrinsic.

- Functionalists can respond to Block's 'China mind' by amending their theory to claim that phenomenal properties are fixed by functional *and physical* properties, taken together.

- Chalmers argues that there are two distinct concepts of mind, phenomenal and psychological. While scientific psychology can explain the functions of psychological consciousness, it cannot explain the subjective quality of phenomenal consciousness.

Summary: functionalism

In this section on functionalism, we have looked at what functionalism is, how it explains the multiple realisability of mental states, and the objection that it cannot explain phenomenal properties. In our discussion and evaluation of these arguments, we have looked at the following issues:

1. What does it mean to claim that mental states are 'functional' states?
2. Why is functionalism compatible with both physicalism and dualism?
3. Is there something about what it is like to have conscious experiences that cannot be analysed in terms of functions?
4. What are thought experiments and how can they be used in philosophy of mind?

V. Dualist theories: property dualism

A. Property dualism

The theory

We saw that SUBSTANCE DUALISM (p. 181) claims that minds are not bodies, nor parts of bodies, nor properties of bodies, but substances that are distinct from bodies. Rejecting this claim led us, in the first instance, to PHYSICALISM (p. 212), the view that not only is the only substance physical, but that everything that exists is either physical or supervenes on the physical properties of physical substances. In the last section, we saw that FUNCTIONALISM (p. 268) is compatible with this claim. Although it claims that mental properties are not themselves physical properties, because they are functional properties they supervene on physical properties.

Property dualism is the view that, although there is just one kind of substance, physical substance, at least some mental properties are neither physical nor functional properties, nor are they behavioural dispositions. Instead, they are properties that do not supervene on physical properties in the way that physicalism claims. While mental properties are possessed by physical substances, they are a *fundamentally* different kind of property from physical properties.

Look again at FIGURE 3.7 'LEVELS' OF EXISTENCE, EACH SUPERVENING ON THE ONES BELOW, p. 214. Property dualists argue that some mental properties, e.g. phenomenal properties, are as fundamental as elementary physical particles, even if correlated with processes of living things.

Property dualism most often defends this claim for phenomenal properties of consciousness. These properties, such as pain, the smell of coffee, the visual experience of a red rose, the feeling of joy, and so on, can't be reduced to physical, behavioural or functional properties. These properties, at least, are a completely new type of property.

Property dualism rejects physicalism, and claims that there are some mental properties that exist that are neither physical nor do they supervene on physical properties. It argues that the properties identified by physics do not form the *complete* fundamental nature of the universe, because in addition, there are properties of consciousness. Physics misses something fundamental. When all the physical properties of the world are finalised, this does not fix or determine the properties of consciousness the way distributing paint on a canvas determines its aesthetic properties.

Property dualists are happy to allow that there may be correlations, even natural (though not physical) laws, that connect particular physical and mental properties. So it may be a law of nature that when a creature has a certain neurological property, it has a certain conscious experience. But it is metaphysically possible for these correlations to be different, for the properties of consciousness to come apart from any physical properties with which they are correlated. Mental properties are an entirely new kind of property in the world, and do not supervene on physical properties in the way that physicalism claims.

We will see in ISSUES FACING INTERACTIONIST PROPERTY DUALISM (p. 323) that some property dualists argue that these mental properties have their own causal powers, which can affect physical events. This is a second way in which property dualism may reject physicalism, in rejecting physicalism's claim that non-physical causes do not contribute to the way the physical world changes over time.

?

What is property dualism?

This article is also reprinted as Chalmers, *The Character of Consciousness*, Ch. 5.

CHALMERS, 'CONSCIOUSNESS AND ITS PLACE IN NATURE', §§2, 3.1

We saw in THINKING HARDER: CHALMERS ON EXPLAINING CONSCIOUSNESS (p. 285) that Chalmers distinguishes between what he calls the 'easy' and the 'hard' mind–body problems. The 'easy' problem involves the 'psychological' concept of consciousness, analysing and explaining the functions of consciousness, e.g. the facts that we can consciously control our behaviour, report on our mental states, and focus our attention. Chalmers thinks that understanding how the brain works will eventually provide the solutions. So this doesn't threaten physicalism. The 'hard' problem relates to the 'phenomenal' concept of consciousness, what it is like to undergo conscious experiences. How and why are certain physical processes in the brain associated with such experiences?

Setting aside philosophical behaviourism, physicalists say that these conscious experiences *just are* certain physical processes or certain physical states playing a particular functional role. But, Chalmers argues, a physical account of something can only explain its physical structure and function – how something is constituted and how it works. And this, he objects, is not enough to explain phenomenal consciousness. Such explanations miss out how experiences 'feel', what it is like to undergo them, their subjective or first-personal aspect. There is more to phenomenal consciousness than structure and function. This thought is fundamental to arguments for property dualism.

> Outline and explain the differences between the 'easy' and 'hard' mind–body problems.

The knowledge argument

JACKSON, 'EPIPHENOMENAL QUALIA', §1

Frank Jackson defends property dualism on the basis of his 'knowledge argument'. He describes the following scenario. Suppose there is a neuroscientist, Mary, who has lived all her life in a room in which everything is black and white. She has never seen any colour other than black, white and shades of grey. However, she has specialised in the science of vision, and through textbooks and black-and-white TV, she has come to know every physical fact there is to know about colour vision – everything about the properties of light, everything about the eye, everything about the nerves and the brain related to vision. So, Mary knows all the physical information there is to know about what happens when we see a ripe tomato. She is then let out of the black-and-white room, and comes to see something red for the first time. Does she learn something new?

Jackson claims that 'it seems just obvious' that she will. She will learn about what it is like to see the colour red. And so she learns something new about our visual experience of the world. However, we said that she knew all the physical facts while she was in the room. So not all the facts are physical facts. It is possible to know all about the physical properties of the brain involved in having an experience and yet not know about the qualia.

P1. Mary knows all the physical facts about seeing colours before being released from her black-and-white room.
P2. On being released, she learns new facts about seeing colours.
C1. Therefore, not all facts are physical facts, e.g. some facts about colours are not.
C2. Therefore, phenomenal properties are non-physical and physicalism is false.

By 'all the physical facts', Jackson means not only what we already know about physics and neurophysiology. Mary knows all the physical facts as discovered by a *completed* physics and neuroscience. Furthermore, she has worked out all the causal and functional facts that are entailed by these facts. Because physicalism claims that the world is entirely physical (if we include causal and functional properties), it must claim that to have complete physical knowledge is to have complete knowledge. But no amount of physical information can enable Mary to know what it is like to see a ripe tomato.

Explain Jackson's knowledge argument against physicalism.

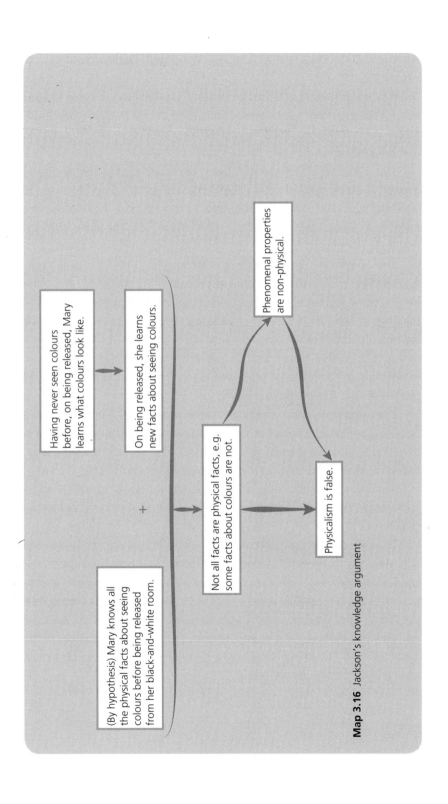

Map 3.16 Jackson's knowledge argument

THE KNOWLEDGE ARGUMENT AS A DUALIST ARGUMENT AGAINST OTHER THEORIES

The syllabus indicates that dualist arguments in general should be considered as objections to philosophical behaviourism and the mind–brain type identity theory, and that we should also consider the knowledge argument as applied to functional facts.

The knowledge argument attacks the mind–brain identity theory directly. The identity theory claims that sensations just are brain processes, so it follows that if Mary knows all about brain processes, she knows everything there is to know about sensations. This is precisely the claim that the knowledge argument attacks.

The argument works against functionalism in the same way. Functionalism claims that phenomenal properties are functional properties (or functional + physical properties). When Jackson says that Mary knows all the physical facts, he includes the functional facts. Mary knows exactly how the brain functions during an experience of seeing red. But the argument is meant to show that Mary doesn't know all there is to know about such an experience, so phenomenal properties are not just functional (+ physical) properties, and functionalism is wrong.

The argument also works the same way against Hempel's hard behaviourism, which claims that we can reduce talk of colour experiences to the conditions of verification. But, the knowledge argument claims, Mary knows all about what conditions in someone's brain would verify whether or not they had a particular colour experience, but she doesn't know all about colour experiences, because she doesn't know what it is like to experience colour.

To object to Ryle's soft behaviourism, we need to extend the knowledge that Mary has. Not only does she know everything that goes on in someone's brain when they experience colour, let us say that she also knows exactly how they are disposed to behave, e.g. what they will say if asked certain questions, what similarity judgements they will make, how they associate colours with emotions, and so on. Still, we can argue, even to know all this is not to know everything about colour experience. Mary still doesn't know what it is like to actually see colours.

We discuss consciousness and Ryle's behaviourism further in PROPERTY DUALISM MAKES A 'CATEGORY MISTAKE', p. 330.

Explain one physicalist account of phenomenal consciousness and how the knowledge argument is an objection to it.

Responses to the knowledge argument

Physicalist responses to Jackson's argument point out that there is more than one meaning of 'to know', more than one kind of knowledge. We can and should accept that Mary gains new knowledge when she sees red for the first time. But this doesn't mean that she gains knowledge of some new *fact*. The three different responses offer alternative accounts of just what Mary learns.

MARY DOES NOT GAIN NEW PROPOSITIONAL KNOWLEDGE, BUT DOES GAIN ABILITY KNOWLEDGE

The first response argues that instead of gaining knowledge of a fact, described by a proposition (e.g. 'that red looks like this'), Mary gains *know-how* – the knowledge involved in certain abilities. For instance, to see red for the first time is to gain the ability to know how to imagine or recognise red. So Jackson hasn't shown that there are any facts that are not physical facts.

We can challenge this objection as follows. Suppose that seeing red gives us these new abilities. Are such abilities *all* that is involved in knowing what it is like to see red? Suppose Mary wonders whether what it is like for others to see red is the same as what it is like for her. She isn't wondering about her abilities to imagine and recognise red. She is wondering about the truth of a proposition. So when Mary first learns what it is like to see red, she *does* gain knowledge of a new fact.

Is the objection even right to think that knowing what it is like to see red involves knowing how to imagine red? Suppose there is someone who (for whatever reason) has no ability to imagine seeing red. Now suppose this person looks attentively at something red. While they look at red, they know what is it like to see red. And yet they cannot imagine seeing red. This shows that the ability to imagine is not necessary for knowing what it is like to see red. Now suppose someone else has the most amazing ability to imagine seeing colours. They are told that there is a shade of red, e.g. burgundy, that is between plum red and tomato red. They are now *able* to imagine burgundy, but as long as they don't *actually* imagine burgundy, they still don't know what it is like to see burgundy. This shows that the ability to imagine a colour is not sufficient to know what it is like to see it. (We can make similar arguments for recognising colours.)

Propositional
Practical
Acquaintance

On ability, acquaintance and propositional knowledge, see Epistemology, TYPES OF KNOWLEDGE, p. 31.

like when you forget your friend's face

Is Mary's learning what it is like to see red just her gaining new abilities?

If the ability to imagine seeing red is neither necessary nor sufficient for knowing what it is like to see red, then when Mary comes to know what it is like to see red, she learns more than simply knowing how to imagine seeing red. The response fails to show that Mary does not learn a new fact. It fails to show that the knowledge argument is mistaken.

MARY DOES NOT GAIN NEW PROPOSITIONAL KNOWLEDGE, BUT DOES GAIN ACQUAINTANCE KNOWLEDGE

A second response to Jackson's argument argues that Mary gains a different kind of knowledge again, not propositional knowledge (knowing that), but not ability knowledge (knowing how) either. Instead, she gains 'acquaintance knowledge' – a direct awareness of the thing. To see red is a *direct* apprehension of red, as contrasted with descriptions of seeing red. How does the objection work?

Suppose that what it is like to see red is a physical property of the visual experience, which itself is a physical process. In other words, the phenomenal property of what it is like to see red is some property of the brain (type identity). Mary can then know all *about* this physical property, about what it is, when it occurs, and so on, before she leaves the room. However, she is not *acquainted* with the property – she doesn't have direct knowledge of it because *her brain has never itself had this property*. When she sees red, this property occurs in her brain and she becomes acquainted with it. She gains new knowledge, but she hasn't learned any new fact. She already knew all about this property before she left the room. (Compare: a friend describes someone you have never met. When you first meet the person and become acquainted with them, you think of them in a new way. But the person you meet was someone you already knew about.)

Patricia Churchland puts the two ~~above~~ responses together. Knowing the neuroscience won't help you experience or identify phenomenal properties in consciousness. For this, the theory needs to be true of your brain, i.e. your brain needs to undergo the processes that the theory describes as constituting colour experience. This fact doesn't mean that there is something that the theory misses out. When Mary's brain actually undergoes the processes that she knows all about, then she will be acquainted with colour and gain abilities of recognition, etc. But that is all the colour experience is. Nothing in addition to the physical processes is needed or occurs.

There are two possible responses to this objection. First, we can argue that acquaintance knowledge involves propositional knowledge. What it is

> Explain the claim that when Mary leaves her room, she gains acquaintance knowledge but not new propositional knowledge. Explain why this claim defends physicalism against the knowledge argument.

to be acquainted with red is to know *that seeing red is like this* (having the experience). Becoming acquainted with red involves learning some new fact. So Mary does learn a new, and therefore non-physical, fact when she becomes acquainted with red. So what it is like to experience red can't simply be a physical property of the brain.

Second, we can argue that the objection misunderstands the argument. The knowledge argument isn't about *Mary's* experience. The argument is that Mary didn't know everything about *other people's* experiences before she left the room, even though she knew everything physical about their experiences. Mary doesn't know what it is like for anyone to experience red. This is a *fact* about experiences that Mary doesn't know. When Mary leaves the room, she realises how impoverished her conception of people's colour experiences has been. So there are facts about other people's experiences of seeing red that Mary learns.

P1. Mary (before her release) knows everything physical there is to know about other people when they see colour.

P2. Mary (before her release) does not know everything there is to know about other people when they see colour (because she *learns* something about them on her release).

C1. Therefore, there are truths about other people (and herself) when they see colour which escape the physicalist story.

C2. Therefore, phenomenal properties are non-physical and physicalism is false.

> Does Mary learn more than acquaintance knowledge about what it is like to see red?

> The distinction between concepts and properties also served in THINKING HARDER: WHAT IS CONCEIVABLE MAY NOT BE METAPHYSICALLY POSSIBLE (I), p. 189, and SMART ON CORRELATION, IDENTITY AND REDUCTION, p. 218, as well as arguments in Metaphysics of God, THINKING HARDER: GOOD IS THE SAME PROPERTY AS WHAT GOD WILLS, p. 47.

Thinking harder: Mary gains new propositional knowledge, but this is knowledge of physical facts that she already knew in a different way

A third response to Jackson's argument distinguishes between two ways we might talk about 'facts' on the basis of the distinction between concepts and properties.

Suppose I know that there is water in the glass. Is that the same as knowing that there is H_2O in the glass? No – because someone may know one of these truths without knowing the other. Someone can have the concept WATER without having the concept H_2O. Or again, someone may have both concepts, but not know that water and H_2O are the same thing. So we can say that to know that there is water in the glass and to know that there is H_2O in the glass is to know two different facts. In this sense of 'fact', we count facts in terms of concepts.

However, in another sense of 'fact', the fact that there is water in the glass *just is* the fact that there is H_2O in the glass, because water and H_2O are identical – one thing. Both of these claims are made true by just one state of affairs in the world. In this sense of 'fact', we count facts in terms of how the world is, not how we think about it. Another way of expressing this is to say that the property of being water and the property of being H_2O are one and the same property. We will use 'fact' in this sense from now on.

We can now apply this to the knowledge argument. Before leaving the room, Mary has a concept of red in physical terms – wavelengths of light, neurons firing, and so on. Call this the 'physical' or again a 'theoretical' concept of red, RED_{TH}. Or again, using Chalmers' distinction between psychological and phenomenal concepts, Mary knows what it is to see red in the psychological sense of 'seeing red'. We can contrast this with a 'phenomenal' concept of red, RED_{PH}. A phenomenal concept of something is the concept by which you recognise something when you experience or perceive it. So we gain the phenomenal concept RED_{PH} by seeing red. Before she leaves the room, Mary doesn't know what it is to see red in the phenomenal sense.

When Mary comes out of the room and sees red, she acquires the phenomenal concept RED_{PH} for the first time. She is now able to think about red in a new way, in terms of what it is like to see red. She couldn't know what it is like to see red before because she didn't have the phenomenal concept. But, we can claim, the phenomenal concept RED_{PH} is a concept of *the same thing* that her theoretical concept RED_{TH} is a concept of – they are two different concepts of a physical property of the brain (like WATER and H_2O are two concepts of the same physical substance). Mary gains new propositional knowledge about seeing red in one sense (because she gains a new concept) but her new knowledge is about a property that she already knew about under a different concept. The theoretical concept RED_{TH} and the phenomenal concept RED_{PH} are two concepts that refer to the same property.

is RED_{PH} qualia?

Plato's Slave boy?

Semantic problems?

RED_{TH} doesn't explain qualia

diagram?

Let us accept that the knowledge argument shows that there are different *ways of thinking* about physical things, some of which depend on experiencing, rather than describing. To know what it is like to see red, you need to have the phenomenal concept RED$_{PH}$, and this you can only gain from experience. So Mary gains knowledge of a new fact, in the sense of fact that relates to concepts.

However, physicalism and property dualism are claims about what exists. They are claims about *properties*, not about concepts. The knowledge argument does *not* show that Mary gains knowledge of a new *property*. It doesn't show that Mary learns about something in the world that she didn't know about before. And so it doesn't show that what it is like to see red cannot be a physical property. So the argument fails to show that there are any non-physical properties. So it fails to show that physicalism is false.

> Explain the knowledge argument and one response to it.

The 'philosophical zombies' argument

It is perhaps worth knowing in advance that the zombie argument and responses to it are probably the most philosophically demanding material on the A level. Understanding the next few pages will require even more careful thought than usual. We will be discussing not only property dualism, but the question of the limits of metaphysics and the relation between philosophy and science.

To understand the 'zombie' argument, we first need to understand the idea of a possible world.

POSSIBLE WORLDS

To start, read again the discussion of the three types of possibility – physical possibility, logical possibility, and metaphysical possibility – in THINKING HARDER: WHAT IS CONCEIVABLE MAY NOT BE METAPHYSICALLY POSSIBLE (I) (p. 189).

To summarise: what is physically possible is what is possible given the laws of nature as they are in the actual world; what is logically possible is whatever is not conceptually incoherent or self-contradictory; and we didn't give a definition of metaphysical possibility, but we said it was constrained by the real nature or identity of things. We discussed it in terms of necessary

Modal logic

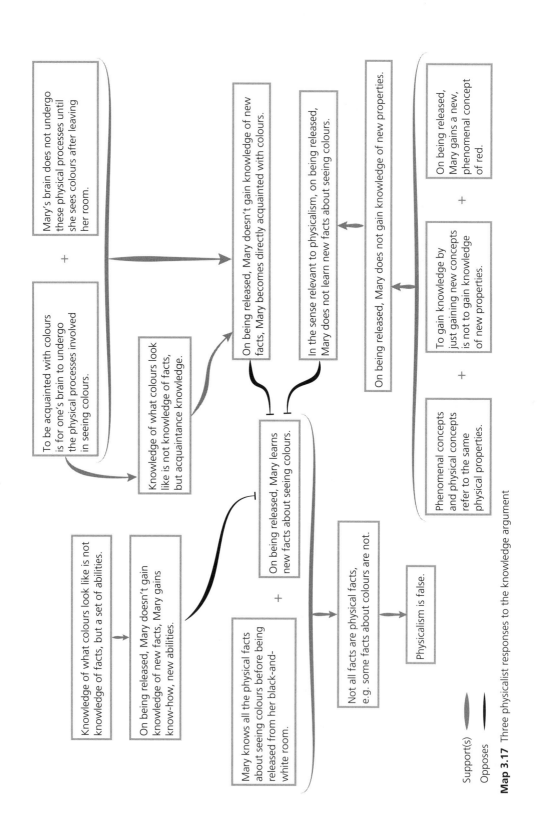

Map 3.17 Three physicalist responses to the knowledge argument

Support(s)

Opposes

truths that are not analytic, such as 'water is H_2O'. We can understand metaphysical possibility better by talking about 'possible worlds'.

Let's start by talking about true and false propositions. Propositions describe 'states of affairs'. Propositions can be true or false. A proposition that is true describes the actual world, the way things are, a true state of affairs. A proposition that is false describes the way things are not, a false state of affairs.

However, false propositions can be necessarily false or just contingently false. A proposition that is necessarily false cannot be true – it is impossible for it to be true (either logically or metaphysically). A proposition that is only contingently false describes a state of affairs that is possible, but false, given how the world actually is. For example, 'I was born in Kenya' is false, but could have been true.

A contingently false proposition describes a way things could be, if they were different. We can say that in some other 'possible world', a contingently false proposition is true, the state of affairs it describes is part of the way that world is. In some other possible world, I was born in Kenya. A possible world is a way of talking about how things could be.

Possible worlds are distinct from one another depending on what we are supposing to be true in that world. So the possible world in which I was born in Kenya is different from the possible world in which I was born in Argentina which is different from the possible world in which I don't exist at all. — can't talk about that

Metaphysical possibility

These examples – of where I was born or even not existing – describe possible worlds that are physically possible as well as metaphysically and logically possible. There is nothing physically, metaphysically or logically impossible about the state of affairs of my being born in Kenya. We can imagine much bigger differences from the actual world without leaving physical possibility, e.g. a world in which the Earth never formed or in which evolution never gave rise to human beings.

But we can also talk about possible worlds that are physically impossible, worlds in which the laws of nature are different, e.g. in which light travels at a different speed, or that contain physically impossible things, perhaps things such as angels and ghosts. If these are genuine possible worlds – ways that a world could be – then they are worlds which are physically impossible but metaphysically possible.

if physics was different things are metaphysically possible?

As we will see, philosophers disagree on which worlds are possible worlds. It is not always easy to tell. For example, is there a possible world in which water is not H_2O? In our previous discussion of metaphysical possibility, we said that 'water is H_2O' is not an analytic truth, so it is conceivable (logically possible) that water is not H_2O. But water and H_2O are identical – just one thing. So it is not metaphysically possible for water to exist without being H_2O. There is no possible world in which water exists, but is something other than H_2O.

We'll return to this discussion when we assess the zombie argument, looking again at arguments for claiming that what is conceivable may not be metaphysically possible (see THINKING HARDER: WHAT IS CONCEIVABLE MAY NOT BE METAPHYSICALLY POSSIBLE (I), p. 189). For now, we can say that what is metaphysically possible is what can exist or occur as part of a possible world. Metaphysical possibility is narrower than logical possibility, since it turns out that not all conceptually coherent propositions describe how things could exist. So physical possibility concerns how things can be given the actual laws of nature; metaphysical possibility concerns how things can be in any possible world; and logical possibility concerns whether a proposition is conceptually coherent.

What is a possible world?

bit circular

CHALMERS' ZOMBIE ARGUMENT

Property dualism claims that phenomenal properties (which many property dualists claim are qualia) are not physical properties, nor do they supervene on physical properties. It rejects physicalism. But how can a property dualist show this? In THE KNOWLEDGE ARGUMENT (p. 293), we saw Jackson argue that knowledge of all physical properties won't include knowledge of phenomenal properties, so they must be distinct. Chalmers uses the idea of possible worlds to reach the same conclusion.

According to physicalism, everything that exists is either physical or depends on what is physical. So if physicalism is true, a possible world that is an exact physical duplicate of our world (the actual world) will be an exact duplicate of our world *in all respects*. This is just the claim of supervenience, but at the level of the world. Consider: a painting that is an exact physical duplicate of another painting has all the same aesthetic properties as that painting. So a whole world that is an exact physical duplicate of another world also has all the same aesthetic properties. But what goes for aesthetic properties goes for all properties, according to physicalism. There can be no difference in, say, mental properties without a difference in physical properties. In other words, it is *metaphysically impossible*, says physicalism, for two worlds to have the same physical properties and different mental properties, because the physical properties determine the mental properties.

Therefore, if there is a possible world that is an exact physical duplicate of our world but is different in any way, e.g. it has different phenomenal properties, then physicalism is false. If two physically identical worlds have different properties of consciousness, those properties of consciousness don't depend on physical properties. This is what Chalmers tries to show with the idea of a philosophical zombie.

Explain physicalism in terms of possible worlds.

CHALMERS, 'CONSCIOUSNESS AND ITS PLACE IN NATURE', §3.2

What is a philosophical zombie?

A 'zombie', in the philosophical sense, is an exact physical duplicate of a person – you, for instance – but without any conscious subjective quality of experience. It therefore has identical physical properties to you, but different mental properties – it has no phenomenal consciousness.

define?

Figure 3.17 This is not a philosophical zombie!

Haha Lacewing you're hilarious

Figure 3.18 This is a philosophical zombie

Of course, zombies are not possible in the actual world. They are not physically possible, i.e. given the laws of our universe, we have every reason to believe that any being that has identical physical properties to you will also have consciousness.

What we are thinking about when thinking about zombies is a different possible world – a world which has all the physical properties of our world but without consciousness. We are describing a world that may be metaphysically possible.

But is such a world really (metaphysically) possible? To argue that a world with zombies is possible is to argue for property dualism. How does the argument work?

The argument

First, it seems that zombies are at least conceivable. I've just described them, and there isn't an obvious contradiction in the idea. Second, given their conceivability, we may argue that zombies

What is a philosophical 'zombie'?

Conceivability! Nooo!

are therefore metaphysically possible. There is a possible world which has all the same physical properties as the actual world, but has no properties of consciousness.

Now, if consciousness were *identical* with physical properties, it would be impossible for a creature to have the same physical properties as you but not have consciousness. This is Leibniz's principle of the indiscernibility of identicals. As we saw with water and H_2O, if *A* is identical to *B* – if *A* is *B* – then you can't have *A* without *B* or vice versa; they are the same thing. So if zombies are possible – if a creature could be physically identical to you but not have consciousness – then consciousness is *not* identical to any physical properties. So, if zombies are metaphysically possible, then consciousness is not identical to any physical properties. Furthermore, if zombies are metaphysically possible, consciousness doesn't supervene on physical properties either, because you and your zombie 'twin' have identical physical properties, but different phenomenal properties. And so property dualism is true: phenomenal properties are neither reducible to nor supervenient upon physical properties.

P1. It is conceivable that there are zombies.

P2. If it is conceivable that there are zombies, it is metaphysically possible that there are zombies.

C1. Therefore, it is metaphysically possible that there are zombies.

P3. If it is metaphysically possible that there are zombies, then phenomenal properties of consciousness are neither physical properties nor supervene on physical properties.

C2. Therefore, phenomenal properties of consciousness are neither physical properties nor supervene on physical properties.

C3. Therefore, physicalism is false and property dualism is true.

Outline and explain the zombie argument as an objection to physicalism.

Conceivability = Facepalm

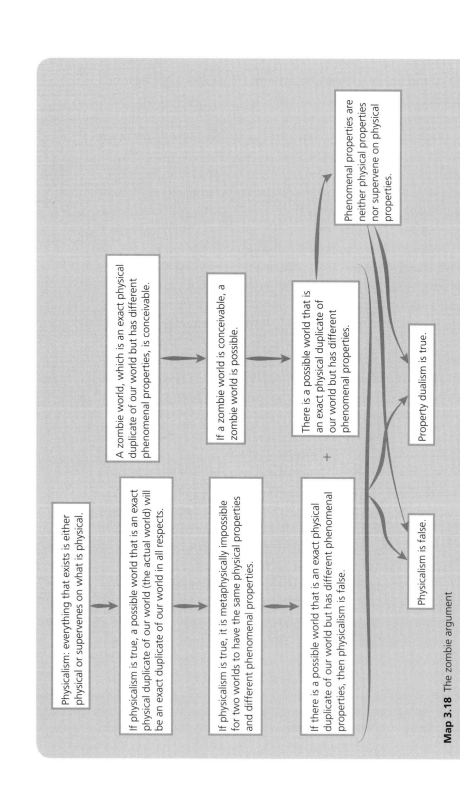

Map 3.18 The zombie argument

Thinking harder: how arguments for property dualism work

The zombie argument has similarities to two arguments we have already discussed. It is similar to DESCARTES' CONCEIVABILITY ARGUMENT (p. 185), but it is about properties not substances. And it is similar to the argument discussed in BLOCK ON THE POSSIBILITY OF A FUNCTIONAL DUPLICATE WITH NO QUALIA (p. 282), but it applies the argument to physicalism generally instead of objecting to functionalism specifically.

Chalmers presents a general analysis of how arguments for property dualism work. He focuses just on the knowledge argument and the zombie argument, but his comments also apply to other arguments from conceivability, including those mentioned above.

CHALMERS, 'CONSCIOUSNESS AND ITS PLACE IN NATURE', §3.4

The zombie and knowledge arguments both start from an *epistemic* claim. In the case of the zombie argument, this is established by reflecting on what is conceivable. The claim is that we can conceive of physical properties existing without the phenomenal properties of consciousness with which they are correlated in the actual world. In the case of the knowledge argument, we reflect on what Mary can know before she leaves her room. The claim is that she cannot figure out, just from her knowledge of all the physical facts, what it is like to experience red.

From the epistemic claim, each argument infers an *ontological* claim – a claim about the nature of what exists. The properties of consciousness are distinct from and do not supervene upon physical properties. In the knowledge argument, this inference is made on the basis of Mary learning a new fact about the world when she leaves the room. In the zombie argument, the inference is made through considering possible worlds. The argument claims that what we can coherently conceive of is possible; and if it is possible for one thing to exist without the other, this shows that they are distinct things.

THE ZOMBIE ARGUMENT AS A DUALIST ARGUMENT AGAINST OTHER THEORIES

Before looking at responses to the zombie argument, the syllabus indicates that the argument should be considered as an objection to philosophical behaviourism and the mind–brain type identity theory.

The zombie argument attacks the mind–brain type identity theory directly. Mind–brain type identity theory claims that phenomenal properties are identical with certain physical properties. If this were correct, then zombies would be metaphysically impossible, as explained above. So if zombies are metaphysically possible, then the mind–brain type identity theory is false.

Hempel's hard behaviourism claims to reduce talk of conscious experience to the conditions of verification. These all involve physical conditions – bodily movement, physiology, brain processes. Zombies have the same physical properties as us, and so we may suppose that they would satisfy all the conditions of verification that we satisfy. If this is all that is required to say that they undergo conscious experiences, then zombies are impossible – nothing could satisfy the conditions of verification for conscious experience and yet lack conscious experience. The zombie argument claims that zombies are possible, so it attacks Hempel's hard behaviourism. If zombies are possible, then our concept of consciousness cannot be reduced to physical concepts that describe conditions of verification.

As we saw in THINKING HARDER: RYLE ON CONSCIOUSNESS (p. 260), Ryle argues that consciousness in the sense that the property dualist talks about it is a 'myth'. Conscious experience is a matter of paying attention, e.g. to experience red is just to pay attention to the colour of something red, and to be conscious of doing this is just to be ready to say what you are thinking or feeling. But, if we understand these activities behaviourally, then it seems that zombies will behave like this, but they won't have conscious experiences of redness. So conscious experiences can't be fully understood in this way. If zombies are possible, then Ryle's behaviourism must be false.

Explain how the zombie argument is an objection to either mind–brain type identity theory or philosophical behaviourism, first in prose, then using an argument map.

wouldn't be disposed to act in a way because they hadn't been aware of their experience. of red

Responses to the zombie argument

We saw in the discussion of DESCARTES' CONCEIVABILITY ARGUMENT (p. 185) that there are different ways in which we may respond to dualist arguments from conceivability. First, we may argue that what is being proposed — in this case, a possible world that contains zombies – is not conceivable. Second, we may argue that although zombies are conceivable, they are not metaphysically possible. Third, we may argue that even though zombies are metaphysically possible, this doesn't tell us what consciousness is, and its relation to physical properties, in the actual world. Thus, we shall revisit these forms of argument that we first saw in response to Descartes, but with a deeper understanding of physicalism, metaphysical possibility and what is at stake in the debate.

A PHILOSOPHICAL ZOMBIE (OR ZOMBIE WORLD) IS NOT CONCEIVABLE

The first premise of the zombie argument claims that we can conceive of beings that have the same physical properties as us but without consciousness. Why think this is conceivable? Because when we think of physical properties, this doesn't determine what we must think of consciousness. By contrast, when we think of the answer to 3 × 4, we must – if we are thinking clearly – think of 12. It is inconceivable that 3 × 4 is anything other than 12. Or again, to use Descartes' example, it is inconceivable that the interior angles of a triangle could add up to anything other than 180 degrees. By contrast, it does not seem inconceivable that there could be a being with identical physical properties to you, but without consciousness.

The first objection to the argument is that, despite appearances, zombies are not conceivable. If we think they are conceivable, we are not thinking clearly or we lack some relevant information. It is difficult to recognise that we are not thinking clearly. But we can spell out where we are going wrong in more detail.

First, if physicalism is true, we should note that something's physical properties determine its functional properties. So a physical duplicate of you is also a functional duplicate of you. (If physicalism is not true, then something's functional properties could depend on its non-physical properties as well. But we cannot *assume* that physicalism is false, since that is what the zombie argument is trying to prove. To assume physicalism is false is to beg the question.)

Second, we need to revisit the arguments that phenomenal consciousness can be analysed in terms of physical and functional properties; there are no qualia. If we are not persuaded by this claim, it is probably because our analysis of consciousness is still underdeveloped. But if we had a complete analysis, we would see that consciousness can be completely explained in these terms. In that case, a physical, functional duplicate of you would also have consciousness.

(handwritten: ?)

(handwritten: This assumes physicalism is true? Begs the question?)

So, once we are clear on a being's physical properties, we can, in principle, deduce how it functions, and from this, with a complete analysis of consciousness, we can deduce whether or not it is conscious. So to imagine a being with identical physical properties to you but without consciousness is confused. It is like accepting the premises of a deductive argument but rejecting the conclusion. In conceiving of a 'zombie' as having identical physical properties, you conceive of it as having identical functions. But to function in certain (highly complex) ways just *is* to be conscious. So zombies – physically identical, but non-conscious beings – are inconceivable. (As Descartes might put it, the ideas of a zombie and of consciousness are not clear and distinct. When we make them clear and distinct, we see the contradiction the idea of zombies.)

(handwritten: using his words against him)

> P1. A zombie is a physical duplicate of a person with phenomenal consciousness, but without phenomenal consciousness.
> P2. (If physicalism is true,) A physical duplicate is a functional duplicate.
> C1. Therefore, a zombie is a physical and functional duplicate of a person, but without phenomenal consciousness.
> P3. (If physicalism is true,) Phenomenal properties are physical properties realising particular functional roles.
> C2. Therefore, a physical and functional duplicate of a person with phenomenal consciousness has phenomenal consciousness.
> P4. A physical and functional duplicate of a person with consciousness cannot both have and lack phenomenal consciousness.
> C3. Therefore, (if physicalism is true,) zombies are inconceivable.

Explain the objection that philosophical zombies are inconceivable, first in prose, then using an argument map.

This objection to the zombie argument depends on there being a complete physical and functional analysis of consciousness. I have inserted the phrase 'if physicalism is true' into two premises, (P2) and (P3), which the property dualist will contest. If there is no such analysis, because an analysis of consciousness in terms of its physical and functional properties doesn't provide an analysis of what it is like to experience something, then it seems that this response to the zombie argument fails.

Should we accept (P2) and (P3)? To do so, we need to have good reasons to think that phenomenal properties can be understood or explained either in terms of physical structure or in terms of functions. But there is nothing in our phenomenal concept and experience of consciousness that supports the claim. And so we can conceive of that same physical thing either with or without phenomenal consciousness.

The debate looks like a stalemate. On the one hand, the zombie argument mustn't assume that physicalism is false, since it is trying to show that physicalism is false. On the other hand, the response seems to assume that physicalism can give a complete analysis of our concept of consciousness.

Many philosophers have concluded that we should grant that zombies are conceivable, and focus the discussion on whether they are metaphysically possible. That takes us to our second response.

> Are philosophical zombies conceivable?

Thinking harder: what is conceivable may not be metaphysically possible (II)

The second response targets the second premise ((P2) on p. 307). Although zombies are conceivable, they aren't in fact metaphysically possible. What we are able to conceive is not always a reliable guide to what is possible.

> This response is similar to that discussed in MARY GAINS NEW PROPOSITIONAL KNOWLEDGE, BUT THIS IS KNOWLEDGE OF PHYSICAL FACTS THAT SHE ALREADY KNEW IN A DIFFERENT WAY, p. 299.

Identity and metaphysical possibility

To understand this, let us return for one last time to the example of water and H_2O. As we saw in our previous discussion of the principle that what is conceivable may not be metaphysically possible (THINKING HARDER: WHAT IS CONCEIVABLE MAY NOT BE METAPHYSICALLY POSSIBLE (I), p. 189) in relation to Descartes' conceivability argument, the two concepts WATER and H_2O are distinct, and it is not an analytic truth that water is H_2O. So it is conceivable (even if false) that water is not H_2O.

Given this, it is easy to think that water could have been different, i.e. in some possible world, water is not H_2O. However, given that water *is*

H_2O, it's not metaphysically possible that water isn't H_2O. This was an important claim about identity first made by Saul Kripke. It's not possible for A to be B and for it not to be B. So if A is identical to B – if A *is* B – then A is B *in every possible world*. Because water is H_2O, it is H_2O in every possible world.

Naming and Necessity

It is possible that the water in the oceans could have been fresh, not salty. Or in other words, in another possible world, the water in the oceans is fresh, not salty. The fact that oceans are salty is a *contingent* property of water in our world. It isn't what makes water what it is. Or again, the fact that water falls as rain is a contingent property of water. If it never rained, this wouldn't change what water is. So in another possible world, water never falls as rain.

But turn now to the question of what makes water what it is. What is the *essential* property of water? The answer: its chemical composition, H_2O. Now, what makes water *what it is* is not a property that water can lack in some possible world. A world without H_2O is a world without water, because water just is H_2O.

Explain why water is H_2O in every possible world.

Suppose there is another possible world in which a transparent, odourless liquid falls as rain, fills the oceans, freezes and evaporates, etc., but isn't H_2O. Is this liquid water? No, says Kripke. It is something *just like* water, in that it has many of the contingent properties of water. But it isn't water, because it isn't H_2O.

Kripke concluded that identity claims – 'A is identical to B' – are necessarily true, if true at all. They are true in all possible worlds.

We said that we can conceive of water not being H_2O. But we have argued that it isn't possible that water is not H_2O. This shows that we cannot always infer metaphysical possibility from conceivability.

The response to the zombie argument

We can now apply the point to zombies. The fact that we can conceive of zombies doesn't show that zombies are metaphysically possible. If phenomenal properties *just are* certain physical and/or functional properties, then it isn't possible for zombies to exist (even if they are conceivable). Given the physical properties we have, if physicalism is true, it just isn't possible for a being with the same physical properties not to have consciousness as well. If physicalism is true, then when we think of phenomenal consciousness and, say, certain neurological or functional properties, we are thinking of one and the same property in two different ways, using two different concepts.

This response doesn't have to claim that phenomenal properties *are* physical properties, that physicalism *is* true. It only has to claim that the zombie argument cannot show that physicalism is false. The premise that zombies are metaphysically possible cannot be defended without assuming that phenomenal properties are not, unknown to us, physical properties.

Explain the objection that philosophical zombies, though conceivable, are not metaphysically possible.

A disanalogy?

This second objection to the zombie argument relies on an analogy between phenomenal consciousness and scientific identities, such as water and H_2O or life and chemical processes. Property dualists can argue that this analogy doesn't work.

Something isn't water if it isn't H_2O, because H_2O is the 'essence' of water. The concept WATER is a concept of something that has a particular structure and causal role, which science can then discover. Water is precisely the kind of thing that could be – and is! – identical with a chemical property. This is why you can't have water without H_2O or H_2O without water.

See also MAP 3.3,
p. 193.

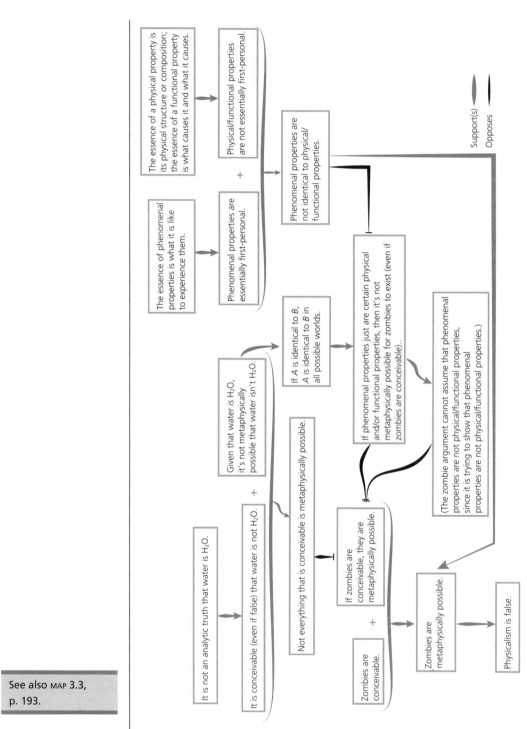

The essence of a physical property is its physical structure or composition; the essence of a functional property is what causes it and what it causes.

Physical/functional properties are not essentially first-personal.

+

Phenomenal properties are not identical to physical/functional properties.

The essence of phenomenal properties is what it is like to experience them.

Phenomenal properties are essentially first-personal.

If A is identical to B, A is identical to B in all possible worlds.

Given that water *is* H_2O, it's not metaphysically possible that water isn't H_2O.

If phenomenal properties just are certain physical and/or functional properties, then it's not metaphysically possible for zombies to exist (even if zombies are conceivable).

(The zombie argument cannot assume that phenomenal properties are not physical/functional properties, since it is trying to show that phenomenal properties are not physical/functional properties.)

It is not an analytic truth that water is H_2O.

It is conceivable (even if false) that water is not H_2O.

+

Not everything that is conceivable is metaphysically possible.

If zombies are conceivable, they are metaphysically possible.

Zombies are conceivable.

Zombies are metaphysically possible.

+

Zombies are metaphysically possible.

Physicalism is false.

Support(s)

Opposes

Map 3.19 Are zombies metaphysically possible?

By contrast, say property dualists, the essence of phenomenal properties is *what it is like to experience them*. The essence of pain – what makes pain pain – is *how pain feels*. Its essence isn't some physical or functional property. The essence of a physical property is its physical structure or composition; the essence of a functional property is what causes it and what it causes. In arguing that neuroscience can tell us what consciousness 'really is', physicalists are assuming that the essence of consciousness, like the essence of water, is something physical. But this is a mistake. Consciousness is essentially first-personal, i.e. what it is like for the person. The concept of consciousness is not the concept of something that has a particular physical structure or set of causal relations that science can then discover. So consciousness is not essentially a set of brain properties described by the neuroscientist.

If this is correct, then the correlation between brain properties and consciousness in the actual world is *contingent*. As it happens, certain brain processes give rise to consciousness. But you could have the brain processes without consciousness and vice-versa. It is only the essential properties of something that can't change in different possible worlds, the contingent properties can. The same physical processes that are correlated with consciousness in the actual world may not be correlated with consciousness in another possible world. Because phenomenal properties have a different essence from physical and functional properties, each can exist without the other. So zombies are possible.

Are philosophical zombies metaphysically possible?

Thinking harder: what is metaphysically possible tells us nothing about the actual world

A third objection to the zombie argument targets the inference from the claim that zombies are *possible* to the conclusion that property dualism is *true*. The zombie argument shows, at best, that *in another possible world*, physical properties and phenomenal properties are distinct. But why does this entail in the *actual* world that they are distinct? Couldn't it be the case that physicalism is true in the actual world, but property dualism is true in

Same as all theories

Explain the argument that if phenomenal properties are physical properties, they are physical properties in every possible world.

Same qualia

a different possible world? Or in other words, the zombie argument only shows that property dualism is possible; it doesn't show that property dualism is true.

We can reply that this objection makes two mistakes. First, the objection misunderstands identity. It suggests that phenomenal properties could *be* physical properties in this world but not in another possible world. But this isn't possible. Nothing can be something else. I can't not be me in another possible world. If 'I' were not me, but you, say, then that person is not me. In any possible world, the only person I can be is me. Likewise, water can't be something other than water. Since water *is* H_2O, it can't be something else in another possible world.

The same goes for phenomenal properties. If phenomenal properties *are* physical properties in this world, then they are physical properties in every possible world. And if they are *not* physical properties in another possible world, then they are not physical properties in any possible world, including the actual world. When it comes to identity, possibility does tell us about reality.

Second, if the objection is intended to defend physicalism, it misunderstands what physicalism claims. Physicalism claims that what exists is either physical or supervenes upon what is physical. We need to be clear about supervenience. As noted in PHYSICALISM (p. 212), in the example of the painting, we want to say that if the physical properties of two paintings are identical, then the aesthetic properties *cannot* be different. It is not strong enough to simply say that they *aren't* different, since that would allow that the physical properties don't 'fix' the aesthetic properties.

What we said about the aesthetic properties applies to properties of consciousness as well, and what applies to paintings is true of whole worlds. According to physicalism, once the physical properties of a world are finalised, then there is no further work to be done to 'add' consciousness. It is already part of the world. Phenomenal properties *cannot* differ independently of physical properties. So physicalism is a claim about what is metaphysically possible.

The zombie argument attacks this claim. It argues that there can be two worlds that are physically identical but with different phenomenal properties. Once the physical properties of a world are finalised, then there *is* still further work to be done to 'add' consciousness. Thinking about possibility does, in this case, tell us about reality.

Patricia Churchland on thought experiments

PATRICIA CHURCHLAND, *BRAIN-WISE*, CH. 4, §2.2

Patricia Churchland is sceptical about the use of appealing to conceivability or metaphysical possibility to discover the nature of the world. In imagining a zombie, we are imagining a being with a brain just like ours. But in imagining that it doesn't have phenomenal consciousness, we are imagining that if we knew everything about neuroscience, like Mary, we still wouldn't have explained or understood consciousness. But all this imagining is really a reflection of our own epistemic limitations and the fact that neuroscience just isn't very developed yet. The thought experiments of Mary and zombies don't tell us anything significant about the nature of consciousness. Property dualists are mistaken in trying to get conclusions about what exists out of epistemic premises.

See HOW ARGUMENTS FOR PROPERTY DUALISM WORK, p. 309.

Suppose someone (perhaps 200 years ago) said 'I just can't imagine how living things could really be composed of dead molecules – how can life arise out of the interactions of things that are not alive?' Or again, suppose someone proposed the thought experiment of 'deadbies', creatures who are physically identical to us, but aren't alive. They claim to be able to imagine such creatures. None of this would persuade us to think again about vitalism and the existence of a special, non-reducible 'life force'. On the current biological theory of what it is to be alive, deadbies are impossible and life really is just the highly complex interactions of molecules.

Similarly, we shouldn't be persuaded by the property dualists' appeal to zombies. First, from what is conceivable we cannot infer anything about the nature of how things are. Our grammar – our concepts as they are now – are not necessarily a good guide to how things really are. We change our concepts as we discover more about the world. Second, the same goes for thought experiments about what is metaphysically possible. What things really are is what they are in the actual world. We discovered what water is through scientific investigation. Similarly, the right way to think about consciousness is through scientific investigation, and we shouldn't let considerations about concepts determine in advance what scientific investigation may or may not discover. For example, contemporary biology argues that genes are DNA. Should we object to this reductive explanation because in another possible world, genes – understood as the units of heredity – might not be DNA? No. What genes are is what genes are in the actual world. And all we need to make this claim is an empirical identity, supported by scientific explanation. The same goes for consciousness.

Churchland is arguing that philosophy simply can't do metaphysics in this way, using thought experiments and possible worlds to discover what something is. Philosophical 'speculation' must give way to experimental science.

Churchland's argument also rejects Chalmers' distinction between phenomenal and psychological concepts of consciousness. She can either argue that Chalmers is just wrong that our normal concept of consciousness is phenomenal, because we can reduce consciousness to brain functions; or she can argue that he is right that we have a phenomenal concept of consciousness, but it is radically mistaken and should be eliminated in favour of a purely psychological one.

Explain Churchland's objection to the zombie argument.

See THINKING HARDER: CHALMERS ON EXPLAINING CONSCIOUSNESS, p. 285.

Does the philosophical zombies argument establish that property dualism is true?

Key points: property dualism

- Property dualism claims that at least some mental properties (usually phenomenal properties/qualia) cannot be reduced to physical properties, nor do they supervene on physical properties. They are a new kind of fundamental property. Therefore, physicalism is false.
- Chalmers argues that a physical account of anything can only explain its structure and function. Phenomenal properties are qualia, and cannot be explained in terms of structure and function.
- Jackson's knowledge argument argues that Mary, a neuroscientist who knows everything physical about colour vision, learns something new, namely what it is like to see colour, upon first leaving her black-and-white room. Therefore, what it is like to see colour is not a physical fact.
- The argument attacks the mind–brain identity theory, functionalism and philosophical behaviourism by showing that these theories have a counter-intuitive consequence. It argues that they must claim that Mary knows what it is like to see red before leaving her room.
- Physicalists can respond that while Mary learns something upon leaving her room, she doesn't gain propositional knowledge of a new fact. On one reply, she gains new abilities. We can object that her new knowledge of what it is like to see red can't be reduced to new abilities.
- On another reply, Mary is said to gain acquaintance knowledge, directly apprehending (the brain property which is) what it is like to see red. We can object that Mary still learns a new fact about other people's colour experience.
- A third response appeals to a distinction between concepts and properties. It claims that Mary gains a new, phenomenal concept of red. However, the concept refers to the same physical property which Mary already knows about by means of theoretical concepts. So although she learns something new – a new way of thinking about the world – this doesn't threaten physicalism.
- A possible world is a way things could be. A contingently false proposition describes a state of affairs that is true in some possible world, i.e. that would be true if that world were the actual world. Some possible worlds are physically possible (they share the same laws of nature); others are physically impossible. A state of affairs is metaphysically possible if it is true in some possible world.

- A 'philosophical zombie' is an exact physical duplicate of a person, but without consciousness.
- The zombie argument for property dualism claims that zombies are conceivable and so metaphysically possible. If consciousness were identical to (or supervened on) physical properties, it would not be metaphysically possible for something to have that physical property without consciousness. Therefore, if zombies are metaphysically possible, then consciousness cannot be identical to or supervene on physical properties.
- The knowledge and zombie arguments, like other arguments for dualism, begin from an epistemological claim and infer an ontological claim.
- The zombie argument attacks the mind–brain identity theory and philosophical behaviourism by arguing against what they entail. If they were correct, then zombies should be metaphysically impossible. But because zombies are metaphysically possible, these theories are mistaken.
- Physicalists can argue that zombies are not, in fact, conceivable if we correctly understand consciousness. A physical duplicate of you is a functional duplicate of you, and consciousness can be completely analysed in physical and functional terms. Therefore, any physical, functional duplicate of you must also be conscious.
- We can object that consciousness cannot be completely analysed in physical and functional terms, as such an analysis cannot capture the intrinsic quality of what a conscious experience is like.
- Physicalists can also object that zombies are not metaphysically possible, even though they are conceivable. Conceivability is not always a reliable guide to possibility. For example, we can conceive that water is not H_2O, but this is not possible. Likewise, if phenomenal properties are physical properties, zombies are impossible. Churchland adds that we cannot use tests of what is conceivable to discover the real nature of things.
- Property dualists can reply that there is a disanalogy between scientific identities and consciousness. H_2O is the essence of water, which is why H_2O without water is impossible. However, the essence of a phenomenal property is how it feels, not some physical property. And so it is metaphysically possible to have the physical property without the phenomenal property.

- A final response is that we cannot infer from what is possible to what is real. However, we can argue this objection misunderstands both identity and physicalism, which make claims about what is possible. Churchland argues that this demands too much of both science and philosophy.

B. Issues facing property dualism

The discussion of this section refers back to and develops some of the ideas in the discussion of ISSUES FACING SUBSTANCE DUALISM (p. 196). It is worth quickly reminding yourself of the points made there.

Property dualism, we said (THE THEORY, p. 291), claims that at least some mental properties, e.g. phenomenal properties of consciousness, are fundamentally distinct from physical properties. They do not supervene or depend on physical properties in the way physicalism claims. However, property dualism is happy to allow that there can be basic or fundamental laws of nature that correlate mental properties with physical and/or functional properties.

Interactionist property dualists argue that these distinct mental properties causally affect both other mental states and physical states. Epiphenomenalist property dualists claim that mental properties have no causal powers. While physical properties cause changes in mental properties, mental properties cause nothing at all. Both views face objections.

Issues facing interactionist property dualism

David Chalmers discusses the conceptual and empirical interaction problems facing property dualism, and argues that neither poses a strong objection.

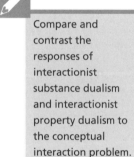

phen props are props of
physical
          e.g. pain
how do mental props
affect phys props
          e.g behaviour

CHALMERS, 'CONSCIOUSNESS AND ITS PLACE IN NATURE', §3.9

Substance dualism faced the challenging CONCEPTUAL INTERACTION PROBLEM (p. 197) in trying to explain how a mental substance not in space could cause physical effects in space. Property dualism doesn't face this particular issue, because mental properties are properties of physical objects. The claim is simply that these mental properties make a difference to how the physical world changes. For instance, having a painful experience makes a difference to what I do next, e.g. jumping up and down – my bodily movements are caused by my being in pain.

How? Can interactionist property dualism provide any details of *how* mental properties would cause physical effects? It seems not. In reply, Chalmers notes that this is true of any *fundamental* causal relationship. For instance, for many years, physicists had no account of *how* gravity works. Then Einstein suggested that it was the result of mass bending space. But at present, we have no account of how mass bends space. But this is no objection to accepting the claim that mass does bend space. Property dualism claims that mental properties are fundamental in the same sense as fundamental physical properties. There is no further explanation in other terms available. But there is no *special* conceptual problem of mental causation here. Causation in general cannot be explained.

We can object, however, that the claim that mental properties cause physical effects is incompatible with physics and with neuroscience. But as discussed in THE EMPIRICAL INTERACTION PROBLEM (p. 199), we don't have strong evidence of this. Chalmers notes that there are interpretations of quantum mechanics that actually *suggest* that consciousness plays a causal role in physical events. (If you are interested in physics: this is the interpretation that maintains that conscious observation of a quantum system collapses its superposed state to a determinate state.) Nor do we know enough neuroscience yet to be able to claim confidently that the causal story of how the brain works is a completely physical story.

Compare and contrast the responses of interactionist substance dualism and interactionist property dualism to the conceptual interaction problem.

Explain one objection to interactionist property dualism and one reply to that objection.

mind has no causal powers

Issues facing epiphenomenalist property dualism

THE PHENOMENOLOGY OF OUR MENTAL LIFE

CHALMERS, 'CONSCIOUSNESS AND ITS PLACE IN NATURE', §3.10

If the knowledge and zombie arguments work, then property dualism is true, it seems. On the other hand, Chalmers argues, the claims of PHYSICALISM (p. 212) that physical laws govern all events in space-time and that every physical event has a sufficient physical cause seem appealing in light of the success of empirical science. Epiphenomenal property dualism allows both sets of claims to be true. Some mental properties are neither physical nor supervenient on physical properties, but they don't make any causal difference to the world. Physicalism is right about causation, it just isn't right about what exists.

We can object, however, that epiphenomenalism is very counter-intuitive. It is part of our experience of having mental states that our mental states, e.g. feeling pain or wanting chocolate or believing that Paris is the capital of France, cause other mental and physical states and events. Most obviously, mental states can cause our behaviour, such as wincing or going to the food cupboard, and they can be part of a causal mental process, such as thinking about how to get to Paris. The 'phenomenology of our mental life' involves experience of such causal connections, doesn't it?

The epiphenomenalist property dualist replies, first, that it is only those mental properties that they are dualist about that are epiphenomenal. So, for Chalmers, it is only phenomenal properties of consciousness that are epiphenomenal. We can say that beliefs and desires have causal powers, since we can analyse these states in terms of physical properties and functions. Nevertheless, that the feeling of pain or longing of love is epiphenomenal is still counter-intuitive. So, second, the epiphenomenalist property dualist offers an alternative explanation of why it *seems* this way to us, even though such mental properties never cause anything.

functionalism !

only consciousness is epiphenomenal

4.12.17

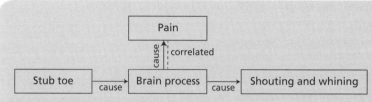

Figure 3.19 An epiphenomenalist property dualist's account of behaviour

Explain epiphenomenalism's account of why it seems that mental states cause physical states.

The physical process in the brain with which phenomenal properties are correlated causes *both* the phenomenal property, e.g. the painful experience, *and* the behaviour which we think is caused by the phenomenal property, e.g. jumping up and down. So the experience and the behaviour are *correlated* because they are both effects of the same cause. It is this correlation that makes us think that the experience causes the behaviour. But it doesn't.

This may be counter-intuitive, but that is not sufficient reason to reject epiphenomenalism.

against epiphenomenalist property dualism

NATURAL SELECTION

The property dualist believes that mental properties are properties of physical objects, namely certain living creatures. Suppose that Darwin's theory of evolution by natural selection is true. According to this theory, millions of genetic alterations randomly take place. Most disappear without a trace. But some that coincidentally help a creature to survive and reproduce slowly spread. That creature and its descendants reproduce more than others without those traits, so more and more creatures end up with them. The features enable the creature to reproduce more, so its descendants also have those features and reproduce more, and so on.

So, according to the theory of evolution, the traits that evolve over time are ones that causally contribute to the survival and reproduction of the creature. We can assume that mental properties, including qualia, evolved. But how, if they make no difference to what creatures do and so whether they survive and reproduce? Epiphenomenalism conflicts with our best account of the origin of consciousness.

Explain the objection to epiphenomenalist property dualism from evolution by natural selection.

Where did consciousness come from?

is it the best account?
Doesn't really tell you where consciousness comes from

JACKSON, 'EPIPHENOMENAL QUALIA', §4

Jackson considers this objection and replies that natural selection is more complicated than just described. In fact, there are lots of traits that have evolved that don't contribute to survival or reproduction, but are instead *by-products* of traits that *do* contribute. For instance, polar bears have thick, warm coats which help them survive in the Arctic. A thick coat is a heavy coat. But having a heavy coat doesn't contribute to the polar bear's survival, because it makes the bear slower. However, it is better to have a thick, warm and heavy coat than a thin, cool and light coat. Having a heavy coat is a by-product of having a thick, warm coat, and having a thick, warm coat contributes to survival.

Likewise, there are brain processes that make a difference to how a creature behaves and which are very conducive to survival. Consciousness, according to epiphenomenalism, is simply a by-product of these brain processes. It just happens to be a fundamental law of nature that these physical properties are correlated with certain properties of consciousness.

We can object that this response presents us with a very divided picture of the world. Consciousness sits entirely outside the rest of the natural world, and has no effect on it.

Jackson accepts this: we shouldn't expect to understand the world. Our abilities to understand the world themselves relate to survival. As a result of evolution, we are equipped to learn about and understand what we need to know in order to survive. Consciousness doesn't make any difference to this, so it is no surprise that we can't understand it well.

how did physical cause mental?

beneficial

only reason our brains work how they do is because we have phen props

Is epiphenomenalism compatible with evolutionary theory? *Yes*

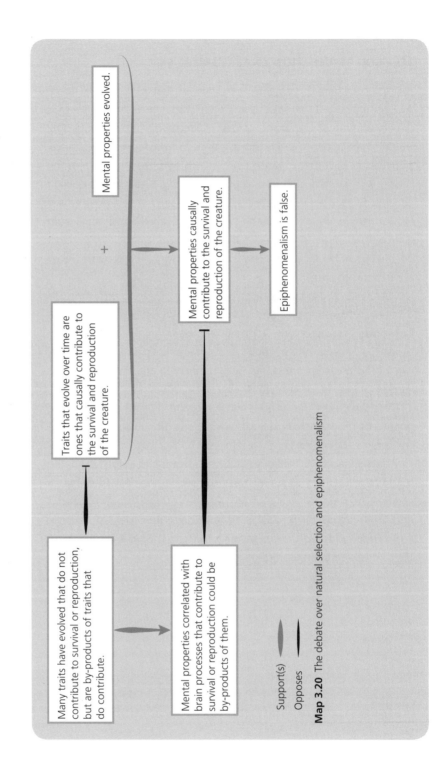

Mental properties evolved.

Traits that evolve over time are ones that causally contribute to the survival and reproduction of the creature.

+

Mental properties causally contribute to the survival and reproduction of the creature.

Epiphenomenalism is false.

Many traits have evolved that do not contribute to survival or reproduction, but are by-products of traits that do contribute.

Mental properties correlated with brain processes that contribute to survival or reproduction could be by-products of them.

Support(s)

Opposes

Map 3.20 The debate over natural selection and epiphenomenalism

5.12.17

Thinking harder: introspective self-knowledge

In our discussion of the ISSUES FACING EPIPHENOMENALIST SUBSTANCE DUALISM (p. 200), we gave reasons to think that if mental states don't cause anything, even other mental states, then this threatens our knowledge of our own mental states. For instance, according to epiphenomenalism, my belief that I am in pain is caused not by the pain but by some brain state. So if that brain state occurs, I would have the belief that I am in pain whatever I actually feel.

Epiphenomenalists can reply that knowledge of something doesn't always require that thing to *cause* one's belief. I can know that I am in pain without the painful experience causing this knowledge. For instance, suppose the brain state that causes my belief that I am in pain is also the same brain state that causes my pain. In this case, I wouldn't, under normal circumstances, have the belief that I am in pain unless I was in pain – the same brain state causes both. So even though my belief that I am in pain isn't caused by the painful experience, I can know that I am in pain because my belief is caused by a reliable mechanism.

Chalmers gives a different response. Knowledge of my experiences is knowledge by acquaintance. I am directly aware of my experiences, but this is not a causal relation. My belief that I am in pain is partly constituted, not caused, by this direct awareness. My being in pain makes my belief the belief that it is. So my knowledge that I am in pain depends on my being in pain, but is not caused by it.

where does the pain come from

relies on specific scientific hypothesis

See Epistemology,
RELIABILISM, p. 55.

Pain ——awareness——> belief

is causal?

1) Explain the objection to epiphenomenalism from introspective self-knowledge and one response to it.
2) Can epiphenomenalist property dualism successfully answer the challenges facing it?

The problem of other minds (II)

Property dualism faces similar difficulties to substance dualism when it comes to the problem of other minds (see THE PROBLEM OF OTHER MINDS (I), p. 201). If phenomenal properties of consciousness are distinct from physical and functional properties, how can we know from how other people behave and how they are physically constituted, whether they have any consciousness at all? In other words, if phenomenal properties of consciousness are distinct from physical and functional properties, how do we know that other people aren't zombies?

Property dualists can appeal to THE ARGUMENT FROM ANALOGY (p. 202). However, as we saw, this response faces the objection that I may be a special case. Perhaps I am the only being that is conscious, while everyone else is not.

A better response, then, is to argue that THE EXISTENCE OF OTHER MINDS IS THE BEST HYPOTHESIS (p. 203). An interactionist property dualist claims that consciousness causes behaviour and other physical effects. Such causal relations don't provide a complete analysis of what phenomenal properties are (which is why functionalism is false), but consciousness does have effects. The best explanation for why people behave as they do, and why we can observe differences in behaviour between conscious and non-conscious creatures, is that people are conscious, i.e. they experience phenomenal properties.

As we have phrased it, the argument depends on accepting mental causation. So what can the epiphenomenalist property dualist say about the problem of other minds? Jackson argues that the same argument can be used, but it becomes a little more complicated. The best explanation of phenomenal properties is that they are the effects of brain processes. I can know that other people have consciousness, because I can know that their behaviour is caused by brain processes and these brain processes cause phenomenal properties.

These responses face the objections raised in our previous discussion of this argument.

> ?
>
> **Can property dualism solve the problem of other minds?**

Property dualism makes a 'category mistake'

In our discussion of whether SUBSTANCE DUALISM MAKES A 'CATEGORY MISTAKE' (p. 207), we saw that Ryle rejects substance dualism because it misunderstands talk about the mind and mental states as talk about substances, properties and causation. We can apply his objection just as easily to property dualism. While property dualism doesn't claim that the mind is a distinct substance, it does think of mental properties – or at least phenomenal properties of consciousness – as part of the same metaphysical framework as physical and functional properties, only not physical.

> See THINKING HARDER:
> RYLE ON CONSCIOUSNESS,
> p. 260.

Ryle would argue that the concept of phenomenal properties (let alone qualia) misunderstands our talk of sensations, feelings, images and so on. These are not each a 'something' that has peculiar properties of 'what it is like'. The whole metaphysical picture here is wrong.

So how should we understand our talk about conscious experiences? On Ryle's behalf, we could argue that when we express our experiences, we use words that derive their meaning from describing physical objects. To say 'what it is like' to see red is simply to describe what we see when attending to the colour of a red object, or if it is not in front of us, we give a report of our memory of seeing it. The redness that we experience is the redness *of the rose*, not a property of our experience of it. *no qualia ?*

People don't normally talk about 'sensations' or 'what it is like' in the sense of qualia in everyday language, before being exposed to some theory. If you ask someone 'what it is like' to see a rose, they will usually respond evaluatively, e.g. 'it's wonderful' or 'it's calming'. Of course, experiences differ from each other. But this isn't because what each experience 'is like' differs. We can express the difference between what experiences 'are like' in terms of what the experience *is of* (red roses look different from yellow roses – this is a difference between roses, not between experiences of roses), and how we evaluate experiences, e.g. whether we enjoy one and find another boring. The property dualist has misunderstood our mental concepts.

For example, in response to THE KNOWLEDGE ARGUMENT (p. 293), what we should say is this. In knowing all the physical facts, Mary can't yet understand our normal way of talking about experiences. She has no experiences of coloured objects that she can express and report, and as a result, she has only a limited understanding of our discussions of them. But none of this has to do with knowledge of facts, either facts about some 'inner' conscious experience or facts about the brain. To think otherwise is a category mistake.

These points can be compared with the argument of direct realism against sense-data. See Epistemology, THINKING HARDER: DIRECT REALISM AND OPENNESS, p. 76, and LOCKE'S DISTINCTION BETWEEN PRIMARY AND SECONDARY QUALITIES, p. 80.

1) Does property dualism make a category mistake? 2) Is property dualism true?

Key points: issues facing property dualism

- Interactionist property dualism claims that mental properties can cause physical (and other mental) events. It faces the problem of explaining how this is possible and empirical objections to whether it occurs.
- Chalmers responds that for *any* fundamental causal relationship, we do not have an account of how it works. There is no special problem here. Furthermore, we have no empirical evidence that mental properties do not affect physical properties, and even some interpretations of quantum theory that support the claim that they do.
- Epiphenomenalist property dualism claims that mental properties, or at least, phenomenal properties, have no causal role. To the objection that

this is counter-intuitive and doesn't reflect our experience of our mental lives, epiphenomenalism can respond that such properties appear to have a causal role because what causes them (a brain state) also causes what looks like their effects (bodily movements, other mental states).

- We can object that epiphenomenalist property dualism is incompatible with evolutionary theory, because evolution only selects properties that make a difference to the survival and reproductive success of the animal.

- Jackson responds that properties that are selected for can have by-products. And consciousness is a by-product of advantageous brain processes.

- We can object that epiphenomenalism entails that we cannot gain knowledge of our minds. The epiphenomenalist can reply that our beliefs about our mental states are caused by the same brain processes that cause those mental states. As this is a reliable process, we can have knowledge of our mental states. Alternatively, the epiphenomenalist can argue that our experiences partially constitute our beliefs about them.

- Property dualism faces the problem of other minds. If phenomenal properties are logically independent of bodies, then no amount of evidence from someone's bodily behaviour could prove that they are conscious. Property dualists can respond by arguing that the claim that other people experience phenomenal properties is the best hypothesis.

- We can apply Ryle's argument that substance dualism makes a category mistake to property dualism. To think of consciousness in terms of phenomenal properties is to misunderstand how we talk and think about the mind.

Summary: property dualism

In these sections on property dualism and objections to it, we have looked at two arguments for property dualism (the knowledge argument and the zombie argument), responses to these arguments, and issues facing property dualism from causal interaction, the problem of other minds, and its understanding of mental concepts in terms of 'properties'. In our discussion and evaluation of these arguments, we have looked at the following issues:

1. What does it mean to claim that phenomenal properties can neither be reduced to nor supervene on physical properties?
2. Is there, in principle, a complete physical/functional analysis of phenomenal consciousness?
3. What, if anything, does Mary learn when she first leaves her black-and-white room?
4. Do we have two different ways – theoretical (physical/psychological) and phenomenal – of thinking about just one set of properties in the brain?
5. Are philosophical zombies either conceivable or metaphysically possible?
6. What are the limits of metaphysics? Can we use thought experiments to learn about the nature or identity of things?
7. Can epiphenomenalism successfully explain our mental life?
8. How should we understand our talk about the mind?

Chapter 4

Preparing for the A level exam

This chapter is about preparing for the A level philosophy exam, covering both Paper 1 (Epistemology and Moral Philosophy) and Paper 2 (Metaphysics of God and Metaphysics of Mind).

To get good exam results, you need to have a good sense of what the exam will be like and what the examiners are looking for, and to revise in a way that will help you prepare to answer the questions well. This probably sounds obvious, but in fact, many students do not think about the exam itself, only about what questions might come up. There is a big difference. This chapter will provide you with some guidance on how to approach your exams in a way that will help get you the best results you can.

It is divided into four sections: the examination, understanding the question, revision, and exam technique. In the last two sections, I highlight revision points and exam tips. These are collected together at the end of the chapter.

The examination

The structure of the exam

There are two papers, each lasting three hours. Each paper has two sections. In Paper 1, these are Section A Epistemology and Section B Moral Philosophy. In Paper 2, they are Section A Metaphysics of God and Section B Metaphysics of Mind. All the questions on both papers are compulsory – there is no choice in what you can answer.

Each section has three types of question. First, there is a 3-mark question that asks you to define a concept or explain a single philosophical idea or brief argument. Second, there are two 5-mark questions and one 12-mark question; these ask you to explain some philosophical material. For the 5-mark questions, you could be asked to explain a claim, theory or argument, or to compare or contrast two theories. The material for the 12-mark question will be more extensive or complex. For instance, you could be asked to explain a complex theory or argument, to compare or contrast two theories, to apply a theory to an issue (in moral philosophy), or to explain both a theory and an argument for or against it. There may be other possibilities as well. Third, there is one 25-mark open-ended essay question that asks you to evaluate a philosophical claim.

Here are the questions from the specimen exam papers:

Paper 1

Section A Epistemology
1. What is philosophical scepticism? (3 marks)
2. Explain *one* way in which a direct realist could respond to the argument from illusion. (5 marks)
3. Explain how Berkeley's idealism differs from indirect realism. (5 marks)
4. Explain how Descartes argues that we can gain a priori knowledge through intuition and deduction. (12 marks)
5. How should propositional knowledge be defined? (25 marks)

Section B Moral Philosophy
1. Briefly explain why Aristotle thinks that pleasure is not the only good. (3 marks)
2. Explain why emotivism is a non-cognitivist theory of ethical language. (5 marks)
3. Explain the analogy drawn between virtues and skills within Aristotelian ethics. (5 marks)
4. Explain how Kant's deontological ethics can be applied to the question of whether we should ever tell lies. (12 marks)
5. How convincing is utilitarianism as an account of what makes an action morally right? (25 marks)

Paper 2

Section A Metaphysics of God

1. Explain the difference between the claims 'God is eternal' and 'God is everlasting'. (3 marks)
2. Explain the evidential problem of evil. (5 marks)
3. Outline Aquinas' Third Way. (5 marks)
4. Compare and contrast Paley's and Swinburne's versions of the design argument. (12 marks)
5. Is religious language meaningful? (25 marks)

Section B Metaphysics of Mind

1. What do eliminative materialists claim about mental states? (3 marks)
2. Outline Descartes' conceivability argument for substance dualism. (5 marks)
3. Explain how Block's China thought experiment can be used to argue against functionalism. (5 marks)
4. Outline mind–brain type identity theory and explain how the issue of multiple realisability challenges this view. (12 marks)
5. Does philosophical behaviourism give the correct account of mental states? (25 marks)

If you've been doing the questions in the margin of this textbook, these kinds of questions should be very familiar.

Assessment objectives

The examiners mark your answers according to two principles, known as 'Assessment Objectives' (AOs). They are:

AO1: Demonstrate knowledge and understanding of the core concepts and methods of philosophy, including through the use of philosophical analysis

AO2: Analyse and evaluate philosophical argument to form reasoned judgements.

AO1 requires you to understand how philosophers have argued, and AO2 requires you to be able to argue – to construct and evaluate arguments – yourself. Except for the 25-mark questions, all the marks available are for AO1. For the 25-mark questions, 5 marks are for AO1 and 20 marks are for AO2. How well you write also makes a contribution, so it is important to write clearly and grammatically, so that the examiner can understand what you mean. Don't try to impress using big words or long sentences – it just gets in the way of clarity and precision.

Understanding the question: giving the examiners what they are looking for

The key to doing well in an exam is understanding the question. I don't just mean understanding the *topic* of the question, like 'religious language' or 'functionalism'. Of course, this is very important. But you also need to understand what the question is asking you to *do*. Each type of question tests different kinds of philosophical knowledge and skill.

> More information on this is available in the Mark Schemes that the AQA publish online.

Three-mark questions

The first question of each section tests the *accuracy* and *precision* of your understanding.

Three-mark questions ask you to define a concept or explain a claim or brief argument. The examiners want you to be *concise*. State the definition/claim/argument as clearly and precisely as you can and then move on. Don't waffle or talk around it. So my answer to 'What do eliminative materialists claim about mental states?' is this:

> Eliminative materialists claim that at least some mental states, as we usually think of them, don't exist. Our commonsense concepts of some mental states are fundamentally mistaken, so nothing exists that corresponds to these concepts. Examples include qualia and propositional attitudes.

> Taken from
> ELIMINATIVE MATERIALISM,
> p. 225.

And my answer to 'Briefly explain why Aristotle thinks pleasure is *not* the only good' is this:

According to Aristotle, what is good is a 'final end', something we aim at for its own sake. Pleasure is not the only good because, he argues, pleasure is not the *only* thing that we aim at for its own sake. There are other things which we seek out, such as knowledge and virtue, that we would seek out even if they brought us no pleasure. The pleasure they bring is not *why* we seek them. They are also final ends, not a means to pleasure.

Taken from Moral
Philosophy,
EUDAIMONIA AND
PLEASURE, p. 294.

Five-mark questions

Five-mark questions ask you to explain an important philosophical concept, claim or argument, or may ask you to compare two theories. Explaining involves not just describing the idea, but giving a sense of the reasoning or thought behind it. It is important not only to state the essential points but to *order* them and *link* them logically. Say enough to give a full explanation, but as with 3-mark questions, stay concise and don't waffle. If you are explaining an argument, it's fine to use numbered premises and conclusion.

My answer to 'Outline Aquinas' Third Way' is this:

Aquinas' Third Way is a cosmological argument from 'contingency'. Something exists contingently if it is possible for it to exist and for it not to exist. Something exists necessarily if it must exist, i.e. if it is impossible for it not to exist.

P1. Things in the universe exist contingently.
P2. If it is possible for something not to exist, then at some time, it does not exist.
P3. If everything exists contingently, then it is possible that at some time, there was nothing in existence.
P4. If at some time, nothing was in existence, nothing could begin to exist.
P5. Since things did begin to exist, there was never nothing in existence.
C1. Therefore, there is something that does not exist contingently, but must exist.
P6. This necessary being is God.
C2. God exists.

Taken from AQUINAS'
THIRD WAY, p. 115.

And my answer to 'Explain how Berkeley's idealism differs from indirect realism' is this:

Berkeley's idealism differs from indirect realism in three fundamental ways:

1. Idealism is anti-realist; it denies the existence of mind-independent physical objects. Indirect realism claims that mind-independent physical objects exist. Berkeley argues that the very concept of mind-independent physical objects is incoherent; indirect realists claim that their existence explains our perceptual experience.
2. Idealism claims that the only objects of perception are ideas, and we perceive these immediately. Indirect realism claims that while we perceive ideas (sense-data) immediately, these are caused by and represent physical objects. Therefore, we can also be said to perceive physical objects (indirectly).
3. Indirect realism claims that there is a distinction between primary and secondary qualities. Primary qualities are qualities, such as size, that physical objects have independent of their being perceived. Secondary qualities are ones, such as colour, which are defined in relation to being perceived. Berkeley argues that there is no distinction between primary and secondary qualities, because all sensible qualities are mind-dependent.

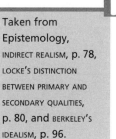

Taken from
Epistemology,
INDIRECT REALISM, p. 78,
LOCKE'S DISTINCTION
BETWEEN PRIMARY AND
SECONDARY QUALITIES,
p. 80, and BERKELEY'S
IDEALISM, p. 96.

Twelve-mark questions

Twelve-mark questions generally ask you to explain a more complex argument or a set of arguments, a theory or a comparison between theories, or some other material. The marks are still all for AO1, your understanding of the argument or theory, so you should not *evaluate* it. This is very important, because any time spent on evaluation is simply wasted – no marks are available, and what you write will be redundant. So if you are asked to explain a theory, you should not discuss whether it is convincing or true. If you are asked to explain an argument, you should not discuss whether it is a *good* argument.

As with the 5-mark questions, the examiners are looking for clarity, precision and an *explanation* that sets out the central claims in a way that

On the difference
between
understanding and
evaluation, see
UNDERSTANDING
ARGUMENTS AND
ARGUMENT MAPS, p. 9,
EVALUATING ARGUMENTS,
p. 12, and EVALUATING
CLAIMS, p. 13.

demonstrates the logical links between them. The answer needs to work as a single 'whole', rather than a number of disconnected 'bits'. In addition, you will need to stay focused and relevant and use technical philosophical language appropriately (i.e. with clarity, precision and only when it is needed).

My answer to 'Outline mind–brain type identity theory and explain how the issue of multiple realisability challenges this view' is this:

> Mind–brain type identity theory claims that mental 'types' of thing (mental properties, states and events) are physical 'types' of thing (highly complex neurophysiological properties, states and events of the brain). Type identity theory is a type of reductive physicalism. It proposes an ontological reduction of mental types to physical types. There is *nothing more* to mental properties than being a certain kind of physical property. So, for example, thinking a thought is exactly the same thing as certain neurons firing.
>
> The identity claim is not a claim about language or concepts, but about reality. So the claim is not, for example, that the concept 'pain' *means* 'the firing of nociceptors'. The identity claim is, therefore, not meant to be *analytically* true. The claim is that both concepts refer to *the same thing* in the world. The firing of nociceptors is what pain is. Two concepts, one property.
>
> Multiple realisability challenges the identity claim, as first argued by Hilary Putnam. Mental properties are not *identical* to physical properties because the *same* mental property can be related to or supervene on *different* physical properties. For example, the brain states that relate to pain may well be different in different species, in humans and birds, say, but pain is the same mental state. If this is true, there are creatures who, when they are in pain, have different physical properties from us when we are in pain. Therefore, 'being in pain' cannot be exactly the same thing as having a particular physical property.
>
> To see this more clearly, suppose pain is identical to some neurophysiological property, N_1, in humans. If they are one and the same thing, then whatever has N_1 is in pain, and whatever is in pain has N_1. Now suppose pain is identical to some *different* neurophysiological property, N_2, in birds. If pain = N_1 and pain = N_2, then $N_1 = N_2$ (because pain = pain!). But we have supposed that $N_1 \neq N_2$. Type identity theory must claim that for *any being*, even extraterrestrials, to be in pain, it

must have N$_1$, rather than another neurophysiological property. This is a highly implausible empirical prediction. It is more reasonable to conclude that neither N$_1$ nor N$_2$ are identical to pain.

The argument from multiple realisability can also be rephrased as an a priori argument from conceivability:

P1. It is conceivable, and therefore possible, for a being with quite a different physical constitution from us to have the same thoughts or sensations.

P2. But it is inconceivable, and therefore impossible, for something both to have and not have a certain property.

C1. Therefore, mental properties can't be the same as physical properties.

> Taken from TYPE IDENTITY THEORY, p. 216.

My answer to 'Compare and contrast Paley's and Swinburne's versions of the design argument' is this:

Paley's and Swinburne's versions of the design argument – like all design arguments – both begin by identifying some empirical feature of the world from which they infer the existence of a designer, which they then argue is God. However, they identify different empirical features. Paley focuses on regularities in 'spatial order' – the property of having parts that are organised and put together for a purpose. This property, he argues, is the mark of design. Of anything that has this property, we can infer that it is designed. Swinburne focuses on regularities of 'temporal order' – an orderliness in the way one thing follows another, described by the laws of nature. The 'design' evident in nature is in the operation of laws of nature.

Both Paley and Swinburne argue that the best explanation for the feature they identify is a designer – an intelligent mind that brings these features about deliberately. Both of them argue that, in fact, this is the *only* possible explanation. Paley uses the example of a watch to make the point, e.g. we cannot accept that something with parts organised for a purpose simply 'happened' by chance to exist. Swinburne argues that scientific explanation cannot explain the laws of nature, because scientific explanations must assume laws of nature in order to provide any explanations at all. That leaves only personal explanation – we can explain temporal regularities in terms of the activity of a designer.

Paley compares watches and living things to make his argument. However, he does not offer an argument from analogy. He does not argue that natural things are *like* watches, so their causes are *like* the causes of watches. He says that natural things have exactly the same property – being organised for a purpose – as watches, and whatever has this property is the result of design. From these premises, he deduces that natural things are designed and so a designer exists. Swinburne, by contrast, does offer an argument from analogy. We can understand the operation of the laws of nature to be *like* our actions, so that we can apply personal explanations in both cases. Just as we can act by moving our bodies, bringing about a sequence of events in time because that is what we intend, a divine person can act on the universe bringing about the effects of the laws of nature.

Taken from PALEY'S DESIGN ARGUMENT, p. 79, and SWINBURNE'S DESIGN ARGUMENT, p. 87.

Twenty-five-mark questions

When you are answering a 3-, 5-, or 12-mark question, what you need to do is straightforward. You don't need to make any choices about *what* concepts or arguments to talk about, since that is specified by the question. By contrast, 25-mark questions are much more open-ended. You are asked to evaluate a claim. To do this, you will need to construct and evaluate arguments for and against the claim. Because there are marks available for AO2, if you do not evaluate the philosophical claims, theories and arguments that you discuss, then you cannot get a good mark for the question, no matter how clear and accurate you are in explaining them.

See EVALUATING ARGUMENTS and EVALUATING CLAIMS, pp. 12–13.

In addition to evaluating individual claims and arguments, your answer as a whole needs to work as one long argument. Arguments have a clear conclusion – you need to decide from the very beginning what your conclusion will be. For 'Does philosophical behaviourism give the correct account of mental states?', your conclusion could be:

1. 'yes', that is, you defend PHILOSOPHICAL BEHAVIOURISM (p. 239);
2. 'no', that is, you argue that philosophical behaviourism suffers from fatal objections;
3. something conditional such as 'yes for some mental states but not all', for example, you may say that it fails for qualia, but is otherwise correct;

4. something sceptical, 'we cannot know because …' (this is quite difficult to defend for this question!).

With your conclusion in mind, you need to select which arguments and theories you will discuss. You want to discuss the arguments that you think are the most critical ones – the ones that either provide the strongest reasons for the claim or the strongest objections to it. You need to evaluate the points and arguments/objections you discuss. Are there false or unknown premises? Is the argument valid – or if it is inductive, is it cogent? Your evaluation should never be simply 'there are points against and points in favour'. If there are points against and points in favour, provide an argument that the points on one side are stronger (more cogent) than the points on the other side. Distinguish the arguments that are crucial for your conclusion from ones that are not.

The examiners are more interested in the *quality* of what you write than the quantity. You have demonstrated what you *know* in the other exam questions. Now you need to show that you can *argue*. Three points are relevant here:

1. Don't aim for a comprehensive discussion of the question, covering all the angles. Perhaps just discuss two arguments – ones that you think are really strong or important – but discuss them with depth and rigour (i.e. for each argument, also consider objections and replies). One good discussion is worth more than many weak or superficial points.
2. The examiners don't expect you to try to provide a 'balanced' account in the sense of trying to find points for and against a particular claim. They are testing your skill at arguing. So your answer can take the form of a very strong argument in favour of your conclusion and then strong replies to objections that can be raised.
3. To make your answer coherent, what you argue at each point in the answer should make some contribution to your conclusion. It fits into a logical structure.

There is no single right way to do all this (which is one reason I don't give a sample answer here). So you will need to plan your approach and answer to the question carefully. How to do this, and much more on answering essay questions, was discussed in WRITING PHILOSOPHY (p. 18). Once again, it's fine to use numbered arguments. It's also fine to use bullet points, particularly if you are running out of time.

Revision: it's more than memory

There are lots of memory tricks for learning information for exams. This section isn't about those. Revision isn't just about learning information, but also about learning how to use that information well in the exam. If you've been answering the questions throughout this book, then you have been putting into practice the advice I give below.

See THE EXAMINATION, p. 334.

In revising for the exam, you need to bear in mind the structure of the exam and the AOs. First, the five questions in each section are all compulsory, and cover different areas of the syllabus, so you'll need to revise the whole syllabus. Second, thinking about the 25-mark questions, structure your revision around the central questions or topics that the syllabus covers. In Epistemology, these are knowledge, perception, innate knowledge, rational intuition and deduction, and scepticism. In Moral Philosophy, they are the three normative theories (utilitarianism, Kantian deontology, Aristotelian virtue theory), the four applied issues (stealing, eating animals, simulated killing, lying), and the debates in metaethics between cognitivist and non-cognitivist theories (covering naturalism, intuitionism, error theory, emotivism, prescriptivism). In Metaphysics of God, they are the concept of God, the arguments for and against God's existence (ontological, design, cosmological, problem of evil), and religious language. In Metaphysics of Mind, they are the six main theories about the mind and body (substance dualism, property dualism, philosophical behaviourism, type-identity theory, eliminative materialism and functionalism), supplemented by the concepts of consciousness/qualia, intentionality and physicalism.

AO1 tests your understanding of central concepts and claims in these areas and how arguments are constructed for or against claims. We can break this down further. For the short-answer questions,

> R1. Learn the concepts and definitions that are central to the philosophical theories studied.

The GLOSSARY (p. 354) can help with this.

For the 5- and 12-mark questions,

> R2. Learn who said what. What are the most important claims they made? What arguments did they use to defend their claims?

However, AO1 tests your *understanding*, not just your knowledge, of these claims and arguments. So you will need to show how the arguments are supposed to work. What are the premises and conclusion, and how is the conclusion supposed to follow from the premises?

> R3. Spend time identifying the main claims and arguments involved in each issue you have studied, putting arguments in your own words, stating clearly what the conclusion is and what the premises are, and constructing argument maps. Explain how the reasoning is supposed to work.

This is difficult, because philosophical ideas and arguments are abstract and complicated, so it can be hard to know just what they mean. But the examiners also want precision. So it is worth thinking further about whatever you find hardest to understand.

> R4. Revise those concepts, claims and arguments that are hard to understand. Try to identify the differences between different interpretations. Which interpretation is best and why?

The exam questions do not explicitly ask for examples, but examples can prove very helpful when explaining a claim, objection or theory. If you are going to use examples, you want them to be good – clear, relevant, and supportive of the point you want to make. You can either remember good examples you have read, or create your own. In either case, you should know precisely what point the example is making. An irrelevant example demonstrates that you don't really know what you are talking about.

> R5. Prepare examples beforehand, rather than try to invent them in the exam. They must be short and they must make the right point – so try them out on your friends and teachers first.

What about AO2? How do you revise evaluation? Twenty-five-mark questions test you on how well you build an argument, deal with objections, and come to a supported conclusion. The best way to prepare for it is to spend time *thinking* about the arguments and issues. For example, you might know and even understand Hume's arguments against rationalism, but you may never have stopped to really work out whether you think they are any good. Get involved!

So think about the different kinds of objection that can be raised to claims and arguments. Relate a particular argument to other arguments and viewpoints on the issue, and reflect on whether the objections to an argument undermine it. Work through the arguments so that you understand for yourself the pros and cons of each viewpoint.

See EVALUATING ARGUMENTS and EVALUATING CLAIMS, pp. 12–13.

> R6. Think reflectively about the arguments and issues. Practise arguing for and against a particular view. Think about the place and importance of the arguments for the issue as a whole.

Your answer needs to work as an argument itself, a coherent piece of reasoning. This means that what you write should also take the form of premises and conclusion. The premises will be your judgements as you go along, in response to this view or that objection. These judgements need to add up to a conclusion. You shouldn't end your essay with a totally different point of view than your evaluations in the essay support. In other words, do the judgements you reach reflect the arguments you have presented?

> R7. Think about how your judgements on the various arguments you have studied add up. Do they lead to one conclusion, one point of view being right? Or do you think arguments for and against one position are closely balanced?

These first seven revision points relate to taking in and understanding information. There are two more points that will help you organise the information, learn it better, and prepare you for answering exam questions. This is especially important in relation to the 25-mark questions.

Twenty-five-mark questions are open-ended, and so you will need to choose to discuss what is *relevant* to the question being asked. Knowing what is relevant is a special kind of knowledge, which involves thinking carefully about what you know about the theories in relation to the question asked. A good way of organising your information is to create answer outlines or web-diagrams for particular issues.

For example, you could create an outline or web-diagram for mind–brain type identity theory. Think about the essential points, and organise them, perhaps like this:

1. What does the claim that mental states are ontologically reducible to brain states mean?
2. Who argued that mental states are reducible to brain states? What are the main arguments?
3. Who argued against this claim, in favour of non-reductivism? What are the most important and powerful arguments?
4. What is your conclusion on the issue, and why?

With an outline structured like this, you should be able to answer any question that comes up on the mind–brain type identity theory.

R8. Create structured outlines or web-diagrams for particular issues. Try to cover all the main points.

Finally, once you've organised your notes into an outline or web-diagram, time yourself writing exam answers. Start by using your outline, relying on your memory to fill in the details. Then practise by memorising the outline as well, and doing it as though it were an actual exam. You might be surprised at how quickly the time goes by. You'll find that you need to be very focused – but this is what the examiners are looking for, answers that are thoughtful but to the point.

R9. Practise writing timed answers. Use your notes at first, but then practise without them.

Exam technique: getting the best result you can

If you've understood the exam structure, and know what to expect, the exam will seem less daunting. You'll have a good idea about how to proceed, and a sense of how the questions are testing different aspects of your knowledge. This section gives you some tips on how to approach the questions when you are actually in the exam.

Exams are very exciting, whether in a good way or a bad way! It can be helpful, therefore, to take your time at the beginning, not to rush into your answers, but to plan your way. The tips I give below are roughly in the order that you might apply them when taking the exam.

First, how long should you spend on each part of the papers? The marks give a rough guide. For each paper, there are 100 marks available, 50 for Section A and 50 for Section B. You have 3 hours or 180 minutes. That's a little under 2 minutes for each mark. However, this isn't exact – the answer for each 3-mark question will probably take less than 6 minutes, while 50 minutes or a little more is about right for each 25-mark question, especially because these answers require more planning. And because the exam covers five topics, you'll probably find that you know the answer to some of the questions better than others. Give yourself a little extra time for the questions you find difficult. You don't need to answer the questions in the order in which they are set. You might want to answer the ones you are confident about first, to get the best marks you can, and come back to the others later on. Don't lose marks on the questions that you can do, by not giving yourself enough time to answer them well.

E1. The number of marks available for each part is a rough guide to how long you spend on it. But allow a little extra time for the 25-mark questions and parts you find difficult. Choose what order to answer the questions in.

Before you start to write your answer to any part, read the question again very closely. There are two things to look out for. First, notice what the question is asking you to do. Remember that you need to display your *understanding*, not just your knowledge, of the philosophical issues. So you'll need to explain claims and arguments, not just state them. Second, notice the *precise* phrasing of the question. For example, in answering the sample question 'Explain *one* way in which the direct realist could respond to the argument from illusion', it would be a mistake to talk about why direct realism is the right/wrong theory, to talk about indirect realism, or to discuss more than one way direct realists deal with illusions. Many students have a tendency to notice only what the question is about, e.g. 'scepticism' or 'functionalism'. They don't notice the rest of the words in the question. But the question is never 'So tell me everything you know about *x*'! Make sure you answer the actual question set, and don't discuss anything that doesn't help answer that question.

See UNDERSTANDING THE QUESTION, p. 337.

> E2. Before starting your answer, read the question again very closely. Take note of every word to make sure you answer the actual question set. Remember to explain, and not just state, claims and arguments.

With 25-mark questions, and for many 12-mark questions as well, before you start writing, it is worth organising your thoughts first. What are you going to say, in what order? Whether you are explaining or evaluating arguments, you need to present ideas in a logical order. Especially for 25-mark answers, if you've memorised an outline or a web-diagram, quickly write it out at the beginning so that you note down all the points. It is very easy to forget something or go off on a tangent once you are stuck into the arguments. Having an outline or web-diagram to work from will help you keep your answer relevant and structured. However, you might discover, as you develop your answer, that parts of the outline or diagram are irrelevant or just don't fit. Don't worry – the outline is only there as a guide. It will also remind you how much you still want to cover, so it can help you pace yourself better. If you do run out of time, you can indicate to the examiners that they should look at your plan – they will give marks for it.

> E3. For longer answers, before you start writing, it can be worth writing out your outline or web-diagram first. This can help remind you of the key points you want to make, and the order in which you want to make them.

Because philosophy is about the logical relationship of ideas, there are a number of rules of thumb about presentation. Here are four important ones.

> E4. Four rules of thumb:
> a.   Use philosophical terms to be precise and concise, not simply to sound 'impressive', and make sure it is clear from the context that you know what they mean.
> b.   Keep related ideas together. If you have a thought later on, add a footnote indicating where in the answer you want it to be read.
> c.   In 25-mark questions, explain a theory before evaluating it.
> d.   In 25-mark questions, apart from the conclusion for the essay as a whole, don't state the conclusion to an argument before you've discussed the argument, especially if you are going to present objections to that conclusion. You can state what the argument hopes to show, but don't state it *as* a conclusion.

If you use examples, you need to keep them short and relevant, and explain why they support your argument. An example is an illustration, not an argument in itself.

> E5. Keep your examples short and make sure they support the point you want to make. Always explain how they support your point.

For 25-mark questions, it is worth noting that evaluation is more than just presenting objections and responses side-by-side. Get the objections and the theory to 'talk' to each other, and come to some conclusion about which side is stronger.

> E6. For 25-mark questions, make sure your discussion is not just reporting a sequence of points of view, but presents objections and replies, evaluates the arguments, and reaches a particular conclusion.

Finally, it is very easy to forget something, or say it in an unclear way. For all the questions except the 25-mark questions, you may have time to write a rough draft and then once you are happy with it, write it out as neat into the answer booklet. The exam should test your ability to think, not your ability to write fast! Accuracy, clarity, concision and logical links can all improve in a second draft. For the 25-mark questions, leave time to check your answer at the end. You might find you can add a sentence here or there to connect two ideas together more clearly, or that some phrase is imprecise. These little things can make a big difference to the mark.

> E7. For questions other than 25-mark questions, you may have time to write two drafts – rough and final. For 25-mark questions, leave time to check your answer at the end. Don't be afraid to add to or correct what you have written.

Revision tips

R1. Learn the concepts and definitions that are central to the philosophical theories studied.

R2. Learn who said what. What are the most important claims they made? What arguments did they use to defend their claims?

R3. Spend time identifying the main claims and arguments involved in each issue you have studied, putting arguments in your own words, stating clearly what the conclusion is and what the premises are, and constructing argument maps. Explain how the reasoning is supposed to work.

R4. Revise those concepts, claims and arguments that are hard to understand. Try to identify the differences between different interpretations. Which interpretation is best and why?

R5. Prepare examples beforehand, rather than try to invent them in the exam. They must be short and they must make the right point – so try them out on your friends and teachers first.

R6. Think reflectively about the arguments and issues. Practise arguing for and against a particular view. Think about the place and importance of the arguments for the issue as a whole.

R7. Think about how your judgements on the various arguments you have studied add up. Do they lead to one conclusion, one point of view being right? Or do you think arguments for and against one position are closely balanced?

R8. Create structured outlines or web-diagrams for particular issues. Try to cover all the main points.

R9. Practise writing timed answers. Use your notes at first, but then practise without them.

Exam tips

E1. The number of marks available for each part is a rough guide to how long you spend on it. But allow a little extra time for the 25-mark questions and parts you find difficult. Choose what order to answer the questions in.

E2. Before starting your answer, read the question again very closely. Take note of every word to make sure you answer the actual question set. Remember to explain, and not just state, claims and arguments.

E3. For longer answers, before you start writing, it can be worth writing out your outline or web-diagram first. This can help remind you of the key points you want to make, and the order in which you want to make them.

E4. Four rules of thumb:

    a. Use philosophical terms to be precise and concise, not simply to sound 'impressive', and make sure it is clear from the context that you know what they mean.

    b. Keep related ideas together. If you have a thought later on, add a footnote indicating where in the answer you want it to be read.

    c. In 25-mark questions, explain a theory before evaluating it.

    d. In 25-mark questions, apart from the conclusion for the essay as a whole, don't state the conclusion to an argument before you've discussed the argument, especially if you are going to present objections to that conclusion. You can state what the argument hopes to show, but don't state it *as* a conclusion.

E5. Keep your examples short and make sure they support the point you want to make. Always explain how they support your point.

E6. For 25-mark questions, make sure your discussion is not just reporting a sequence of points of view, but presents objections and replies, evaluates the arguments, and reaches a particular conclusion.

E7. For questions other than 25-mark questions, you may have time to write two drafts – rough and final. For 25-mark questions, leave time to check your answer at the end. Don't be afraid to add to or correct what you have written.

Good luck!

Glossary

(with Joanne Lovesey)

a posteriori: Knowledge of propositions that can only be known to be true or false through sense experience.

a priori: Knowledge of propositions that do not require (sense) experience to be known to be true or false.

ability knowledge: Knowing 'how' to do something, e.g. 'I know how to ride a bike', 'I can imagine seeing the colour red.'

abstract: Theoretical (rather than applied or practical) and removed from any concrete objects or instances.

acquaintance knowledge: Knowledge of someone or something gained by direct experience (not description). For example, 'I know the manager of the restaurant', or 'I know the colour red.'

actual world: The world as it is. The actual world is a possible world, specifically the one we live in.

ad hoc: A statement or a move in an argument that suits the purpose at hand but has no independent support.

analogy: Similarity in several respects between different things.

analogy, the argument from: The argument that I can use the behaviour of other people to infer that they have minds because they behave as I do, and I have a mind.

analysis: Process of breaking up a complex concept, expression or argument in order to reveal its simpler constituents, thereby elucidating its meaning or logical structure.

analytic: A proposition that is true (or false) in virtue of the meanings of the words. For instance, 'a bachelor is an unmarried man' is analytically true, while 'a square has three sides' is analytically false.

antecedent: The proposition that forms the first part of a conditional statement, usually the part of the sentence that comes after 'if'. E.g. in both 'If it rains then I will get wet' and 'I will get wet if it rains', the antecedent is 'it rains'.

Aquinas' First Way: A form of cosmological argument presented by Aquinas, said to be from 'motion'. By 'motion', Aquinas means 'change' from the potential to actual state of something. Such change must be caused by something that is already actual. If the cause was previously potential, then it must in turn have been caused to become actual. There must be a 'first cause' of change in this sequence, a cause that is not itself changed from actual to potential. This is God.

Aquinas' Second Way: A form of cosmological argument presented by Aquinas, said to be from 'atemporal' or 'sustaining' causation. As nothing depends on itself, things are sustained in their continued existence. Therefore, there must be a first sustaining cause, which does not depend on any other cause. This is God.

Aquinas' Third Way: A form of cosmological argument from contingency by Aquinas. Anything that exists contingently, at some time does not exist. If everything exists contingently, then at some point, nothing existed. If nothing existed, then nothing could begin to exist. Therefore, something must exist necessarily, not contingently. This is God.

argument: A reasoned inference from one set of claims – the premises – to another claim, the conclusion.

argument map: Visual diagram of the logical structure of an argument, i.e. how the premises logically relate to one another and to the conclusion.

assertion: The claim that a proposition is true.

assumption: A proposition accepted without proof or evidence as the basis for an inference or argument.

atemporal: Not existing in time or subject to the passing of time.

attitude: A mental state regarding how the world is or should be. A cognitive attitude, e.g. belief, has a mind-to-world direction of fit. A non-cognitive attitude, e.g. desire, has a world-to-mind direction of fit.

begging the question: The informal fallacy of (explicitly or implicitly) assuming the truth of the conclusion of an argument as one of the premises employed in an effort to demonstrate its truth.

behaviourism, 'hard': Hempel's version of philosophical behaviourism that claims that statements containing mental concepts can be reduced or translated into statements about behaviour and physical states containing no mental concepts, only physical ones. Also known as 'analytical' behaviourism or 'logical' behaviourism.

behaviourism, methodological: The theory that claims that because science can only investigate what is publicly accessible, psychology is concerned only with the explanation and prediction of behaviour and not with any 'inner' mental states.

behaviourism, philosophical: The family of theories that claim that our talk about the mind can be analysed in terms of talk about behaviour. The meaning of our mental concepts is given by behaviour and behavioural dispositions. Also known as 'logical' behaviourism.

behaviourism, 'soft': Ryle's version of philosophical behaviourism that claims that our talk of the mind is talk of how someone does or would behave under certain conditions. However, behavioural dispositions are not reducible to a finite set of statements about how someone would behave, nor to a set of statements containing no mental concepts.

belief: Affirmation of, or conviction regarding, the truth of a proposition. E.g. 'I believe that the grass is green.'

blik: An attitude to or view of the world that is not held or withdrawn on the basis of empirical experience.

category mistake: Treating a concept as belonging to a logical category that it doesn't belong to, e.g. 'this number is heavy' commits a category mistake as numbers are not the sorts of things that can have a weight.

causal closure: Another term for the completeness of physics.

causal principle: The claim that everything that exists has a cause.

China thought experiment: A thought experiment by Block, presented as an objection to functionalism. If the population of China, using radios, duplicated the functioning of your brain, would this create conscious experiences (just as your brain does)? If not, functionalism (about consciousness) is false.

circular: An argument is circular if it employs its own conclusion as a premise. An analysis or definition is circular if the term being analysed/defined also appears in the analysis/definition.

claim: A proposition that is asserted or affirmed to be true.

cogent: An inductive argument in which the truth of the premises (significantly) raises the probability that the conclusion is true.

cognitive: Language or thought that can be true or false and aims to express how things are.

cognitivism: A cognitivist account of religious language argues that religious claims express beliefs, can be true or false, and aim to describe the world. So 'God exists' expresses the belief that God exists, and is either true or false.

coherent: A set of statements are coherent if they are consistent and increase each other's probability.

common sense: The basic perceptions or understandings that are shared by many (most) people.

compatible: Two claims are compatible if they are consistent. Two properties are compatible if it is possible for something to have both of them at once.

compatibilism: The theory that the causal determination of human conduct is consistent with the freedom required for responsible moral agency.

completeness of physics: The thesis that every physical event has a sufficient physical cause that brings it about in accordance with the laws of physics. Also known as causal closure.

composition, fallacy of: The informal fallacy of attributing some feature of the members of a collection to the collection itself, or reasoning from part to whole. E.g. 'sodium and chloride are both dangerous to humans, therefore sodium-chloride (salt) is dangerous to humans'.

conceivability argument: Arguments for dualism from the conceivability of mind and body being distinct. Descartes argues that 1) it is conceivable that the mind can exist without the body; 2) conceivability entails possibility; so 3) it is possible that the mind can exist without the body. Therefore the mind and body are distinct substances. The zombie argument is a form of conceivability argument for property dualism.

conceivable: Capable of being imagined or grasped mentally without incoherence or contradiction.

concept: Any abstract notion or idea by virtue of which we apply general terms to things.

conclusion: A proposition whose truth has been inferred from premises.

conditional: A proposition that takes the form of 'if …, then …'. The conditional asserts that if the first statement (the antecedent) is true, then the second statement (the consequent) is also true. E.g. 'If it is raining then the ground is wet' asserts that if it is true that it is raining, it is true that the ground is wet.

consciousness: The subjective phenomenon of awareness of the world and/or of one's mental states.

consciousness, easy problem of: The problem of analysing and explaining the functions of consciousness, e.g. that we can consciously control our behaviour, report on our mental states, and focus our attention. According to Chalmers, it is 'easy' to provide a successful analysis of these facts in physical and/or functional terms.

consciousness, hard problem of: The problem of analysing and explaining the phenomenal properties of consciousness, what it is like to undergo conscious experiences. According to Chalmers, it is 'hard' to provide a successful analysis of these properties in physical and/or functional terms.

consequent: The proposition that forms the second part of a conditional statement, usually the part of the sentence that occurs after 'then'. E.g. In both 'If it rains then I will get wet and 'I will get wet if it rains', the consequent is 'I will get wet.'

consistent: Two or more claims are consistent if they can both be true at the same time.

contingent: A proposition that could be either true or false, a state of affairs that may or may not hold, depending on how the world actually is.

contingent existence: The type of existence had by a being, such as human beings, that can exist or not exist.

contradiction: Two claims that cannot both be true, and cannot both be false. Or one claim that both asserts and denies something. E.g. 'It is raining and it is not raining.'

correlation: A relationship between two things whereby one always accompanies the other, e.g. the properties of size and shape are correlated. Correlation should be distinguished from identity.

cosmological argument: Arguments for God's existence that claim that unless God exists, the question 'why does anything exist?' is unanswerable. Oversimplified, arguments from causation claim that everything must have a cause, and causal chains cannot be infinite, so there must be a first cause. Arguments from contingency claim that every contingent thing must have an explanation for its existence, and this can ultimately only be provided by something that exists necessarily.

counter-argument: An argument that attempts to establish a conclusion that undermines another argument, or the conclusion of another argument.

counterexamples, method of finding: If a theory makes a general claim, such as 'all propositional knowledge is justified true belief', we only need to find a single instance in which this is false (a counter-example) to show that the general claim is false and so something is wrong with the theory.

counter-intuitive: Something that doesn't fit with our intuition.

deduction: An argument whose conclusion is logically entailed by its premises, i.e. if the premises are true, the conclusion cannot be false.

defence, free will: An argument to show that there is no inconsistency between the existence of evil and the existence of God, because it is possible that God would allow evils that arise from free will in order that we (or other beings) can have free will.

definition: An explanation of the meaning of a word. Philosophical definitions often attempt to give necessary and sufficient conditions for the application of the term being defined.

design argument: Arguments for God's existence that claim that there is complexity in the world that is evidence of design, and design requires a designer, which is God. The evidence of design that is appealed to is usually the organisation of parts for a purpose or temporal regularities expressed by the laws of nature. Also known as teleological arguments.

desire: A state of mind that motivates a person to act in such a way as to satisfy the desire, e.g. if a person desires a cup of tea, they are motivated to make and drink a cup of tea.

determinism: Commonly understood as the claim that everything that happens, including each human choice and action, has a cause, in accordance with laws of nature. Many philosophers argue that given a particular cause, only one outcome is possible.

dilemma: Two mutually exclusive and exhaustive options (horns), both of which face significant objections.

direction of fit: The direction of the relation between mind and world. In one direction, the mind 'fits' the world, as in belief. We change our beliefs to fit the facts. In the other direction, the world 'fits' the mind, as in desire. We act on our desires to change the world to satisfy our desires.

disanalogy: A point of dissimilarity between two things, something that two things don't have in common.

disjunction: An either/or claim. An example of a disjunction is: 'Either it will rain or it will be sunny.'

disposition: How something or someone will or is likely to behave under certain circumstances: what it or they would do, could do, or are liable to do, in particular situations or under particular conditions, including conditions that they are not in at the moment. For example, sugar is soluble (it tends to dissolve when placed in water) while someone who has a friendly disposition tends to smile when they are smiled at.

distinction: A difference or contrast between things.

dualism, interactionist: The theory that mental and physical events can cause one another even though the mind and body are distinct substances (interactionist substance dualism) or mental and physical properties are distinct fundamental properties (interactionist property dualism).

dualism, property: The theory that there is only one kind of substance, physical substance, but two ontologically fundamental kinds of property – mental properties and physical properties.

dualism, substance: The theory that two kinds of substance exist, mental and physical substance.

elimination: Ceasing to use a concept on the grounds that what it refers does not exist, e.g. the idea of 'caloric fluid' was eliminated by a new theory of heat as molecular motion.

eliminative materialism: The theory that at least some of our basic mental concepts, such as consciousness or Intentionality, are fundamentally mistaken and should be abandoned, as they don't refer to anything that exists.

empirical: Relating to or deriving from experience, especially sense experience, but also including experimental scientific investigation.

empiricism: The theory that there can be no a priori knowledge of synthetic propositions about the world (outside my mind), i.e. all a priori knowledge is of analytic propositions, while all knowledge of synthetic propositions is gained through sense experience.

enumerative induction: The method of reasoning that argues from many instances of something to a general statement about that thing. E.g. the sun has risen in the morning every day for x number of days, therefore the sun rises in the morning.

epiphenomenalism: The theory that mental states and events are epiphenomena, by-products, the effects of some physical process, but with no causal influence of their own. Often combined with property dualism.

epistemology: The study (*-ology*) of knowledge (Greek *episteme*) and related concepts, including belief, justification, and certainty. It looks at the possibility and sources of knowledge.

equivocation, fallacy of: The use of an ambiguous word or phrase in different senses within a single argument. E.g. 'All banks are next to rivers, I deposit money in a bank, therefore I deposit money next to a river.'

eschatological: The study (*-ology*) of the 'last things' (Greek *eskhatos*) – death, the final judgement, and the ultimate destiny of human beings.

eternal: Timeless (atemporal). What is eternal cannot have a beginning or end.

Euthyphro dilemma: Does God will what is morally good because it is good, or is it good because God wills it? If the former, God is not omnipotent, if the latter, morality is arbitrary and 'God is good' is tautologous.

everlasting: Existing throughout all time, without beginning or end.

evil, moral: Bad things that arise as the result of the actions of free agents, e.g. murder.

evil, natural: Bad things, especially pain and suffering, that arise as the result of natural processes, e.g. people dying in earthquakes.

explanation: An intelligible account of why something happens. The thing to be explained (explanandum) is usually accepted as a fact, and what is used to explain it (the explanans) is usually plausible but less certain.

faculty: A mental capacity or ability, such as sight, the ability to feel fear, and reason.

fallacy/fallacious: An error in reasoning. More exactly, a fallacy is an argument in which the premises do not offer rational support to the conclusion. If the argument is deductive, then it is fallacious if it is not valid. If the argument is inductive, it is fallacious if the premises do not make the conclusion more likely to be true.

false: A proposition is false if things are not as it states. E.g. the proposition 'grass is always purple' is false, because there is grass that is not purple.

falsifiable: A claim is falsifiable if it is logically incompatible with some (set of) empirical observations.

falsification principle: A claim is meaningful only if it is falsifiable, i.e. it rules out some possible experience.

fatalism: The belief that human choice and action makes no (important) difference to what will happen in the future.

folk psychology: A body of knowledge or theory regarding the prediction and explanation of people's behaviour constituted by the platitudes about the mind ordinary people are inclined to endorse, e.g. 'if someone is thirsty, they will normally try to find something to drink'.

free will: The capacity of rational agents to choose a course of action from among various alternatives.

function: A mapping from each of the possible inputs to some state to its output. The description of a state's function describes what that state does.

functionalism: The theory that mental states are (can be reduced to) functional states, i.e. what it is to be a mental state is just to be a state with certain input and output relations to stimuli, behaviour and other mental states.

functionalism, causal role: The version of functionalism that interprets the function of mental states in terms of the role they play in a network of causes and effects. A mental state can be 'realised' by any state that plays that causal role.

Ghost in the Machine: Ryle's name for substance dualism.

Hume's 'fork': We can have knowledge of just two sorts of claim: the relations between ideas and matters of fact.

hypothesis: A proposal that needs to be confirmed or rejected by reasoning or experience.

hypothetical reasoning: Working out the best hypothesis that would explain or account for some experience or fact.

idealism: The theory that minds are the only kind of substance. Therefore, all that exists are minds and what depends on them (ideas).

identical, numerically: One and the same thing. Everything is numerically identical to itself, and nothing else.

identical, qualitatively: Two or more things are qualitatively identical if they share their properties in common, for example, two separate copies of the same picture.

incompatibilism: The belief that determinism and free will cannot both be true. If human beings have free will, determinism is false; if determinism is true, human beings do not have free will.

inconceivable: Impossible to imagine, think or grasp without contradiction or incoherence.

inconsistent: Two claims are inconsistent if they can't both be true at the same time.

indefinitely heterogenous dispositions: Dispositions that can be manifested in many, many different ways. Ryle argued that mental states are indefinitely heterogenous behavioural dispositions, so that while mental concepts can be analysed in terms of behaviour, they cannot be reduced to talk about behaviour. *See* entry on 'behaviourism, "soft"'.

indiscernibility of identicals: Leibniz's principle that if two things are identical (i.e. are just one thing), then they share all their properties and so are indiscernible; i.e. you cannot have numerical identity without qualitative identity.

indivisibility argument: Descartes' argument that bodies are divisible into spatial parts, but minds have no such parts. Therefore, the mind is a distinct substance from the body.

induction: An argument whose conclusion is supported by its premises, but is not logically entailed by them, i.e. if the premises are true, then this makes it (more) likely that the conclusion is true, but it is still possible that the conclusion is false.

inference: Coming to accept a proposition as true on the basis of reasoning from other propositions taken to be true.

inference to the best explanation: An inductive argument form where the conclusion presents the 'best explanation' for why the premises are true.

infinite: Without any bounds or limits. E.g. the natural numbers form an infinite series, the numbers continue in both directions (positive and negative numbers) without any end point.

intention: A mental state that expresses a person's choice. It specifies the action they choose and often their reason or end in acting.

Intentionality: The property of mental states whereby they are 'directed' towards an 'object', that is they are 'about' something; e.g. the belief that Paris is the capital of France is about Paris and the desire to eat chocolate is about chocolate.

interaction problem, conceptual: The objection to interactionist dualism that mind and body (or mental and physical properties) cannot interact causally, because they are too different in nature, e.g. the mind is outside space while the body is in space.

interaction problem, empirical: The objection to interactionist dualism that the claim that the mind or mental states cause changes to the body or physical states conflicts with scientific theory or evidence, e.g. that the total energy in the universe stays constant.

intrinsic/extrinsic: Distinction in the properties of things. The intrinsic properties of a thing are those which it has in and of itself, e.g. the size of a physical object; its extrinsic (or relational) features are those which it has only in relation to something else, e.g. the function of a mental state.

introspection: Direct, first-personal awareness of one's own mental states.

intuition: Direct non-inferential awareness of abstract objects or truths.

invalid: Not valid. A deductive argument is invalid if it is possible for the premises to be true while the conclusion is false.

inverted qualia: The thought experiment that supposes that two people experience subjectively different colours when looking at the same object, but otherwise think and behave in identical ways; e.g. they both call the same object 'red'. The argument is presented as an objection to a functionalist account of phenomenal consciousness.

justification: What is offered as grounds for believing an assertion.

Kalām argument: A form of cosmological argument that claims that everything that begins to exist has a cause, and that the universe began to exist because it is impossible for a temporal sequence of things to be infinite, and so there is a cause of the universe.

knowledge argument: Jackson's argument for property dualism, presenting the thought experiment of Mary, a neuroscientist who has lived her entire life in a black-and-white room, but who knows all the physical information there is to know about what happens when we see a ripe tomato. When she first leaves the room and comes to see something red for the first time, does she learn something new? If so, some properties are not physical properties.

laws of nature: Fixed regularities that govern the universe; statements that express these regularities.

Leibniz's principle of the indiscernibility of identicals: *See* entry on 'indiscernibility of identicals'.

logical positivism: The twentieth-century philosophical movement that used the verification principle to determine meaningfulness.

machine table: A table listing every possible combination of input and output for a machine, describing the operations of its software.

Masked Man fallacy: A fallacious form of argument that uses what one believes about an object to infer whether or not the object is identical with something else; e.g. I believe the Masked Man robbed the bank; I do not believe my father robbed the bank; therefore, the Masked Man is not my father. This is a fallacy, because one's beliefs may be mistaken. More generally, it is said to challenge the use of conceivability to infer what is possible/actual.

materialism: The theory that the only substance is matter (or physical substance). Everything that exists, including the mind, depends on matter (physical substance) to exist.

meaningful: Having a linguistic (semantic) meaning.

mental states: Mental phenomena that can endure over time, such as beliefs and desires. The term is sometimes used more broadly to cover mental phenomena or mental properties in general (states, processes and events).

metaphysics: The branch of philosophy that asks questions about the fundamental nature of reality. *Meta-* means above, beyond, or after; physics enquires into the physical structure of reality.

monism: The theory that only one kind of substance exists. Both materialism (physicalism) and idealism are monist theories.

monotheism: The view that there is only one God.

motion, argument from: *See* entry on 'Aquinas' First Way'.

multiple realisability: 1) The claim that there are many ways in which one and the same mental state can be expressed in behaviour. This is presented as an objection to the claim that mental states are reducible to behavioural dispositions. 2) The claim that one and the same mental state can have its function performed by different physical states. This is presented as an objection to the claim that mental states are identical to physical states.

multiverse theory: The claim that there are or have been (many) other universes. It can be used as an objection to the argument from design, to argue that the chance that some universe with laws that enabled order is high. So we shouldn't infer that there is a designer.

necessary: A proposition that must be true (or if false, it must be false), a state of affairs that must hold.

necessary condition: One proposition is a necessary condition of another when the second cannot be true while the first is false. For example, being a man is a necessary condition of being a bachelor, as if you are not a man you cannot be a bachelor.

necessary existence: The type of existence had by a being, such as God, that does not exist contingently, but must exist.

non-cognitive: Language or thought that cannot be true or false and does not aim to express how things are.

non-cognitivism: The theory that claims that religious claims express non-cognitive attitudes. Religious language does not make claims about reality and is not true or false (it is not fact-stating).

objection: A claim or argument that is given as a reason against the truth of another claim or argument.

objective: Independent of what people think or feel. A claim is objectively true if its truth does not depend on people's beliefs.

Ockham's razor: The principle that states that we should not put forward a hypothesis that says many different things exist when a simpler explanation will do as well. 'Do not multiply entities beyond necessity'. A simpler explanation is a better explanation, as long as it is just as successful.

omnibenevolent: Being perfectly or supremely good. Often defined as being perfectly morally good.

omnipotent: Having perfect power. Often defined as having the ability to do anything it is possible to do.

omniscient: Having perfect knowledge. Often defined as knowing everything that it is possible to know.

ontological argument: Arguments that claim that we can deduce the existence of God from the concept of God.

ontologically distinct: Two things are ontologically distinct if they are not the same thing, neither is able to be reduced to the other, and the existence of one is not determined by the existence of the other, e.g. substance dualists claim that mind and body are ontologically distinct substances.

ontologically independent: Not depending on anything else for existence. According to traditional metaphysics, only substances can be ontologically independent.

ontology: The study (-*ology*) of what exists or 'being' (Greek *ont-*).

paradox: A claim or set of claims that are contradictory but present a philosophical challenge, e.g. 'This sentence is false' (if the sentence is true, it is false; if the sentence is false, it is true).

paradox of the stone: Can God create a stone that he can't lift? If the answer is 'no', then God cannot create the stone. If the answer is 'yes', then God cannot lift the stone. So either way, it seems, there is something God cannot do. If there is something God can't do, then God isn't omnipotent.

para-mechanical hypothesis: Ryle's name for understanding mental states and processes as akin to physical states and processes, but non-spatial and non-mechanical.

phenomenal concept: A concept by which you recognise something as of a certain kind when experiencing or perceiving it, e.g. a phenomenal concept of red as 'this' colour. Contrasted with theoretical concepts, which describe something in theoretical terms, e.g. a theoretical concept of red as light with a frequency of 600 nanometres.

phenomenal consciousness: A form of consciousness with a subjective experiential quality, as involved in perception, sensation and emotion. Awareness of 'what it is like' to experience such mental phenomena.

phenomenal properties: Properties of an experience that give it its distinctive experiential quality, and which are apprehended in phenomenal consciousness.

physicalism: A modern form of materialism, which claims that everything that exists is physical, or depends upon something that is physical. More precisely, the theory that everything that is ontologically fundamental is physical, that is comes under the laws and investigations of physics, and every physical event has a sufficient physical cause.

physicalism, reductive: A form of physicalism that claims that mental properties are physical properties. *See* entry on 'type identity theory'.

plausible: Fits with what else we already know.

possible: Capable of happening/existing/being the case. If something is possible, it could be true.

possible world: A way of talking about how things could be. Saying that something is possible is saying that it is true in some possible world. Saying that something is impossible is saying that it is false in all possible worlds.

possible, logically: Something is logically possible if it doesn't involve a contradiction or conceptual incoherence.

possible, metaphysically: Something is metaphysically possible if there is at least one possible world in which it is true.

possible, physically: Something is physically possible if it could be true given the laws of nature in the actual world.

predicate: The part of a sentence or clause containing a verb or adjective and stating something about the subject. E.g. in 'Jane is happy' the predicate is 'is happy'.

premise: A proposition that, as part of an argument, provides or contributes to a reason to believe that the conclusion is true.

preservation of truth: Valid deductive arguments preserve truth, meaning that when the premises are true, anything that logically follows from them will also be true.

presuppose: To require or assume an antecedent state of affairs, e.g. if Jones has stopped playing basketball, this presupposes that he was playing basketball.

principle of sufficient reason: the principle, defended by Leibniz, that every true fact has an explanation that provides a sufficient reason for why things are as they are and not otherwise.

private: Capable of being experienced or known by no one other than the subject themselves.

problem of evil: The existence of evil either logically rules out or is evidence against the existence of an omnipotent, omniscient, supremely good being.

problem of other minds: The question of how we can know that there are minds other than our own, given that our experience of other minds (if they exist) is through behaviour.

proof: The demonstration of the truth of a proposition using a valid deductive argument from known or certain premises to that proposition as its conclusion.

property: An attribute or characteristic of an object. E.g. the property of being green, or being tall. Physical properties are those properties of objects investigated by physics, or more broadly, the natural sciences. Mental properties include mental states, such as beliefs, and mental events, such as having a thought or feeling pain.

property, Intentional: A property of a mental state that enables it to be 'about' something, to represent what it does. It is an extrinsic or relational property (*see* entries on 'intrinsic/extrinsic' and 'Intentionality').

property, relational: A characteristic that something has only in relation to another thing. E.g. 'Pete is taller than Bob', or 'Alice loves Jack.'

proposition: A declarative statement (or more accurately, what is claimed by a declarative statement), such as 'mice are mammals'. Propositions can go after 'that' in 'I believe that …' and 'I know that …'.

propositional knowledge: Knowing 'that' some claim – a proposition – is true or false, e.g. 'I know that Paris is the capital of France.'

prove: To demonstrate that a proposition is true by giving a valid deductive argument from known or certain premises to that proposition as the conclusion.

qualia: Phenomenal properties understood as intrinsic and non-Intentional properties of mental states.

rationalism: The theory that there can be a priori knowledge of synthetic propositions about the world (outside my mind) gained through rational insight and reasoning.

reason: A statement presented in justification for a claim. A good reason in some way raises the probability that the claim is true.

reasoning: The process of thinking about something in a logical way, in particular, drawing inferences on the basis of reasons.

reducible: A phenomenon or property is reducible to another if the first can be completely explained in terms of, or identified with, the second (which is considered more ontologically fundamental), e.g. type identity theory claims that mental properties are reducible (identical) to physical properties.

***reductio ad absurdum*:** A form of argument that shows that some claim leads to a contradiction.

reduction: The reducing of one thing to another. An analytic reduction claims that one set of concepts can be translated without loss of meaning into another set of concepts, e.g. Hempel's 'hard' behaviourism claims that mental concepts are reducible to behavioural and physical concepts. An ontological reduction claims that the things in one domain are identical with (or can be completely explained in terms of) some of the things in another domain, e.g. type identity theory claims that mental properties are reducible to physical properties.

reductionism: The belief that statements or properties of one sort (in one domain, e.g. the mental) can be reduced to statements or properties of another, more basic kind (in another domain, e.g. the physical).

redundant: Superfluous, not adding anything.

sceptical: Not easily convinced, or having doubts or reservations. (Not to be confused with scepticism.)

self-evident: A proposition that can be known just by rational reflection on that proposition.

sensation: Our experience of objects outside the mind, perceived through the senses.

signposts: Sentences that indicate what the text is about, what has been, is being, or will be argued. E.g. 'I will now argue that …'.

simultaneous: At the same time. (Stump and Kretzmann argue for new definitions of simultaneity that allow temporal and eternal beings to be said to be simultaneous.)

sophism: The use of plausible arguments that are actually fallacious, especially when someone dishonestly presents such an argument as if it were legitimate reasoning.

soul: The immortal, non-material part of a person.

sound: A deductive argument is sound if it is valid with true premises.

subjective: That which depends upon the personal or individual, especially where it is supposed to be an arbitrary expression of preference.

substance: Something that does not depend on another thing in order to exist, which possesses properties and persists through changes.

sufficient condition: One proposition is a sufficient condition for another when the first cannot be true while the second is false. For example, being a dog is sufficient for being an animal, because something can't be a dog without also being an animal.

super-spartans: People (or creatures) in Putnam's thought experiment who so completely disapprove of showing pain that all pain behaviour has been suppressed, and they no longer have any disposition to demonstrate pain in their behaviour. The thought experiment is presented as an objection to philosophical behaviourism.

supervenience: A relation between two types of property. Properties of type *A* supervene on properties of type *B* just in case any two things that are exactly alike in their *B* properties *cannot* have different *A* properties, e.g. aesthetic properties supervene on physical properties if two paintings that have identical physical properties cannot have different aesthetic properties.

sustaining cause: A cause that brings about its effect continuously, rather than at a specific moment, such that the effect depends on the continued existence and operation of the cause. Sometimes also called an atemporal cause.

synthetic: A proposition that is not analytic, but true or false depending on how the world is.

tautology: A statement that repeats the subject in the predicate, that 'says the same thing twice'. E.g. 'Green things are green.'

teleological argument: Another term for the design argument.

temporal cause: A cause that brings about its effect at a time, such that the effect comes after the cause and can continue after the cause ceases.

theodicy: An attempt to explain how or why an omnipotent, omniscient, supremely good God would allow the (apparent) presence of evil in the world.

theodicy, soul-making: God allows evil because it is necessary for us to develop virtue.

thought experiment: A philosophical method designed to test a hypothesis or philosophical claim through imagining a hypothetical situation and coming to a judgement.

timeless: Not in time (atemporal, eternal).

true: A proposition is true if things are as it states. E.g. the proposition 'the grass is green' is true if the grass is green, and otherwise it is false.

type identity theory: The theory that mental properties are identical (ontologically reducible) to physical properties. Mind–brain type identity theory claims that mental properties are identical to physical properties of the brain.

unanalysable: Not subject to analysis.

unconscious: A mental state is unconscious if the subject is not aware of having that mental state.

universalise: To apply to everything/everyone.

unsound: A deductive argument is unsound if it is either invalid or has at least one false premise.

valid: An argument in which, if the premises are true, then the conclusion must be true. In this case, we say that the conclusion is entailed by the premises. Only deductive arguments can be valid.

verifiable, empirically: A statement is empirically verifiable if empirical evidence would go towards establishing that the statement is true or false.

verification, eschatological: Verification of God's existence in the afterlife or at the end of time.

verification principle: The principle that all meaningful claims are either analytic or empirically verifiable.

verificationism: The thesis that the verification principle is the correct account of meaning.

zombie argument: The argument for property dualism that if consciousness were identical to some physical properties, it would not be metaphysically possible for something to have that physical property without consciousness. However, 1) philosophical zombies are conceivable, and so 2) philosophical zombies are metaphysically possible. Therefore, 3) consciousness is non-physical and physicalism is false.

zombie, philosophical: An exact physical duplicate of a person, existing in another possible world, but without any phenomenal consciousness. It therefore has identical physical properties to the person (and identical functional properties, if these are fixed by physical properties), but different mental properties.

Index by syllabus content

Metaphysics of God

Set texts

Metaphysics of Mind

Index

Page numbers in **bold** refer to figures, page numbers in *italic* refer to argument maps.